Burying the Dead
but Not the Past

CIVIL WAR AMERICA

Gary W. Gallagher, *editor*

*Burying the Dead
but Not the Past*

Ladies' Memorial Associations
and the Lost Cause

CAROLINE E. JANNEY

The University of North Carolina Press   *Chapel Hill*

© 2008 The University of North Carolina Press
All rights reserved
Manufactured in the United States of America

Designed by Michelle Coppedge
Set in Minion by Tseng Information Systems, Inc.

The paper in this book meets the guidelines for permanence
and durability of the Committee on Production Guidelines
for Book Longevity of the Council on Library Resources.

Library of Congress Cataloging-in-Publication Data
Janney, Caroline E.
Burying the dead but not the past : Ladies' Memorial
Associations and the lost cause / Caroline E. Janney.
p. cm. — (Civil War America)
Includes bibliographical references and index.
ISBN 978-0-8078-3176-2 (cloth : alk. paper)
1. Ladies' Memorial Association—History. 2. Southern States—
Civilization. 3. Popular culture—Southern States. 4. United
States—History—Civil War, 1861–1865—Influence. I. Title.
E483.99.L33J36 2008
369'.17—dc22   2007026904

12 11 10 09 08   5 4 3 2 1

For my parents,

Robert & Sharon Janney,

and in memory of my grandfather,

Roby Janney

Contents

Illustrations

Acknowledgments

I first discovered the Ladies' Memorial Associations as an undergraduate in the spring of 1998, and in the ten years since they have become part of my life to no small degree. In the process of preparing this book (something I certainly never envisioned a decade ago), I have accumulated an untold number of debts. In particular, I wish to thank Gary W. Gallagher. I was fortunate to take his Civil War class in my second year of graduate school at the University of Virginia, and I was elated when he subsequently agreed to serve as my dissertation advisor. Since that time, he has continued to inspire me with his wisdom, generosity, and passion for history. Much of what I have learned about both writing and teaching history I owe to him. His support as a mentor, colleague, and friend has been essential, not only to this book, but also to my development as a scholar. Working with him has been the best and most rewarding experience of my academic life.

In Charlottesville, I was also privileged to be part of an incredible scholarly community. Along with Gary Gallagher, Cindy Aron, Edward L. Ayers, and Steve Cushman proved to be an exceptional dissertation committee. Cindy Aron shared her vast knowledge of women's history and also pushed me to make larger claims about the centrality of the Ladies. Steve Cushman helped me to craft my prose and urged me to think more about the symbolism inherent in Confederate memorials and cemetery art. Not only did Ed Ayers lend his expertise in southern history during the course of this project, but he must likewise be held accountable for stirring my excitement for history while I was an undergraduate. Grace Hale, Peter Onuf, Joe Miller, Lori Schuyler, and Franny Nudelman all provided extraordinary advice and encouragement. My fellow graduate students, Kristin Celello, Carl BonTempo, Aaron Sheehan-Dean, Ethan Sribnick, Chris Nehls, Kurt Hohenstein, John Mooney, and Andre Fleche, challenged my thinking and all the while made my time at Virginia more enjoyable. Rob Parkinson deserves special thanks for his diligent reading and commentary on countless drafts and for his endlessly intellectually stimulating discussions (even when they drifted to talk of the Revolution). Kate Pierce and Laurie Hochstetler read early drafts and listened to infinite chatter about my research, and from them I learned untold amounts about press culture and the many dilemmas of Puritans. For their keen intelligence, wonderful company, and charming humor, I will always be thankful.

I have likewise benefited from the wisdom of numerous scholars beyond Charlottesville, most especially Joan Waugh, Bill Blair, Peter Carmichael, Matt Gallman, and Katrina Powell. I would also like to thank the anonymous readers of the manuscript who vastly improved this book. My summers at Shenandoah National Park added to my appreciation and dedication to public history. My coworkers there were incredibly supportive of my decision to pursue a career in academia. In particular, Reed L. Engle and Joanne Amberson read and commented on numerous early drafts of this manuscript. I am also grateful to my new colleagues at Purdue University, especially Jennifer Foray, who has encouraged me to think in a broader fashion about issues of memory, power, and nationalism. David Perry, Paula Wald, Dorothea Anderson, and the entire staff at the University of North Carolina Press have likewise been unrelentingly supportive throughout this process.

I could not have written this book without the patient and constant help I found at the archives. I am especially appreciative of the Museum of the Confederacy. Not only did the museum prove to be the repository for two of the Ladies' Memorial Associations, but its entire collection is among the best in the country for studying the Lost Cause. Beyond its archives, the museum's true treasures are John and Ruth Ann Coski. Amid talks about our dogs and the ravages of Hurricane Isabel, John and Ruth Ann proved overwhelmingly helpful, insightful, and efficient. Because of them, this project was made all the more enjoyable. A number of other archival institutions and individuals have also been very helpful. For sharing their knowledge and expertise, I would like to thank the staff of the Albert and Shirley Small Special Collections Library at the University of Virginia; the Manuscript Department of the William R. Perkins Library, Duke University; Nelson Lankford and staff at the Virginia Historical Society, Richmond; the archivists at Handley Regional Library, Winchester; Sandra Treadway, Rebecca Dobyns, and the entire staff at the Library of Virginia, Richmond; the staff of the Jones Memorial Library, Lynchburg; Ted Delany at Old City Cemetery, Lynchburg; Robert E. L. Krick at Richmond National Battlefield Park; the staff of the Central Rappahannock Regional Library, Fredericksburg; and the Earl Gregg Swem Library, College of William and Mary, Williamsburg, Virginia. I also wish to express my deep appreciation to the always patient staff of Interlibrary Loan at Alderman Library, University of Virginia. Robert K. Krick proved invaluable when it came to Fredericksburg and the Army of Northern Virginia. Barbara Crookshanks of Fredericksburg and Alice L. Everitt of Petersburg graciously shared their experiences and knowledge of their respective Ladies' Memorial Associations. Finally, I am appreciative of the financial support I received from the University of Virginia, Virginia Historical Society, and Duke University to complete my research and writing. Even with all the assistance throughout this project, the flaws that remain are solely mine.

I owe more than can be expressed to my family, for their encouragement and faith during the past seven years. I want to give special thanks to my parents, Robert and Sharon Janney, for teaching me to ask the hard questions and to follow my dreams. From them I have learned the value of finding a profession that you love. Thanks also to Andrew, Marc, Monica, Isa, and Conner for their constant love and support. My grandparents are no doubt responsible for the nature of this project. It was my grandfather, Roby Janney, a veteran of World War II, who whetted my appetite for history by taking me to Civil War battlefields as a young child. He passed away this spring just as I was completing the manuscript, but his legacy will live on in all his grandchildren's passion for history. My grandmother, Marion Janney, only encouraged my obsession with the past by telling me stories of her own grandparents and parents in late-nineteenth-century Virginia. Finally, my husband, Spencer Lucas, deserves more thanks than can be rendered in words. He has endured more of the Ladies over the years than should be necessary. He has inspired me to work hard, and he has tirelessly given me the inspiration and encouragement that I needed. For that, I will always be grateful.

Introduction

And when the bright sun of peace shall gleam refulgent
from the murky clouds of War, a band of battle scarred
veterans, a still unfainting few bearing their tattered
standards to the scenes of home, beneath peaceful skies,
shall gladly pay a life long homage at the shrine of the
patriotic ladies of the South, at their feet shall be laid
the brightest laurels and fairest fruits of peace.
—WICKHAM'S BRIGADE TO MRS. RALEIGH COLSTON,
JANUARY 23, 1865

A few short miles from busy U.S. I-66, which carries throngs of politicians, bureaucrats, and visitors to the nation's capital each day, rest the remains of more than two hundred Confederate soldiers in a small, unassuming cemetery. Located on the property of the Manassas National Battlefield Park, the Groveton Confederate Cemetery serves as a reminder of the nation's bloodiest war. In this burial ground there is but one inconspicuous interpretive sign intended to provide at least a bit of the field's turbulent history. The sign gets the story wrong, however, indicating that the cemetery had been established by the United Daughters of the Confederacy in 1866. The Daughters could not have done so: they did not organize for another thirty years. Instead, it had been members of the local Ladies' Memorial Association, established in 1867, who had secured the land, located the bodies to be reinterred, created the cemetery, maintained it for more than forty years, and honored the Confederate dead through annual Memorial Day celebrations. Like their counterparts in communities throughout Virginia and the South, the Manassas Ladies' Memorial Association had created a shrine to the Confederacy and had helped perpetuate the memory of their dead—only to be forgotten or mistaken for the Daughters by the time the interpretive plaque was installed by the National Park Service in the late twentieth century.[1]

As the historical marker at Manassas indicates, historians and contemporary Americans have tended to forget the role the Ladies (as they called themselves) played in crafting a positive memory of the Confederacy.[2] When women have emerged as primary actors in what has become known as the Lost Cause, they do so only in the 1890s and early 1900s with the United Daughters of the Confederacy. Ladies' Memorial Associations have essentially become either invisible or tangential to the development of the Lost Cause.[3] This book restores these women's place in the historical narrative by exploring their role as the creators and purveyors of Confederate tradition in the post–Civil War South. Through a study of Virginia's Ladies' Memorial Associations from 1865 to 1915, it examines how and why middle- and upper-class southern white women came to shape the public rituals of Confederate memory, Reconstruction, and reconciliation.

Contrary to contemporary understandings, between 1865 and 1915 white southerners frequently hailed the critical role Ladies' Memorial Associations (LMAS) had played in crafting the traditions that honored the Confederate cause and keeping alive a sense of white southern solidarity. They understood that it had been the Ladies, not Confederate veterans, former politicians, or even the Daughters, who had established Confederate cities of the dead and had organized elaborate Memorial Day celebrations where they might gather to mourn their failed cause. "Thanks to the ladies' memorial associations," one Richmond newspaper editor noted, "once a year, all the people ceasing from labor, turn their thoughts back to the war [and] revive the memories of those days of heroism and suffering." The *Southern Opinion*, an anti-Reconstruction newspaper, further commended the annual Memorial Days organized by women throughout the South for "keeping alive that nationality and hereditary feeling that our destroyers would systematically crush out." Former Confederate general Robert E. Lee, too, understood the ramifications of the women's commemorations. He extolled the women's "noble efforts, to protect the graves of those enshrined in our hearts," though he consistently declined to attend Memorial Day exercises because he believed such celebrations engendered northern hostility and slowed reconciliation. Even the northern press held the Ladies responsible for "inflaming the passions" through their commemorative traditions. Forty years after the war, the tributes to women continued when General Stith Bolling heralded the "untiring and faithful efforts of the Ladies of the Memorial Association to perpetuate [veterans'] memory."[4] White southerners and northerners of the late nineteenth and early twentieth centuries clearly recognized the efforts of these southern "Ladies" in perpetuating nostalgia for the Confederate past, or for what has come to be known as the Lost Cause.

The rhetoric and traditions of the Lost Cause developed in the postwar climate of economic, racial, and gender uncertainty as many white southerners began to cultivate a public memory of the Confederacy that sought to present the war and its outcome in the best possible terms. Rather than forsaking the defeated Confederacy, they created and romanticized the "Old South" and the Confederate war effort, often factually and chronologically distorting the way in which the past would be remembered. This nostalgia for the past accompanied a collective forgetting of slavery, while defining Reconstruction as a period of "Yankee aggression" and black "betrayal." The Lost Cause provided a sense of relief to white southerners who feared being dishonored by defeat, and its rituals and rhetoric celebrated the memory of personal sacrifice in a region rapidly experiencing change and disorder.

One of the reasons historians may have overlooked the relevance of women and gender in memorializing the past, especially between 1865 and 1890, is that most have focused on national organizations and trends, such as the United Confederate Veterans and the United Daughters of the Confederacy. Because of this national scope, not only have they disregarded community-based groups such as the LMAs, but they have also failed to examine the fractures within postwar memory and the cyclical nature of Confederate celebration. Likewise, historians have vastly underestimated the number of women involved in efforts to enshrine the Lost Cause, proposing that only a handful had the energy, resources, and inclination to engage in memorial activities. Evidence from Virginia proves that a solid core of dedicated women emerged as early as 1865 and 1866 to serve as guardians of what they deemed to be a sacred past; more than three hundred women organized into three different LMAs in Richmond alone only one year after the surrender. Furthermore, these organizations did not disappear by the 1870s but endured well into the twentieth century. Like the Lost Cause as a whole, the LMAs experienced a period of depressed interest in the late 1870s and 1880s, but the associations managed to revitalize themselves and continued to influence Lost Cause traditions for several more decades.[5] The women of the LMAs, and not the United Confederate Veterans nor the United Daughters of the Confederacy, were responsible for remaking military defeat into a political, social, and cultural victory for the white South.[6]

By considering women's earliest mourning activities as a political response to Reconstruction, much of our understanding of Lost Cause historiography can be revised. The traditional narrative argues that celebrations of the Confederacy emerged with the die-hards, such as former Confederate general Jubal A. Early, in the 1870s, flourished in the mid-1880s with veterans' groups, and reached a pinnacle of popularity early in the twentieth century in un-broken continuity. But this chronology assumes that men alone directed the

movement. By placing women at the forefront of this movement, the nature of Confederate traditions and memory is altered in several ways. First, it be-comes apparent that the Lost Cause began *immediately* after the war, as soon as May 1865 in some localities. Second, contrary to the assumptions of many historians, the memorial work of the Ladies was intensely political and should not be cast aside as insignificant.[7] Finally, the notion of an ever-increasing momentum toward the Lost Cause is replaced with a more complicated pic-ture of the tensions within postwar memory and the cycles of celebration.[8]

Scholars have increasingly recognized that memory is not a passive act, but that people actively engage in selecting what should be remembered and what should be omitted from the historical record. Historians such as William Blair, David Blight, John Neff, W. Fitzhugh Brundage, Joan Waugh, and Alice Fahs, among others, have demonstrated the ways in which northerners and southerners, white and black, participants and civilians, interpreted Civil War memory through veterans' reunions, memorial celebrations, and the con-struction of monuments. Through these acts, memories of the past became a shared creation, providing a sense of community for those with "common remembrances." As Fitzhugh Brundage has so powerfully argued, this process allowed those who wrote the history to stake claims of power and status—in the case of ex-Confederates and their heirs this translated into claims about who was and who was not a legitimate southerner.[9] But in order to thoroughly understand this process of memory making, we need to start at the beginning. The foundation for Confederate nationalism and solidarity had been crafted during the war, but the postwar beginnings of the Lost Cause originated in the hands of the LMAs.

Exploring the Lost Cause through the lens of the LMAs also challenges the conventional narrative of southern women's history. The LMAs were the first systematic and enduring organizations among southern white women twenty to thirty years before the establishment of national groups such as the United Daughters of the Confederacy, the Daughters of the American Revolution, and the Woman's Christian Temperance Union. LMAs, therefore, provide evidence of a collective southern white woman's consciousness and activism (what historians have labeled "organized womanhood") much earlier than many historians have supposed. Through their experiences with the Ladies, middle- and upper-class southern white women altered their relationships to each other, to men, and to the state. They redefined what it meant to be both an "ex-Confederate" and a "southern lady" in the postwar South.

Historians of southern women generally agree that the war offered many white women a chance to step beyond the traditional boundaries of their gender. During the four years of civil war, white women in Virginia and throughout the Confederacy expanded on the civic duty they had embraced since the Second Great Awakening. They saw their loved ones off to war, endured the hardships of the home front, nursed the wounded, and, most important, formed a myriad of patriotic and benevolent associations to support the cause. Confederate women moved more directly into the political realm by coordinating regional supply networks, sponsoring gunboats, undermining the orders of Union soldiers, participating in military funerals, and fanning the flames of Confederate nationalism. As Anne Firor Scott argued more than thirty years ago, the war helped to emancipate southern white women, allowing them to take on both new activities and new ideas about gender.[10]

[margin note: ✓ war pushed S. women into new roles]

Historians such as Suzanne Lebsock, George C. Rable, Drew Gilpin Faust, and LeeAnn Whites have since challenged Scott's findings. They maintain that southern white women returned to their antebellum roles immediately after the war in large measure to prop up southern patriarchy, failing to participate in organized clubs or public life until the latter part of the nineteenth century. But an examination of the LMAs demonstrates that, for many Confederate women, devotion to the cause and participation in female-driven organizations did not end with Appomattox but grew stronger in the postwar period. The war proved to be a pivotal moment for white women, creating unusual opportunities and amplifying their activities.[11] Most important, the war politicized them far more than partisan rallies or benevolent societies ever could have. Middle-class and elite southern white women emerged from the war more active, both socially and politically, than at any previous time in their history and immediately directed their energies into memorial societies. The LMAs, therefore, served a critical role in the evolution of southern white women's societies.[12]

[margin note: ✓ war was pivotal -- did NOT revert back to household after]

Here a definition of politics is necessary. Rather than a strict nineteenth-century understanding of the term as confined to voting and political parties, the definition must be broadened. Politics as I have chosen to employ it, is the ability of individuals or groups to wield influence in their communities, state, or region. As historian Lori D. Ginzberg has pointed out, virtually all early-to-mid-nineteenth-century female activists "recoiled from a public association with the potentially partisan nature of their efforts . . . but they lived with the contradictions of exerting their influence in decidedly political ways toward clear political ends." Antebellum and wartime women, both North and South, attempted to and succeeded in influencing their respective governments through legislative petitions, voluntary associations, reports, appeals, and even novels. As historian Elizabeth Varon has shown, in some instances women expressed their allegiance to a particular political party on the campaign trail, and during the sectional crisis southern white women acted first as mediators and then as advocates of southern rights. During the Civil War, Confederate women continued to petition the government, criticize military and bureaucratic leadership, help to supply the Confederate armies, and claim to be the most ardent of patriots. Although Victorian culture assumed that women were indifferent to politics, this was hardly the case.[13]

Women's interest in politics continued after the war across a wide range of issues, including the political reconstruction of the South. It was in this realm that women found a way to further deploy politics in the interest of their state (by which they still meant the Confederate nation), and they were successful in part because white men presumed them to be "apolitical." LMAS actively rejected northern attempts to remake southern identity, even as they fashioned material for remembering the past. White women's postwar memorialization efforts were therefore an extension of their deep devotion to the Confederate nation and of the time-tested vehicles of benevolent societies, memorial associations, and partisan campaigns. As Anne Firor Scott has argued, "It was in the Reconstruction period that the first foreshadowing of a new style of woman began to appear." LMAS, therefore, reveal not only well-laid networks of southern white women, but also the highly bureaucratized, political nature of such women's organizations.[14]

This book, therefore, explores how gender infused efforts to commemorate the past and to define what it meant to be an ex-Confederate after defeat. Women's postwar organizations not only employed the skills they had gleaned from decades of experience, but they also served an even more valuable purpose to their male counterparts. Because women, and not ex-Confederate soldiers, directed early memorialization efforts, white southerners hoped that northerners would perceive their work as less politically motivated and threatening. Just as members of the southern Whig Party had done since the 1830s, postbellum Virginian men and women agreed that because the Ladies were by nature uninterested in politics, their motives must be pure. If women were not political, then, by extension, their actions could not be either. Memorial activities lay clearly within the province of female mourning and posed no threat to sectional reunion. Because women were able to lay the groundwork for commemoration immediately after the war, ex-Confederates could later glorify their past without much resistance from northern observers. Although disputes over control of the movement arose between male and female leaders

[margin handwritten note:] Cloak of gender made it seem less political

in the 1870s and 1880s, LMA women secured the foundation for national reconciliation of northern and southern whites by providing the domestic legitimization of mourning that Confederate men lacked.

The Ladies shrewdly manipulated the political conditions of Reconstruction and the New South to maintain widespread southern support and broadened their public role by serving as surrogate government agencies for the defeated Confederacy. While northern women such as Elizabeth Cady Stanton, Susan B. Anthony, and Lucy Stone debated woman suffrage and the Fifteenth Amendment, the LMAS were likewise busy redefining southern women's relationship to men and the state, thus creating an alternate (and uniquely southern) form of women's political engagement. They staged elaborate public spectacles; moved beyond the local nature of earlier southern benevolent work that had focused on orphanages and almshouses; and called on municipal and state governments to support their projects. Expanding on their wartime roles, the LMAS allowed southern white women to engage in civic life as never before. In between the localized benevolent societies of the 1830s and the women's club movement of the 1880s and 1890s, the LMAS served as a transitional group in the evolution of southern white women's organizations.

The very nature of the LMAS' work forced them to craft a new relationship with both men and the state. Female club members hired and managed men for reinterment projects; they drew public attention to themselves when they organized and took center stage at memorial activities; they solicited support from the most powerful men in their communities, state, and region to accomplish their goals; and they fought off those men who attempted to thwart their efforts. Not surprisingly, too, male/female relations were not uniform throughout Virginia. For example, in Petersburg the elite white women of the LMA and the city's male leaders often disagreed over the necessity of maintaining the Confederate cemetery, while in Winchester the men and women worked closely together to provide a unified front. In many cases, men supported LMAS financially and otherwise, and men certainly found a valuable political reason for supporting women's efforts that allowed all former Confederates to honor their past. But, regardless of the specific situation, gender patterns did not return to their antebellum status, as some historians have posited; rather, women of the LMAS proved determined to control the direction of their associations, expand their civic duties, and redefine the very nature of southern femininity.[15]

Because the Ladies had taken the center stage at the end of the war, these women came to believe that they were equally valuable participants in the state, setting in motion debates regarding women's influence over Confederate memorialization as Reconstruction came to an end. Despite the diversity of male/female relations among Virginia's LMAs, the general pattern confirms that LMAs did not simply organize to bolster southern white men's masculinity in the face of defeat, as some historians have maintained.[16] It is true that the LMAs' primary objective was to honor the sacrifices and lives of those Confederate men who had fallen in battle. But if LMA women wanted only to reassure men of their virility, they would have played a more submissive role. Although men certainly encouraged female-dominated memorial associations for their own political reasons, the LMAs never served as mere puppets for male ambitions. Neither did women refrain from criticizing men, including veterans, when they failed to provide adequate support for the memorial associations. Above all, these women saw themselves as patriots performing vital civic duties for their communities and the larger South, rather than as purveyors of male confidence. Thus, in this manner, the Ladies not only honored those men who had fought for the South, but they also secured their own legacy as devoted citizens and participants in the cause.

The Old Dominion was certainly not the only southern state in which LMAs organized. Georgia, South Carolina, North Carolina, Mississippi, and Alabama also witnessed a proliferation of such groups in the war's aftermath; all told, between seventy and one hundred such associations were established throughout the South.[17] But Virginia offers the most fruitful study because of its prominence during the years of the Confederacy and its significance as a bastion of Lost Cause rhetoric and figures. As the center of the war's Eastern Theater, Virginia experienced more battles on its soil, sent more men to fight, and lost more sons than any other state.[18] Many of the war's most famous heroes hailed from the Commonwealth, including Thomas J. "Stonewall" Jackson and Robert E. Lee, and the state capital of Richmond served simultaneously as the Confederate capital beginning in May 1861. Between the 1870s and early 1900s, several of the most important male-dominated Lost Cause organizations called Virginia home, such as the Southern Historical Society, the Lee Monument Association, the Lee Memorial Association, and the Grand Camp of Confederate Veterans (Robert E. Lee Camp in Richmond).

But Virginia also fostered the organization of extremely active LMAs that were well connected with other women's groups both within their state and across the region at large. By the fall of 1868, at least twenty-six such societies, including those at Appomattox Court House, Bristol, Charlottesville, Danville, Emory and Henry College (Washington County), Fairfax Court House, Fredericksburg, Front Royal (Warren County), King George County, Gordonsville (Piedmont), Leesburg, Lexington, Loudoun Park, Lynchburg,

Manassas and Bull Run, New Market, Orange Court House, Petersburg, Portsmouth, Richmond (three different associations), Spotsylvania, Staunton, Warrenton, and Winchester, were enthusiastically establishing cemeteries and arranging Memorial Days throughout the state. With a conservative estimate of 50 members per association, more than 1,300 of Virginia's elite and middle-class women joined the ranks of the LMAs in the years immediately after the war.[19]

I selected the cities of Winchester, Fredericksburg, Petersburg, Lynchburg, and Richmond because of the diversity of wartime and postwar experiences they offer. I use the terms "city" and "town" interchangeably, as the residents did, but these communities represent a range of populations, with the largest being Richmond and the smallest being Winchester. Likewise, they offer a wide geographic base, extending from Winchester in the far northern corner of the state, to Lynchburg on the median between the Piedmont and Blue Ridge, and then to Petersburg in the Southside. Most importantly, within these five communities alone, women of the LMAs reinterred the remains of more than 72,520 Confederates, nearly 28 percent of the 260,000 Confederate soldiers who perished in the war.[20]

Although it would ultimately have one of the smaller Confederate cemeteries, Winchester proved to be the first community to establish an LMA. Located in the famous Shenandoah Valley twenty-five miles south of Harpers Ferry, the town became a military command post and major supply depot for the Confederacy in April 1861. Most of the community's 3,000 white residents supported the Confederate effort, but throughout the Lower Shenandoah Valley (as it was designated because the Shenandoah River ran north to meet the Potomac), pockets of staunch Unionist sentiment persisted for the course of the war. Because of its strategic importance within the Valley and its proximity to the U.S. capital in Washington, D.C., Winchester remained contested territory throughout the conflict, occupied by one army or another at all times and witnessing five major battles.[21]

Situated on the fall line of the Rappahannock River, Fredericksburg had been a mercantile center in colonial times, but much of its glory had waned by the Civil War as a result of the tobacco depression in the 1840s. Fredericksburg's 5,000 residents, along with those in the surrounding counties of Spotsylvania and Stafford, endured four major battles during the war—Fredericksburg (December 1862), Chancellorsville (May 1863), the Wilderness (May 1864), and Spotsylvania (May 1864). These battles claimed more than 100,000 causalities, necessitating makeshift hospitals throughout the town and countryside. Union troops occupied the town on five separate occasions during the conflict, the first beginning on April 19, 1862. During the bombardment by Union forces under the command of General Ambrose E. Burnside on December 11, 1862, the town suffered nearly as much destruction as the more famed cities of Atlanta and Charleston. Testimony from both civilians and the armies reported rampant looting and destruction by the Union forces as they marched through town. According to historian William Blair, soldiers "entered homes, stripped clothing from bureaus, defaced walls with their unit numbers, and tossed contents into the streets." Word of the sacking spread quickly throughout the South and served to intensify hatred toward the Union soldiers. Although subsequent battles in the area continued to drain the city's resources and increase privations, the winter of 1862 had been seared into Fredericksburg's memory.[22]

In 1860, Petersburg had been a bustling manufacturing and transportation hub for the South, with a population of 18,266 and the largest free urban black population in Virginia. Between 1850 and 1860, the population had expanded by nearly 30 percent, and the value of all real estate, personal property, and slaves had increased by 82 percent. The second-largest city in Virginia, and fiftieth-largest in the country, its five railroads extended in several directions, shipping products from the city's cotton mills, ironworks, slave trade, and tobacco manufacturers. The Confederate army understood that Petersburg's link between Richmond and supplies in the west and south made it a prime target for Union armies, and during the summer of 1862 southern engineers constructed a ten-mile line of fortifications around the city. On June 9, 1864, Union forces, led by Major General Benjamin F. Butler, threatened the town, and a small force described as 129 "grey haired sires and beardless youths" of the home guard held off the Federal soldiers until the Confederate forces arrived, sustaining 15 deaths and 18 wounded. For the next ten months, Union forces commenced a steady siege on the Confederate line, the railroads, and the city itself. On April 2, 1865, General Lee ordered the soldiers defending Petersburg to evacuate and to set fire to several of the city's tobacco warehouses, bridges, and railroad stations. The following day, Union soldiers took possession of the shell-shocked city.[23]

Like Petersburg, Lynchburg experienced a period of rapid growth and prosperity in the years immediately preceding the Civil War. Its financial base of tobacco "flowed into the city in increasing quantities," but the city's other industries, such as iron foundries, gristmills, and clothing manufacturers, also contributed to its success. The city lay 110 miles west of Richmond along the James River and the Kanawha Canal and at the convergence of six major turnpikes, thus making it an important link in the transportation network of the state and the Confederacy. Lynchburg's 6,000 residents experienced only one major battle in the immediate vicinity of their city, and that battle paled in comparison to military action near the other cities of this study. But its rail, canal, and road access rendered Lynchburg an important supply and hospital center. By the end of the war, Lynchburg's tobacco warehouses, empty buildings, and private homes had been converted into more than 30 hospitals with a staff of approximately 50 military surgeons and several hundred women nurses/matrons who treated more than 20,000 patients (nearly 3,000 of whom died in the city).[24]

Richmond, the City of Seven Hills, had grown up along the fall line of the James River as a trading town in the eighteenth century. It had served as the Commonwealth's capital since 1780 and was named capital of the Confederacy in May 1861. During the antebellum period, the capital city, like Petersburg and Lynchburg, thrived as an industrial complex and commodity broker. Companies such as Tredegar Iron Works, the Crenshaw Woolen Mills, the Franklin Paper Mill, seven major flour mills, and fifty tobacco factories depended on slave labor, and the slave trade became the city's most profitable business. In 1860, the city's population was 37,916 (including 11,699 slaves and 2,576 free blacks), but refugees, soldiers, and government officials arrived during the war to swell the population to more than 100,000. Throughout the conflict, the city remained a constant target of the Union army, most famously during the 1862 Peninsula campaign and again in the 1864 Overland campaign. As one historian has noted, "The city was, at times, almost an annex of the battlefield, surrounded by armed encampments, thronged with wounded and with prisoners, infused with the sights and smells and sounds of death."[25]

Rather than focusing on one community at a time, I have woven the stories of each locale together into one narrative, allowing me to highlight and explain the differences between cities while simultaneously drawing general conclusions. Chapter 1 examines the ways in which Virginia women supported the war effort through their "patriotic" activities. Women's wartime conduct simultaneously transformed their relationships with each other and the state and heightened their public role in mourning traditions, all of which became crucial to the establishment of LMAS (and therefore the Lost Cause) in the years after Appomattox. Chapter 2 traces the development of seven LMAS in Virginia, focusing on which women were most likely to join the cause and elaborating on the political dimension of white women as the guardians of Confederate memory. Chapter 3 follows the LMAS during their years of prominence from 1867 through 1870. In these years of Congressional or "Radical" Reconstruction, Virginia's white women continued to dominate and dictate the path of Confederate celebration. Chapter 4 explores the increasing tension between male and female Lost Cause representatives. As the political necessity of white women leading the commemoration diminished, white men, especially former Confederate leaders such as Jubal Early, attempted to wrest control of the movement from the Ladies. Chapter 5 explores the resurrection of the LMAs during the so-called height of the Lost Cause in the last two decades of the century and considers how the associations were able to transition from a period of gender strife into an era of gender cooperation. Finally, chapter 6 examines the relationship between the Ladies and the new generation of women devoted to the Lost Cause, the United Daughters of the Confederacy.

A word about what this study does not explore is in order. First, I have focused on African American commemorations of the Civil War only where they bear directly on the activities of the LMAs. This is in part because historians such as Kathleen Clark, William Blair, David Blight, and Antoinette Van Zelm have provided an extensive and well-developed literature on the subject. Equally important, African American women, like white women who supported the Union, could follow a path different from their ex-Confederate counterparts in memorializing their Civil War experiences. When it came to burying the Union dead, including those of the U.S. Colored Troops, the federal government and not women's organizations performed the work. Moreover, African American men and women tended to work together in Emancipation Day ceremonies. Although there were often clear distinctions between men's and women's spheres in celebrations, African American women, unlike members of the LMAs, did not have to take the lead to shield their men from charges of treason.[26]

This does not mean that race was unimportant in the making of the Lost Cause. On the contrary, it played a vital role in shaping the social, cultural, and political dynamics of the postwar South. For example, an African American celebration of Richmond's evacuation appears to have helped spark the city's Confederate memorial movement in 1866. Similarly, although LMAs frequently touted the "loyal" black people who attended their memorial services, the word "Confederate" in their writings clearly indicated that their associations were for whites only. It was not until the surge in white supremacy and violence against black people in the closing decades of the nineteenth century that Confederate memorial groups believed it necessary to designate their organizations for "whites only"—as one Richmond LMA did in the 1890s. In the years that followed, as the Ladies began to fade from the spotlight, the newly organized United Daughters of the Confederacy more directly endorsed white supremacy by indoctrinating schoolchildren and poor white southerners with racial stereotypes and exaggerations about the benevolence of slavery. But in the earlier period examined in this study, the Ladies were not predominantly concerned with race (no doubt because they assumed white supremacy).[27]

Likewise, this is the story of women who joined the LMAs, and as such it does not engage in a systematic fashion the women who did not join. The majority of southern white women in the postwar South did not enroll in the LMAs, either for financial or social reasons. The associations were the province of well-connected, middle- and upper-class white women who had the resources and time to focus on the past. Even so, the activities of the LMAs touched the lives of white women from all social classes. In many instances, the Ladies provided burials for Confederate soldiers that their own mothers and families could not afford. Most important, the Memorial Day services organized by the Ladies allowed tens of thousands of white southerners, rich or poor, to perpetuate a sense of latent Confederate nationalism.

Neither do I attempt to analyze the organization of men's memorial associations and veterans' associations.[28] But this book does add to the scholarship on men's organizations in a couple of important ways. First, when women's mourning ceremonies of 1865 and 1866 are taken as evidence of a collective Confederate response to defeat, it helps restore men to the earliest Lost Cause activities. And second, it also suggests that men were in fact motivated to celebrate the Confederacy, at least in part because of their competition with women and gendered assumptions about battlefield glory.

In terms of sources, I have tried, to the extent possible, to retrieve the voices in the form of diaries and letters of individuals from each of the selected communities. When necessary, however, I have incorporated evidence from other places in the state that appeared to reflect the attitudes and activities of those who experienced the war or were involved in memorial work in the Commonwealth. Most of the information regarding individual LMAs comes directly from their minutes and correspondences, except in the case of the Winchester association, whose organizational records no longer exist. Newspapers, pamphlets, circulars, and publications such as the *Confederate Veteran* rounded out the research.[29]

Ultimately, this book reveals the ways in which middle- and upper-class southern white women of the LMAs played a vital role in shaping the politics, culture, and society of late-nineteenth-century Virginia. Through their activities and membership bases, the Ladies helped sustain a sense of Confederate pride and white southern solidarity in the face of battlefield defeat. My hope is that this book illuminates an all-too-often-neglected aspect of southern women's history, highlighting the ways in which gender affected how Americans remembered—and continue to remember—the Confederacy and the Civil War.

Patriotic Ladies of the South

1

Virginia Women
in the Confederacy

While Virginia's men and boys gathered their muskets and marched off to battle in the spring of 1861, the Commonwealth's women understood that they, too, had an important role to play during this time of national crisis. Women willingly sent their husbands, brothers, and sons off to war; they helped supply the armies with clothing, food, and bandages; they endured countless hardships on the home front; they nursed the wounded and helped bury the dead; and they championed the southern cause.[1] Sixteen-year-old Lizzie Alsop not only supported the war effort by helping to send supplies to Confederate hospitals in Richmond, but she also demonstrated her loyalty to the rebel nation when she denounced the Union soldiers who had taken over Fredericksburg in the summer of 1862. "I never hear or see a Federal private or officer riding down the street that I don't wish his neck may be broken before he crosses the bridge," she proudly noted. She praised the local women for treating the Yankees "with silent contempt" and declared that the northern soldiers "little know the hatred in our hearts toward them." That same summer when she and several friends passed a store where a Union flag flew, they "all went into the street preferring to get our dresses dirty to *bending our heads* beneath the 'Stars & Stripes.'"[2]

This deep loyalty to the Confederate nation had profound implications for individual Virginia women as well as for their organizations and female networks. Building on a tradition of antebellum benevolent societies, Confederate women elaborated a more public and political role for themselves by way of their patriotism in aid societies, hospitals, and cemeteries.[3] They coordinated regional supply networks, sponsored gunboats, defied orders of Union soldiers, and participated in military funerals. These wartime experiences heightened the nature of women's associations, broadened their base, and extended their geographic reach across the state and region, thereby transforming women's relationships with one another and with the state. This expansion of women's organizations and activity, moreover, did not end when the armies laid down their guns. The networks and support bases these women established during the war became crucial to the establishment of the Lost Cause in the years after Appomattox, as women like Lizzie Alsop extended their wartime patriotism into Ladies' Memorial Associations (LMAS). The battlefields of Virginia did more than alter forever the lives of thousands of her sons; it transformed the patriotic fervor, political horizons, and civic responsibilities of many of her leading daughters as well.

As had been the case prior to the outbreak of hostilities, during the war Virginia's white women paid close heed to what was happening in the larger political world. They read newspapers and corresponded with friends and family to keep abreast of the happenings throughout the North and the South. In their diaries and letters, women detailed the maneuverings of armies and commented on the capabilities of officers and government officials. In May 1862, Betty Herndon Maury of Fredericksburg criticized General Joseph E. Johnston for not attacking McClellan during that spring's Peninsula campaign. Adelaide Clopton voiced similar frustrations in the summer of 1862. She berated Confederate leaders for their many "useless, profitless battles." If only the army would pursue the Union forces and not allow them to recuperate after every encounter, she argued, the war might end. But beyond merely watching and listening, Virginia's women launched their own war effort in their homes and churches, at hospitals, and, eventually, in their cemeteries.[4]

Prior to the Civil War, northern and southern white women alike had been largely excluded from the nation's narratives. According to one scholar, in the antebellum years, "literature on the nation, with its focus on governments, public parties, and military heroes, simply ignored the roles of women." Women had served as spies and aided the Continental Army during the American Revolution, but this activity was not deemed equivalent to that of the male citizen-soldier. While women might contribute to the well-being of the nation by raising good republican sons, citizenship had been defined by service to the state and so remained restricted to white men. But the Civil War fundamentally blurred this line. The scale of the war necessitated the mobilization of men as well as women in both the North and the South, leading the press, pulpits, and politicians alike to call on "patriotic ladies" to support their respective political communities.[5]

Like their female counterparts in the Union and elsewhere in the Confederacy, at a rapid pace Virginia's white women transformed their antebellum benevolent, school, and church associations into ladies' relief and soldiers' aid societies. Women, who had previously spent their afternoons visiting, now found themselves busy seamstresses. "The click of the sewing-machine was the music which most interested them," recalled one Richmond woman. "The 'stitch, stitch, stitch,' from morning to night" filled the parlors and church halls as women plied their new trade. Women went to work carding lint, rolling bandages, and sewing jackets, trousers, and haversacks. They made heavy tents from cumbrous sailcloth, leaving many delicate fingers stiff, swollen, and bleeding. Those who had little experience in sewing also volunteered their limited skills. "Even tents were made by fingers that had scarcely ever used a needle before," observed Winchester's Cornelia McDonald.[6]

Nearly every town and city in the Commonwealth became the site of some ladies' association. Lynchburg's town leaders called on the women to aid in the "patriotic act" of furnishing supplies for the volunteer companies. The young girls of the Lynchburg Female Seminary donated the funds they had raised for their May festival to purchase knapsacks for the Rifle Greys. On April 20, nearly 500 of the city's women organized the Ladies' Relief Society to outfit the poorer regiments. Within weeks, they had equipped several companies and were making uniforms for a company organized in nearby Nelson County. By the following January, the women reported that they had provided 1,789 coats, 2,195 pairs of pants, 1,454 shirts, 493 pairs of drawers, 523 pairs of gaiters, 1,175 cartridge boxes, 66 beds, 10 overcoats, and many other necessary articles. As one Virginia woman aptly observed, "Our needles are now our weapons."[7]

At least six church-based sewing societies formed in Petersburg to support the troops. In July 1861, the women of the Washington Street congregation organized a society to "aid in both clothing and contributing to the relief of the soldiers of the Confederate Army." A separate group of Petersburg women picked up their needles to aid the cause and also to provide relief on the home front. Bessie Callender, Jane Simpson, Evelyn Walker, and several others (most of whom would later join the LMA) organized a society to provide work to the wives of those who had enlisted. Collectively, the disparate women's groups made arrangements with the Commissary Department in Richmond to have materials delivered each week to Tabb Street Church. There the cotton cloth would be distributed to the city's sewing societies; a tailor was employed to cut the drawers and shirts. "I cannot tell how many thousands were made," Callender later recalled, noting that she often found it difficult to get home to dinner. But with the exhausting work, the women kept the men in uniform and reached out to their less fortunate sisters. Callender claimed that her group paid good prices; the payroll often amounted to a $1,000 a week in Confederate scrip. "In this way I became well acquainted with a class of women I had not known before." The war, it seemed, was quickly breaking down many long-standing class barriers.[8]

Sewing societies in the capital city also multiplied. Within two weeks of the bombardment on Fort Sumter, female members of the Grace Baptist Church began to meet after Sunday services to sew for the soldiers. The women of the First and Second Baptist Churches, West Point Church, and four Methodist churches all helped sew uniforms and tents for local military companies. Lucy Bagby and her mother joined yet another association that met daily at St. Paul's Church. Under the auspices of Miss M. E. Woodward, women in the neighborhood of Ridge Church met in August 1861 to form the Ladies' Ridge Benevolent Society. The society's goals included alleviating the suffering of sick and wounded soldiers and, like Callender's association, also providing "work and other comforts for such families as have been left by the soldiers in our neighborhood without a sufficient support." The women initially agreed to meet every Saturday, with a goal of darning at least 500 pairs of socks for the army.[9]

Mary Adams Randolph, wife of Secretary of War George Wythe Randolph, served as president of the city's most prestigious organization, the Richmond Ladies' Association. It included wives of government officials, such as Mary Boykin Chesnut, but the association consisted primarily of "old [women] who wanted their way." Chesnut mused that the women, excluding Randolph, were often "crossgrained" with "sharp tempers." At one meeting, the group became rankled when Randolph proposed dividing all the goods sent to the organization equally with the northern wounded and sick prisoners. Some women believed it was indeed the Christian thing to do, but others were less generous. "Some shrieked in wrath at the bare idea of putting our noble soldiers on par with Yankees—living, dying, or dead," recalled Chesnut. She believed that these "august, severe matrons" had not been accustomed to hearing the other side of an argument from anyone. They were, rather, "just old enough to find the last pleasure in life in power—and the power to make their claws felt." Despite the bitter infighting that these meetings endured, the association proved remarkably efficient at collecting and distributing goods to needy and wounded *Confederate* soldiers.[10]

The Ladies' Soldiers' Relief Society of Fredericksburg included a similar makeup of women from the town's most prominent families—many of whom would play a leading role in the postwar memorial associations. Mary Gordon Wallace, wife of medical director, bank president, and former mayor John H. Wallace, served as president. Bella Little, a journalist and sister to the town's local newspaper editor, acted as secretary. Other members included Sallie Braxton Slaughter, wife of a banker, Lucy A. Broaddus, wife of the Fredericksburg Baptist Church's minister, Elizabeth Gordon, wife of a bank cashier, and Mrs. F. A. Knox, wife of a merchant and wheat speculator.[11]

Perhaps it was this elitism within the groups that led some women to complain that members were merely using aid societies to gain notoriety. An unnamed "lady" from Lynchburg went so far as to write a letter to the editor disparaging the local women's organizations. She believed that "certain cliques" monopolized these groups. It was her observation that the "few" consult, form the basis for the societies, agree on officers, and then place a notice in the papers calling for a mass meeting. "When we go," she wrote, "we find the project all cut and dried—a fixed matter—between these few leaving the masses . . . with nothing to do, but to expend their money for the credit of a few women."[12]

Many women, nevertheless, devoted substantial amounts of time and energy to such work. Sallie Munford of Richmond apologized to her brother Charles for not writing more frequently in June 1861. "My opportunities for writing are very small now, for I really feel as if I was neglecting a positive duty every moment taken from work on the soldiers' clothes," she confessed. Twenty-one-year-old Abby Gwathmey told her parents she had spent the better part of a week making six large jackets, each with sixteen buttonholes. In Fredericksburg, Betty Herndon Maury, daughter of the world-famous oceanographer Matthew Fontaine Maury, recorded her hard work in her diary. In three days, she managed to complete six pairs of pantaloons, six jackets, eight shirts, and haversacks. Overwhelmed at first, she quickly found women willing to assist in the work. "Every one that I asked took a part," she noted; "the work is now comparatively easy." Even Mary Custis Lee, wife of the Confederacy's acclaimed general, spent her time knitting gloves and socks for the soldiers.[13]

Confederate men lauded and encouraged women's nationalistic and philanthropic efforts. In Lynchburg, the local paper heralded the "moral heroism and fortitude evinced by the women of this city" engaged in preparing their men for the upcoming struggle. According to the paper, the women had made themselves "useful in the present emergency, and deserve great praise for their patriotic spirit." Men in Richmond urged women to help provide clothing for the soldiers. "Let the spinning wheel and the handloom and the knitting needle supply the deficiencies of our factories, and provide our soldiers for the rigors of the coming winter," one newspaper requested. The *Richmond Whig* published and warmly endorsed an appeal from Sally Mosby of

Powhatan calling on all Virginia women to contribute their gold and silver for the cause. "There is not a true-born Virginia woman, young or old, who would not gladly strip herself of every ornament, of every vase, goblet, urn or spoon, to uphold the freedom and independence of this State," wrote the editor. Likewise, he seconded Mosby's proposition that every county or town should organize a ladies' aid society.[14]

Rather than seeking women's support, the governor's proclamation of July 1861 called men to arms by touting the eager volunteer efforts of the state's female population. "Our gallant sisters of the South are hurrying to our assistance," noted the governor. "Be ready to lock arms with them, to rush unitedly upon and crush the foul invaders," he advised. What seems especially notable is that this appeal to arms placed women on an equal footing of importance to the war effort. Even the Confederacy's beloved General Stonewall Jackson expressed his "deep and abiding interest in our *female soldiers*." In a letter to a Winchester woman, Jackson noted that the South's women were "patriots in the truest sense of the word, and I more than admire them."[15] Both government officials and army officers recognized the early mobilization of sewing and aid societies, and they encouraged men to join the defense of the Confederacy already under way by women. Although women were obviously not members of the electorate or (usually) army volunteers, Confederate officials considered them a vital component of the nation.[16]

Men and women alike employed the rhetoric of the Revolutionary spirit of 1776 to motivate the state's female population.[17] One reporter pointed out that the women of the Confederacy might not realize how their activities mimicked those of the founding mothers. Quoting Washington Irving, the reporter recounted how Martha Washington had spent her time in the wintry encampments at Valley Forge. There she "set an example to her lady visitors by diligently plying her needle, knitting stockings for the poor, destitute soldiers." Confederate women were, no doubt, "worthy descendants of the matrons of the revolution." In Sally Mosby's plea, she also invoked the Revolution. "Let us emulate our revolutionary matrons," she wrote, to show the entire world "that Virginia's present daughters are not unworthy or degenerate descendants of their noble and patriotic grandmothers."[18]

Women who joined soldiers' aid societies believed that they were fulfilling a necessary patriotic role. Less than a week after Virginia's vote to secede, several Fredericksburg women organized a Soldiers' Relief Society. In resolutions printed in the local newspaper, Mary Gordon Wallace, president of the group, elaborated on the relationship between women and their new nation. The group deeply deplored the sad necessity of war, as women often do, but they would "cheerfully" submit to any privations their husbands or government might direct. They agreed to deny themselves "all the luxuries of dress and table that our men may expend more for the defense of our homes and liberties." Following in the tradition of women during the American Revolution, these women submitted to a self-imposed ban on any article not grown, produced, or manufactured by the Confederacy—although it is unclear whether or not they followed through on their declaration. Confederate women insisted that throughout the secession crisis they had been "silent observers" but "not uninterested spectators of the condition of our State and nation." "We firmly believe the course pursued by Virginia has been ever true and just," they proclaimed.[19]

A month after the first major battle of the war at Manassas, another group of Fredericksburg's women organized the city's second patriotic society. Acting on the suggestion of Captain Matthew Fontaine Maury, the women held a meeting on August 21 to discuss whether a new flag should be adopted by the Confederate states. Calling themselves simply the Ladies of Fredericksburg, they elected Betty Maury president and Mrs. William T. Hart secretary. Maury's cousin, Ellen Mercer Herndon, wrote the petition to Congress citing their objections to the "Bars and Stars," as they called it, on the grounds that it was an ugly, "servile imitation" of the U.S. flag that conveyed "no idea of principle to the eye of the stranger or the citizen of our nation." Instead, the women suggested that the national flag be a "Southern Cross" upon "an azure field." Mrs. S. B. French, Sallie Slaughter, Lizzie Braxton, and Nannie Taylor then drafted a circular addressed to the women of the Confederacy, asking them to hold similar meetings and petition Congress for the flag's adoption. Although the reception of the women's petition remains unclear, sentiment such as theirs no doubt led to the Joint Committee on Flag and Seal's task in April 1862 to propose a new standard for the fledgling nation.[20]

Philanthropic associations and flag petitions were not the only goals of Virginia's women. Gunboat societies, organized by women in coastal cities from Virginia to Alabama, represented what one scholar has deemed "genuine military intervention" on the part of women.[21] On March 27, 1862, Richmond's women first called for a Gunboat Association, or Ladies' Defense and Aid Association, which would further the defense of the city.[22] As the soldiers' aid societies and Ladies of Fredericksburg had done, the women quickly elected officers, adopted a constitution, and organized fund-raising events. It was not until early April that the women, on advice from Captain Maury, decided to raise money for a gunboat to protect the city following the battle of the ironclads, the USS *Monitor* and the CSS *Virginia*, at Hampton Roads. Under the direction of Maria Clopton, a committee of women met with President Jefferson Davis to request that he allow the society to raise the necessary funds for the first gunboat built in the city. Davis immediately endorsed the plans and encouraged the women to meet with the secretary of the navy.[23]

Foreshadowing the organizational networks used by the LMAs following the war, these women immediately set about soliciting funds and materials from each corner of the state. They called upon the tobacconists of Richmond and Lynchburg for old iron and requested donations from other women's organizations and private individuals. Women in Prince Edward, Goochland, and Louisa Counties, along with those in the cities of Fredericksburg and Lynchburg, formed quasi-auxiliary associations to aid the gunboat society. They sent scraps of iron, silver plate, gold watches, metal kettles, and thousands of dollars to the Richmond association. By the end of April, the group's treasurer, Martha Maury, reported that they had collected upwards of $10,000. Within a year, the Gunboat Association had handed the iron and the money over to the government so that the women might rightly call the *Lady Davis* their own.[24] With the ironclad built, the women found it no longer necessary to meet and disbanded the organization in the spring of 1863.[25]

Contrary to scholarly claims that women were expressing displeasure with the government's inability to protect them, these women appear to have simply been looking for yet another outlet to support the Confederacy. After noting in her diary that the Richmond women had organized a gunboat society, Harriette Branham of Louisa offered a positive pronouncement. "Everyone seems to be in good spirits about the war," she wrote. In fact, rather than suggesting a failure on the part of their men, women in these associations viewed themselves as rough partners in the defense of their homes. A resolution from Lynchburg's women supporting the Gunboat Association acknowledged "the vital importance of resisting the march of our invading enemies by all means that can be employed." They vowed "never to surrender our homes and country while life is left in *man or woman* to defend them." Cynthia Coleman of Williamsburg endorsed the plan because she "lov[ed] Virginia too faithfully to see her over-run by a vindictive foe." These women did not believe their men had failed them, but they saw the war as *their* war, too. Southern white women had been attending political rallies prior to April 1861, but the war now offered them an outlet and reason to move more predominantly into the public sphere. Although they could not vote or don a gray uniform, they could provide invaluable services to their state and nation.[26]

As the efforts to build a gunboat reveal, the war provided southern white women with an opportunity to forge networks with like-minded women from across the state and region. Scholars of southern women have argued that until the late 1870s southern culture "inhibited the formation of women's consciousness, collective identity, and self-assertion." This model maintains that the South's evangelical community and kin-dominated society discouraged the development of independent women's networks, even during the Civil War. But evidence abounds to suggest otherwise. Using the organizational skills they had learned from antebellum orphan asylums, benevolent associations, and church groups, along with the continuance of correspondence to friends and family, Confederate women developed substantial female networks that continued into the postwar period.[27]

Virginia's Confederate women went to great lengths to inform white southerners about the Gunboat Association, soldiers' aid societies, and relief efforts. Many relied on time-honored familial and kinship ties, writing to their mothers, sisters, aunts, cousins, and in-laws to solicit support. Living in Fredericksburg, Betty Maury heard continuous reports about the activities of women in the Confederate capital from her many cousins who resided there, including Martha Maury, president of the Gunboat Association. "I wish I were one of the women in Richmond," she wrote in 1862. "They have made for themselves a name that will be handed down with praise and honour for many generations." Later that month, Maury sent $800 to Richmond to help care for wounded soldiers.[28] But the political geography of Virginia also operated as a conduit for women's networks. As both the state and the national capital, Richmond served as a temporary home to bureaucrats, statesmen, and military officials—and their wives—from across the Confederacy. This created immediate ties from the capital city to places as distant as Louisiana and Texas. The famous diarist/memoirist, Mary Boykin Chesnut, wrote letters to her sister-in-law in Camden, South Carolina, with implicit instructions for aiding the war effort. Chesnut informed Harriet Chesnut Grant that a great deal was needed in the capital city for the South Carolina wounded. "Whatever you send," Chesnut wrote, "direct to Mrs. G. Randolph, Franklin St., Richmond. Always send by express." Finally, she noted, "Ask Kate Williams to get us arrowfoot from Florida." Soon after Chesnut's letter, supplies began pouring in from South Carolina.[29]

Newspapers, too, proved an invaluable source for communication among women both within and beyond the state borders. Women devoured newspapers whenever they were available, filling letters and diaries with tidbits of news or gossip they gleaned from the daily or weekly rags. And leaders of women's organizations knew it. Announcements and calls for help from associations regularly appeared in the state's papers, both as a forum for appealing for additional support and as a public reminder of women's dedication to the war effort. The Lynchburg Ladies' Hospital, for example, not only published a detailed list of contributions on a weekly basis but also used the space to invite the cooperation of women from across the state. The Fredericksburg women did the same in their efforts to change the Confederacy's flag. Ladies' associations from other states frequently wrote to Virginia newspapers thanking the local women for tending to their wounded husbands and sons. Finally, the long-standing practice in which editors reprinted articles from other papers vastly increased the circulation of women's appeals. Notices about women's organizations in Richmond, Petersburg, and Winchester often reached the far corners of the state and Confederacy, no doubt inspiring other women to participate in similar associations, just as women's efforts in these locales in turn motivated the Commonwealth's women.[30]

Even more than their northern counterparts, Confederate women found themselves in the midst of a revolution in females' relationship to the state. On June 9, 1861, an order by the U.S. secretary of war had authorized the creation of the U.S. Sanitary Commission to coordinate the volunteer efforts of northern women. The objectives of the commission were to collect supplies, support soldiers' homes, transport the sick and wounded, and provide relief for discharged soldiers. But without such an organization, the Confederacy relied heavily on women's volunteer organizations—a trend that would continue even after the rebel government ceased to exist in April 1865.[31]

In some instances, the Confederate government called on women to aid procurement efforts. Colonel Daniel Ruggles issued General Order No. 4 in July 1861, requesting that the women of Fredericksburg contribute to the war effort in accordance with "the patriotic offer" made by them, by tending "to the comfort and well-being of the sick" in the nearby hospitals. In the spring of 1863, E. W. Johnson of the Medical Purveyors Office too requested that the women of Virginia "render the Confederacy very essential service" by sending a generous supply of garden poppies for the production of opium.[32] But, by and large, women's associations throughout the state initiated the volunteer drives on their own. Even before the first major battle of the war, a group of prominent Richmond churchwomen, led by Nancy MacFarland (future president of the Hollywood Memorial Association), Catherine Myers, Mrs. Frank G.

Ruffin, and several others, formed the Soldiers' Aid Society of Virginia. The association consisted of delegates from the city's various churches, who met frequently to collect and dispense garments for sick and wounded soldiers. In June 1861, the women called on their "sisters throughout the State" to form similar groups that would forward donations to the capital city. The Soldiers' Aid Society received almost immediate response from groups such as the Ladies of Lewisburg and the Ladies of Henry County, who agreed to form an auxiliary of the Richmond group.[33]

Despite the positive response from Virginia's women, by July it became evident that the society would need to look beyond the state for additional resources. Presuming the importance of Virginia as a battleground, the women requested that their sisters throughout the Confederacy unite with them, given that "most of those who may be wounded in any battle that may take place will be brought here." The Ladies' Hospital Association of Charleston, South Carolina, immediately sent supplies of whiskey obtained via blockade runners from Nassau to Richmond's Winder Hospital. During the summer of 1862, the Greenville (South Carolina) Ladies' Association sent trunks filled with drawers, sheets, towels, shirts, soap, brandy, books, herbs, and tin cups to hospitals in Richmond, Fairfax, Culpeper, and Charlottesville. Materials were either dispatched directly to a hospital or were forwarded (free of charge) by the Adams Express Company to the association, which would then distribute the provisions to hospitals from Winchester to Culpeper.[34]

Coordinating regional supply networks often led women into more formal means of caregiving, such as nursing.[35] In Lynchburg, several of the women from the Soldiers' Aid Association enlarged their volunteer activities during July 1861 by establishing the Ladies' Relief Hospital. Given the city's position along important rail lines and the James River canal, Lynchburg rapidly filled with more than 3,000 wounded soldiers sent to the twenty-plus hospitals that had been improvised from tobacco factories, the old college, and various other buildings. Led by the tall and commanding Lucy Mina Otey (who would likewise lead the city's memorial association in 1866), the women established a hospital in the old Union Hotel. During the hospital's first few weeks, they asked citizens of comfortable means to donate meals, bedding, clothing, or any other necessary article to provide for the sick soldiers.[36] Contributions, including firewood, clothing, bedding, an assortment of foods, and cash, poured into the Ladies' Relief Hospital.[37] In October 1862, as Virginians began to face their first difficult winter of the war, hospital directresses Lucy Otey and Susan Speed requested that the secretary of war grant women hospital workers the same opportunity officers benefited from of purchasing goods from the city's commissary. Despite their intense work at the Ladies' Relief Hospital, the government denied their petition.[38]

Although cities and towns across the Commonwealth operated hospitals, Richmond served as the hospital center of the Confederacy. Using some of her substantial means and the residence of friend Judge Robertson, thirty-one-year-old Sally Louisa Tompkins opened Robertson Hospital shortly after the war began. When the government took over private hospitals in mid-1861, President Davis commissioned her a captain of cavalry so that she might continue to operate her hospital for the duration of the war.[39] Maria Clopton, widow of a Virginia Supreme Court justice and president of the Ladies' Gunboat Association, established her hospital in the spring of 1862.[40] A tiny woman, less than five feet tall, with striking blue eyes and dark hair, Clopton operated the hospital largely at her own expense and through subscriptions she obtained from the public. According to the surgeon's report, she ran an efficient and clean hospital, primarily because of the wealth and patriotism of the neighborhood's generous inhabitants.[41] Jane Coles Fisher, Caroline Mayo, and Lucy Webb, too, operated their own private hospitals.[42]

For those women who lacked the means to furnish their own hospitals, nursing provided an opportunity to comfort wounded and dying soldiers. Moreover, nursing not only afforded some elite women an outlet to directly serve their government (and thus claim to be patriotic citizens of the Confederacy) but, like the soldiers' aid societies, also created bonds and networks among individuals separated by hundreds of miles who otherwise would not have met. When a wounded Alabama soldier returned home after being nursed by Janet Cleiland Weaver and her daughters (one of whom would become a leading figure in the Hollywood Memorial Association), his mother frequently wrote his caregivers expressing appreciation for their devotion.[43] "Such kindness bestowed on my son when he lay wounded, sick and out of reach of a Mother's care has awakened a gratitude in my heart too deep for utterance," she wrote. Winchester's Kate Kern likewise reached out to comfort a distant mother who had lost her son. The young soldier had asked that Kate write his mother, Mrs. C. J. Presnell, of North Carolina, telling her not to worry about him. She conveyed the manner of his death and informed his mother that he had spoken of his faith before passing. Because Kate had spent so much time with the soldier, she told Mrs. Presnell that she no longer felt that the two women were strangers. Kinship and church ties were not the only connections among women during the tumultuous war years. Like the soldiers' aid associations, the maternal nurturing and letter writing by women close to battlefields helped knit together a community of women from the far corners of the Confederacy.[44]

　　Virginia's women demonstrated their loyalty to the Confederacy through their volunteer associations and nursing but also expressed their ardent support in other less organized ways. Confederates who resided in occupied areas often affirmed their patriotism through "noncooperation or passive resistance." Many openly shunned the Federals, refused to cooperate with them, and spurned offers of conciliation. Union officials often encountered the most stalwart resistance when it came to oaths of loyalty. The nineteenth-century South's culture of honor meant that oaths were deeply revered, and breaking one was near sacrilege. In occupied regions of the Confederacy, Federal authorities were charged with bringing white southerners back into allegiance to the Union, and they often relied on oaths to ensure loyalty. But Federal attempts to pressure leading citizens and common folk into taking oaths rarely succeeded. Despite the low success rate, Federals often required Confederates to pledge an oath of loyalty in order to receive passes and permits that were required for travel, trade, work, and, occasionally, food rations.[45]

Many Virginia women adamantly refused to take oaths of allegiance to the Union out of loyalty to their new country and their male relatives. In Winchester, Confederate women balked at the April 14, 1862, Federal order forbidding clergy to marry individuals who had not signed the oath. General Robert H. Milroy, who occupied the town in January 1863, further declared that all citizens not signing the oath be denied essentials such as food and firewood. "Milroy is trying to starve us into loyalty," Laura Lee seethed. Refugee Judith McGuire scoffed at the notion that rations could be obtained by taking the oath. "Who is so base to do that?" she asked. "Can a Southern woman sell her birthright for a mess of pottage? Would she not be unworthy of the husband, the son, the brother, who is now offering himself a willing sacrifice on the alter [sic] of his country?" Fredericksburg's women expressed similar sentiments. Following the arrest of the town's most prominent men in the spring of 1863, the U.S. Army announced that a loyalty oath would be offered to the women. If they chose not to take the oath, Union officials warned, they would be arrested. Writing to her daughters Lizzie and Nannie who were at school in Richmond, Sarah Alsop declared that her fate had been sealed. "I would suffer confinement and death before I would give up my principles," she informed them. The next day she dressed in her best, convinced that she would be spending that evening and many more in the Old Capitol prison. Much to her surprise, however, the Federals left town and released ten of the imprisoned men.[46]

Interactions with northern soldiers and reports of Federal brutality served simultaneously to deepen Virginia women's antipathy toward the Yankees, engender a renewed loyalty to the Confederacy, and strengthen bonds among the southern populace. Even in parts of the Commonwealth that remained unoccupied until the last days of the war, Confederate women sympathized with their sisters, both literal and figurative, who had to endure interactions with the Union forces. Emily Aylett of Richmond could not bear to hear how the Yankees had treated her sisters, Alice and Etta. The reports made her, if possible, "feel more bitter and intense in my hatred of the Yankees than ever," she wrote. "I feel now almost as if I could enjoy shooting them myself." Incensed by accounts of General Sheridan in the Shenandoah Valley, Richmond resident Lucy Fletcher claimed never to have heard of "such barbarism . . . by any nation pretending to be civilization." Nurse Phoebe Yates Pember described the equally hostile opinion of northern soldiers among other Richmond women: "The feeling here against the Yankees exceeds anything I could imagine, particularly among the good Christians. I spent an evening among a particularly pious sett [sic]. One lady said she had a pile of Yankee bones lying around her pump so that the first glance on opening her eyes would rest upon them. Another begged me to get her a Yankee Skull to keep her toilette trinkets in."[47]

Although volunteer activities such as the gunboat or soldiers' aid associations ensured connections of a bureaucratic nature among women, the shared experience of a common enemy, one that was threatening women and children on the home front, provided a powerful and deep emotional connection among Confederate women. From the capital city of Richmond, the Shenandoah Valley, and beyond Virginia's borders, Confederate women from widespread parts of the South shared a common bond because northern soldiers were killing their men on the battlefield, occupying their communities, and destroying their homes. Women might not experience the fraternal attachment that soldiers developed in camp and on the battlefield, but they were waging their own valiant war effort in their cities and homes. In her analysis of the Confederate home front, Jacqueline Glass Campbell has demonstrated that women understood that along with their husbands and sons, "they had a vital role in defending the institutions on which southern society and its way of life depended." Confrontations with Federal soldiers thus allowed Confederate women on the home front to think of themselves as warriors, "giving them material and ideological reasons to resist."[48]

Although common wisdom holds that women in other regions of the Confederacy may have grown disgruntled with the war effort and lost confidence in those who were to protect them, most middle- and upper-class Virginia women remained steadfast patriots during the course of the war.[49] Their letters and diaries testify to the fact that many still expected the Confederacy to succeed during the last two years of the war, a time in the war at which many scholars have claimed that southern women felt despondent.[50] Lucy Otey, of the Lynchburg Ladies' Hospital Association, observed in March 1864 that so long as the men remained in the field, "there are loving hearts and busy hands *at home*—praying and toiling, for their preservation and success." A month later, Lucy Fletcher of Richmond saw hope amid all of the turmoil: "While the most intense anxiety prevails in regard to the fate of friends in the Army, and every one is more or less straitened by the scarcity of provisions, and the enormous prices of every article of food and clothing, our people are hopeful as to the result of the war." That same summer, Maria Peeks of Richmond told her future husband that regardless of the many fearful odds, "our cause is just." In January 1865, Kate Mason Rowland observed that the people were even willing to give up slavery if the Europeans would then acknowledge the Confederacy's independence. "Anything, everything, will we sacrifice rather than come again under the same government with the hated Yankee! Such are the sentiments of everyone I have seen," she declared. Lucy Bagby remembered feeling anxious during February and March 1865, but claimed that her faith in the cause never wavered. "Rumors were rife, but they did not break through our abiding faith in our army," she wrote. In Fredericksburg, Lizzie Alsop, too, felt that military affairs were gloomier than at any other period during the war but believed that "with God's help, we *shall* be victorious."[51]

Faith alone did not guide the state's female population. Patriotic contributions to the war by Virginia's women also continued through the spring of 1865. Numerous associations had suspended meetings by the fall of 1862, but many women persisted in their hospital work and individual sewing efforts. In some communities, such as Fredericksburg, the momentum shifted from sewing societies, as supplies dwindled, to the tending of sick and wounded soldiers. Richmond's elite women donated expensive materials such as furs to the patriotic fund in the spring of 1863. The following November, General Lee requested that the women of Richmond assist him in procuring socks for his army. By the winter of 1864, when conditions were bleak throughout the state, the Lynchburg Relief Society maintained their patriotic activities. During that time, they organized a library, volunteered at the hospitals, and established a knitting society. In February and March, they made more than one thousand pairs of socks for the soldiers. As General Grant's army began to lay siege to Petersburg, the city's women rallied behind the troops, rushing out to the streets, cheering the soldiers and waving handkerchiefs. Six months later, even as many of her neighbors had evacuated the city, Bessie Callender continued in her devotion to the Confederacy through small acts such as mending and washing soldiers' clothes. As late as March 1865, a woman penned a letter to the *Richmond Examiner* asking all "patriotic" women to donate their jewels to the Confederate government so that soldiers might be paid.[52]

All of this confirms what historians have been increasingly willing to accept: southern white women were equally, if not more, complicit in Confederate nationalism as the men of their own race and class. This loyalty to an independent Confederate nation came from a variety of sources, including military service of loved ones, the experience of war on the home front, a desire for revenge, powerful symbols such as flags, and a deep-seated belief that white southerners shared little in the way of cultural values with northerners. Whether through their acts of sewing, raising funds for a gunboat, nursing, or otherwise, many women saw themselves as invaluable citizens—even as political actors—in the Confederate nation, with the same goals as their male counterparts. This desire to defend their homes, families, and cultural values served as an unrelenting well of nationalistic spirit and hope in their cause. Through the spring of 1865, most of Virginia's Confederate women, along with many of their comrades to the south, held onto their faith in Robert E. Lee, the Army of Northern Virginia, and the Confederate nation. Moreover, this patriotic fervor among the state's women did not diminish after Lee's surrender in April. Instead, women mobilized to redirect their energies and unrelenting Confederate nationalism into memorial societies.[53]

The Civil War not only rapidly altered the relationship between women and the state, but it also transformed the ways in which individuals and communities responded to death and heightened women's public role in mourning traditions. In the antebellum period, high infant mortality, epidemics, poor sanitary conditions, and limited medical knowledge meant that most Americans had experienced the death of at least one member of their nuclear family before adulthood. Victorians' preoccupation with death and its meaning dictated elaborate and structured mourning customs, especially for women. For example, widows who could afford to do so were expected to respect a minimum two and a half years in mourning. In the period immediately following the death of one's husband, a wife embarked on heavy-mourning in which she was compelled to wear only black clothing and to keep her face concealed with a black, crepe veil when she left her home. This was followed by full-mourning, during which she continued to don black garments and a veil, but lighter shades of lace and cuffs were allowed to adorn her outfit. The final stage, half-mourning, permitted the widow to wear solid-colored fabrics of lavender or gray. Clothing, however, was not the only thing that demanded strictures during mourning; widows were also obliged to wear only appropriate jewelry (usually jet black or tokens containing a lock of the deceased's hair), avoid social functions, and correspond on appropriate black-lined stationery.[54]

Although women had held prominent roles in mourning rituals through-out the Victorian era, the astronomical number of casualties brought on by the war necessitated significant alterations in their responses. During the first year of fighting, many women tried to maintain the rituals of dress and be-havior that accompanied death. But with the increasing economic hardships, many middle- and upper-class southern women simply could not afford to continue to abide by the etiquette. When Varina Davis went into mourning for her young son in April 1864, she wore a black dress of inexpensive cotton. Susan Caldwell's husband advised her in the fall of 1864 against wearing black following the death of their young daughter. With "war and penury upon us," he thought it unwise to spend the money on an unnecessary purchase. Young Lizzie Alsop and her sisters were undecided about wearing black after the death of their grandmother in March 1863. "For tho' we should like to, mourn-ing is so high that I do not know whether it would be right for us to wear it or not," Lizzie commented. Many of Cornelia McDonald's Winchester neighbors continued to dress in black after the death of a family member, but others wore dark colors simply because they anticipated the loss of a loved one. With as many as one out of every four Confederate soldiers dying, women across the region were thrown into a perpetual state of mourning and were often forced to abandon their rituals of dress and self-imposed seclusion.[55]

As women's ability to observe strict mourning rituals of dress and appear-ance declined, the number of funerals they witnessed increased. Prior to the war, funerals tended to be private affairs situated firmly within the domestic sphere. But as the death toll rose, funerals became daily, public events in cities across the state. An unknown woman writing to Sallie Munford in the winter of 1863 mourned for the gay life of the antebellum period: "Instead of parties we have been almost every week to a funeral." In 1864, Lucy Fletcher tearfully watched her young son witness one of many military funeral processions pass through the capital's street. During the siege of Petersburg, Mary Rambant Morrison watched as her husband and Rev. Churchill Gibson interred an unknown Confederate soldier. "A band of weeping women, of which I was one," she wrote, "looked on from a North window of a house in Perry Street, commanding a full view of the Second Presbyterian church yard," where the "sad scene was being enacted." Not far away, Dr. John Herbert Claiborne also beheld the city's continuous obsequies, writing to his wife that "yesterday was a gloomy day here—funerals all day and the enemy constantly looked for in force."[56]

Early in the war, nearly all deaths received elaborate funerals, especially in the capital city of Richmond. Nineteen-year-old Henry Lawson Wyatt was one of the war's first casualties, killed at the battle of Big Bethel on June 10, 1861. As such, Richmonders orchestrated an elaborate service to mourn the loss of one of their own. His body was brought by train to Richmond and buried in Hollywood Cemetery with full military honors. But as the casualty lists mounted, the elaborate rituals declined and in some places ceased all together. Constance Cary Harrison later recalled watching the daily funeral processions for soldiers from her Richmond window. Most followed a similar pattern: "The coffin crowned with cap and sword and gloves, the riderless horse following with empty boots fixed in the stirrups of an army saddle." "One could not number those sad pageants," Harrison lamented.[57] As the death toll rose, increasingly only the corpses of officers received individual funeral services in the presence of their families.

With men dying hundreds and thousands of miles away from home, strangers increasingly performed many of the rites associated with death.[58] Rather than finding eternal rest in a family plot, most Civil War soldiers were buried on the fields where they had died. Commanders of the victorious army would detail units to serve as burial parties for their own soldiers, but those of the enemy were most often consigned to mass graves. At Antietam, for example, "details from each [Union] regiment gathered up the dead of their own command and in most cases provided individual graves, while the Confederate prisoners were directed to inter their countrymen in groups of 50–100 to a trench." In some communities, such as Winchester, local residents helped tend to the dead once the armies had left the field. After the first battle of Kernstown, Kate Sperry and Joanna Krebs accompanied several male relatives to the battlefield. There the men quickly buried seventy-nine men in a tiny trench before bringing back six others to be claimed by friends or relatives.[59] When Confederates died in Richmond's hospitals, detailed and convalescent

Confederate soldiers laid out for burial near Mrs. Alsop's farm in Spotsylvania, May 20, 1864. During the war, detailed and convalescent Confederate soldiers as well as slaves often performed the anonymous task of burying the dead. (Courtesy Collection of the New-York Historical Society)

soldiers as well as slaves often performed the anonymous task of burying the dead in Hollywood and Oakwood Cemeteries. James C. Reed of the Bedford Artillery recalled witnessing such mass burials at Oakwood: "A great trench as wide as the length of a coffin was dug and the coffins were placed one upon the other, two deep, and then they were covered with earth." By the war's end, more than 11,000 soldiers from battlefields across Virginia had been buried in Hollywood. Thousands more were interred in Oakwood Cemetery, just north of Chimborazo Hospital.[60]

Despite the staggering numbers of dead, during the war elite and middle-class southern women frequently tried to mitigate the impersonal and anonymous burials of Confederate soldiers by attending services, writing letters to soldiers' families, and placing flowers on military graves. Nurse Lucy Mason Webb almost daily closed the eyes of her deceased patients and wrote consoling letters to their friends and families. Kate Sperry and other Winchester women who volunteered in the town's makeshift hospitals helped to wash the faces of the dead in preparation for burial. With family and friends often hundreds of miles away, nurses such as Kate Mason Rowland regularly performed funeral services. "I went to the hospital this evening to read a chapter over the body of a young soldier who died here yesterday," young Kate wrote from Lynchburg. Surrounded by the slaves who labored at the hospital, she read the burial service out of a prayer book while her mother guided a hymn. "It was raining hard while his comrades carried the beardless soldier to his lonely grave," she later remembered.[61]

The frequency with which Confederate women performed funeral rites for their nation's dead helps to explain the enormous popularity of the painting *The Burial of Latané*. In June 1862, Captain William D. Latané of the 9th Virginia Cavalry was the only Confederate killed during Brigadier General J. E. B. "Jeb" Stuart's first ride around General George McClellan's Army of the Potomac. Latané's body was subsequently taken to the plantation home of Mrs. William Spencer Brockenbrough. The much-publicized incident inspired John R. Thompson to compose a poem eulogizing Latané's fate. The poem read in part: "But woman's voice, in accents soft and low, / Trembling with pity, touched with pathos, read / Over his hallowed dust, the ritual for the dead!" Two years later, William De Hartburn immortalized the scene on canvas. The story that circulated with the image noted that in the absence of a minister—or any men for that matter—the soldier's last rites had been read by the lady to whose home he had been taken. Years later, Mrs. Brockenbrough, the "lady" of the painting, revealed that in fact she did not perform the service. Although she and several other women had prepared the body and were about to perform the funeral, a Methodist minister arrived just in time. In any case, the painting commemorated women's special responsibility for mourning, suggesting that their presence at grave sites not only assured the slain of spiritual immortality, but also helped to consecrate the deaths of Confederate soldiers.[62]

As the painting suggests, the transformation in women's wartime mourning marked an increasingly political tone of the formerly private grieving process. Virginia's residents might have grown accustomed to the sight of horse-drawn hearses winding through their streets, but the death of a famous officer usually led to grand public spectacles. When General Turner Ashby, hero of the Shenandoah Valley, died in June 1862 near Harrisonburg, Virginians reeled with sorrow. "Another noble sacrifice to the cause of freedom," lamented Winchester's Laura Lee. Following his death, Ashby's body was transported to Charlottesville, where it lay in state while hundreds of tearful visitors covered the corpse with wreaths of laurel and roses. The next day, an elaborate procession of his cavalry and two slaves, all dressed in black, accompanied his remains to the University of Virginia cemetery, a newly designated resting place for Confederate dead. Behind the hearse followed the black horse on which his brother had been killed, also trimmed in mourning crepe.[63]

Within a year of Ashby's death, Virginians found themselves in the depths of despondency as they mourned an even more popular Confederate leader. "Gen. Jackson is dead! There is a wail of woe throughout the South," cried Laura Lee of Winchester. On May 2, 1863, General Stonewall Jackson was mistakenly shot by some of his own men near Chancellorsville. Eight days later, he succumbed to pneumonia. Immediately his body was transported to Richmond, where it was embalmed and lay in state at the governor's mansion. All businesses and government offices closed, and flags were suspended at half-mast. Mourners from all parts of the South flocked to the capital to pay their final tributes to the general, including a large number of women, who wept and left floral offerings on the casket. On May 13, members of the Stonewall Brigade and the general's famous warhorse accompanied the general's body as it left Richmond on a journey to its final resting place in Lexington. His remains were sent via the Orange and Alexandria Railroad first to Lynchburg, where they received the second military processional of the day. Guns were fired and bells of the city tolled as a procession of citizens and 1,500 convalescent soldiers marched solemnly through the streets. One newspaper reported that "it was an affecting sight to see those maimed and suffering men draw up in line to receive the remains of the glorious hero." In Lexington, Jackson's casket was met by the Virginia Military Corps of Cadets and professors and a large group of local citizens. Again his body lay in state, this time in his former classroom. As he had requested, Jackson was then buried in the Valley of Virginia.[64]

The women of Winchester felt an especially deep sense of loss upon hearing of Jackson's death. Jackson had defended the town during the first years of the war, and his wife, Mary Anna, had spent a great deal of time there residing in the home of Lieutenant Colonel Lewis T. Moore. Upon hearing of his death, Winchester resident Mary Lee confessed in her diary that "a gloom, still deeper, is over our whole town; the sad news is kept as far as possible out of hearing of the sick & fevered patients; men, women, and children weep for their hero." Not content to mourn in private, she made a crepe rosette, with a Virginia button in the center, as a badge of mourning for Jackson. Although friends warned her that the Federal commander in the city, General Milroy, would not allow such a memorial to be worn, she defiantly displayed her loyalty to the fallen general and the cause he represented. Within a week, however, she heard that Federal soldiers had been removing rosettes from women's coats and that any woman caught wearing the memorial was to be arrested. In fact, Union soldiers ripped a rosette from the dress of Julia Clark, commenting that it was an insult to their soldiers. But Lee ignored the warning. "I have worn and shall continue to wear mine," she stubbornly insisted. As would be the case during the postwar period, northerners recognized that Confederate women were often intensely patriotic and capable of treasonous behavior—even in mourning.[65]

The funerals and resting places of common soldiers also took on partisan meaning, as Confederate cemeteries increasingly became sites of national mourning and pride. In the North, Union legislation required that a headboard identifying the remains be placed on each grave, and the U.S. Sanitary Commission helped to register deaths and notify kin. But the limited resources in the South had left the Confederate government unable adequately to reclaim and reinter bodies. Extending their patriotism into the world of the immortal, Confederate women quickly took up the task of helping to identify and pay tribute to the nation's slain. Following the battle of Second Manassas, Janet Henderson Weaver (later Randolph) and several women of Warrenton constructed makeshift headstones for the Confederate soldiers buried in the town. Allegedly, Federal soldiers later used those wooden headstones for their campfires. By the summer of 1864, the women of Richmond's Church Hill district frequented Oakwood Cemetery to lay flowers on the graves of deceased Confederate soldiers. But simply marking the graves was not enough. Southern white women wished their dead to find eternal rest in cemeteries reserved exclusively for Confederates. Like so many other women, Kate Sperry abhorred the idea of Yankees finding their eternal rest next to the graves of brave Confederate soldiers. "It's a desecration," she declared.[66]

It was Lynchburg's women, however, who began turning the soldiers' burial grounds into Confederate shrines as early as May 1863. Foreshadowing their postwar activities, Lucy Otey and the women of the relief hospital requested that every woman in the city undertake the task of tending one grave. "The ladies of Lexington, Kentucky, have turfed the grave of every Confederate soldier buried in their city," wrote Otey. "The Ladies of Lynchburg will do the same." If competition was not enough to motivate the women, Otey invoked the Confederacy's noble cause. "Shall we not mark the resting place of those who have fought and died for us?" she queried.[67] Mourning Confederate soldiers was not then an activity that southern women took up only in the wake of defeat. Instead, the rituals in which Otey and her compatriots took part marked the dead as symbols of the Confederate cause—a fact that would become especially important in the weeks and months after Appomattox, when Otey and her band of sisters would continue their cause under the banner of the Lynchburg LMA.

Many of Richmond's female diarists noted that April 2, 1865, was a clear, beautiful morning. "Nature seemed as if in mockery of our woe to have put on her loveliest dress to meet the conquering foe," Mary Morrison later remarked. Mary Fontaine agreed that she had never seen a calmer or more peaceful Sabbath morning, or a more confused evening. During the packed morning service at St. Paul's Episcopal, a messenger handed President Davis a telegram from Lee informing him that the city was to be evacuated. Church services across the city ended abruptly, as residents rushed home to prepare for the worst. Some, such as Mrs. William A. Simmons, chose to flee. Others, such as Mary Fontaine, bade farewell to their friends and settled in for a long night. Just before dawn, explosions of gunboats and magazines rocked the city, shattering glass and crumbling numerous homes. Retreating Confederate troops set fire to the city's tobacco and cotton warehouses and ignited arsenals stocked with munitions. "Fear and dread fell over us all," one Confederate woman remembered, describing the horrifying scene as fires engulfed the capital city, leaping "from house to house in mad revel." Years later, she could scarcely forget "the terrified cries of women and children [that] arose above the roaring of the flames, the crashing of falling buildings, and the trampling of countless feet." The next morning, Mary Fontaine watched as two Union soldiers unfurled a tiny American flag on the Capitol. "Then I sank to my knees," she wrote, "and bitter, bitter tears came in a torment."[68]

The fall of Richmond was not enough to quell the loyalty of some women to the Confederacy. In Lynchburg, Mary Cabell believed that Lee had experienced just a temporary setback. Though her spirits rose and fell throughout the week with each new report, by Friday, April 7, she felt strength enough to endure the city's surrender, the evacuation of the state, and everything else, "if Lee can save his army and make a stand." The day before Lee surrendered his army at Appomattox, Cabell recorded the remarkable tranquility of the Virginia spring. "The sky, the clouds, the delicate verdure and bloom, the weeping willows that bordered the canal, the birds' songs, all made a fairy land," she wrote. "Never have I seen so beautiful a spring," Cabell concluded. Amid such a lovely setting, she could not have fathomed the next day's news.[69]

But Lee's surrender did not mean the end of women's deep devotion to the Confederacy. The war had necessitated the development of a collective woman's consciousness and a new sense of direct participation in the state as women rallied to support their soldiers. Lizzie Alsop, Janet Weaver (Randolph), Lucy Mina Otey, Susan Speed, Mary Gordon Wallace, Bessie Callender, Lucy Webb, Sally Tompkins, and Nancy MacFarland were just a few of the several hundred Virginia women who would build upon their new female networks and extend their intense feelings of patriotism into the postwar period. Hardly relics of the war, soldiers' aid societies, sewing circles, and Ladies' hospitals would transform into equally devoted LMAs that honored the soldiers who had not received proper funerals or burials during the war. Southern white women's patriotism and nationalism would find a new outlet and purpose in the memorialization of the Confederacy.

A Fitting Work

The Origins of Virginia's
Ladies' Memorial Associations,
1865–1866

2

The spring of 1865 brought peace to Virginia, but the scars of war remained visible throughout the state. During the past four years, graves of southern soldiers had been scattered across the Commonwealth, and with each passing month, residents uncovered more and more decomposing bodies and bleaching bones as they resumed their farming activities. Winchester's Mary Dunbar Williams was especially disturbed by the lack of proper burials for the Confederate soldiers who had so ardently defended the Shenandoah Valley town. In May 1865, Williams visited her sister-in-law, Eleanor Williams Boyd, and recounted the story of a farmer who had plowed up the bodies of two Confederate soldiers while preparing his land for corn. The two women decided that they should call a meeting of all the women who had volunteered in the hospitals during the war, with the objective of forming a memorial society to gather all the dead within a radius of twelve to fifteen miles and inter them in one graveyard. Additionally, they agreed it was imperative that the entire town establish an annual tradition of placing flowers and evergreens on these graves. Less than a month after Robert E. Lee surrendered at Appomattox, the first Ladies' Memorial Association (LMA) in Virginia had organized to honor and eulogize the fallen South.[1] Within a year, white southern women from Virginia to Alabama followed suit, establishing no less than seventy LMAs.[2]

These organizations, however, did much more than provide centralized resting places for fallen Confederates. Many of the same women who had sewn battle flags, volunteered in hospitals, and snubbed Yankee soldiers during the war turned to the LMAS so that they might continue to express their Confederate patriotism through memorial activities. Such work allowed them to expand on two trends that had developed during the war: the creation of an organized womanhood among southern white women and a sense of white southern solidarity among ex-Confederates. But equally important, southern men and women realized that these Ladies, as they called themselves, might deploy gender in the interest of Confederate politics. Relying on the mid-nineteenth-century assumption that women were naturally nonpolitical, ex-Confederate men recognized that women might be best suited to take the lead in memorializing the South's Lost Cause. After all, if women were not political, then their actions could not be construed as treasonous to the U.S. government. Middle- and upper-class women of the LMAS thus served in the forefront of the postwar battle over Confederate memory, simultaneously allowing men to skirt the issue of treason and inaugurating the traditions of the Lost Cause as early as 1865 and 1866.[3]

"Although no State of the South had been exempt from the scourge," wrote Sallie Ann Brock in 1867, "Virginia had borne the brunt of the war." She detailed the destruction of the once-grand state in her postwar memoir: "Wherever the foot of the invader had been pressed, it left its mark in desolation. Along the Potomac River scarcely a dwelling remained to indicate that that fair region had once been the abode of one of the happiest, most refined and intelligent communities in our country, but charred monuments of destruction betokened the work of the incendiary and the despoiler." Lucy Fletcher walked along the ruins in Richmond only days after Lee's surrender. She noted that from the south end of Capitol Square to the river, from Eighth Street to Eighteenth Street, scarcely one building remained standing. "All was in ruins and desolation," she exclaimed. Smoke billowed from the city's burned business district, where brick chimneys stood as stark reminders of the city's antebellum industrial strength. As in Winchester, throughout the Commonwealth the signs of lost lives were omnipresent. Writing to her family in the North, one Union woman recounted the landscape surrounding Petersburg: "We saw many, very many obtruding feet of the dead, some heads were uncovered, and, in many instances, the whole figure was easily traced under a thin covering of earth." Virginians, like those elsewhere in the former Confederacy, looked around to see burnt cities, exhausted farms, torn-up railroads, battlefields littered with soldiers' remains, and a disrupted labor force. Four years of war had left the region devastated.[4]

Surrounded by the chaos of destruction and exhausted from four years of battle, Virginia's ex-Confederate soldiers joined most other white southerners in grudgingly accepting defeat. A few fiery souls like Colonel Thomas T. Munford attempted to keep troops in the field following Lee's surrender and

Remains on the Manassas battlefield. In 1865 and 1866, Virginia's landscape was littered with the signs of war, including the bones and other remains of soldiers. (Courtesy Collection of the New-York Historical Society)

others like Jubal A. Early and George E. Pickett fled the country, but most soldiers and citizens admitted that their quest for independence had failed. They agreed that Confederates had tried their hardest and had fought honorably, but that they could not overcome the superior manpower and military strength of the well-supplied U.S. Army. Virginia's white residents laid down their guns, abandoned secession, and acknowledged the abolition of slavery, although they remained loyal to old political values and the principle of white supremacy. As historian Anne Sarah Rubin has pointed out, even when Confederate men felt disdain toward the Union, they recognized that it was in their best interest to profess loyalty to the Union in order to regain their confiscated property and political rights. Restoring and rebuilding the defeated South became the primary objective for most ex-Confederate males.[5]

Having no guns to put down, white southern women often found surrendering their service and devotion to the Confederacy more difficult.[6] In fact, many of Virginia's elite women continued to proclaim their allegiance to the Confederacy even after Appomattox. Two days after Lee's surrender, Mary Cabell still held out hope of "yet seeing the Southern flag float over my beloved Richmond," noting that rumors circulated that France might yet help save the Confederacy. On April 12, 1865, Fredericksburg's Lizzie Alsop scribbled passionately in her diary that "Gen. Lee has surrendered! I pray God that I may yet live to see his vengeance exercised against our enemies." In December 1865, Isabel Maury wrote to her cousin, who had moved to England following Appomattox, boldly announcing that two flags hung on the family's Christmas tree—the Confederate flag and the battle flag. "Gen. Lee, bless his soul, was hung immediately below" the flags, she remarked. And on New Year's Day, Maury proudly claimed that white southerners did not take part in any celebration of receiving visitors, as such was a northern tradition. "We are a distinct and separate nation, and I wish our customs to be as distinct as we are," she declared.[7]

Not only did many upper-class women grieve for their lost cause, but they remained the fiercest opponents of the U.S. government.[8] When Union troops marched into Richmond, numerous white women fumed about the Yankee invaders. A few openly turned cold shoulders on the occupying forces, as they had done during the war. Lucy Fletcher observed the "capitol square lined with blue coats" and resented the fact that these were "the people who for 4 years have been slaying our brethren, and desolating our land, burning and ravaging our homes insulting and robbing our defenceless women and grey haired men." As Federal troops flooded the streets of the former capital, Confederate women who appeared in public at all did so in mourning dress. Mrs. Charles Ellis noted that the "young ladies have scrupulously avoided the acquaintance or recognition of any of the Enemy and for the first two or three weeks when they went on the streets wore veils 2 or 8 fold." Similarly, Emmie Sublett confided to a friend that she always went out "thickly veiled and never notice[d] the Yanks in the least." In fact, she proudly claimed, having northern soldiers in the city "makes us fifty times more southern in our feelings." Many other women claimed to be too heartbroken to leave their homes. Rather than accept invitations from Union soldiers to come to Capitol Square for fresh air and music, they remained quietly indoors.[9]

But Confederate women did more to indicate their continued devotion to the failed cause than simply rant about Yankee soldiers. Although the U.S. government provided transportation for men to return home, Confederate soldiers often found themselves hundreds of miles from their homes with no means to get there. Ex-Confederate women frequently took the lead in fulfilling what should have been a government responsibility. Women in both Petersburg and Lynchburg, for example, supplied food and aid to the "famished and shivering Confederate" soldiers returning home from northern prisons; the Petersburg association alone provided aid to more than 12,000 parolees. The Ladies' Soldiers' Aid Society of Richmond likewise discovered even more duties for itself in the wake of defeat. The women cared for wounded Confederate soldiers in hospitals, furnished means for them to reach their homes, and proposed education for those soldiers who had been disabled from wounds so that they might have the means to provide a living for themselves. Confederate women furnished poor, maimed soldiers with artificial arms and legs, helped feed and clothe their destitute widows and children, and generally assisted in relieving the suffering and poverty caused by war. In short, because the now-defunct Confederate government would never be able to extend aid, women took up the banner. Beginning in the spring of 1865 and 1866, these white southern women took on yet another task that should have fallen to the government—that of honoring the Confederate nation's soldiers.[10]

During the summer of 1865, the women of the Winchester LMA met frequently at the residence of Eleanor Boyd and continued in their efforts to locate the graves of Confederate dead surrounding the town. Late that fall, they issued an appeal to the entire South for aid. The appeal described the destruction in the Valley and noted that "the dead were generally buried where they fell, and their rude graves are fast disappearing beneath the feet of men and beasts." Appearing in newspapers throughout Virginia and into the Deep South, the appeal explained that Winchester's resources had been greatly reduced by the war. "We are therefore induced to appeal to you for aid in this matter, encouraged by the belief that you will feel it a privilege as well as duty to pay this tribute of respect to the memory of those who fell in your cause." Because every former Confederate state was represented among the fallen, the Winchester LMA believed that each should feel obliged to aid the town's efforts.[11]

Despite the South's devastation, donations for Winchester's cemetery fund began to pour in from across the South.[12] In early March 1866, the local paper in Montgomery, Alabama, reported Winchester's efforts and advocated that the "daughters of Alabama" should "assist their sisters in Virginia in this pious undertaking." By spring 1866, Winchester had received $14,000 in contributions ($1,200 from Alabama alone), and the Winchester LMA in conjunction with the Stonewall Monumental Association purchased five acres for a Confederate cemetery to be named after General Jackson. Mary Williams and Eleanor Boyd then organized a public meeting at which they assigned a group of men to begin collecting the remains of the dead for reinterment prior to the coming summer heat. By late May, men employed by the Winchester LMA had collected the dead from a radius of fifteen miles around Stonewall Cemetery and buried them in individual graves. Within a year, the Winchester LMA had directed the reinterment of 2,489 Confederate soldiers, providing separate lots for the dead of each state and a section for the 829 unknown.[13]

While the Ladies of Winchester were busy creating their Confederate cemetery during the summer and fall of 1865, Union burial crews had begun the process of recovering the remains of their own soldiers from shallow and mass graves on the southern battlefields. Roused by reports of Union grave desecration throughout the South, the northern public had demanded that its war dead be provided honorable interments such as had been afforded those at Gettysburg.[14] By early June 1865, the quartermaster general had issued orders sending Captain James Moore, assistant quartermaster, to the battlefields of the Wilderness and Spotsylvania to bury the remains of Union soldiers. Captain Moore and his crew successfully interred more than 700 remains, making an effort to inscribe the names of the deceased on wooden headboards at each grave. In early July, Moore and his men were sent to the site of Andersonville prison in Georgia, where they would work (often acrimoniously) with Clara Barton to create a national cemetery, and thus their work in Virginia was suspended.[15]

By the spring of 1866, Congress had finally provided the financial support for gathering all the remains of Union soldiers still reposing in "the States lately in rebellion." This massive reinterment project would send crews across the South to scout for grave sites and organize cemeteries for Union soldiers similar to those that had been created during the war at Gettysburg, Arlington, Chattanooga, Knoxville, and Stones River.[16] As early as February, officers and work crews began arriving in Richmond to gather the remains of northern prisoners who had been buried at Hollywood and Oakwood Cemeteries and at Belle Isle. Modeled after the national cemetery at Gettysburg, the burial corps laid out the grounds so that each grave was of equal importance and provided individual headstones for all remains. From Richmond, the Union detail moved on to Cold Harbor, Seven Pines, Hampton, City Point (near

Union soldiers' graves near the General Hospital, City Point, Virginia. In the spring of 1866, the U.S. Army sent crews across the South to scout for grave sites and organize national cemeteries for Union soldiers. (Courtesy Collection of the New-York Historical Society)

Petersburg), Fredericksburg, and Winchester, repeating the process of identifying the remains and arranging the graves in orderly burial grounds. By 1870, 300,000 Union soldiers had been reinterred in 73 national cemeteries, at least 17 of which were in the Commonwealth.[17]

There appears to have been virtually no dissent within the U.S. Army ranks to interring only loyal soldiers; northerners clearly understood that providing proper burials implied bestowing honor on the dead. As historian John Neff argues, "The drive toward honoring the lives and deaths of Union soldiers seems to have necessitated, perhaps understandably, the neglect of the Confederate soldier dead."[18] But ex-Confederates often deeply resented the decision. With the presence of the U.S. Burial Corps on the outskirts of Richmond, residents became increasingly angered by the lack of provisions for Confederate soldiers—and by the atrocities they believed were being committed by the Union burial crews. An article in the *Richmond Daily Examiner* opined that "the nation condemns our dead," leaving them "in deserted places to rot into oblivion." Newspapers in Petersburg reported stories that Union crews were "digging up skeletons of [Confederate] soldiers" and "selling them to be ground for manure." Still other Virginians accused the federal government of contracting the labor out to those who would "place a sufficient number of bones in a coffin" to make it "rattle, and then marking the same by imaginary names" so as to make a profit of "$8 per body." To increase the compensation, the report alleged that "some parties cut the bodies in four pieces, burying the same in four pieces, and thus receiving $32 instead of $8."[19]

Not only were the Union soldiers purportedly desecrating the Confederate dead, but the well-tended, neatly organized Union cemeteries stood in stark contrast to the shallow graves of Confederate soldiers, which were being uprooted by farmers and scavenging animals.[20] The real issue, however, was the underlying message of these new "national cemeteries" (as they had been designated by Congress). According to historian William Blair, such a designation suggested that ex-Confederates were second-class citizens within the new nation. The care rendered only to the Union dead "proved to them that northern officials intended to subjugate the Confederate South rather than place the region on an equal footing with the North." Providing national cemeteries for the northern dead carried the message that these soldiers had given their lives for a noble cause while the Confederate soldiers, alternatively, had died in vain.[21]

Even though the Winchester women had begun preparing Confederate cemeteries in the spring of 1865, the intensified Union practices of expressly ignoring the Confederate dead during elaborate reburial efforts incited the further organization of LMAs and the cult of the Lost Cause during the spring of 1866. In Petersburg, for example, it seems to be no coincidence that the city's women called for a formal meeting to discuss the plight of the neglected Confederate graves only two weeks after a Union detail began surveying a location for a permanent national cemetery in the vicinity.

But even more galling to Richmond whites than the U.S. Burial Corps was the Evacuation Day ceremony sponsored by the city's black residents. Much like Emancipation Days staged by African Americans throughout the South after the war, the event was to occur on April 3, 1866 (exactly one year after the city surrendered), and was to include a parade of ex-slaves taking to the streets to celebrate their newfound freedom. When white residents learned of the planned festivities, they reacted viscerally, vowing to "prevent any demonstration by the negroes." One Richmond newspaper editor proclaimed that April 3 was no time for merriment but rather "a day of gloom and calamity to be remembered with a shudder of horror by all who saw it, whether it be the Federal soldier, or the resident, whether white or black." Although the city's black residents published a notice stating that they did not intend to celebrate the failure of the Confederacy but to commemorate their liberation, their efforts did not prevent violence. Just days before the ceremony, an unknown (no doubt white) person burned the Second African Baptist Church, a freedmen's school, and the meeting location for those planning the event.[22]

Despite the church razing, rumors that effigies of Jefferson Davis and Robert E. Lee were to be burned, and threats by whites that they would "wade through blood" before allowing the celebration, the festivities took place with only one minor incident and no bloodshed. Gathering at the fairgrounds to the northwest of the city, approximately 1,000 to 1,500 black men, many dressed in uniform and carrying muskets, marched, while several hundred more rode horses down the city's streets. As the procession wound down Broad Street to Capitol Square, a crowd of 15,000 spectators cheered them along. White Richmonders did little to stop the event but warned that black people who had abandoned their work "to engage in the jubilee" would "not be employed again by their old masters."[23]

This combination of the former slaves' Evacuation Day celebration and the "neglect" of rebel graves by the federal government fueled the fires of resistance and outrage among ex-Confederates. Moreover, President Andrew Johnson's fairly lenient Reconstruction policies had provided southern sympathizers the climate in which they might freely commemorate their failed rebellion. In the spring of 1865, many ex-Confederates had wondered about their fate. Would they be tried as traitors? Would their leaders be hanged? Would the Federals confiscate all rebel property?[24] By the following year, white southerners felt confident that they had escaped their worst nightmares. In fact, members of the Freedmen's Bureau and military officials testifying before Congress's Joint Committee on Reconstruction in March 1866 believed that Virginians were more disloyal to the Union at that time than they had been immediately after Lee's surrender. Under the "benign influence" of the Johnson administration, they claimed, ex-Confederates had become "arrogant, exacting, and intolerant."[25]

Given this political atmosphere, Virginia's white residents refused to sit idly by as the South's sons continued to molder in unidentified mass graves. It is no coincidence that within two weeks of the Evacuation Day ceremony, Virginia's white women began to call for the organization of LMAs throughout the state. On April 19, 1866, Richmond women representing the eastern portion of the city known as Church Hill gathered to organize the Oakwood Memorial Association (OMA); by year's end, it claimed 328 members.[26] Picking up on their wartime practice of placing flowers on Confederate graves, within a week at least forty women of the Lynchburg Ladies' Relief Hospital, motivated by "humanity and patriotism," agreed to formally transform their organization into a memorial association.[27] Between May 3 and 10, some of the most prominent women of the state formed the Hollywood (based in Richmond), Petersburg, and Fredericksburg LMAs. Realizing that Jewish soldiers who had perished in Richmond would not be embraced by either the Oakwood or Hollywood groups, the Hebrew Memorial Association organized on June 5. Within a matter of two weeks, several of the most influential and active LMAs in the state, and in the South, had come into being.[28]

While the Ladies in several cities appear to have met of their own accord as an extension of their wartime aid societies, women were not the only impetus behind such organizations. Colonel Thomas A. Ellis, president of Richmond's Hollywood Cemetery Corporation, issued a call in the papers inviting all citizens interested in tending the cemetery grounds to meet in St. Paul's Church on May 3, 1866.[29] Richmond's women, many of whom had probably been members of the postwar Ladies' Soldiers' Aid Society, responded en masse.[30] As in the state capital, the men of Fredericksburg and Lynchburg called for LMAs in their respective communities, recognizing that memorial tributes from the "gentle hand of woman" would be less threatening to the federal government. Even though Lynchburg's women had been tending to the graves of Confederate soldiers since the spring of 1863, the local paper encouraged their efforts. "A fitting work lies before the ladies," the paper wrote in April 1866, concluding that "we doubt not they will do it well and promptly." Fredericksburg's clergy held a meeting on May 10, 1866, so that the city might make arrangements for the Confederate dead. On that Thursday, the city's stores and businesses closed to commemorate the death of Stonewall Jackson, while women, children, and old men gathered at the Episcopal Church to mourn the Confederacy. Following an address by J. Horace Lacy, the women in attendance, including young Lizzie Alsop, agreed to organize an LMA for the purpose of taking care of the numerous Confederate graves that dotted the landscape, as well as those at the city cemetery. Immediately thereafter, the women elected officers and appointed several men to serve on committees to aid their endeavors. After the meeting ended, a large number of women formed a procession to the city cemetery, where they decorated Confederate graves with flowers and evergreens.[31]

Like most of the wartime associations, the LMAs were organized by women at the community level, and they operated independently of one another. But such local origins did not mean that the groups failed to interact or support each others' efforts. Lynchburg's women, for example, had been especially tied to the Richmond groups through the Gunboat Association. It seemed only natural that they might build on these connections in their efforts to commemorate the Confederacy. The Lynchburg LMA adopted the OMA constitution and followed the Richmond women's lead in selecting May 10 as their Memorial Day. Fredericksburg, too, borrowed from the Richmond memorial associations. Less than a month after first meeting, the Fredericksburg LMA distributed a copy of the Hollywood constitution and bylaws as a model for its own founding documents.[32]

At least four LMAs discussed the possibility of uniting their organizations. Less than two weeks after the Hollywood Memorial Association (HMA) first met, the women of the Oakwood association proposed that the two groups unite so that they might have more success in raising money and tending to the soldiers' graves. The groups agreed that each would select two men to represent their interests at a meeting on May 24. Before that meeting could take place, however, three HMA women attended an OMA meeting, proposing that the two associations be dissolved and then reorganized under the name "The Memorial Association of the Ladies of Richmond." Though the OMA had initiated talks, its members rejected the HMA plan, anticipating a loss of both financial and political control of the association, presumably because of the HMA members' more elite status. Regardless, it is obvious that as discussions continued, the OMA became increasingly concerned about its tenuous status as the capital city's inaugural memorial society. At one point during the talks, the OMA representative even suggested dividing Richmond so as to leave "an equal portion of the city open to the collectors of the Oakwood Association." Surprisingly, the suggestion "met with the entire approbation of the HMA" and the city was thus divided between those in the east who supported the Oakwood association and those in the west who donated to the Hollywood women.[33]

Fredericksburg's LMA also sent a delegation of men to speak with the neighboring Spotsylvania LMA regarding a union between the two societies. The Richmond groups had commenced talks as a way to aid their memorial work, but the Fredericksburg Ladies exhibited a far more pretentious reason for negotiations with Spotsylvania. In early June 1866, neither community had yet established a Confederate cemetery. The groups agreed to meet to discuss the practicality of establishing a single cemetery in which both LMAs would cooperate. Fredericksburg LMA representative J. Horace Lacy enumerated the reasons why their city should be selected. First, the city commanded better transportation accessibility with its railroads, thereby making it an obvious place for common interment of the dead. Transportation to Spotsylvania, however, was all but impossible. Perhaps most audaciously, Lacy claimed that Fredericksburg's battle and siege made it of "greater . . . historic celebrity." The Spotsylvania LMA unsurprisingly turned down these overtures to join with its Fredericksburg neighbor.[34]

These early attempts at unification should not be interpreted as failures to create statewide organizations. Instead, they suggest that women of the LMAs wanted to preserve the autonomy of their local relief associations even as they understood that collaboration among groups would benefit all. Rather than creating a state or regional organization, the LMAs remained independent but agreed to cooperate with one another.

In order to reach those sympathetic to their cause, LMA women employed the gendered language of family. As they had during their wartime nursing activities, women of the LMAs saw themselves as filling the symbolic role of the grieving mother. They believed it was their Judeo-Christian duty to serve as surrogate mothers (and thus mourners) for boys and men who had died beyond the reach of their families. The women of the Petersburg LMA specu- lated on the importance of this work in one of their early meetings: "We can picture to ourselves the aged mother as she seeks the column that reports our celebration. Her son was in the army in Virginia . . . but she thinks of the simple bouquet affections offering, placed by the woman's hand on the green mound, and her heart echoes the thought—perhaps my child lies there. This is but one ray of that consolation we seek to afford. Who will refuse it? None—no, not one!" Their cemetery work offered comfort to mothers across the South, creating a common bond among all southern women who had lost a loved one to the war. Just as important as maternalism, however, was the notion of sisterhood. Through sewing societies and other wartime asso- ciations, Confederate women had found a community of women who shared their passions, worries, and tribulations. But with the end of the Confeder- acy and the reduced need for such societies, many women looked to rekindle those female networks and redirect their energies through memorial work. Playing on a latent Confederate nationalism, the Ladies of Charlottesville, Virginia, urged all those who wished to "embrace the sisterhood of those who once called the Confederate cause their own" to enlist.[35]

To attract members to the ranks of their family of ex-Confederates, the LMAS frequently relied on well-established personal and political networks. Nancy MacFarland, president of the Hollywood association, asked the vice presidents and managers to nominate suitable persons who might "represent the association in the different cities of the South." Because the husbands of many HMA members had been government officials during the war, these women presumably had many connections throughout the South. These networks, along with family ties, surely helped bolster the HMA's fund-raising efforts. The Fredericksburg LMA began its campaign by writing letters to those persons who previously had lived in the city as well as those who might consider themselves "friends of the Society," including Robert E. Lee. The LMAS in Petersburg, Richmond, and Lynchburg likewise invited the former leader of the Confederacy to participate in their own memorial activities. Though Lee gratefully accepted their honorary membership, he offered neither financial nor other support to any of the associations.[36]

All of the LMAS relied heavily on circulars, either reprinted in southern newspapers or sent by mass mailings, to rally white southerners and especially other women to their cause of tending to Confederate graves.[37] In February 1866, Colonel T. B. Roy, former chief of staff to Lieutenant General William J. Hardee, sent a letter to the *Montgomery (Alabama) Mail* requesting that the editor publish the enclosed circular soliciting contributions for the Winchester LMA. Roy asked that several Alabama women volunteer to collect subscriptions, as he was "impressed with the belief that ladies are more successful in such enterprises." The Winchester Ladies managed to muster a significant sum of money, and their efforts subsequently encouraged the women of Montgomery and other southern locals to organize similar associations. The HMA Ladies likewise issued an appeal addressed to "the Women of the South," in which they reminded their "southern sisters" that they remained united even if the Confederate war effort had failed. "The end we propose is the cause of the South . . . the permanent protection and adornment" of at least 13,000 "Confederate dead interred in Hollywood Cemetery." Even in defeat, the women claimed to have an "inextinguishable sympathy" for the Confederate cause.[38]

LMA relationships with other women's organizations both within and beyond the state reveal that white southern women's associations were both more established and better connected than historians of women have often assumed. Some historians have argued that southern women failed to participate in organized clubs or public life until the latter part of the nineteenth century because of a distinctive southern gender system. But evidence from

LMAS reveals that white women in fact expanded on their feminine role as caregivers, mourners, and, ultimately, Confederate nationalists, to elaborate a more public and organized role for themselves after the war. In Richmond, Fredericksburg, Winchester, Lynchburg, and Petersburg, no fewer than 500 women immediately joined the ranks of the LMAS, and that number fails to take into account at least 19 additional associations active in the state.[39] These women expected other LMAS to support their projects and, as the Richmond and Fredericksburg cases indicate, initially considered merging their organizations. These extensive networks among associations and the speed with which women joined and supported LMAS throughout Virginia and the region suggest that, contrary to numerous historians' assertions, women's associations were not absent in the mid-nineteenth-century South, nor did they vanish with the Civil War. On the contrary, they were alive and flourishing.

Theoretically, any woman in the community could join these associations. In fact, nearly every society created committees to canvass particular sections of the city and solicit membership or, as in the case in Fredericksburg, placed a register at a local store for women to enroll. Those who pledged to join the association were then expected to provide their "subscription," or dues, ranging from fifty cents annually for the OMA and the Fredericksburg LMA to fifty cents monthly in Petersburg. Despite the claim that "every person [woman] of good character properly vouched for" could become a member, the membership rolls of each group reflected an obvious elite bias.[40] Not surprisingly, women who joined LMAS between 1865 and 1870 were overwhelmingly the wives and daughters of the cities' businessmen and civic leaders.[41] The LMAS' executive boards generally included women whose husbands or fathers were politicians, physicians, insurance agents, merchants, tobacco manufacturers, and lawyers.[42]

Most of the women who joined the LMAS were born between 1830 and 1850, and therefore, had experienced the Civil War as young women. Thirty-four-year-old Bessie Meade Callender, member of the Petersburg LMA, was representative of the earliest members of the memorial associations. She was born to John and Rebecca Meade in Prince George County at the family home, Cedar Level, in 1832, where her father made his living as a wheat and tobacco planter. Bessie married David Callender, a cloth manufacturer, in 1855, and moved to Petersburg, where she gave birth to three children. During the war, David sold cloth to the Confederate army, and Bessie proudly served as treasurer of a soldiers' relief society while enduring the siege of the city. Like many of her counterparts in Petersburg, she continued to demonstrate her allegiance to the Confederacy as a founding member of the Petersburg LMA in 1866.[43]

Although older than many of her counterparts, Mary Gordon Wallace was also a typical LMA member when it came to class and wartime experiences. The former president of the Fredericksburg Soldiers' Relief Association, she was sixty-three-years-old when the war ended. After the battle of Fredericksburg, Wallace and her husband, Dr. John H. Wallace, had become refugees from the sacked city. They returned in 1865 to find that their house had been spared, but their provisions had been reduced to one hen, a cow, and a small supply of cornmeal. Despite her impoverished condition, Wallace's leadership ability made her the natural selection for president among the members of the LMA. Her fellow members of the Soldiers' Relief Association, including Sarah Alsop and Mrs. James H. Bradley, also served on the Fredericksburg LMA board of directors.[44]

Women in the capital likewise adapted their wartime organizational skills to postwar memorialization projects. Nancy MacFarland's position as president of the HMA was a natural outgrowth of her experiences during the war. MacFarland had served as the president of the Soldiers' Aid Association of Virginia, organizing a network of the women's volunteer societies throughout the state and the Confederacy. She had declined the treasurer's office for the Gunboat Association, noting that although her heart was in the cause she would not be able to do it justice, given her other commitments. Her colleague in the Soldiers' Aid Association, Mrs. Samuel Price, transferred her role as treasurer to the OMA.[45] Members of Richmond's Gunboat Association also joined memorial associations in the capital city: Martha Greenhow Maury, Mrs. George Gwathmey, Mrs. F. Nelson, Mrs. John Purcell, and Mrs. B. Smith all joined the HMA in 1866.[46]

Proximity to Civil War deaths likewise prompted membership in the LMAs. Many of the women who believed it their duty to provide centralized cemeteries for Confederate soldiers had first witnessed the anonymous and lonely deaths of soldiers in wartime hospitals. Eleanor Boyd and Mary Williams, founders of the Winchester LMA, had fed, clothed, and nursed wounded soldiers in the town's numerous hospitals. Nora Davidson, who operated a school for young children after the war, had frequently tended to wounded soldiers in Petersburg. Some women, such as HMA's Janet Henderson Randolph, had welcomed wounded soldiers into their private homes. A handful of LMA members had served in the more official capacity of nurse. "Captain" Sally Tompkins, who had operated her own private hospital in Richmond, was quick to join the HMA, as was fellow Richmond nurse Lucy Mason Webb.[47]

Lynchburg provides one of the most direct examples of women transforming their soldiers' aid societies and nursing activities into an LMA. The president of the Lynchburg Hospital, Lucy Mina Otey, realized that a cemetery for soldiers would be needed to deal with the mounting death toll in the city's hospitals. Though busy with the arduous task of managing the hospital in 1861, Otey attended to the last rites of the first soldier buried in the town, Private Robert Feemster of the 11th Mississippi. Soldier burials in the Old Methodist Cemetery continued throughout the war, and in April 1866 several of Otey's colleagues at the hospital organized a memorial association to enclose the graves and arrange an annual Decoration Day. Although Otey died at age sixty-five in May 1866, hospital directors Susan Speed, Cornelia Christian, and Mrs. Robert L. Brown helped continue her work through the town's memorial association.[48]

For some, simply having endured the devastation of their communities was enough to sustain their Confederate patriotism after the war. At least two of the Fredericksburg LMA vice presidents had witnessed the destructive battle of their city. Fannie S. White, a widow and mother of three small children, had remained in the town during the 1862 Union shelling and occupation. Friends and family had desperately urged her to leave, but she had thought it best to remain in her home to protect her household. When the bombardment began on December 11, she hurried to the cellar with her children, slaves, and two men visiting from Stafford. After the shelling stopped at one o'clock in the afternoon, she surveyed the damage to her property. Cannon balls and broken shells littered the garden, limbs had been knocked off trees, and several large holes had been torn through the house. Given the condition of her property, the two men from Stafford finally convinced White to take refuge near Salem Church. Anne F. Fitzhugh, too, endured staggering losses following the battle. When an effort began in December 1863 to compensate Fredericksburg citizens who had lost property during the shelling, Fitzhugh reported a list of losses, including $3,845 in household items and $15,000 in damage to the residence and outbuildings. The families of HMA members Mrs. Lewis Crenshaw, Anne Grant, Alice Brown Haxall, and Nancy MacFarland reported losses ranging from $3,000 to $68,000 following Richmond's evacuation.[49]

Though a systemic survey of every LMA member is virtually impossible, most members had supported the war effort and had experienced its hardships in some fashion. These wartime experiences had generally intensified women's bitterness toward Federal soldiers (who now occupied their communities and focused reburial efforts solely on the Union dead) and strengthened their identities as Confederates. What better way to demonstrate their disdain for Yankees and their undying loyalty to the Confederate cause than by honoring the South's dead?

Along with their intense and continued loyalty to the defunct Confederate nation, women who joined memorial associations were also motivated by more personal reasons. Namely, membership in the Ladies served as a marker of class status. In the antebellum South, a "lady" had been defined as a white woman of the slaveholding class who was delicate and refined, exhibited exceptional manners, and remained obedient and submissive to the men in her life. Although the reality of even elite southern women's lives often contradicted this image, the ideal "lady" was one who was freed from the burdens and drudgery of work because of her reliance on slave labor. But slavery as a marker of elite status had vanished with the surrender, and former white slaveholders were forced to find alternative markers of class status. One such symbol of class for women was membership in a memorial society. As the membership rolls suggested, only the community's wealthiest women, the wives of doctors, lawyers, and business owners, could afford to join the LMAs. Membership required dues and free time, both no doubt difficult to come by for many families immediately following the war. But even more important was the name the women selected for themselves. Hardly anyone could dispute their position and purpose when they declared themselves "the Ladies." These women were not only ranking members of society but (presumably) were confined to the domestic sphere and therefore naturally disinterested in anything political. Elite white women, then, would employ their class status as a political shield.[50]

Although many historians have described LMAs as merely "memorial," and by implication, irrelevant, these associations demonstrated continued evidence of Confederate nationalism and had profound implications for southern identity in the postwar period. Recent scholarship suggests that even though the Confederate state ceased to exist, many white southerners continued to identify themselves as a distinct cultural group well into the late nineteenth century. LMAs, more than any other individual or group in the immediate postwar period, cultivated this notion of southern distinctiveness and fostered a residual Confederate nationalism that would endure for generations.[51]

Beyond establishing Confederate burial grounds, LMAs sought to make the cemeteries physical reminders of the cause, albeit a lost one. The women of the OMA, for example, believed that "it is for the living . . . that such memorials are held, to inspire their lives with the memory of the lives and deeds of the great and noble dead." As such, the OMA laid out its long-term goals: to turf and mark each of the 16,000 graves, to lay out and decorate the grounds, and in the future when finances would permit, to replace the wooden headboards with those of "enduring marble." Similarly, women in Lynchburg agreed that they should enclose the space around the graves in order to protect them for future generations. The local newspaper concurred, arguing that leaving the thousands of graves exposed to the elements would be "a shame, and a reflection on the people of Lynchburg."[52] That is, if contemporary white southerners did not act quickly, future generations would never know of the sacrifice and devotion of their Confederate forefathers and mothers.

These southern cities of the dead bound the slain soldiers together in eternal rest and created opportunities for surviving Confederates to foster a sense of white southern solidarity. From Winchester to Lynchburg, Ladies appealed to a unified South to raise funds to continue their work.[53] Both the Fredericksburg and Winchester associations called on every state of the former Confederacy, observing that scarcely a town or a county was unrepresented on the city's battlefields. The Hollywood women's appeal addressed "the South as one family" and believed that "the southern heart throbs with one impulse." The OMA women declared that their work was to be performed "for the honor and credit of the entire South."[54] The Petersburg LMA claimed that the entire South should be expected to provide "aid of a work which has equal claims on them as on ourselves." These pleas for aid did not go unanswered. Donations reached the women of the LMAS from as far away as Louisiana and Texas. Because of the number of Alabama soldiers who reposed in the Old Dominion, the state's women were especially generous in their donations to Virginia's LMAS, sending contributions to the Winchester, Hollywood, and Fredericksburg associations. An anonymous gift of twenty dollars in gold arrived for the Fredericksburg LMA from Mobile. The Montgomery LMA not only offered its cooperation in caring for Alabama's dead but also pledged to donate the proceeds from a charity ball held in Montgomery.[55]

Two surprising but important membership characteristics confirm that continued patriotic devotion to the Confederacy rather than mere sentimentalism motivated the women of the memorial associations. First, many of the LMAS' male relatives, especially husbands, did not serve in the Confederate military; rather, they tended to remain in the community, either because of job obligations or of age. For example, Rev. Andrew H. H. Boyd, husband of Winchester LMA vice president Eleanor Boyd, was an adamant supporter of the Confederate cause but remained in the town throughout the war because of his position as minister of the Loudoun Street Church. Phillip Williams II, Boyd's brother-in-law and husband of Winchester LMA president Mary Williams, probably did not join the army because of his position as a town councilman and his age of fifty-nine when the war commenced. Both men, along with several other prominent townsmen, however, were taken prisoner during the course of the war by Federal forces. Charles Button, husband of Lynchburg LMA vice president Mary Button, stayed in Lynchburg to operate his paper, the *Virginian*. HMA president Nancy MacFarland's husband, sixty-two-year-old William H. MacFarland, served as a Virginia delegate to the Confederate Provisional Congress from 1861 to 1862 and therefore did not join the military. The same held true for HMA member Henrietta Lyons's fifty-nine-year-old husband, James.[56]

Second, it appears that even when their loved ones did serve in the military forces, most of the Ladies in Virginia did not lose male relatives in the war. Captain Charles Tackett Goolrick, brother to Fredericksburg LMA member Virginia Goolrick, was wounded at Chancellorsville and resigned due to disability in February 1864, but he survived the war. Colonel Robert S. Chew, the brother of another Fredericksburg LMA member, Ellen P. Chew, served as an officer with the 30th Virginia Infantry and returned home safely in 1865, as did Lizzie Alsop's uncle, William Alsop. Captain Richard Pegram, husband of Petersburg LMA member Helen Pegram, and Major General William Mahone, husband of Petersburg LMA vice president Otetia Mahone, likewise returned home after the war. The LMA women, then, were not grieving for their own kin. As the OMA's constitution expressly noted, a "deep and living sympathy for bereaved families" motivated the women. The notion of "our" bereaved families was conspicuously absent.[57]

The fact that LMA members tended not to be the widows and orphans of men who died in the fighting reveals in part their political agenda. The "mourning" demonstrated by these women at Memorial Days and cemetery dedications was not of a personal nature; they were not there to secure the proper burial of their own fathers, sons, and brothers, or, in most instances, even to decorate the graves of a loved one. But that does not negate the very real mourning they felt, which was the bereavement for the loss of the Confederacy, for the death of their cause. The act of hiring burial crews, establishing cemeteries, and organizing elaborate Memorial Day spectacles all represented means by which they could keep alive their intense feelings of Confederate patriotism and demonstrate their continued commitment to the cause. Moreover, these projects gave them reason to foster ties with other like-minded southern "ladies," providing for greater coordination and cross-fertilization among the region's women than historians have previously acknowledged.

Clearly, these women did not see the end of the war as severing their cultural and emotional ties to the former slave states. Rather than fading, their identification with other ex-Confederates seemed only to intensify after the war. The LMAS called on the entire white South, not just their own communities or even states, issuing appeals to people hundreds of miles away to aid in their efforts. Virginia's Ladies, moreover, petitioned the whole region for good reason—they cared for a substantial percentage of the Confederate graves. Within just the seven LMAS located in Fredericksburg, Lynchburg, Richmond, Petersburg, and Winchester, the Ladies would eventually reinter more than 72,520 remains, nearly 28 percent of the South's total war dead. At a minimal estimate of one dollar per body, that was a hefty price tag for these organizations to assume, especially given the financial circumstances of the postwar South.[58]

But it was more than just a need for pecuniary support that led them to contact their southern sisters and brethren. These women considered themselves loyal Confederates and identified with the common plight of white southerners across the region who had sacrificed sons, brothers, fathers, and lovers. The LMAS maintained that their men had fought a gallant fight, and now the women bore responsibility for keeping alive their cause and memory. These women, from Virginia to Texas, were united by common losses—the experience of so much death and destruction as well as the loss of their Confederate nation. More than just having a mutual understanding of each other's suffering, women in Virginia, North Carolina, Alabama, and beyond expected a collective and cooperative effort to bury the dead. Although the South had been defeated on the battlefield, Confederate sentiment continued to thrive for decades in the South's cities of the dead because of the Ladies.

If establishing Confederate cemeteries motivated Virginia's women to organize LMAS, their most visible and popular activity was the annual celebration of Memorial or Decoration Days. White southerners celebrated these days in the spring as a sign of renewal and rebirth, but each community chose its own symbolic date on which to gather. Fredericksburg, Lynchburg, and Oakwood in Richmond all selected May 10, the anniversary of Stonewall Jackson's death. The women of Hollywood agreed on May 31, the anniversary of the day Richmonders first heard the cannons of war. Schoolchildren repaired to the graves of Blandford Cemetery for an informal ceremony under the direction of Petersburg LMA member Nora Fontaine Maury Davidson on May 26, but the Ladies selected June 9 for their official services. It had been on that day, two years prior, that the "grey haired sires and beard-

Petersburg's First Memorial Day, June 9, 1866. The recently remounded graves were adorned with floral tributes typical of Confederate Memorial Days regardless of date or location. (Courtesy Museum of the Confederacy, Richmond, Virginia, copy photography by Katherine Wetzel)

less youths" of the home guard defended the city until Lee's troops could arrive.[59] Finally Winchester's Ladies settled on June 6, the day the Valley's hero, General Turner Ashby, was killed.

Regardless of the date, Memorial Days tended to follow similar patterns. The women of the LMAs gathered on the days preceding the event to make evergreen and floral arrangements and requested that young men or boys perform any physical work, such as remounding. On Memorial Day, hundreds and even thousands of citizens gathered at some central location in town, perhaps a church or town hall, and then marched in procession to the cemetery, where the Ladies and children decorated the graves with flowers and evergreens. Subsequently, orators chosen by the LMA delivered prayers and evocative speeches. Even though women selected men to serve as the featured guests and speakers, everyone understood that the Ladies ran the show. As city newspapers noted, Memorial Day was "under the direction of the Ladies"—they selected the date, chose the orators, invited groups to participate in the procession, and even picked the musical selections.[60]

Despite the omnipresent rhetoric of mourning at these Memorial Days, white Virginians knew they were treading on dangerous ground when they invoked the "sacred" memory of the Confederacy so soon after defeat. Petersburg's Sara Pryor later recalled that the Ladies recognized the need for discreet behavior, given the continued presence of the Federal Army in the city. In order to avoid any confrontations with the Union soldiers, Petersburg LMA president Margaret Joynes had quietly sent notes to all the members, requesting their presence at Blandford Church on the afternoon of June 9, from which the services would commence. Perhaps it was an effort to prevent Federal Army censure that the Ladies also decorated the Union graves that were scattered among those of the Confederates.[61] On Lynchburg's first Memorial Day, May 10, 1866, the city newspaper admitted that the services would "doubtless excite harsh and malignant remarks in certain quarters of the North, and be taken as evidence of a mutinous, malcontent spirit pervading our people." But, the writer maintained, "we are sure" that "this sentiment will for the main part be confined to men who took no active *battle-part* in the war." Northern soldiers, and perhaps their devoted wives and daughters, would surely recognize the need to honor the remains of those who had died "valiantly in the opposite ranks."[62]

Indeed, ex-Confederates had every reason to suspect that the U.S. Army and northern press closely monitored their actions. In May 1866, an unidentified northern paper charged that the money obtained for the dead should have been donated to the destitute living. The southern press defended the actions of their women, pointing out that "they can bury the dead but once; they are feeding the poor daily." White southerners, however, knew the real motive behind the accusation. "The secret of this carping is not because the fund was not applied to the relief of the poor, but because it was applied to preserving the memory of our dead," a Lynchburg newspaper insisted. Representative Thomas Williams of Pennsylvania clearly indicated the political significance of Confederate memorializing, noting that "the memories of the traitor dead have been hallowed and consecrated by local public entertainments and treasonable utterances in honor of their crime." In the days following the first Confederate Memorial Days, an anonymous northern woman lamented that "we have few flowers for the graves of our heroes, but we have crowns and honors for the heads of traitors." She implored her fellow northerners to "not forget Andersonville, nor Libby, nor Castle Thunder, nor Belle Isle! Let banishment at least be meted to this man who tortured and slaughtered our brothers." The *New York Times* concurred, warning northerners that the "Southern Spirit" was continuing to grow "with wonderful rapidity." "Its most fruitful feeders," it noted, "are the Memorial Associations." The paper reminded its readers that these seemingly "noble" Memorial Days provided forums for ex-Confederate men to make speeches, "wherein [they] adroitly inculcat[e] hatred of the North. . . . These memorial days have now become painfully frequent, and on every one of them recruits are gathered to the Democratic banner." The *Chicago Tribune* agreed, denouncing the Ladies of Richmond for strewing flowers on the graves of the Confederate dead, charging that these women sought "to keep alive the political feeling of hostility to the Union."[63]

Northerners perhaps were inclined to view southern white women's behavior as overtly political because of female activism in their own region. Women had long been active in the abolitionist movement, and in 1848 Elizabeth Cady Stanton and Lucretia Mott had called the first women's rights convention at Seneca Falls, at which they declared that men and women were created equal. During the next seventeen years, a small but growing number of northern women began to demand rights, such as control of their own earnings, guardianship of their own children in cases of divorce, and, eventually, the right to vote. During the war, Anna Dickinson embraced partisan politics when the New Hampshire State Republican Committee invited her to speak in favor of the Republican gubernatorial candidate in the spring of 1863. By the end of year, Dickinson had helped the Republicans defeat Democrats in four states, soon thereafter becoming the first woman ever to address Congress. In the wake of the war with emancipation secured, northern women like Dickinson, Mott, and Stanton once again turned their attention to the vote, pressing for an amendment that would ensure universal adult suffrage. Northern critiques of southern women's graveside services, therefore, came from a context in which women were increasingly seen as overtly public and political.[64]

But safe within the cloak of "motherly and sisterly undertaking," former Confederates defended these floral tributes under the direction of the Ladies. "This poor privilege is all that is left us now," they claimed. The *Richmond Whig* likewise responded that "political significance is not attached to these funeral ceremonies in the South," as it was not the habit of southern women to form political conspiracies. Rather, the paper proclaimed, "if the men of the South contemplated treason and 'civil war,'" they would not put "forward their wives and daughters to do the dangerous work." But for all their reasoning and justifications, southern white men did just that.[65]

If southern men simultaneously recognized and denied the political nature of the women's activities, the LMAS clearly understood that their work spoke to issues of loyalty and bordered on treason.[66] The Petersburg LMA, for example, invoked the military leadership of both the Revolution and the Confederacy in its founding documents. The Ladies believed that they would be untrue "to our birthright of glory—untrue to the hand of a Washington and a Lee did we not give every energy to this work." Here, the Ladies continued the tradition of equating the American struggle for independence with that of Confederate hopes and also noted their continued devotion to the South's unsuccessful rebellion. In Georgia, members of the Athens LMA recalled years later that their men had initially discouraged memorial efforts, as they had sworn an oath to the Union. The women pointed out that they were under no such parole and so would continue in their work.[67]

Such carefully chosen rhetoric confirms that Ladies' associations throughout the former Confederacy recognized the political implications and the religious symbolism inherent in their floral graveside tributes. Minutes from the Ladies' meetings, speeches delivered at Memorial Days, and even newspaper accounts were filled with biblical overtones. At the HMA's first meeting, Rev. Charles Minnegrode opened the gathering with a prayer and then commenced to speak "of the sacredness of the movement and offered up an earnest petition that success might attend the holy enterprise about to be inaugurated." In a reference surely intended to invoke the image of Mary Magdalene at Christ's grave, a Winchester newspaper noted that "while man had shown energy and industry in preparing and mounding the graves of the dead, the hand and heart of woman had been enlisted in the decoration of the sacred ground." These floral tributes revealed that Virginia's "sympathizing daughters" had been first at the tomb. Several years later, in Wilmington, North Carolina, former general Raleigh E. Colston used the same analogy: "Unwearied by all their labors and self-sacrifice during four years of war, they were, like Mary, the first at the graves of their beloved dead. Therefore, to them we may safely entrust the holy ark of our Southern faith."[68] By framing their discourse in the language of a pious undertaking, the Ladies hoped to further remove themselves from the political sphere. The divine, of course, was beyond the realm of partisan and sectional politics. But even more, such rhetoric suggested that the Confederacy, like Christ, might yet rise again.[69]

During 1866, inaugural memorial celebrations occurred throughout the South. On May 10, the third anniversary of Jackson's death and the very day that Elizabeth Cady Stanton, Susan B. Anthony, and other northern women were congregating to form the American Equal Rights Association in New York, the OMA paid tribute to their dead Confederates for the first time. Richmonders suspended business, and more than a thousand gathered for religious services at St. John's Church, where Patrick Henry had given his "Give Me Liberty or Give Me Death" speech, before marching in a procession to

Oakwood Cemetery. At the burial grounds, the participants scattered flowers on the 16,000 graves, before listening to Rev. Manning appeal to God to console and bless the wives and orphans of those Confederate soldiers who had fallen in war. Robert E. Lee had been invited to be the day's orator but declined the invitation. Instead, the final speaker of the afternoon was Raleigh E. Colston. After his speech stressing the loyalty of the enlisted men to the Lost Cause, 200 Confederate survivors saluted him with a rebel yell. Despite this blatantly militaristic display, Richmonders were quick to remind any unionists who might be watching that women had directed the entire affair. The officers of the OMA and their invited guests, the HMA, occupied center stage on the speakers' stand, and newspapers pointed out that the day's activities were "under the management of the ladies." Richmond's ex-Confederates hoped that women had depoliticized the event by their leadership and presence, thereby providing a forum for Lost Cause advocates such as Colston to voice their unwavering support of the Confederacy.[70]

Not to be outdone, the HMA organized an even more impressive, and more militaristic, memorial celebration. Prior to the day's affair, Major Thomas A. Brander offered the services of the city's military companies to the HMA. The men formed themselves into companies and marched out to Hollywood on May 28 and 29 to remove weeds, remound, and place properly marked headboards on nearly 6,000 graves. One observer commented that "the arms worn on that day and the duties to be performed were quite different from what they were some months ago. The musket, the sword, and the bayonet, gave place to the spade, the shovel, the pick, and the rake."[71] Replicating the freed slaves' Evacuation Day procession a month earlier, on May 31, twenty-three military companies participated in what could only have appeared to many northern observers as a military demonstration. Wearing their uniforms without military insignia or buttons as the law required, thousands of Confederate veterans made their way to Grace Church where they joined the HMA. From there, the men and women formed a single procession to the burial ground. "It was a strange and splendid spectacle," one newspaper reported. "The carriages, filled with lovely women, were covered with flowers; wreathes and garlands decked the roofs of the omnibuses usually devoted to baser burdens, and all the treasures of Spring seemed to blush and tremble."

Stores across Richmond, except those owned by Republicans or African Americans, remained closed for the day, and an estimated 20,000 people congregated in Hollywood Cemetery. Although no ceremonies or speeches occurred, the HMA members placed evergreens and garlands on the graves while the veterans solemnly paid tribute to privates and generals alike. Again the newspapers tried to assure everyone that the affair was not intended to provoke Union authorities; rather it had been formulated by the "spontaneous demonstration" of "self-sacrificing" Richmond women.[72]

Though smaller than the Hollywood ceremony, white southerners argued that the festivities in Winchester on June 6, 1866, were equally free of treason-ous spirit. As in Richmond, businesses closed, while thousands of locals and visitors filled the town's streets for its inaugural Memorial Day. Three hundred former Confederates, primarily survivors of the Stonewall and Arnold Elzey brigades, were followed by fourteen young girls wearing white dresses and black sashes, accompanied by other citizens in a procession traveling from the Episcopal Church to the new cemetery. Upon reaching the site, the women and young girls decorated every grave with wreaths and garlands of fresh flowers and greenery. Finally, the crowd gathered to hear three speakers, all former Confederate majors, pay tribute to the fallen soldiers. Surely northern troops stationed in Winchester must have—or at least should have—frowned upon the large gathering of southern sympathizers, not to mention the hundreds of ex-Confederate soldiers who paraded through town only a year after the war's end.[73]

In order to avoid cries of treason from northerners, Winchester's men, like their counterparts in Richmond, consciously framed the day's blatant displays of Confederate patriotism within the domestic sphere of women. "The mothers and daughters of Virginia are the chief mourners and actors in these touching obsequies," one of the day's speakers, Major Uriel Wright, pro-claimed. For Wright and other former Confederates, the language of mourn-ing and feminine virtue were virtually inseparable when justifying tributes to their "lost cause." This rhetoric, if not full-fledged belief, allowed them subtly to protest not only the outcome of the war, but also the uncertainty of what a reconstructed South might look like in those first years after Appomattox. Who knew what changes might lie ahead? Already the region's labor and racial systems had been overturned. By placing the responsibility for protecting the past in the firm but gentle hands of women, white southern men could claim that memorializing the Confederacy was by no means a political gesture.[74]

Wright made sure that white southerners, as well as any northerners who might be watching, understood that despite Confederate veterans' support, these ceremonies were solely the work of the South's women. "Mothers and daughters of Virginia," he exclaimed, "this noble enterprise is your work. Scenes like this, rising up wherever our dead lie, gild with melancholy light the desolation of the land. They took their origin in the brains of no poli-tician, no schemer, seeking individual distinction or plotting the renewal of strife." Because this tribute had been born in the heart of women, he argued, it could only be interpreted as true and pure. These women certainly could not be viewed as traitorous—they were simply exhibiting the qualities nineteenth-century Victorian ideology attributed to women: sentiment, emotion, and devotion to one's menfolk. In fact, Wright declared that southern white women "were not political casuists." They had not paused "to enquire whether the teachings of Jefferson, Madison, or Mason furnished the true interpretation of the Constitution, and correctly marked the boundaries of State and Federal powers." Just as members of the southern Whig Party had done since the 1830s, postbellum Virginians agreed that women were naturally "disinterested" in politics and therefore must possess pure motives. In denying the political nature of women, Wright simultaneously denied the very political nature of their work: if women were not political, then, by extension, their actions could not be construed as such. Therefore, memorial activities, clearly within the province of female mourning (and hence the domestic sphere), posed no threat to sectional reunion.[75]

What he failed to mention, however, was that under the direction of the Ladies, Memorial Days provided legitimate venues for ex-Confederate veterans to march into towns, for thousands of white southerners to gather in a central location, and for former generals and political figures to praise the Confederate cause in a public forum. Protected by their gender, white women were able to escape charges of treason during Reconstruction, for which men, as "political-beings," would have been found guilty. Moreover, ex-Confederate men could practice what Anne Rubin has termed "political ventriloquism." That is, by allowing white women to take center stage at memorial activities, men could both express their bitterness toward Yankees and assure the federal government of their loyalty.[76]

If Winchester's Memorial Day celebration in June 1866 should have been enough to raise northern eyebrows, then the elaborate reburial of General Turner Ashby and three other Confederate officers the following autumn should have been seen as outright treason. Believing that Winchester rather than Charlottesville would be a more appropriate burial location for the Valley's dashing hero, the Winchester LMA proposed that Ashby and his brother Richard, killed fighting on Kelly Island, Maryland, in 1861, be reinterred in Stonewall Cemetery.[77] Joseph Holmes Sherrard and James Averitt, writing on behalf of the LMA, drafted a letter to the Ashbys' sisters in August 1866 requesting permission to reinter the bodies. The men assured one of the sisters, Mary Moncure, that both the brothers "seemed attached to our people, where they had hosts of warm and instant friends." They claimed that "there are none to whom the guardianship of these remains would be more appropriately committed than those whose homes and firesides they tried to defend." The sisters willingly consented to the reburial.[78]

In early October, men hired by the LMA exhumed the bodies of both Ashbys and prepared them for transfer to Winchester. They placed Turner Ashby's body in an elaborate coffin paid for by the "patriotic women" of Jefferson County, West Virginia. Made of black walnut and covered with black cloth of the finest fabric, it was, the newspaper noted, "nearly enveloped in silver fringe and platings." The brothers' bodies were transported first to Charles Town, West Virginia, and then on to Winchester, where they joined the remains of two other comrades on the night of October 24. The hearse, drawn by four white horses and accompanied by sixty former military officers and local officials, wound through small Valley communities until reaching Stonewall Cemetery. The elaborate processional must have been a spectacle reminiscent of Confederate military parades through towns during the war.[79]

On Thursday morning, October 25, nearly 10,000 Valley residents and guests gathered to await the reburial of the Confederate officers and dedication of Stonewall Cemetery.[80] Morning trains on the Winchester and Potomac line brought eleven passenger cars crowded with enthusiastic spectators from Virginia and Maryland. Even West Virginia was well represented by the "fair women and brave men" of Jefferson and Berkley Counties. According to the local paper, they ignored "their unnatural separation which has, temporarily we trust, deprived them of their birth rights as Virginians" and "gathered around the tombs of the Confederate dead." Men and women alike thronged the bustling streets of Winchester, and all recognized the vital role the fairer sex played in the day's events. One observer noted that "an early visit to the cemetery revealed to us the fact that, while man had shown energy and industry in preparing and mounding the graves of the dead, the hand and heart of woman had been enlisted in the decoration of the sacred ground." Women from West Virginia to North Carolina had contributed to the affair. A collection of flowers sent by the women of Shepherdstown, West Virginia, and an elegant floral cross, a gift of women from North Carolina, decorated Ashby's grave. Monuments marking the lots appropriated to each state had been "wreathed and twined with evergreens, myrtle, and cedar, whilst the numberless bouquets resting on the hills marking the repository of the heroic dead, told plainly the sympathizing daughters of Virginia had been thus early at the tomb."[81]

The Ladies of Winchester and their sisters from surrounding areas, however, served a more valuable purpose than mere decorators. As had been the case only months before, at Winchester's first Memorial Day, women once again proved to be an important political symbol for the ex-Confederacy's message of triumph through defeat. As the keynote speaker at the dedication, former governor Henry A. Wise spoke neither of mourning nor of reunion. Instead, he encouraged the crowd to look to the dead for the power and strength to deal with surrender and submission. He told them to ask themselves what the Mighty Stonewall would do in their situation. "Would he have praised proclamations of peace! Peace! When there is no peace?" he asked. "Would he not have demanded as lawful rights the withdrawal of military force and of Freedman's Bureau, and the restoration of Civil Rule and the writ of Habeas Corpus?" Responding to the frequent and hearty applause, Wise declared that Jackson would have never disavowed the cause for which his comrades died. Again referencing Jackson (and invoking the biblical rhetoric so common at Lost Cause gatherings), Wise proclaimed: "The Captain of our Salvation was conquered; He died that the cause might live." With the Federal troops watching from across the field, he thundered: "A lost cause! If lost it was false; if true, it is not lost!" He closed his remarks by noting that the state of West Virginia was "the bastard child of political rape," but promised that "there is still substance enough left in Virginia to insure her honor and more than restore her preeminence." With this, Wise stepped down from the podium. Surely U.S. troops stationed in the town must have looked on in astonishment. As historian William Blair has pointed out, Turner Ashby had been reinterred in a town in which he had never resided, in a cemetery named after Jackson (who was buried in Lexington as opposed to Winchester), at a dedication that featured a recalcitrant rebel in Wise. How could northerners look upon the spectacle in the Valley as anything other than pro-Confederate political behavior?[82]

Women of the LMAs were not puppets of the South's men; they clearly orchestrated the creation of Confederate cemeteries and Memorial Days. But it was equally clear that men supported these displays of residual Confederate patriotism. In several instances, men had encouraged women to form associations and, in nearly every instance, had provided the labor for preparing the Confederate graves. They could claim that these "Ladies" were disinterested in politics, but women had literally provided the platform from which ex-Confederate men could lament their defeat. This fact was not lost on Republicans and Union occupying forces and did little to persuade them that these displays had no political content. On the day of Hollywood's services, for example, some Federal soldiers arrived in Richmond from Fredericksburg to prevent any emergency or hostility that might arise between the white southerners and the occupying forces. Governor Francis Pierpont believed that the observance at Hollywood indicated that treason remained alive in the former Confederacy.[83] The U.S. Burial Corps stationed in Winchester had refused the request of a woman to lower the flag at its camp during Ashby's reinterment and later that afternoon brandished their weapons at a group of the town's residents. Despite these close encounters, Union forces did relatively little to prevent these intense displays of Confederate patriotism in the spring and fall of 1866. Under the auspices of the Ladies, from Winchester to Petersburg, Virginia's first Memorials Days passed without incident.[84]

Within a year of Appomattox, white women had successfully launched an effort to venerate the defeated Confederacy. Hundreds of Virginia's leading daughters transformed their wartime aid societies into memorial associations and launched campaigns throughout the South to raise funds for their national Confederate cemeteries, which only furthered the sense of southern solidarity and sectional animosity. Ex-Confederate men and women alike recognized the pivotal role women played in maintaining and re-creating Confederate identity in the aftermath of defeat. The LMAs had created a permanent reminder of the Confederate war effort through their cemeteries. They had provided a forum through Memorial Days and tributes such as the Ashbys' reinterment that allowed white men like Wise to expound on the virtues of the Confederacy and advocate resistance to Reconstruction. Although challenges awaited the women after implementation of more rigid Reconstruction policies in 1867, using the cloak of feminine mourning, the LMAs had set in motion Lost Cause traditions that would continue into the next century.[85]

The Influence and Zeal of Woman

3

Ladies' Memorial Associations during Radical Reconstruction, 1867–1870

Even in the "tender" hands of southern women, Memorial Days and cemetery dedications smacked of unrepentant rebellion. The relatively lenient period of presidential Reconstruction had not quelled the Confederate spirit; in fact, it appeared to have stoked it. Southern Unionists and northerners fumed over such reports, repeatedly declaring that they were attempting reconciliation while ex-Confederates continued to exhibit bombastic and sectionalist behavior. One Unionist newspaper editor condemned the federal government's policy of avoiding controversy: "Union men must keep quiet, hang their heads, and look on in submission, allowing young loyalists of the South . . . to do as they please and to vaunt as they choose about the past." Some white northerners even denounced the commemoration of Confederate heroes and "the annual floral decoration of soldiers graves" as a "deeply laid plan in Virginia extending throughout the South, to keep alive for future use the hopes, purposes, and organization of the late disunion conspiracy." Others claimed to have discovered the real motives of Confederate memorial services: to "keep alive the rancors of hate." Moreover, the elaborate memorial celebrations of 1866 led U.S. major general Philip H. Sheridan to declare that an "undoubted change for the worse" in the attitude of white southerners had occurred in the last six months.[1]

Former Confederate soldiers parading through the streets, the southern press's tirade against Reconstruction policies, southern whites' treatment of freedmen, and President Andrew Johnson's moderate policies toward the South all prompted Congress to begin passing a series of Reconstruction Acts in March 1867. The first of the acts stipulated the terms by which the southern states might reenter the Union. Each of the eleven Confederate states, excluding Tennessee, would be required to write a new constitution that provided for manhood suffrage, to approve the new constitution by a majority of voters, and to ratify the Fourteenth Amendment. Equally important, the act divided the region into five military districts, whose commanders could use the army to protect life and property. Virginia was designated Military District Number 1. Under the command of Major General John M. Schofield, it had a total of 2,087 Federal soldiers, which occupied twelve camps scattered throughout the state, with the largest concentration of 1,031 in Richmond.[2]

Despite the tightening of Congressional Reconstruction measures, Ladies' Memorial Associations (LMAS) throughout Virginia persevered in their efforts to commemorate the Confederacy. Between 1867 and 1870, women of the LMAS continued to direct Confederate traditions, in a period of gender cooperation, with the endorsement and support of most southern white men. They shrewdly manipulated the conditions of Reconstruction to maintain a sense of white southern solidarity and broadened their public role by serving as surrogate government agencies for the defunct Confederacy. While northern women such as Elizabeth Cady Stanton and Susan B. Anthony debated woman suffrage and the Fifteenth Amendment, LMA members were likewise busy redefining southern women's relationship to the state, thus creating an alternate form of women's political engagement. The Ladies staged elaborate public spectacles, moved beyond the local nature of earlier southern benevolent work that had focused on orphanages and almshouses, and called on municipal and state governments to support their projects. Expanding on their devotion to the failed Confederate cause, LMAS allowed southern white women to engage in civic life as never before.

Although U.S. troops had occupied cities across the Commonwealth since the surrender of Lee's army in April 1865, the first two years of Reconstruction in Virginia were a fairly lenient period for former rebels. The military presence was minimal (estimated at less than 200 soldiers as of April 1866), and the state was jointly governed by both the Freedmen's Bureau and the provisional government, run by Unionist Republican governor Francis H. Pierpont.[3] The governor proved to be an early, if unexpected, ally for former Confederates. Like President Andrew Johnson, Pierpont believed that the most appropriate response was to reestablish civil order throughout the state. Pierpont recognized that he needed more than the support of the state's Unionists, and therefore he restored political rights to former Confederates so long as they repudiated secession and appeared reasonably repentant. By the summer of 1865, many of the Commonwealth's offices were filled by men who only months before had been enemies of the state.[4]

This relatively peaceful political environment, however, soon gave way to increasing tension and controversy. With the exception of Tennessee, the southern states adamantly rejected the Fourteenth Amendment and black suffrage, thereby infuriating Republican leadership and pushing even moderate northerners toward more punitive measures. After gaining control of Reconstruction policies in the spring of 1867, moderate and radical Republican congressmen denied all former Confederates political power, instituted martial law, directed southern states to provide freedmen with political rights, including access to the ballot box, and laid out the means by which civil governments might be restored. Despite General Schofield's attempts to implement Congressional Reconstruction in Virginia with impartiality to both whites and blacks, several riots occurred and political tension mounted as ex-Confederates were disenfranchised while freedmen increasingly occupied public office.[5] In May 1867, violence erupted in Richmond after police arrested three black men of the Mounted Negro Guard for sitting in the white section of a horse-drawn streetcar.[6] That same month, two other riots occurred in the capital city following incidents involving the black community and police. Although aggression continued between individual whites and blacks in Richmond, there were no riots in 1868 or 1869. Nevertheless, throughout the Old Dominion, a loose coalition of newly enfranchised blacks, southern Unionists, and transplanted northerners garnered control of the state and local governments.[7]

Virginia's Conservatives, the label Democrats adopted, did not attempt to hide their disdain for the new political order. According to historian Steven Tripp, Lynchburg's old elite "condemned the opposition with a ferocity seldom seen in prewar political contests." They portrayed the Republican leaders as illegitimate aliens who had gained power by misleading the "ignorant and misguided" blacks and poor whites. Conservatives believed that the Republicans' intention was to "humiliate the Southern people as they stole from state coffers and raped the South of its resources." In order to stop the carnage, conservatives believed they must unite and reelect "traditional" leaders to power.[8]

Women, too, expressed outrage toward the federal government and Republican politics, just as they had during the secession crisis and war. Maria Louisa Carrington lamented that Virginia's political prospects were "more and more dreadful" during Reconstruction because radicals were "filled with every fiendish feeling." Lizzie Alsop voiced a similar despair. "The political horizon, never clear, has recently become so dark and threatening that I shudder at the bear [sic] possibilities of the troubles in store for us," she wrote in the spring of 1867. Later that summer, Maria Louisa Wacker Fleet reported that Richmond had been "beset by a fresh influx of Yankee officers and carpetbaggers trying to register the negroes and influencing them to vote against us." But, she countered, "I will not dwell on this as it is too dreadful even to contemplate."[9]

One of the most vocal public opponents of so-called Radical Reconstruction was a new weekly Richmond newspaper, the *Southern Opinion*. Established only three months after the Reconstruction Act by avowed secessionist H. Rives Pollard, wartime editor of the *Richmond Daily Examiner*, the paper's expressed purpose was to foster a distinctive southern culture. Pollard advised the people of the South to "comply in good feeling with the requirements of the military bill" and vowed that his paper would not obstruct the military "in any of its operations through our influence." In fact, the first edition of the paper described Schofield as "on the whole, as moderate and just as could be expected." The South might be "politically dead," reasoned Pollard, but it was not "socially or intellectually dead." Echoing much of the LMAs' sentiment, he repeatedly encouraged former Confederates to "foster in the hearts of our children the memories of a century of political and mental triumphs," and preserve the heroism and endurance of their cause. By the spring of 1868, the paper regularly printed weekly indictments of the Republican government, Schofield, and the freedmen. Pollard's paper would become a mouthpiece for continued Confederate memorialization, especially the LMAs of Virginia and the South at large.[10]

In the months following the 1867 Reconstruction Acts, Union authorities had begun restricting expressions of Confederate sentiment throughout the South. In Raleigh, North Carolina, occupying troops ensured that the local Ladies organization abstained from organizing a procession on Memorial Day. Members of the association later recalled that "indeed the threat was made that if the Ladies' Memorial Association, chiefly women and children in mourning, did form a procession, it would be fired on without further warning." The LMAs throughout the state were thus prohibited for five years from marching in processions to cemeteries, although women in groups of two and three quietly made their way to the burial grounds to lay wreaths and flowers under the watchful eye of Federal soldiers. The Union commander in Memphis likewise refused to allow any processions, speeches, or public demonstrations for that city's 1867 Memorial Day. But New Orleans, under the military command of Major General Philip H. Sheridan, experienced some of the harshest constraints. The general forbade residents of the city from participating in fund-raising endeavors for monuments and broke up organizations dedicated to supporting widows and orphans of Confederate soldiers. The orders eventually led the Ladies' Confederate Memorial Association of the city to drop "Confederate" from its name.[11]

Although there was no official crackdown on memorial celebrations or cemetery projects in Virginia, the commencement of Congressional or Radical Reconstruction, along with the various riots in the capital city, prompted Virginia's LMAs to institute at least a voluntary curtailment of their memorial activities.[12] In 1867, the commanding Federal officer in Lynchburg prohibited H. Rives Pollard from delivering a lecture regarding the chivalry of the South during war. That spring, the local LMA chose only to gather at the cemetery to deposit flowers on the graves. Fredericksburg's activities remained relatively low-key as well. There was no official procession, although advance cars and wagons led by citizens brought loads of sod to the cemetery early in the morning. On this fourth anniversary of Stonewall Jackson's death, the Fredericksburg LMA and "a number of gentlemen repaired to the cemetery near town where they spent the day sodding and decorating with strewn flowers and evergreens" the graves of more than 200 southern soldiers. The Oakwood Memorial Association (OMA) refrained altogether from organizing a decoration day. Although Richmond's businesses closed as if for a Sabbath and between 15,000 and 20,000 people turned out to place flowers on the graves at Hollywood, the Hollywood Memorial Association (HMA) likewise held no formal procession and prohibited orations in eulogy of the dead. As several newspapers indicated, the majority of those in attendance were women and children.[13]

The significance of this overwhelming feminine presence was not lost on James Henry Gardner of Richmond. Witnessing the day's activities, he noted that even without the parades and speeches, if the affair "had not been under the control of the Ladies," then a "thousand bayonets would have bristled to prevent the celebration." But such a display of arms, Gardner believed, still would not prevent the LMAs from their memorial work. "Nothing," he maintained, "can subdue the deep seated sympathy of noble women of the Southern Confederacy." The stiffening of Reconstruction policies in 1867 had made it all the more necessary for Memorial Days and Confederate cemeteries to be under the leadership of women. Despite the presence of General Schofield and his Federal troops stationed throughout the Commonwealth, the LMAS defiantly claimed that "we yet have left us the right to love and to mourn."[14]

Memorial celebrations did not diminish under Radical Reconstruction but continued to grow in popularity with the passing of years. In 1869, "nearly all the people" of Fredericksburg and the surrounding countryside paid tribute to the Confederate dead in an elaborate ceremony. An assemblage primarily of Sunday schools began at the Presbyterian Church and formed a procession that extended for three city blocks. That same year, Winchester's tribute attracted between 6,000 and 8,000 people, including, according to the local paper, the town's black residents. Hundreds of citizens attended the Hebrew Memorial Association's third Memorial Day, even though the cemetery contained only a small number of Confederate dead. Services at Hollywood continued to generate substantial crowds, often ranging close to 20,000. At Petersburg's third memorial celebration on June 9, 1868, people from throughout the state sent flowers, local businesses provided hacks and wagons, and a great many locals participated in decorating the graves. The whole city came to a virtual standstill on that day, as businesses closed their doors and thousands of white citizens paid homage to the dead heroes of the Lost Cause. In all, they decorated between 2,500 and 3,000 graves in Blandford Cemetery with offerings of flowers, evergreens, and tiny flags stamped with the Confederate motto. Support for the Petersburg LMA and its cemetery abounded, and it exclaimed that "on no previous occasion has there been manifested by our people more cordial sympathy with the objects of our Society." The Petersburg LMA rejoiced: "Our hearts are thus encouraged, and we are stimulated to a more lively zeal."[15]

Memorial Days allowed ex-Confederates to honor their war dead, but these services also provided an opportunity for white southerners to devise their own interpretation and model of southern race relations during the uncertain years of Reconstruction. Even though the Ladies overwhelmingly tended to avoid discussions of race, they made a concerted effort to praise instances of African American loyalty to their former masters. In accounts of Winchester's inaugural Memorial Day, for example, several African Americans joined ex-Confederates in the procession to Stonewall Cemetery. Fredericksburg's LMA likewise invited those members of the "colored population who may desire to honor the Confederate dead" to join their exercises.[16] If "faithful" ex-slaves were encouraged to participate in memorial services, white southerners also exalted them for their individual and more personal tributes to the Lost Cause. Ned Richardson, a freedman in Richmond, was allegedly dressed in a

Mourners at Stonewall Jackson's grave in Lexington, Memorial Day, 1866.
(Courtesy Museum of the Confederacy, Richmond, Virginia)

Confederate uniform when hauled before the court for a minor charge of selling chickens. Local whites enthusiastically observed that he seemed as "proud
as a cat wearing shoes" in the rebel garb. While visiting his brother's grave at
Lynchburg, a white man noticed three of his former slaves placing flowers on
the tomb. Not only did the white man tearfully watch the scene, but the local
newspaper dedicated a whole column to the incident, recounting the "tender
relations which existed under the old dispensation between the two races"
and encouraging similar devotions from the city's black residents.[17]

Ex-Confederates deliberately published such accounts with two audiences
in mind: white northerners and black southerners. Bloody race riots had occurred in Memphis, New Orleans, and Norfolk during the spring of 1866, and
there were smaller outbreaks in Richmond during 1867, but white southerners'
emphasis on black participation in memorial ceremonies strove to suggest
that peaceful relations between the races were possible. Such touching obsequies, former Confederates believed, ran contrary to northern tales of racial
conflict in the South—and demonstrated that white southerners should be
left to manage their own affairs, free from federal government oversight. But
the message was also directed at shaping the behavior of southern freedmen.
Immediately following the account of freedmen visiting a Confederate grave,
the Lynchburg newspaper quoted a local African American proclaiming that
"the negroes' duty is to labor. Politics was the rock on which the Union was

dissolved, and I advise my race to steer aloof from it." Less than a year later, the Ku Klux Klan organized in Lynchburg to frighten those less "devoted" blacks into submission.[18] As long as African Americans acknowledged the supremacy of whites, shunned Republican politics, and especially if they joined in mourning the Confederacy, they would be safe from violence. Applauding freedmen who participated in Confederate commemorations allowed southern whites to praise those black people who knew their "place" in society— those who did not question the authority of whites, meddle in politics, or stage Emancipation Day celebrations.

Highlighting freedmen's devotion to their former masters and willingness to participate in Confederate mourning made it possible for white southerners to gloss over, or outright ignore, the persistent racial violence sweeping the region. Moreover, as historian Joan Marie Johnson has posited, celebrating "loyal" African Americans allowed white southerners to reinforce the justness of the Confederate cause and underscore black dependence on whites at a time when the legal, political, economic, and social climate of the South was in a state of flux. It seems small wonder that ex-slaves following their old masters to the cemetery and placing flowers on the graves of the men who had fought so hard to keep them enslaved would surely remind both whites and blacks of the "appropriate" relationship between African Americans and whites in the post-emancipation South.[19]

Like Confederate cemeteries, LMAs never intended Memorial Days to be exclusively local affairs. Rather, as had been the case with their circular campaigns and cemetery projects, the women saw memorial celebrations as an opportunity for all white southerners to extend their identity as loyal Confederates. Openly defying occupying Federal forces, LMAs directed city councils, newspapers, and businesses in encouraging the largest possible crowd for each celebration. Often, LMAs requested that free transportation for visitors and floral arrangements be provided by the local railroads and express companies. General William Mahone of Petersburg, his wife a member of the city's LMA, agreed to issue round-trip tickets at half fare along any of his three railroads to anyone wishing to attend the memorial celebration at Lynchburg in 1869. The reduced rates appeared to have been successful, as locals reported a great number of strangers arriving to witness the celebration.[20]

But Confederates were not the only ones who felt compelled to honor their war dead. In the spring of 1868, former general John A. Logan, commander-in-chief of the northern veterans' association, the Grand Army of the Republic

(GAR), instituted the first "Union Memorial Day."[21] In General Order No. 11, May 5, 1868, Logan called on GAR posts throughout the country to organize ceremonies on May 30 in which they might honor the Federal dead.[22] The *Richmond Times Dispatch*, disparaging the GAR as a "secret political society," fumed that the Federals had selected the same day reserved for Hollywood's celebrations. The *Southern Opinion* likewise seethed that the "memorial tributes paid the Federal dead is [sic] a miserable mockery and burlesque upon a holy and sacred institution, peculiar to Southern people, and appropriately due only to the Confederate dead."[23]

Some northerners agreed. The Philadelphia *Sunday Dispatch* (labeled by the *Opinion* as "radical") rebuked the GAR for modeling their celebration after the "rebel practice." The *Dispatch* declared that "the custom is intensely secessionist" and it "would be better to adopt a form not founded upon a slavish imitation of rebel customs." The Philadelphia paper reminded its readers that the southern Memorial Day celebrations were in fact treasonous affairs, revealing "that the living are still traitors at heart." The paper shuddered to think that tributes to their own noble dead should mimic those honoring rebels. The *New York Times* concurred, noting that the "ladies of the South instituted" Memorial Day to "keep alive the rancors of hate" and "to annoy the Yankees." "Now the Grand Army of the Republic, in retaliation, and from no worthier motive, have determined to annoy them by adopting their plan of commemoration. The motives of both are unworthy," the writer exclaimed. The paper begged both the Ladies and the GAR to cease their activities and focus instead on the living.[24]

Nevertheless, the Union ceremonies took place as planned. On May 30, 1868, U.S. Army veterans across the nation followed Logan's orders and initiated memorial services in 183 cemeteries in 27 states—including Virginia. That day, Richmond's GAR branch held their services at the National Cemetery located two miles from the city where 6,200 Federal soldiers had been buried. Approximately 3,000 people attended, primarily Federal officers and their wives, government employees, the newly appointed city officers, and "nearly all of the Richmond Radicals, accompanied by their families." Of those 3,000, the *Richmond Daily Dispatch* estimated that only 400 were white. The paper was not surprised that Confederate sympathizers failed to engage in "these ignoble pursuits" because Logan's order had been "couched in words libeling us and insulting our own noble dead."[25]

Union Memorial Days, such as those held annually at U.S. national cemeteries in Richmond and Winchester, were remarkably similar to those organized by Confederates.[26] Crowds gathered at the cemetery (either on their own or via a procession), decorated graves with flowers and evergreens, and listened to orators discuss the soldiers' patriotism and virtue. But there was one key difference between the celebrations of Confederates and Federals; Confederate Memorial Days had begun and remained under the auspices of women, but Union celebrations were the province of men, most often military men. It had been northern men, rather than women, who formed cemetery associations, such as the Antietam National Cemetery Association, and directed reburials. And such distinctions did not go unnoticed. The southern press lauded women for undertaking memorial societies, and the northern press likewise acknowledged that the leadership of the respective Confederate and Federal commemorative activities was delineated by gender. When calling for the end of Memorial Day celebrations, for example, the *New York Times* expressly addressed the "ladies of the South, and Grand Army of the North" to cease and desist.[27]

Unionist women certainly attended Federal Memorial Days, but they played no role in organizing the events. Nor did Union orators pay tribute to women's wartime sacrifices and devotion to the cause, as was common rhetoric at Confederate exercises. In fact, the Northern Women's Relief Corp, a group of women who later in the century helped organize Memorial Day events, was not recognized by the GAR until 1883. Historian Stuart McConnell notes that "'loyal women' could participate in the patriotic project, but only within a clearly delimited sphere. They were to inculcate patriotism in children; otherwise, they were to wait on the wishes of the ex-soldiers."[28] Northern women, then, were to play supporting but not lead roles in Union Memorial Days.[29] The fact that the GAR *did not* encourage women to be the centerpiece of these mourning rituals bolsters the notion that Memorial Days were indeed fraught with political meaning. As the victors, Union soldiers were primarily responsible for honoring their war dead. Unlike ex-Confederate soldiers, Federals saw no reason to turn over their tributes to the feminine sphere.

The same held true of African American Emancipation Day and Fourth of July celebrations in the South. In contrast to the role of white women in Confederate Memorial Days, African American women served only as participants and not as the leaders of such ceremonies. As with Confederate celebrations, "men dominated the speech-making and grabbed center stage in many parades" while "women marched as members of schools and civic associations."[30] But like northern white men, African American men did not find it necessary to defend their actions as being "under the influence" of the women. There simply was no need for African American men to appear nonpolitical, especially during the years of Congressional Reconstruction, and therefore for African American women to take the lead.

Moreover, white interpretations of African American women's involvement in freedom celebrations highlighted a racial hypocrisy toward female memorialization. In direct contrast to defenses of southern white women's participation in Confederate Memorial Days, historian Kathleen Clark notes that white observers frequently condemned the high visibility of freedwomen in Emancipation Days and Fourth of July celebrations as a sign of illicit sexual activity. Here the racial double standard of female participation in Civil War commemorations was most visible: white women at Confederate services not only reaffirmed their status as "ladies," but they also legitimized the events. The participation of black women at commemorations of freedom, however, confirmed that they were not capable of exhibiting ladylike behavior, thus undermining the proceedings. In spite of this hypocritical interpretation, it is clear that African American women shared one similarity with women of the LMAS: both were struggling to assert their own unique form of political participation in the postwar South.[31]

Regardless of the gendered organization of Emancipation and Memorial Day celebrations, as late as 1868 and 1869, some white northerners continued to protest demonstrations of residual Confederate nationalism that appeared to be gaining rather than losing momentum under the LMAS' direction. The *New York Times* disparaged the *Petersburg Daily Express* for draping its masthead in mourning on the city's Memorial Day. Petersburg responded in defiance: "The North may as well understand at once and forever, that no prosecution, however severe; no malignity, however envenomed . . . can withdraw the great Southern heart from its ceaseless ward and watch at the graves of those who vainly died that their people might be free." Neither Unionists nor ex-Confederates seemed ready to embrace reunification and forgiveness.[32]

Thus former Confederates claimed their right to mourn their dead, and they also continued to insist that the actions of their LMAS were not treasonous. "We have no desire to connect these memorial tributes with the political agitations of the hour," the *Daily Express* maintained. Lynchburg, too, continued to defend its memorial celebrations. Following the largest Memorial Day celebration to date in 1869, the local paper warned those who "scent treason in every breeze wafted from the South" that the demonstration was of "no political significance." A Fredericksburg paper pointed out that "there was no uncalled for demonstration such as flying of Confederate flags, or cemetery gates being dressed in mourning or high sounding speeches in eulogy of the soldiers or the cause in which they fell." Rather, the day was marked by somber silence. Petersburg's white residents, however, remained less placating in their stance. Following the June 9, 1868, celebration, a city newspaper longed for southern unity in the face of Reconstruction, regretting that there was not yet a single Memorial Day for the entire South. In words that resonated with the very treason many had tried to dispel, the paper hoped that the South would never again celebrate July 4, "until our Lees and our Jacksons, instead of being stigmatized as 'rebels' shall have a place alongside Washington and Jefferson." Like Fredericksburg, the Petersburg paper saw June 9 as a day for solemn reflection. "With the heel of the oppressor on our necks," the paper concluded, "we have no use for a day of rejoicing now; but rather a day of mourning and humiliations." Clearly, the LMAS' "mourning rituals" had infused the South with a lasting sense of Confederate identity that was not about to yield to northern criticisms, even under Reconstruction.[33]

Throughout Reconstruction, Virginia's memorial movement remained firmly under the control of the state's middle- and upper-class white women. Women's leadership, however, did not preclude men from involvement in the movement. As the previous chapter explained, men had initially urged women within their respective communities to organize and had defended women's memorial work as explicitly nontreasonous. Between 1867 and 1870, middle- and upper-class white men continued to support the Ladies' efforts. Although the level of male-female cooperation varied significantly among the different memorial associations, a gendered division of tasks developed within Lost Cause traditions that would substantially alter the very nature of public male-female relations in the South.[34]

In keeping with the notion that mourning belonged in the feminine realm (thus remaining ostensibly "nonpolitical"), men tended to play supporting roles in early memorial activities. Most of the societies permitted men to serve as "honorary members" by paying dues, but reserved full membership for females. Several societies, including the HMA, offered honorary membership to specific groups of men, such as ministers or Confederate generals (and often their wives). In some instances, such as with the OMA, the women held that any person of good standing in the community might become a life member by payment of dues, but only active, female life members had the right to vote.

The women in these associations generally agreed that although men might aid their endeavors, offices should always be filled by women.[35] This, however, did not preclude men's aid to the LMAS. Both the Fredericksburg and Winchester associations officially appointed males as advisory committee members to provide legal and financial advice to the associations. Captain C. T. Goolrick, for instance, served as the chairman of the Fredericksburg LMA's Committee on Constitution and Bylaws. But even in associations such as Hollywood, Petersburg, and Oakwood where men did not serve in an official capacity (at least until the 1890s), men played supportive roles to the associations. For example, Charles Dimmock helped the HMA plan their memorial pyramid, and Henry D. Bird, Esq., designed the layout of Petersburg's Blandford Cemetery. Beyond administrative functions, men's most conspicuous role was as Memorial Day speaker. Former Confederate generals, state and local municipal officers, and ministers were the most common orators on such occasions.[36]

Men also frequently served as agents for the women's associations. Because Victorian morals and the doctrine of separate spheres held that it was unacceptable for women to speak in public settings, LMAs often appointed men to do so on their behalf. Typically, these men, who were relatives of the most active female members, served as liaisons between women and their communities—and, on occasion, between LMAs. When the Oakwood and Hollywood groups discussed the possibility of union, each association asked men to write and present the proposals. The same held true during talks of collaboration between the Fredericksburg and Spotsylvania associations. Both the Fredericksburg and Petersburg societies chose men to act on their behalf during negotiations for cemetery land. Like the women they represented, these men were always from the upper echelons of society and were generally either church leaders or former Confederate military personnel.[37]

Initially, the Fredericksburg women had agreed that no man was to be admitted to any monthly or called meeting unless he was an advisory member or had been specially invited by the president or board of directors. Perhaps this was to dissuade members' husbands from attempting to usurp authority from the LMAs. Nevertheless, by May 1867, the women had relaxed their policy regarding men. "Any gentlemen in connection with the society," the women noted, "shall be admitted at all times." Still, the three men who composed the cemetery committee, all of whom had been active advisory members of the organization since its inception, were the only men who ever appear to have attended the Fredericksburg LMA's regular meetings.[38]

Men also aided LMAs in their fund-raising endeavors. When the Fredericksburg women found themselves in "urgent need of funds" to continue their repatriation activities in the spring of 1868, they turned to Major J. Horace Lacy, husband of Fredericksburg LMA vice president Betty Churchill Lacy and prominent city resident. The association requested that Lacy represent them "wherever and whenever he may think the cause would meet with sympathy and support." He traveled first to Baltimore, where a southern sympathizer introduced him throughout the port city, enabling him to raise $2,000. His speaking circuit eventually took him as far north as New York and as far south as New Orleans. In the Crescent City, Lacy received endorsement of the women's efforts, garnering the signatures of prominent Confederate generals, including Dabney H. Maury (Fredericksburg resident and LMA advisory board member), P. G. T. Beauregard, James Longstreet, and Joseph E. Johnston, as well as of Jedediah Hotchkiss, Stonewall Jackson's celebrated cartographer. Surprisingly, Louisiana's predominantly African American legislature donated $5,000 for the cause. Lacy's efforts paid off handsomely for the Fredericksburg Ladies, eventually raising nearly $10,000 that the association used to build a cemetery wall, monument, and gate.[39]

In addition to lecturing circuits such as Lacy's, men frequently offered their forensic talents more locally. In May of 1866 alone, the OMA requested that a Mr. Pleasants and a Mr. Farrar deliver addresses on topics dear to the hearts of white southerners, such as Farrar's talk on "Johnny Reb." Colonel George Wythe Munford, of Gloucester, Virginia, agreed to render his services to the HMA. In the winter of 1867, he gave a lecture in Richmond titled "The Jewels of Virginia," which praised the heroics of the Commonwealth's famous sons; the lecture was subsequently published for the benefit of the HMA. Dr. Hunter McGuire, too, donated his oratory skills to the HMA in 1866 when he provided a benefit lecture on the life of Stonewall Jackson.[40]

Occasionally, it was men who contacted the LMAs with strategies for raising money. In December 1866, General Jubal A. Early, who had left the United States following the war, wrote to memorial associations in Richmond and Lynchburg, offering to donate the proceeds from his memoirs about his campaigns. The Lynchburg LMA accepted his offer, and in a February 1867 circular requesting money, advertised the publication of Early's second edition memoir for the benefit of the LMAs of Virginia.[41] Perhaps the most bizarre proposal was that made by W. Webb of the Old Dominion Soap Works. Webb contacted both the HMA and the OMA in the winter of 1866–67 with a plan to increase the groups' bank accounts through the sale of "Branded Memorial Soap." No doubt the exact details of this fund-raiser remain obscure because the LMAs thought it quite odd, rejecting the proposal at once.[42]

Finally, and most importantly to the women, men provided the arduous labor necessary for the disinterment and reburial of thousands upon thousands of Confederate dead. Although mid-nineteenth-century mourning rituals held that women were usually the ones to wash and dress the deceased, the women of the LMAs did not go so far as to handle the decaying corpses of soldiers. Women might accompany the men as they scoured the countryside, with picks, wheelbarrows, and wagons, looking for signs of graves, such as indentations in the earth or possibly crudely constructed headboards. But, overwhelmingly, local men and young boys provided the labor of disinterring and reburying the dead once they had been located. In many instances, men volunteered their labor when local military companies assisted the LMAs. But the women also paid men to do the work; in 1866, the Petersburg LMA hired fourteen local men to haul the bodies, inter them, lay off cemetery plots, and mark and paint 500 headboards for the identified graves. These men also performed general upkeep of the new burial plots, such as remounding sunken graves or weeding.[43]

Winchester provides the most striking example of male/female cooperation in the earliest years of the Lost Cause. In many ways, the relationship between men and women in Winchester mimicked other Virginia cities. For instance, the Ladies selected a committee of six men to superintend removal of bodies, and they presided over Memorial Day activities. But the number of men involved in the reburial process appears to have been substantially higher in Winchester than in other Virginia cities. In early 1866, the women appointed eight subcommittees of five to eleven men each to search for graves around the city. In all, approximately forty men assisted the women on a continuing basis (as opposed to those cities where large numbers of men aided LMAs only in preparation for the first Memorial Day).[44]

More unusual, the city claimed both an independent women's society and a male-female association. Although Mary Williams and Eleanor Boyd had initiated the city's reburial efforts and had organized an LMA in the spring of 1865, Winchester's citizens held a public meeting in February 1866 at which they appointed a committee of the town's most prominent men to cooperate with the women. That spring, the men joined the Winchester LMA to form the Monumental Association of Stonewall Cemetery. Although the Winchester Ladies remained an independent organization from its inception, both Williams and Boyd served as vice presidents within the eleven-member Monumental Association. The women and men appear to have worked harmoniously together, as no records remain indicating disputes between the sexes.[45]

Winchester's memorial associations, therefore, were qualitatively different from other Confederate organizations within Virginia—and from southern benevolent societies, in general. Men and women had jointly been members of antebellum organizations such as orphan asylums, but men had held the administrative authority in these groups. No other scholarly evidence exists pointing to societies in which both sexes served as officers. But here men and women worked together, both sexes taking care of the business aspects of memorial associations. Yet, in many respects, the relationship between the men and women reflected the organization of LMAS throughout the state. The women controlled the nature of Memorial Days, the reinterment process, and all other matters of bereavement, while the men spoke at public events and on behalf of the women.[46] As with every other memorial association, the Monumental Association in Winchester always attributed the idea of caring for the dead to the women. Winchester's men commended the noble manner in which the city's women had "performed their trust" and noted in 1869 that it was "peculiarly appropriate" that women were the "principal actors in this 'labor of love.'"[47]

Looking around at the joint cooperation of men and women in other Virginia communities, the Petersburg Ladies expected that they too would lead the memorial effort and that men would support their endeavors. But the city's men had other ideas about how the commemorations should take shape, electing to organize one of the only known, exclusively male memorial organizations, the Gentlemen's Memorial Society, in May 1866. Despite the fact that the men called for a committee from the LMA to meet with them, they evidently did not help to disinter the bodies on Petersburg's battlefields, and they refused to assist the LMA in their "work of love." The men, as it turned out, had wanted the women to act as a joint committee "for mutual aid." The Ladies were initially open to the idea and repeatedly asked the men's group to aid in their cemetery work, but they would not submit to the role of auxiliary society—foreshadowing disputes that would occur between the veterans and Ladies in the 1880s. President Margaret Joynes noted with extreme regret in December 1866 "the failure of the Gentlemen's Memorial Society to extend us aid which we had a right to expect from them in this cause."[48] She sadly commented that "patriotism and heroism appear entirely dead" among the men of the city. But the memorial association would not be deterred by the men's lack of enthusiasm, subsequently vowing to "take the matter in hand; and persevere over every difficulty until its object is accomplished."[49]

Petersburg's LMA could not comprehend the lack of interest exhibited by the city's men toward Confederate memorial work. The women argued that the cares of business and demands of life in the postwar South could not excuse the "luke warmness of southern men" in the cause. "It is as much their duty to assist in the sacred undertakings as it is that of the ladies," the LMA charged in the local newspaper. It pointed to other cities, such as Lexington, Winchester, and Richmond, where men and women were united to advance their cause, believing that the failure of Petersburg's men would be a stain on the "high character" of the city. Nevertheless, the Ladies believed that men's indifference only further strengthened the need for southern women to control the movement. The reasons why the Gentlemen's Association refused to cooperate with the Petersburg LMA remain unclear. Perhaps the pressure from Union occupying forces prevented them from openly memorializing the Confederate past. Nevertheless, after the Gentlemen's Association failed repeatedly to support the women, the LMA invited individual men to become active and honorary members. In July 1867, the Ladies requested that the Gentlemen's funds be turned over to the women. Just under a year later, the men finally relented and presented a balance of $30.75 to the women's association.[50]

This unusual response among Petersburg's men may have arisen because of the city's history of male and female organizations. According to historian Suzanne Lebsock's study of antebellum Petersburg, the city's upper-middle-class white women organized and managed a variety of autonomous benevolent associations between 1811 and the late 1850s. Following religious revivals of 1858 and 1859, however, women lost their monopoly on organized charity, "as men reclaimed voluntary poor relief as a legitimate male concern." In nearly every type of association after 1859, from the Sons of Temperance to the Library Association, men ran the organizations while women filled auxiliary roles. With a great many men enlisted in the army or focused on other governmental duties during the war, women returned to the helm of autonomous female organizations. In the postwar period, Petersburg's middle- and upper-class white men sought to resume control of organizations—or at least to form their own groups, such as the Gentlemen's Memorial Association. Those women who had been most active during the war would have none of this and fought to retain their dominance in benevolent associations.[51]

With the exception of Petersburg, most former Confederate men wholeheartedly endorsed the Ladies' work. H. Rives Pollard's *Southern Opinion*, read throughout the South between 1867 and 1869, repeatedly offered praise for the devotion of the female sex and acknowledged the centrality of women to the Lost Cause. A July 1867 article noted that "southern women were the most ardent of original secessionists, the most hopeful and indefatigable of belligerents, and to-day their submission is the most tardy and reluctant." The editor recognized that "*they* are now the pious custodians of all that is Confederate memory." As winter gave way to spring in 1868 and the third season of Memorial Days commenced, Pollard echoed the sentiment of many Petersburg LMA members: "Woman—'last at the cross, and earliest at the grave'— has been foremost in memorial work. Men have proved false to their Con-

Even the masthead of the anti-Reconstruction Virginia-based newspaper the Southern Opinion, *1867–69, depicted women's fundamental place in the pantheon of Confederate memory. (Courtesy Library of Virginia)*

federate professions, and have turned away from the neglected graves of their comrades, who unlike themselves, sealed their devotion with their lives; but women never!"[52]

Even the paper's masthead points to women's fundamental place in the pantheon of Confederate memory. On the extreme right, a woman kneels over the grave of a Confederate soldier; standing beside her are two young children. All three appear to be visiting the grave of a loved one, as a wreath of flowers has been placed upon the mound. A Confederate cemetery appears over one side of the mourners, and a small village is visible above the woman's shoulder. On the extreme left, a battle is raging, replete with gun smoke and bodies reeling from wounds. Seated nearby is the Goddess of Fame, watching over the soldiers and recording their deeds of valor in a book. In the center of the picture looms a vignette of General George Washington, surrounded by the paraphernalia of war. Beneath the sketch, a scroll reads: "My Country— May she always be right; but right or wrong—My Country." Men are clearly visible in the illustrations of soldiers and Washington, but the largest images in the print are those of the women. Furthermore, if read as a chronology of the war and its aftermath, women appear to unite the home front and battle-front, as well as the war years and postwar years. As Pollard suggested in his editorial, the masthead conveys the notion that women were devoted Confederates from the beginning to the end.[53]

Desiring to make the *Opinion* an "organ for the promulgation" of information on the women's work, Pollard offered to print the LMAS' reports on Memorial Day celebrations, reinterments, and any other projects the women deemed worthy. The memorial associations took the request to heart, and reports began flooding the paper as the LMAS in Spotsylvania, Lynchburg, Winchester, Petersburg, Richmond, Raleigh, Tallahassee, Vicksburg, Louisville, and beyond sent notices of their work. During the 1868 memorial season, nearly every LMA in the South reported on their communities' memorial celebrations. Pollard published pleas for financial assistance from the LMAS (Petersburg being one of the most active groups on this front) and reported extensively on monument campaigns. The *Opinion*, therefore, served as an even more systemized link between the various women's organizations, helping them to gauge their own efforts against their peers and to make valuable contacts with like-minded women. Although accounts of Confederate leaders and anecdotes about the war appeared in every edition of the paper, Pollard and his associates clearly viewed the LMAS as the centerpiece of early Lost Cause sentiment.[54]

Despite the variations of male-female relations among Virginia's LMAS, the general pattern confirms that LMAS were not simply organized in the South to bolster southern white men's masculinity in the face of defeat, as numerous historians have argued. The LMAS' primary objective was to honor the sacrifices and lives of those Confederate men who had fallen in battle. If LMA women had wanted only to reassure men of their virility, they would have played a more submissive role. Although men certainly encouraged female-dominated memorial associations for their own political reasons, the LMAS never served as mere puppets for male ambitions. And the women did not refrain from criticizing the men, including veterans, when they failed adequately to support the memorial associations. Above all, these women saw themselves as patriots performing vital civic duties for their communities and the larger South rather than as mere boosters of male confidence. LMA women were not only honoring those men who had fought for the South but were securing their own legacy as devoted citizens and participants in the cause.[55]

The LMAS, therefore, marked a pivotal transition in the gender relations of middle- and upper-class southern whites between 1867 and 1870.[56] In many cases, men supported LMAS financially and otherwise, and men certainly found a valuable political reason for doing so: supporting women's efforts allowed *all* former Confederates to honor their past. But as Anne Scott and Jane Censer have argued, middling and elite southern white women emerged from the war more active than at any previous time in their history. Married women, along with their single daughters and nieces, carved out a new space for women's activism. They solicited contributions from friends, local businessmen, and strangers throughout the region; they hired and managed men for reinterment projects; and they drew public attention to themselves when they organized and took center stage at memorial activities. Rather than returning to antebellum gender patterns, as Whites, Faust, and Rable have posited, the women of the LMAs proved determined to control the direction of their associations, expand their civic duties, and redefine the very nature of southern femininity.[57]

"Federal cemeteries have sprung up around the city, in sight of the very fields on which the Confederates fought so bravely," Petersburg LMA president Margaret Joynes pointed out in the fall of 1867. "They are adorned, so neatly and tastefully arranged," she continued, "that it makes one sad to look upon them and think how the bones of Southern men and soldiers lie scattered among the weeds." But the South had no National Cemetery System, no government agency, and no designated organization to oversee the tremendous responsibility of caring for the nation's dead. Neither were the "restored" state governments of the former Confederacy likely to step forward and offer assistance in burying the dead under the conditions of Reconstruction. By necessity, Virginia and other states of the former Confederacy instead relied upon LMAs to raise funds for collecting and transporting remains, hiring burial crews, and securing appropriate locations for the new cemeteries. "To *us* history, which has no page for the unsuccessful, commits the guardianship of the name and fame of our departed brothers," Joynes claimed.[58] Memorial women were determined not to let their nation's dead rot in the woods and forests of the South.

By depicting the LMAs as merely decorators of graves, historians have overlooked one of the Ladies' pivotal roles in the evolution of women's relation to the state. In the absence of a Confederate government, the LMAs acted as surrogate government agencies, or what Theda Skocpol has termed "shadow governments," to care for the defunct nation's dead. Elaborating on their skills of meticulous bookkeeping, petitioning, and networking acquired through wartime soldiers' aid societies, the LMAs appointed committees to oversee reburial projects and monument building, recorded burial information, and provided a systematic finance plan for such projects. Central to the women's work was the process of administering the reburial and identification of the dead. Mary Gordon Wallace, president of the Fredericksburg association, assigned a committee of six women to register and "preserve as far as possible the head boards and any other marks necessary to the identification of the graves of Confederate dead." Most often, however, LMA officers selected a committee of women whose primary responsibility was to hire men who would disinter, remove, and reinter the dead.[59]

An Alabama man, searching for his brother's grave in Fredericksburg, described in detail the process memorial associations had devised for reinterring hundreds of bodies: "Before the work of the removal was done, every Confederate grave in the whole country was marked by a stake made of locust wood and on which the numbers were burnt. When this was being done all information that could be found about each grave was carefully recorded in a book together with the number of the grave. When the remains were taken up, they were placed in boxes about 3½ or 4 feet long, and as soon as each box was closed, it was numbered the same as the stake which was established at that grave." The boxes and stakes were then transported to Fredericksburg where they were laid into newly dug graves, making sure that the box numbers matched the number on the stake. Though men might have performed the labor, it had been the Ladies who organized the undertaking and subsequently took responsibility for housing the documentary records.[60]

Providing information regarding the deceased's final resting place to family members and loved ones throughout the South proved to be a significant quasi-bureaucratic function of LMAS. Mothers had frequently written to nurses during the war inquiring about their sons' health, or in many instances, their burials. This practice continued through the 1860s as families feverishly wrote to LMA presidents in cities where their loved ones had last been known to visit in hope of learning the whereabouts of a husband, son, or brother. T. B. Shepherd, of Charleston, West Virginia, forwarded a letter to Mary Williams of Winchester in 1866 from a widowed mother wishing to retrieve the body of her young son. Three years later, Nancy MacFarland of the HMA was receiving similar requests from desperate parents who lived throughout the South. One father, writing from Austin, Texas, inquired as to whether his son had been buried in Hollywood. If so, he wished to send the HMA a contribution to help care for the grave so far from the young man's home. Having responded to hundreds of such requests, in 1869 the HMA published the "Register of the Confederate Dead." This pamphlet included the names and locations of those buried in the soldiers' section and sold for fifty cents in bookstores throughout the South.[61]

Even though historians have interpreted LMAS as "local organizations," the Ladies did not limit their reburial activities simply to the soldiers from their respective communities.[62] Indeed, women organized and ran associations at the local level, but their initial focus had been on the remains of all Confederate soldiers. LMAS saw themselves as representatives of the Confederacy and therefore placed the needs of their defeated nation above that of their towns and cities when it came to honoring the Confederate dead. It was not until after they finished the initial work of interring the dead from surrounding battlefields that the Ladies began to search for the remains of men from their own cities lying in unmarked graves elsewhere. In their efforts to establish fitting resting places for the South's dead, the Ladies thus were responsible for creating *national* Confederate cemeteries.[63]

Just as the U.S. Burial Corps reinterred U.S. soldiers from every state in their "national" cemeteries, LMAs too laid the remains of soldiers from every Confederate state (as well as those from the border states that fought for the South) in the same cemetery. Replicating the national U.S. Army cemetery in Gettysburg, the Ladies grouped Confederate soldiers from the same state together and designated a separate location for the unidentifiable remains. The LMAs did not discriminate in their devotion to the dead or provide preferential treatment to soldiers from one state over another. In fact, both the Winchester and the Oakwood associations listed among their goals the erection of a monument for each state of the South in their respective cemeteries. In the absence of a Confederate government to honor its dead, LMAs executed what the Petersburg Ladies had noted "would otherwise have been a nation's pride to perform."[64]

Historian Gary Gallagher has argued that during the war Robert E. Lee and his Army of Northern Virginia became the most important national institution in the Confederacy.[65] But even with the collapse of the Confederate state and military apparatus, white southerners looked for other unifying symbols to express the emotional bonds and sense of sectional identity that had been created by war. Under the strictures of Reconstruction, ex-Confederates could no longer wave their flags or wear their military insignia, but they could gather in Confederate cities of the dead to mourn. Not only did Confederate cemeteries offer white southerners a permanent, physical reminder of their cause, but they also allowed Lee and his army to maintain their vaunted position as a visible national symbol. Most of the soldiers buried in Virginia's Confederate cemeteries had belonged to the Army of Northern Virginia and continued to be a source of pride and cohesion for the southern populace, even as they lay in graves. As had been the case during the war, the Army of Northern Virginia served as a rallying point for white southerners in the postwar years largely because of the Confederate cemeteries created by Virginia's LMAs.[66] If, as historian John Neff argues, "the creation of national cemeteries represents the greatest single expression on the part of the federal government about the war and its importance to the national existence," the same must be said of the Ladies' Confederate national cemeteries.[67]

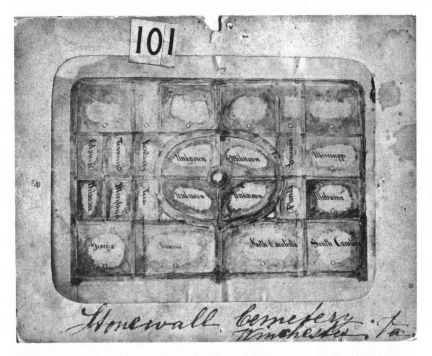

Plan for Stonewall Cemetery, Winchester. These Confederate national cemeteries replicated the U.S. Army's national cemeteries by grouping Confederate soldiers from the same state together and designating a separate location for the unidentifiable remains. (Courtesy Museum of the Confederacy, Richmond, Virginia)

The Ladies were well aware of how important Lee's army had been to the Confederate war effort, and so they called on the entire South to provide support for their cemetery projects. Often, the LMAS targeted specific communities they believed owed a debt of sorts to their association. For example, in August 1868, the Petersburg association issued a circular in the *Montgomery (Alabama) Mail* seeking financial support. After reinterring the bodies of 700 soldiers in the Blandford Cemetery at a cost of nearly $3,000, the LMA reported that it was "entirely out of funds." The Petersburg women informed the Alabamians that many of their state's noble soldiers belonging to the 4th, 5th, 11th, and 12th Regiments remained in unsuitable graves. The *Mail* endorsed the LMA's efforts, noting that they "should have helped them long ago." Less than a month later, however, the Petersburg association issued yet another appeal to the entire South. "We *must* have help, and where can we more properly seek it, than from the bereaved ones," they pleaded. Begging for aid, the Ladies asked only "that the families here represented take this matter in hand." Struggling for assistance, the memorial association pointed fingers not only at the apathetic members in their own community who failed to donate to the cause, but also at soldiers' families throughout the region.[68]

Calls for assistance and donations to LMAs persisted well into 1867 and 1868 as the price of reinterring more than 70,000 corpses continued to rise. Not only did individuals and cities make substantial contributions to the women, but state governments increasingly began to furnish support to bury their dead. In the absence of a federal agency to direct interments or reinterments, combined with the fact that states could not directly hire reburial crews, legislatures frequently funneled money through at least one LMA. The OMA most actively recruited state support for the 16,000 soldiers buried in Oakwood. Sometime in the fall of 1866, the women sent forth an appeal to every state of the South, asking each to contribute the sum of $1,000 so that the "names and graves of your noble sons are saved from oblivion." "The Association is poor, the people of Richmond are poor, and the work to be done is for the honor and credit of the entire South," the OMA reminded everyone. The following January, the governments of South Carolina and Georgia appropriated the requested amount to the Oakwood Association. By April, North Carolina had followed suit and sent their $1,000 and, in September 1868, Mississippi donated $750. Municipal governments, such as Louisville, Kentucky, also contributed money to the various Virginia LMAs.[69] Curiously, Virginia's legislature does not appear to have contributed to the LMAs' work in the 1860s, probably because the House of Delegates and the Senate were both composed of antisecessionist Whigs and not inclined to support Confederate memorialization.[70]

Women of the LMAs pushed the boundaries of the domestic sphere outward to fill the space left vacant by the Confederate government, offering an efficient and bureaucratic method by which white southerners could honor their war heroes and identify their loved ones who had fallen on distant battlefields. In doing so, they were able to more fully enter public service under the banner of grieving mothers on behalf of deceased soldiers and their families. Historians of Progressive Era women have considered the ways in which federations of women's clubs and mothers' clubs in the 1890s and early 1900s extended the moral values and motherly caring of the home into the nation's public life through maternalist social policies, such as mothers' pensions. Although LMAs were certainly not reform organizations in the truest sense of the term, their efforts to coordinate national Confederate cemeteries made them critical to the expansion of white women's influence on electoral politics and government agencies in the postwar South.[71]

In addition to creating national cemeteries for the Confederate soldiers, the LMAs also established national monuments to these war dead. As early as the spring of 1866, members of various memorial societies began to discuss the possibility of erecting monuments or other suitable tributes within their newly refurbished cemeteries.[72] In order to raise enough money for such a grand project without appearing to ask too much from the war-impoverished South, the HMA sponsored lecture series and at least six benefit productions. By far the grandest and most successful moneymaking venture undertaken by the HMA was the gala bazaar held in the spring of 1867. Even in preparation for the event, the HMA was careful not to exaggerate its call for aid. Noting that the association could not "afford to lose the *time* which private solicitations require," President Nancy MacFarland requested that the board of managers donate $154.10 from HMA coffers to purchase materials for the bazaar. "The committee has been anxious not to embarrass the cause by making *too many* appeals to the public for separate interests of the Association," MacFarland wrote. Nevertheless, contributions for the event came not only from throughout the South but also from Confederate sympathizers in New York, Canada, England, and France.[73]

At noon on April 23, 1867, the bazaar opened to the public in grand style. War mementos and other donated articles filled two floors of a Richmond warehouse owned by Colonel Robert G. Morris. Tables representing each of the former Confederate states had been "pillared and canopied with flowers and entwining evergreens" and outfitted with items for purchase—needlework, letters written by Confederate generals, inkstands carved from bones of horses killed in battle, and paintings. HMA members sold raffle tickets for special prizes, including buttons from Stonewall Jackson's coat, a piano, a miniature house, the "Buckeye Reaper," and other agricultural implements. The warehouse's third floor had been reserved exclusively for refreshments and dinners. Young Virginia women served as the waiters in the restaurants, which offered sumptuous dishes such as mock turtle soup, roast lamb, lobster salad, and strawberry cream. The bazaar was such a sensation that the HMA extended it for two weeks. When throngs of people arrived for the final auction, many had to be turned away for lack of space. The event had had great appeal, and it had been even more financially successful than the HMA had imagined. Within days, the Ladies claimed to have earned more than

$10,000 dollars, and by the close of the affair, they had garnered more than $18,000.[74]

At least one member of the HMA recognized that the bazaar was not only a financial boon for the Ladies but also served as a rebuke to federal officials. Writing to her stepdaughter, member Imogen Lyons chastised General Schofield as "a vile Radical," whom she believed had led Richmonders to become the most "oppressed and degraded people on the face of the globe." She no doubt found it amusing that the Ladies had sent him "complimentary tickets" to the bazaar. "I hear he particularly requested none of his Staff go near the place," she quipped. Although Union troops might have ignored the HMA's invitation to join the festivities and discouraged any formal procession to the cemeteries, the bazaar's popularity revealed how deep Confederate sympathy—and women's control of the movement—still ran. When the bazaar finally closed on May 8, the *Richmond Whig* proudly noted the HMA's achievement: "In every respect it was a success, and affords new evidence of the influence and zeal of woman." The bazaar's success, coupled with other less grandiose fund-raising efforts, allowed the women of the HMA to embark on their proposal for a monument to the South's dead, yet another outlet for the women to display their persistent Confederate nationalism.[75]

During the antebellum period, all-male groups most frequently led efforts to erect monuments to national heroes or battlefields, although women, on occasion, did aid men in their memorial endeavors. The Continental Congress had first proposed an equestrian statue of George Washington in 1783, but it was not until September 1833 that the Washington National Monument Society was chartered by Congress under the leadership of Chief Justice John Marshall. After years of faltering and limited success, a group of women organized to help the cause, under the name the Ladies' Washington National Monument Society. Although this group of women proved incapable of saving the Washington Monument, in other instances women were more successful.[76] For example, Bostonian women organized a fair in the 1840s to raise the necessary funds to finish the obelisk memorial to the battle of Bunker Hill, although they immediately gave over their earnings to the all-male group in charge of building the monument. As Kurt Piehler has demonstrated, even in memorial work, northern antebellum women frequently remained subordinate to men.[77]

In the South, and specifically in Virginia, middle- and upper-class women initiated the erection of at least one monument prior to the Civil War. A group of women that supported the Whig Party organized at Richmond in December 1844 under the auspices of the Virginia Association of Ladies for Erecting a Statue to Henry Clay. Although men could make donations to the project, women alone served as officers and collectors. At least 2,236 Virginia women acted as subscribers to the project, raising $5,000 for the marble statue. On April 12, 1860, the eighty-third anniversary of Clay's birth, the women unveiled their statue in Richmond's Capitol Square. The reasons why southern women began to take the reins of monument building in the antebellum period remain uncertain. Nevertheless, their success laid the foundation for women to be seen as the "natural" leaders of memorial projects.[78]

This regional pattern of monument building continued during Reconstruction. Like Federal cemeteries, most Union monuments were built by citizen groups, state or local governments, or veterans' organizations, with the aid of women's organizations.[79] At least two examples exist of southern veterans erecting a monument to their fallen comrades. In the spring of 1866, an association of officers and cavalry of the late Army of Northern Virginia organized to erect a marble bust at the grave of General J. E. B. Stuart. The bust was unveiled that May at the HMA's inaugural Memorial Day. Two years later, Captain Whipple's Company (Leon Hunters) of the 5th Texas Regiment erected a monument of white marble to their captain in Oakwood Cemetery. At least one monument was erected by a foreigner. In 1875, a British admirer donated a life-size statue of Stonewall Jackson that was placed on the State House lawn in Richmond. But, overwhelmingly, in the South, LMAs were the primary impetus behind Confederate memorials in the 1860s and 1870s. Middle- and upper-class women of the LMAs publicly claimed that monument building was clearly an extension of the feminine sphere into the public domain. No longer would men alone choose the setting, design, and dedication of monuments. Tributes to the war dead naturally belonged in cemeteries; therefore LMA women declared that they would have total control of such projects—with men to aid them rather than vice versa.[80]

In the spring of 1867, the HMA requested that engineer Charles H. Dimmock submit a design for a memorial to be completed for less than $15,000 and constructed "as far as possible" with material and labor exclusively from the South. Dimmock eagerly undertook the task but informed the women that their funds were insufficient for a cut-stone monument or memorial chapel. Rather, he suggested erecting a ninety-foot pyramidal structure of large blocks cut from James River granite. Springing from the base, he envisioned ivy, climbing roses, and other creeping plants that would "soon give a grace beyond the reach of art." The granite was to represent the unwavering virtue of the soldiers, while the tendril and rose would be emblematic of woman's love. The HMA resoundingly agreed to the proposal and suggested that the

Watercolor by W. L. Sheppard of the Hollywood Memorial Pyramid or Memorial Pile, erected in 1869. (Courtesy Museum of the Confederacy, Richmond, Virginia, copy photography by Katherine Wetzel)

pyramid rest on a hill overlooking the entire Soldiers' Section. There it would no doubt be the first thing visitors saw upon entering the burial ground.[81]

At a small ceremony attended by the HMA officers and a few Masons, the Memorial Pile's cornerstone was laid on December 3, 1868. The women placed a variety of Confederate relics and symbols in the stone: the first Confederate flag made in Richmond; Confederate insignia; Confederate money and postage stamps; a fragment of the coat worn by Stonewall Jackson the day he was wounded; photographs of Jefferson Davis and Confederate generals; along with many other similar objects. Finally, the women placed a copy of the Bible, the Virginia Masonic textbook, the *Richmond Daily Dispatch*, the *State Journal*, and the records of the HMA into the cornerstone. After nearly a year of construction, the pyramid's capstone was ready for placement on November 6, 1869. The HMA subsequently adopted the pyramid as the symbol of their association, and an engraving of the monument appeared on their stationary and on the frontispiece of the "Register of the Confederate Dead."[82]

The HMA's granite pyramid might have been the most spectacular of the early Confederate monuments, but it was not the only one erected—or at least discussed—by Virginia's LMAs in the 1860s. As early as August 1866, the Fredericksburg women agreed that a primary objective of their organization would be the procurement of a memorial to honor the Confederate dead, but serious work on the monument would not begin until 1873. Petersburg remained focused on the reburial of soldiers throughout the 1860s. After acquiring the deed to the Blandford property in 1868, the city's LMA proposed constructing a monument to overlook the graves, but like their counterparts elsewhere, the women failed to acquire sufficient funds for many years. After Lynchburg's LMA had refurbished the graves and enclosed the cemetery with a wall, the association purchased a monument and dedicated the cornerstone in May 1869. When completed, the memorial pillar was composed of fourteen marble blocks representing each of the states whose dead rested in the cemetery.[83]

The women of the OMA also discussed the possibility of a monument in September 1868 after receiving substantial donations from the states of Georgia and Mississippi. Perhaps competition with the HMA sparked their vigorous pursuit of the monument, but, regardless, the OMA envisioned a different style of memorial—one constructed exclusively of marble. The ostentatious design proved impossible to fund without additional support, and, in April 1870, the OMA appealed to each state that had not contributed to the association, as well as to the members of the Virginia legislature. Although it remains unclear how many states or individuals sent contributions, by the following spring the

OMA had garnered enough money to lay a cornerstone for a twenty-five-foot granite (not marble) shaft, and the monument was officially dedicated in May 1872.[84]

Whether a marble shaft, memorial pyramid, or national Confederate cemeteries, the Ladies' efforts to alter the southern landscape were indeed powerful, if passive, political statements in the midst of Congressional Reconstruction and in the presence of federal occupying forces. Protected by the cloak of feminine mourning, the LMAs secured lasting representations of *their* interpretation of the past—not that of the region's African American population or of the victorious North. Consciously or not, the Ladies seemed to understand what historian Fitzhugh Brundage has recently argued: "Physical space is central to southern historical memory and identity." The Ladies' early memorial work thus would prove invaluable as physical reminders of the Confederacy for generations to come.[85]

Women's efforts to lobby city councils and state legislatures and erect monuments on behalf of the Confederacy marked a change in southern women's relationship to the state. White women, North and South, had enjoyed the right to petition the state legislatures since the 1780s, even though they could not vote or hold office. Many taxpaying widows had exercised this right as individual proprietors, in order to protect their personal property. But women had also turned to this tactic for their benevolent and reform work. The Lowell Female Reform Association circulated petitions calling on the Massachusetts legislature to establish a ten-hour workday for women. Female members of antislavery societies had used petitions to seek the abolition of slavery in the District of Columbia and citizenship for black inhabitants of Pennsylvania. Historian Lori Ginzberg has demonstrated that, through petitioning, "women sought political access and obtained significant political favors in a manner that generally excited little public attention."[86]

During the Civil War, countless southern white women continued to enlarge the feminine sphere of domestic concerns when they wrote to and petitioned the Confederate government—and President Davis, in particular—demanding aid and protection. Women's letters frequently apologized to the government official for writing, often noting that male family members would have written had they been available. As Drew Faust points out, women's writings in these circumstances proved to be an explicit and bold claim to public voice and political identity.[87]

In the postwar period, Confederate women not only continued the tradition of writing to government officials, but they also expanded their requests beyond the needs of the individual or benevolent society. What was new and different about the LMAs' political activism was that the women claimed to be representatives of an entire southern "nation." Wartime women had humbly sought food relief or their husbands' pardon, but LMA women were more assertive in their requests for assistance. Gone was the apologetic tone, and in its place were circulars that invited states to join ranks with the LMA in this "sacred duty" for the Confederacy. Cemeteries were public statements about the community's relationship with the Confederate nation, and if the southern states and cities refused to cooperate in the LMAs' endeavors, their devotion to the cause might be questioned. These women believed that their wartime efforts, coupled with their memorial work, validated them as devoted members of the Confederate nation and entitled them to the privileges afforded citizens to demand state support of their activities. As they had done in petitions to Congress and through soldiers' aid societies during the war, LMA women continued their role as vocal activists on behalf of the defunct Confederate state.[88]

Memorial women were able to venture into the public sphere for two reasons. First, southern white women of the LMAs employed strategies that were more acceptable to the southern male populace than the strategies of some northern women, such as Susan B. Anthony and Elizabeth Cady Stanton, who had intensified their fight for woman suffrage following the adoption of the Fifteenth Amendment.[89] Southern white men believed that allowing women to "dabble in politics" would "soil their skirts." An article from the *Wilmington Star* reprinted in Winchester claimed that "we [white southern men] believe it would be the beginning of national decadence whenever the women of the country turned to politicians," as it would signal the degradation of the female sex. "We respect and reverence the fair gentle women of the South far too much to ever favor any change that shall rob them of any of their glory or benign power or loveliness."[90] But these men found no such signs of rebellion against male hegemony from memorial women. Rather, they saw LMAs as "gigantic agent[s] of benevolence." Organizing cemeteries, directing fundraising ventures, and erecting monuments were entirely appropriate forums for women's influence, as opposed to women's efforts to vote. As one Richmond newspaper noted: "These efforts make no noise. They are silent, but full of power."[91]

Second, LMAs claimed to be representatives of the Confederate nation—a nation that no longer existed in a political or physical sense. Just as having women organize Memorial Days offered little "threat" to the U.S. government, they posed little threat to ex-Confederate males' political ambitions. How could women possibly exceed their acceptable political boundaries when no nation existed in the first place? But the lack of a "real" Confederate nation did not diminish the LMAS' influence on the state governments of North Carolina, Alabama, and others. Rather, as illustrated by the substantial sums of money the LMAS acquired from such states, women had clearly entered the world of lobbying government officials and agencies, foreshadowing the strategies their daughters and granddaughters would employ in the Progressive Era of the late nineteenth century.

Even while Memorial Days continued to draw thousands of Confederate sympathizers to cemeteries, participation in memorial work among Virginia women had begun to decline by 1868–69. The OMA, which had claimed upward of 300 members in 1866, recognized by 1868 that the interests of the living absorbed most white Virginians much more than the care of the dead. "The public feeling on the subject naturally declines with the lapse of time," they admitted. During 1866, an average of twelve members had attended the monthly meetings of the Fredericksburg LMA, but by 1868 that number had dropped to nine. By January 1869, the Petersburg Ladies began to note a decrease in popular support among middle- and upper-class women of their city. President Joynes implored southern women to forever remember those who "vainly died for southern independence" and lamented "that more of the ladies of our city do not lend the aid of their presence and their purses to our sacred undertaking." Petersburg's most prominent women had been enthusiastic about memorial work in 1866, but during the next few years the association gradually began to lose momentum.[92]

The frequency and urgency of their meetings also decreased. When the memorial associations had first organized in 1865 and 1866, they met at least once a month, if not more often. But by 1868 and 1869, most of the associations were meeting only in April and May to make arrangements for their memorial celebrations. At least a few LMA members believed that their only objective was to create and preserve Confederate cemeteries. Ida L. Dodge, first secretary of the Lynchburg LMA, had packed away the group's minutes book upon moving in 1867 or 1868, as she supposed that "all official action of the association was at an end." As the women completed projects, such as reinterments, monuments, headboards, and cemetery walls, they found less need for regular meetings. Without a project at hand, many LMA members simply found other, more pressing issues to fill their time.[93]

Competition among Richmond's three associations for funding and support may have accounted for some of the decrease in popular appeal in the

capital city for at least two of the LMAs. With only a handful of graves to decorate and a very specific membership base, the Hebrew Memorial Association
attracted very little attention on its Memorial Days. But even the more numerous Oakwood Ladies had trouble garnering support. Only a few days before their 1868 memorial tribute, the OMA women pleaded with the people
of Richmond to join in their procession. "There are fourteen thousand very
lonely graves at Oakwood Cemetery" in need of floral tributes, they reminded
the city.[94] Nevertheless, only 2,000 to 3,000 Richmonders participated in the
day's events. "The procession was not a long one," the OMA sadly noted, "for
the ladies of other parts of the city seem strangely to have forgotten the thousands of dead at Oakwood." In comparison, Hollywood's annual tribute did
not fail to attract a bustling crowd of all ages and classes, sometimes in the
range of twenty thousand.[95]

Although not the first LMA to organize, by 1870 the HMA had become somewhat of the flagship memorial association for the state. On top of drawing
enormous crowds to its memorial celebrations, the association had managed
to pull off an elaborate fund-raising bazaar that netted more than $18,000,
while other LMAs desperately begged for funds. The Ladies had overseen the
reburials for 12,000 Confederate soldiers—at that date, the second-largest
burial ground for soldiers in the state. Moreover, their cemetery served as the
final resting place for several Confederate generals, including J. E. B. Stuart,
A. P. Hill, and John Pegram.[96] Finally the HMA had erected a spectacular
monument to the Lost Cause in the state's preeminent cemetery. The HMA's
location in the former capital of the Confederacy gave it a degree of exposure
and political connectedness that might not have been available to women in
cities such as Lynchburg or Winchester. Likewise, the overwhelmingly elite
status of HMA members no doubt helped contribute to their success. While
each of the other LMAs had performed many of the same tasks, the size and
grandeur of the HMA's efforts increasingly overshadowed those of their sisters
throughout the state—a fact that would grow in importance during the next
two decades.

As the conditions of Reconstruction in Virginia eased,
the state's white men began to seek a larger role for themselves within the
Confederate memorialization effort. In the spring of 1869, a handful of former
Confederate military leaders issued a call for a meeting to discuss the establishment of a Confederate historical society to shape how future generations
would interpret the war. Dabney H. Maury, a Virginian and supporter of
Fredericksburg's LMA who had moved to New Orleans following the war, sug-

gested the establishment of a society in the Crescent City that would collect and preserve papers "valuable in preserving the true history of the causes, events, and results" of the late war. Maury, Richard Taylor, Braxton Bragg, and several others formally organized the Southern Historical Society in late April 1869. The men appointed Benjamin Morgan Palmer as president and Dr. Joseph Jones as secretary-treasurer and selected other prominent Confederates as vice presidents of each southern state. Although the Southern Historical Society had a regional scope, Virginia remained a powerful base, as a substantial number of the members hailed from the Old Dominion—including Maury, Governor John Letcher, General Fitzhugh Lee, General Thomas T. Munford, Reverend J. William Jones, and General Jubal A. Early.[97]

While the LMAS' primary mission was to honor fallen soldiers and preserve their heroic memory, the Southern Historical Society's expressed purpose was to craft the "true history of the war." Women had called for financial contributions to fund their cemeteries, but these ex-generals requested both material support and military accounts of the Confederate war effort. Although the Southern Historical Society mailed 6,000 circulars across the South, during 1869 the society gained little support outside of New Orleans. After several months, fewer than a hundred members had joined, and by early 1870 only forty-four members had contributed dues.[98]

But two factors converged in 1870 that helped to stimulate the efforts of the Southern Historical Society. First, after five years of military occupation, on January 26, 1870, the Commonwealth of Virginia was readmitted to the United States of America and Federal troops were withdrawn from the state. Richmond's city council rejoiced at the receipt of news that the state was to be readmitted, ordering a 100-gun salute in honor of the event. The following day, General E. R. S. Canby directed all military commissions acting under the Reconstruction Act to be dissolved, all citizen prisoners turned over to state courts, and all civil officers appointed under the provisional government to vacate their seats upon election of new officials. With the formal end of Reconstruction, Virginia's white men began more openly and forthrightly to claim that it was *their* duty and obligation to honor the likes of Jackson and Lee. They no longer needed to leave the task of praising the Confederacy to women. But even more important to these former generals, the death of Robert E. Lee on October 12, 1870, ignited an outpouring of Confederate sentiment among many of the state's elite men.[99]

Even as some LMAS experienced a decline in participation during 1868 and 1869, memorial tributes became more elaborate, with the erection of cemetery walls, headboards, and, ultimately, monuments. Memorial Days, which had never been exclusively about mourning, were moving beyond eulogies of the dead into a more celebratory phase. But, most significant, the struggle over how to remember the Civil War was no longer merely a battle between Unionists and ex-Confederates. As the state's white men regained their political clout free from the cries of treason, a tense and sometimes bitter contest over Confederate memory ensued between Virginia's white men and women.

4

A Rather
Hardheaded Set
Challenges for the Ladies'
Memorial Associations,
1870–1883

On the night of October 12, 1870, a brief and solemn telegram reached Richmond announcing the death of the South's famed chieftain, Robert E. Lee. The news of Lee's passing brought a deep wave of mourning throughout the city, not experienced since the surrender at Appomattox five years earlier. The following morning, bells on all public buildings commenced tolling from sunrise to sunset as the news of the death spread through the city. The Tobacco Exchange, the city council, and the public offices of the state government immediately suspended all business, and the Chamber of Commerce encouraged all places of commerce to do likewise. By ten o'clock that morning, tacked to the door of nearly every shop on Main, Broad, and Cary Streets was a simple message: "Closed in consequence of the death of Gen. Robert E. Lee." The U.S. and the Virginia flags were both lowered to half-mast on the ships in the river and in front of nearly every public building. The council chambers were to be draped in mourning for six months, and members of the council were to wear mourning badges on their left arms for thirty days. Private residences covered their doors with black mourning cloth or hung photographs of the late general in their windows. Throughout the evening, the capital's streets were unusually quiet, as theaters, the Academy of Music, and other places of amusement remained closed.[1]

Such bereavement was hardly confined to the capital city. Scarce was a community in the entire state where some eulogy to the general could not be found. In Lexington, where Lee had been residing and serving as president of Washington College, exercises at both the college and the Virginia Military Institute were suspended, and it was reported that the students appeared to take the general's passing "as an irreparable personal bereavement." Groups of Lee's formers soldiers, along with grief-stricken citizens in Lynchburg, Fredericksburg, and Petersburg, found comfort in their common loss, meeting "to take some action upon the death of our beloved Lee." The Petersburg Ladies' Memorial Association (LMA) urged a more specific response to Lee's death. Calling a special meeting, the association implored its members and "all ladies of our city," as well as all Confederate veterans, to wear a rosette of black and white ribbon as a badge of mourning for thirty days. Newspapers from Staunton to Norfolk likewise expressed their condolences and sense of loss by draping their mastheads in black or outlining their columns with black borders. In the words of one Lynchburg newspaper, "the head of Virginia is bowed in mourning at the grave of her greatest and noblest son."[2]

Lee's death invoked similar reactions well beyond the borders of the Old Dominion. In Atlanta, both houses of the Georgia legislature adjourned for several days to attend the obsequies in honor of Lee. Bells tolled for hours in the streets of Memphis following the sad news. New Orleans's editors dressed their papers in mourning, and flags throughout the city were flown at half-staff, many draped in black. White southerners in Selma, Alabama, called his death a "national calamity." Even some northern papers appeared to sympathize with the ex-Confederates' loss. The *New York Tribune* admitted that Lee "was not absolutely without honor and even affection in the North," and the *New York World* remarked that his death brought "a chord of profound and sincere regret in the hearts of Americans of all sections and of the most diverse public opinions."[3] But, as they would do for the next three decades, Virginians claimed that *they* held a special place in the loss of Lee and the cult of Confederate memory. "Nowhere will his loss be mourned with such profound grief as in this State," one Richmond newspaper proclaimed.[4]

In many ways reminiscent of 1865 and 1866, this period of deep mourning inspired former Confederates to honor their past. But with the immediate threat of Union troops removed and some vestiges of reunion apparent, southern white men were not content simply to follow women's lead in memorializing Lee. They had agreed that it was both politically and socially expedient for women to lead the memorial movement in the first years after the war, but Confederate veterans—especially officers—saw Lee's death as the first real opportunity to glorify their war effort and honor their own martial spirit. Former officers such as Jubal A. Early, William N. Pendleton, and Bradley T. Johnson believed that men rather than women should lead this effort. Men, not women, were best equipped to protect and pay tribute to the great general, they claimed. But the Ladies were not so convinced. Despite a decline in popular support for the Ladies in recent years, they saw the men's newfound quest for more authoritative roles as an intrusion into the sphere they had so arduously and exhaustively carved out for themselves—and they refused to surrender so easily.[5]

Having toiled for five long years in their memorial work, a handful of Virginia's middle- and upper-class white women refused to relinquish their status as policy shapers of memorialization and protectors of the Confederate past. During the 1870s, the battles over the Lost Cause evolved from tensions among federal officials and Confederate sympathizers into more intimate rivalries among southern white men and women who competed to control Confederate memory. Through wartime associations and their early years of memorial work, LMA women had proven their dedication to the Confederate cause. But more important, *they* had organized Memorial Days, directed reinterments, raised funds for monuments, and made celebrations of the Confederacy tolerable if not palatable to Union troops and the northern populace alike. They had invested precious time and energy in this work, creating networks of like-minded females and an outlet for women beyond the domestic sphere. Why should they be asked to abandon their positions of leadership and surrender their organizations?

As Virginia's Reconstruction came to an end in 1870, the feminine image of passivity and nonpartisanship was no longer necessary to skirt charges of treason, providing instead an opportunity for the veterans to more openly celebrate the failed Confederacy. The LMAs had supported men's efforts to dictate the tenets of the Lost Cause through speeches and writings (even providing occasions such as Memorial Days for them to do so), but some of the most prominent Ladies balked at men's attempts to dominate Confederate traditions that had originated under their guidance, especially monument building and reinterments. Even as the memorial associations began to lose popular interest among the state's women, a handful of dedicated LMA leaders rebuffed men's efforts to control the Lee monument and Gettysburg reinterment projects. In doing so, their efforts forever altered the course of the Lost Cause by ensuring that women would remain central to the Confederate traditions (and transmission of those traditions to the next generation) during the last years of the century.

The initial reburial and memorialization efforts of the LMAs in 1865 and 1866 caused tension between the defeated Confederates and victorious northerners, but Lee's death unleashed its own set of bitter disputes among former Confederates. The first of these debates, regarding where the general's body should lie in rest, arose within forty-eight hours of his death. Many simply presumed that his remains would be interred in Lexington. A group of ex-Confederates, under the leadership of Rev. William N. Pendleton, former chief of artillery in the Army of Northern Virginia, met on the very day of Lee's death in Lexington to form the Lee Memorial Association, with the expressed purpose of erecting an equestrian statue on the Washington College grounds, a bust in the chapel, and a recumbent statue on Lee's tomb.[6] But other Virginians, namely those in Richmond, believed the general should be laid to rest in Hollywood Cemetery, where so many of his men now reposed. The day after the Lee Memorial Association had organized, the Richmond City Council formally resolved that it was "eminently appropriate" that Lee's body should "rest in the metropolis of his native state" and in the city "in whose defense he was so often called." Mary Custis Lee, the general's widow, temporarily put an end to disputes over his burial by agreeing to have him interred in a vault beneath the college chapel in Lexington.[7]

The women of the Hollywood Memorial Association (HMA), claiming to be the guardians of Confederate memory, wasted no time in initiating their own organization to memorialize Lee. Only a week after his death—and prior to the announcement in Richmond papers of the Lexington association— HMA members Nancy MacFarland, Sarah Randolph, Mary Adams Randolph, Henrietta Watkins Lyons, Mrs. William Brown, and Elizabeth (Lizzie) Byrd Nicholas proposed that a bronze equestrian monument to the general be erected in Hollywood Cemetery where thousands of his soldiers slumbered. Even if Lee's family chose to inter his remains elsewhere, the HMA believed that the cemetery overlooking the James River offered the most fitting locale for an eternal tribute. Relying on the same strategies they had employed to raise money on previous occasions, the women designated Sunday, November 27, as a Memorial Day for General Lee and requested that the nearly 25,000 congregations in the South, both Christian and Hebrew, take up collections for the monument. The women invoked the spiritual nature of their cause, asking that on days of religious worship, every congregation in the South make their contribution to this worthy endeavor.[8]

The elite and formidable Sarah Nicholas Randolph served as the secretary and spokeswoman for the HMA committee on the Lee monument. Randolph, great-granddaughter of Thomas Jefferson and granddaughter of former Virginia governor Wilson Cary Nicholas, was a member of one of Virginia's oldest families and an exemplar of white southern womanhood. She was born at her family's home of Edge Hill in Albemarle County in 1839 to Thomas and Jane Randolph. During the Civil War, with the family in financial straits, Sarah, her mother, and her sister opened the Edge Hill School for Girls, which catered to Virginia's wealthiest daughters. She chose never to marry, but along with running the school, she followed in her father's footsteps by writing histories. Throughout the 1870s, she published several popular works, including her most famous title, *The Domestic Life of Thomas Jefferson*.[9] The social standing of Sarah Randolph and her fellow members of the HMA gave them the clout to enter into the fray over the Lee monument.

In accord with their previous calls for aid, the women published a list of more than a hundred prominent Confederate leaders and soldiers, including nearly every member of the new Lexington association, whom they wished would "*act as assistants*" to their committee. Even prior to inquiring, let alone receiving an acceptance, the HMA "appointed" these men "to assist in the work by collections and otherwise." Clearly, the women of the HMA believed that a memorial to Lee fell under their domain, and that the men should support the women's efforts just as they had done for the past five years. Notably present on the list of "assistants" was Jubal A. Early of Lynchburg.[10]

An irreligious and often profane man known by many to be eccentric, Early was perhaps the most outspoken and unreconciled figure of the Lost Cause. Born to a family of means in 1816 near Rocky Mount, Virginia, Early graduated eighteenth in his class at West Point. Following graduation, he served in the Seminole War and then the Mexican wars but spent most of his time practicing law and won election to one term in the Virginia legislature. When the secession crisis commenced, Early was staunchly in favor of union in the hope of avoiding war, but he acquiesced and joined the Confederacy once Virginia seceded in April 1861. He immediately accepted a colonel's commission in the Virginia militia, and during the war he steadily rose to the rank of lieutenant general as one of Lee's corps commanders. But after a failed campaign in the Shenandoah Valley during the fall of 1864, Lee sent a very gentle letter relieving Early of his command in March 1865, citing negative public opinion regarding the faltering general. Having missed the surrender at Appomattox, Early traveled to Cuba, Mexico, and eventually Canada in a self-imposed exile before returning to the United States in 1869.[11]

Despite the fact that Lee had removed him from his command, Early was moved by the general's passing and wished to honor him in some grand way. He had been unable to attend the funeral in Lexington because of pressing legal business and had written to Pendleton expressing his regret. But, departing from his tone of condolence, Early pointedly informed Pendleton that he disproved of the family's decision to inter Lee in Lexington and believed that his remains should have been entrusted to the surviving members of the army. Early apparently did not care about the family's wishes; rather he viewed Lee's death as a public loss. "His fame belongs to the world, and to history, and is beyond the reach of malignity," Early wrote in late October. As such, he hoped to launch a public display of admiration—simultaneously promoting his own interpretation of the war. As with both the Lexington association and the HMA, Early believed that the most appropriate tribute to the late general should take the form of a grand equestrian monument. But like the HMA, he believed that the most suitable location for such a tribute was the former Confederate capital, not Lexington.[12]

Just days after the Hollywood women met and issued their appeal to the veterans for assistance, the former Confederate general published a call in the newspapers soliciting support for his project from the men who had served in Lee's army. Acting with haste to preempt the efforts of both Pendleton's group and the HMA, Early invited the veterans to meet during the state fair on November 3 and 4 to form two complementary organizations: one to sponsor a monument (to be called the Lee Monument Association—not to be confused with Pendleton's Lee Memorial Association) and another to perpetuate the veterans' legacy, the Association of the Army of Northern Virginia (AANVA).[13] In rhetoric no doubt aimed at Randolph and the other women of the HMA committee, Early believed that any effort to honor Lee should come from those who had fought under the general. "A sacred duty devolves upon those whom . . . he led so often in battle," Early claimed, although he had no intentions of confining the contributions to veterans alone, encouraging all those who "admire[d] and revere[d] true greatness" to donate.[14] Approximately 150 veterans from across the state attended the meeting, not surprisingly electing Early president of both the AANVA and the Lee Monument Association.[15]

Early, describing himself as "the senior in rank of all the officers of the Army of Northern Virginia now living in the State," crowned himself as the spokesperson for all things Confederate. He accused Pendleton and other members of the Lexington group of taking advantage of Mary Lee's grief to secure the burial there, yet it was Early's association that continually pressured the widow to reinter her husband's remains in Richmond. The Monument Association/AANVA further advised both the governor and legislature of Virginia that the question of Lee's resting place was not a government issue but one that belonged under the domain of the veterans. Early thoroughly resented any other endeavor to memorialize Lee, especially the Lee Memorial Association's efforts to enshrine Lexington as a memorial to the Confederate leader and similar projects under way in New Orleans and Atlanta. Rather than encouraging white southerners to dot their landscapes with memorials to the famed general, Early insisted that there be only "one grand Confederate Monument" situated in the heart of Richmond—one that was under his control.[16]

By mid-November, Early and the members of the AANVA had invited the HMA to "lend . . . their assistance" in collecting contributions. The women promptly agreed and formed auxiliary committees throughout the South—on the condition that they were to be considered equal partners in the endeavor. But Early and his associates had other motivations. If the men could keep the women close enough, the women could not best the veterans' efforts to honor Lee. The AANVA and Lee Monument Association certainly knew how successful the HMA and other LMAs had been in raising funds for their cemeteries and other projects, and these networks and money-generating capabilities must have been attractive to the men. The HMA women, however, were not nearly so naive and passive as the men expected. Even though the women agreed with Early on several counts, including that the monument belonged in the former capital, they proved an especially troubling thorn in the side of the former rebel commander, demanding full recognition and cooperation throughout the process. By 1871, a bitter and often cantankerous rivalry had arisen between the HMA (recasting themselves as the Ladies' Lee Monument Committee) and Early's Lee Monument Association, a rivalry that would last for nearly two decades.[17]

Relying on the network of women's associations (most importantly the LMAs), as well as on churches, the Ladies' Lee Monument Committee's (LLMC) fund-raising campaign was off to a rapid start throughout the South in the fall of 1870. Reiterating its earlier call for a Memorial Sunday in early November, the committee issued a statement, "To the Women of South," in the region's newspapers (no doubt, a response to Early's appeal, "To the Survivors of the Army and Navy of the Confederate States"). The women referenced the veterans' recent meeting and reported that the soldiers had asked for their help in erecting a monument to Lee. Reminding their female counterparts that the LLMC had already formed an organization for that purpose prior to the veterans' plea, they nevertheless implored women from "Maryland and to Texas" to set aside Sunday, November 27, as a day when their congregations might collect funds. If Early had called upon the veterans' masculinity by invoking the martial spirit of camaraderie and loyalty, the LLMC, too, could employ gendered notions in its pleas for support by linking women's contributions to their churches.[18]

Much to the chagrin of "Old Jube," as Early was often called, donations from across the nation immediately began pouring in to the women's association. Thomas F. Davis, a bishop from South Carolina, had written to encourage the LLMC's endeavor even before Early inaugurated the AANVA. He informed the women that he had received the circular by the end of October and had immediately forwarded the announcement to the diocese in Charleston, asking them to endorse the effort. Indicating the feeling for Lee outside of the South, a little girl from New York earned the honor of making the earliest official contribution during the first week of November when she sent the women a gold dollar. But, as the LLMC would later remind Early and his colleagues, the Deep South would be the most generous: Savannah, Georgia, alone sent $3,000 that fall.[19]

By January, momentum had waned and donations slowed to a trickle. Doubly discouraging to the LLMC was the lack of experience on the part of the men representing the soldiers' association. In two-months time, the men had raised little-to-no money (as compared to several thousand dollars collected by the women), and the LLMC was growing impatient. Randolph, MacFarland, and several other women approached some of the most judicious and high-ranking men of the city (including many of their kinsmen) and determined that it was in the LLMC's best interest to appoint an agent who would canvass the South on its behalf. The women quickly chose B. Frank Moore, a move that touched off an episode illustrative of Early's vindictiveness and desire to monopolize the monument undertaking.[20]

In February 1871, Moore received his instructions from the LLMC and set off on a tour of the Deep South. He arrived first in Mobile, Alabama, a city that had generously supported the HMA and other Virginia memorial projects for the past five years. But upon arriving in the city, he found that his efforts had already been hampered by an unfortunate or "rather imaginary" conflict. Apparently, Mobile's auxiliary committee to the Lee Monument Association had not been informed that Moore was representing the LLMC on behalf of the Monument Association and considered his presence unwelcome. Rather than creating undue controversy, he abandoned his canvass of the city and traveled on to Galveston, Texas, where he managed to solicit $1,000 for the statue, before heading northwest to Houston. There he learned that the *Galveston News* (and more than likely other newspapers, such as those in Mobile) had just published a card from Early warning of imposters, such as himself, who were traveling throughout the South collecting money under the false pretenses of representing the Lee Monument Association. Galveston residents were irate. Believing that they had been duped, they demanded that he explain his connection to the association. Houston's residents were equally angered, declaring that they would not give one cent until Early himself clarified the matter.[21]

Although Moore managed to clear his name in Texas, Early's letter to Galveston and other southern cities revealed his tense relationship with the women's organization. He had not only implied that men such as Moore were not connected with his association, but he also had outright denied affiliation with the LLMC—even after inviting them to cooperate with the Monument Association and AANVA in November. The women were outraged. Sarah Randolph quickly fired off a spirited letter to the general demanding that he rectify the situation. "We have over seven thousand dollars in hand," she reported. "I think, General, that we have done well, for the times, with the work with which you have entrusted us," she flatly noted. The women had accomplished such a feat by hard work, patience, and perseverance, and they believed it insulting to have their efforts thwarted by the former general. Randolph insisted that Early publicly acknowledge that the LLMC was working jointly with his organization and that the money was to go toward erecting a single monument. Moreover, she took the liberty of preparing a card to be published by Early explaining Moore's connection and underscoring the women's affiliation with the Monument Association.[22]

Early refused to accommodate the women. Rather than sending the card Randolph had written for him, he sent his own version to the *Galveston News*. In his letter, he neglected to endorse Moore and cautioned would-be contributors against persons pretending to act in the name of the monument association. He also asked prospective contributors to recognize the distinctions between his group, the Lexington group, and the "project of the Ladies of the Hollywood Memorial Association." In an obvious slight to the women, he even declined to recognize the name "Ladies Lee Monument Committee," choosing instead to identify them by their earlier memorial work alone. He went so far as to blame the "inconsiderable sum" raised by the Lee Monument Association on the "misunderstanding" generated by the LLMC. But, most poignantly, Early revealed the true nature of the dispute: "Over the operations of the Ladies Hollywood Association I have not control whatever." Early's efforts to sabotage the LLMC did not end there. The Monument Association employed its own professional agent to canvass the South and eventually hired a spy to attend the women's meetings and report on their plans. For the next fifteen years, the fires of hostility between Early and the women burned intensely as the agents for competing associations flooded towns and cities throughout the South.[23]

Beyond the obvious and blatant attempts of the AANVA and Monument Association to undermine or at least control the LLMC's efforts, Early's feelings about women, and theirs about him, were complex and often contradictory. A lifelong bachelor (though he had a common-law wife and several illegitimate children), he had been known in many female circles as a misogynist. Ellen Bernard Fowle Lee, the nineteen-year-old wife of Fitzhugh Lee, noted that she had always believed him to be a "woman hater." Early later maintained that he was not, nor had he ever been, such a thing. During the war, he had objected to officers bringing their wives into camp, believing that it fostered a sense of dissatisfaction among the soldiers who witnessed the lavish lifestyle of many wives while their own were at home toiling for the necessities of life. He also believed that women who ventured into camp, even officers' wives, placed themselves on the same social standing as a camp follower, that is, a prostitute. "Besides," he noted years later, "I really thought they had better be at home working and praying for those that were fighting for the common cause, and ministering to the wants of the families of the poor soldiers." Like many white southern men, he believed that the archetype of southern womanhood was represented by the "pure and devoted women who follow[ed] with their prayers the armies of the Confederate States through all their struggles and trials."[24]

Although many women openly questioned his attitude toward the female sex, those in his hometown of Lynchburg felt differently. They repeatedly expressed a great fondness for the general whom they believed had saved their city from destruction in the summer of 1864.[25] When Early first returned to the city, in 1869, the LMA requested he deliver the Memorial Day address, although he ultimately declined. In the summer of 1871, the women of Lynchburg's Methodist Protestant Church held a ceremony honoring Early. They anointed him "the defender of the mothers and the protectors of the daughters" of the city and presented him with an ornate gold-headed cane.[26]

He, in turn, recognized women's importance to the Confederate tradition. In 1866, Early offered to donate the proceeds of his memoirs recounting his campaigns to memorial associations in Richmond and Lynchburg. He likewise expressed his appreciation for female support of the Lost Cause when he thanked the women of Winchester for their "patriotic attention" to his fallen comrades. Wherever he might wander, he promised to carry with him "the knowledge that my countrywomen . . . remain true to the memories of the dead." He graciously contributed to various LMA efforts to mark soldiers' graves, sending at least fifty dollars to the Fredericksburg association. In 1872, on the anniversary of Lee's death, he heralded women's special ability to instill Confederate pride in the next generation. At the annual address of the Southern Historical Society, in 1873, he called for women to be enrolled in the ranks of the society as "the representatives of lost fathers, brothers, cousins, friends, and sweethearts." During the following year's conference, he anointed the women "conspirators with the society in the new rebellion it [the Southern Historical Society] was accused of fomenting." Several years later, at Winchester's memorial celebration, he claimed that "there were no truer adherents of the cause than the ladies of Valley." Clearly, Early understood the vital role southern white women had played in sustaining the memory of the rebellion both during and after the war.[27]

Why then did he take issue with the women of the LLMC if they were integral to the Confederate cause and capable of generating so much money? Although part of the answer resides in the notion that Early simply wanted to dictate every facet of the Lost Cause, except perhaps Memorial Days, the underlying reasons are far more complex. First, with the passing of Lee and the end of Reconstruction, the Lost Cause—and the Lee monument in particular—became an outlet for all Confederate men to reclaim their honor and manhood. As historians of southern masculinity have posited, for white southern men raised in the culture of honor, the Civil War became a test of manhood. Writing home to their loved ones, soldiers filled their letters with passages about courage, bravery, and valor, and (even more frequently) about honor. Honor, it seems, was often valued more than life itself, giving way to the frequent utterance among soldiers (of both sides), "death before dishonor."[28]

Indeed death appeared to be the most honorable status for Confederate soldiers by April 1865; the immediate focus on cemeteries and Memorial Days rather than the welfare of veterans gave proof of that. With battlefield defeat and the implementation of Reconstruction, ex-Confederate men had not only been denied much of their previous wealth and political positions, but they also felt humiliated by their loss to northern soldiers, the emancipation of their slaves, their impoverished financial conditions, and Republican control of state and local politics. Their honor—their manhood—had been called into question. In an effort to counter this emasculated image, Early urged all former Confederate soldiers and sailors to tell the world that they were not "ashamed of the principles for which Lee fought and Jackson died" and implored them to "perpetuate the honors of those who have displayed eminent virtues and performed great achievements" during the war.[29] As Gary Gallagher has demonstrated, in Early's interpretation of the war, Lee and the Army of Northern Virginia "set a standard of valor and accomplishment equal to anything in the military history of the Western world until finally, worn out but never defeated, they laid down their weapons at Appomattox." Ex-Confederate soldiers, then, could take pride in their battlefield performance, admitting defeat only at the hands of overwhelming odds.[30]

Early's desire to control the Lost Cause also stemmed from far more personal reasons. The war had been fought by men, and so he believed that the postwar battles should be led by men. With the passing of Lee, who better to direct the movement than one of his most trusted generals who had served with the Army of Northern Virginia throughout the ordeal? But Early had been dismissed from the Confederate army by the very man he sought to pay tribute to. Having failed in his final mission as a general during the war, he needed to launch a successful campaign in the postwar period to vindicate himself, to regain his own military reputation and therefore his pride, honor, and manhood. Other ex-Confederate generals turned to business, such as John Imboden; to politics, such as John Brown Gordon and Fitzhugh Lee; or to both, such as William Mahone. Early, however, positioned himself as the most commanding authority on the Lost Cause. He seldom missed an opportunity to remind Confederate sympathizers, be they veterans or civilians, that he was the surviving senior officer of Lee's army—at least living in the state of Virginia (which he deemed to be the most important state in the Confederacy).[31] He thus surrounded himself with veterans, whom he could lead in his battle to venerate the name of Lee, thereby "return[ing] to an undefeated Confederacy" and claiming the nobility of honor he insisted had never been lost.[32]

Women might be especially well suited for organizing Memorial Days and honoring the common soldier, but Early did not consider them fit to lead the most important Lost Cause task, that of honoring Lee. As he had indicated in numerous speeches, he believed that women were best used as auxiliaries to men's efforts. Because they had not participated in camp life or engaged in battle, he held that they should not dictate the grandest and most public tribute to the Confederacy's greatest hero. But the women of the LLMC refused to acquiesce to such a position. In fact, Early described Randolph and her fellow members of the LLMC as "a rather hardheaded set" and refused to cooperate with them even after they promised to contribute their funds to his project. If women controlled the monument project, then whom would he lead to regain his stature as a great general? Would his "troops" consist of an army of women? And could women vindicate the martial spirit of the Confederacy that he so desperately wanted to restore? Allowing women to lead Confederate traditions after Reconstruction when the political climate no longer dictated a "feminine" response could serve only to emasculate the veterans. Confederate men could salvage their reputation as courageous, loyal men only if they could reunite for the postwar battle over memory—without the ever-present intrusion of women's groups.[33] Early and his band of veterans were thus attempting to co-opt the memorial associations by taking over their projects and forming a rival organization that required women to serve as mere auxiliaries to the men.[34]

The divisiveness between Early's men and the women of the LLMC, combined with the confusion of multiple groups canvassing the region for contributions, managed to slow the Lee monument's progress to a near standstill within just a few years. By October 1875, Virginians had turned their attention toward plans for the dedication of the Stonewall Jackson monument on the State House lawn, while the Lee monument faded into the background. Just a month prior to the unveiling of Jackson's monument, Governor James L. Kemper, a Confederate veteran, stepped forward to take the reins of the stalled Lee memorial campaign. With Early's collaboration, Kemper commissioned a board of managers, consisting of himself, ex-officers of the Confederate army, the state auditor of public accounts, and the state treasurer, whose purpose would be the erection of a "Colossal Equestrian" statue of Lee on the Capitol Square. Early thus relinquished control of the movement and handed over his meager funds to the governor's board. There are some indications that the Ladies were approached to unite with the men, but it appears that Kemper never intended to give the women a position on the executive board. Because the women refused to give over full control to the men, like Early's Monument Association, the governor's group remained exclusively male.[35]

Kemper's initial goal was to expand the fund-raising endeavors by reaching into every available pocket in the South. Circulars were to be addressed to courts, judges, and treasuries of counties throughout the state. All officers of the Commonwealth were likewise requested to contribute one day's pay to the fund. To reach those beyond Virginia's borders, Kemper appointed Colonel Samuel Bassett French to the association's board of managers and encouraged him to launch a town-by-town canvass of the entire South. Enthusiastic about the project, French promptly requested that every southern mayor provide a list of prominent local citizens who would be likely to give their "earnest support." Reminiscent of the LMAS' earliest efforts to recruit members, the mayors were then asked to lay out their cities "into numerous and convenient divisions, and appoint canvassers for each." Even the youngest white southerners were to contribute, as schoolchildren were encouraged to donate their prized pennies. Perhaps in an effort to thwart the fund-raising abilities of the Ladies' group, the Monument Association also invoked maternal sentiment to win support for its cause. The men invited all women of the southern states, "and especially of Virginia," to aid the board in its "labor of love." In January 1878, as fund-raising efforts slowed, the men once again called on the "daughters" of the South for support, requesting that women be appointed in every southern city and town to solicit subscriptions. Revealing the manner in which they thought women must able to contribute, the association recommended that on the night of January 19, the anniversary of Lee's birth, "tableaux, balls, musical soirees, dramatic representations, feasts, or some like entertainment" be given by the women.[36]

Despite the very public solicitations of the men's group, throughout the 1870s the LLMC continued in its own fund-raising ventures. But disputes over who would collect the most money proved to be only a skirmish in the male/ female war over Lee's monument; the real battles unfolded over the statue's design.[37] Early and the men preferred the selection of Edward Valentine, a Virginia sculptor who had crafted the recumbent Lee statue at Lexington. Wanting the monument to be seen as a masterpiece of art, reflecting the greatness of southern culture, Randolph and the women favored French artist Jean Antoine Mercié.[38] "We cannot forget that the fine equestrian statues now existing have been produced by the highest efforts of matured genius, and that such monuments must ever be the noblest and most elaborate form of sculpture," they insisted. In a moment that appeared to invoke "traditional" gender codes, the LLMC members noted that they were "anxious . . . to hold our opinion and judgment in the matter subservient to your own." But, they continued, rebuffing any pretense of female passiveness, "we cannot do so without betraying the trust which has been confided to us by the contributors of the sums in our hands." Randolph and her cadre insisted, yet again, that *they* were the true and undisputed leaders of the memorial effort and would submit to no man, including the governor. "Better no monument at all than an inferior one," they concluded.[39] Even as Confederate veterans in New Orleans managed to complete and dedicate a memorial to Lee in 1884, the LLMC continued to forestall the Richmond project. Rejecting nearly every design model and refusing to relinquish their funds, the women resisted ceding their authority over public representations of the Lost Cause. But Early and his men would not be alone in their attempt to challenge the women. Yet another group of veterans would seek to impose themselves on what the women saw as their most sacred work, that of Confederate cemeteries.[40]

As it had demonstrated with the LLMC, the HMA proved capable of transforming its objectives as the immediate postwar years of Reconstruction gave way to the 1870s. From cemeteries and monuments to the common soldier and grander memorials such as the one to Lee, the Ladies reshaped and redirected their efforts to maintain control over Confederate traditions. Men might have legitimate reasons for competing with women regarding the erection of monuments infused with so much military significance, but the women of the memorial associations insisted that cemeteries remained their province alone. As such, the HMA's elaborate project of bringing Virginians who had fallen at Gettysburg back to their native soil was one arena in which the women believed they had exclusive domain. Just as with the Lee monument debate, Virginia's white men and women again clashed when men attempted to influence the project.

Concern for the Confederacy's dead had persisted among the southern populace well into the 1870s. Although most white southerners felt comfortable that the remains resting within their own region had been well tended to, questions regarding the status of those reposing on northern battlefields, specifically Antietam and Gettysburg, had begun to surface as early as December 1865.[41] Disturbed by such reports, a few individuals had ventured north to reclaim the bodies of their loved ones or of those from their hometowns. But as spring approached and farmers both North and South returned to their fields, accounts of Confederates "rotting far away in a strange land and foreign soil" began to flood southern newspapers. A southern woman visiting Gettysburg wrote to a Mississippi paper decrying the state of Confederate graves that would soon fall victim to the farmers' spring plows, a plea that was reprinted in newspapers throughout the region.[42] According to the *Charleston Mercury*, a South Carolinian who had relocated to Alexandria, Virginia, volunteered to remove the bodies of South Carolina soldiers from Sharpsburg (Antietam) and suggested that Virginians should do the same. "Her gallant sons lie mouldering far and wide in neglected and almost forgotten graves," he lamented. The soldiers, he insisted, had wished to "live and die in Dixie" and "should at least be sepulchered in her soil." The *Southern Opinion* concurred: "The whole South has sons at Gettysburg and Sharpsburg, in the midst of an unsympathetic people. Shall we not rescue them from the foe?" In Staunton, the *Valley Virginian* published a list of Virginians still interred on the northern battlefield, and resident L. B. Waller offered to retrieve the remains for "any one having friends buried there."[43]

Adding to this issue was the elaborate dedication of the national cemetery and a monument at Sharpsburg, Maryland, on September 17, 1867, the fourth anniversary of the battle of Antietam. President Andrew Johnson, the governors of numerous northern states, members of various foreign legations, and a great many veterans and civilians attended the elaborate celebration. In full Masonic ritual, the cornerstone of a monument to the common soldier was laid, followed by speeches by Johnson, Governor Swann of Maryland, and others. Though the spectacle did not differ substantially from those held in southern communities honoring dead Confederates (except that, as with Memorial Day celebrations, women took the lead in the South and not the North), former Confederates decried the commemoration. "The melancholy reflection that must arise in every right Southern mind is that the brave Confederates who fell in this same fight of Antietam have no part in the cemetery, were unhonoured in the ceremonies, and are not commemorated by the monument," complained the editor of the *Southern Opinion* (though failing to mention that Federal soldiers had received similar treatment, or lack thereof, by ex-Confederates). In a bit of revisionist history, or selective memory at the least, the former Confederates claimed that the South's dead "were the victors on this field of Antietam or Sharpsburg" and should therefore be honored. A year later, the remains of Confederates continued to lie scattered throughout the fields and woods surrounding the Maryland town.[44]

Gettysburg, however, particularly troubled former Confederates. In 1867, the small Pennsylvania hamlet still bore the signs of the three-day battle, in the form of thousands of unidentified Confederate graves that dotted the nearby countryside. A general, writing in the *Army and Navy Journal*, sadly noted that within a year all evidence of the sepulchers would be obliterated. "In very few cases the graves are respected," he observed, but, more often than not, "the ground is cultivated without regard to the remains of the misguided men who lie beneath it." This letter, reprinted in the *Southern Opinion*, garnered a great deal of emotion and indignation on the part of white southerners. The columnist pointed out a famous letter from Louis Napoleon to Lord Hood that stated: "Soldiers who fall upon a foreign soil are the property of the country, and it is the duty of all to honour their memory." All "chivalrous men and nations" had honored this obligation, the writer claimed, but the "Yankees, alone, of all Christendom, have been insensible to it." Finally, he lamented that "the government that takes such vast care of the Northern dead seems to desire that the Southern dead should rot in infamy."[45]

Rather than calling on former veterans, the *Southern Opinion* naturally called on the region's women to rescue the slumbering Confederates from the heights and valleys of Gettysburg. "Where is the memorial association whose kindly arms can open wide enough even to embrace those of our dead who are vilely trampled on in Pennsylvania?" it asked. Several LMAS responded, including the women in Raleigh, North Carolina, and Charleston, South Carolina. By 1870, several state legislatures had also decided to appropriate assistance for the return of the Gettysburg dead.[46]

Along with a handful of LMAS, these states turned to Samuel Weaver, a drayman from the Pennsylvania town who had assisted with the reinterment and identification of Federal soldiers in the autumn of 1863. Upon Weaver's death, in 1871, white southerners asked his son, Dr. Rufus Weaver, for help. Dr. Weaver initially was uninterested in assisting the former Confederates, but, after frequent appeals, he agreed to take on the enormous project. During the spring and summer of 1871, he exhumed and shipped Confederate bodies south, including 137 to Raleigh, North Carolina; 74 to Charleston, South Carolina; 101 to Savannah, Georgia; 73 to individual families; and an unnamed number to several locales in Maryland.[47]

Of the Virginia LMAS, Hollywood seemed the most likely to secure the return of the state's deceased sons. These women were substantially more wealthy and well connected than many of their statewide counterparts, and Hollywood Cemetery certainly appeared a natural resting place for the dead from one of the most famous Civil War battles. So it was only fitting that the HMA received a petition some time between June 1867 and the fall of 1869 requesting that it aid in the retrieval of the Gettsyburg dead. Mary Barney, an HMA member, remembered years later that the subject was "warmly discussed after hearing the heart rendering accounts" of the graves. But the HMA declined to act at that time, noting that its primary duty was to protect the graves of soldiers already resting in Hollywood.[48]

The HMA eventually changed its position, and by October 1869 the women had begun soliciting funds for the reburial of an estimated 3,000 remains, prompting the Ladies to designate a section of Hollywood Cemetery specifically to receive the Gettysburg dead. With a firm reburial location established, the Virginia General Assembly agreed to appropriate $1,000 to the HMA to reinter the soldiers in the state capital the following year. But the women quickly learned from Dr. Weaver that this paltry amount would not begin to cover the costs for such a reburial effort. To supplement the state's money, the HMA would need private donations. On their 1871 Memorial Day, the women thus decided to place donation boxes throughout the cemetery. Heavy rain discouraged some Richmonders from attending the sixth annual celebration, but many turned out to see the graves of the unknown soldiers recently reinterred from Fort Harrison and Arlington Heights and to lay eyes upon former Confederate president Jefferson Davis. Although collections on Memorial Day proved promising, the women could only claim a fund of $4,000, not nearly sufficient to cover Rufus Weaver's estimated expenses of $3.25 to disinter, box, and ship each body.[49]

Even though the full amount for the reburials had yet to be raised, on November 8, 1871, HMA recording secretary Elizabeth H. Brown wrote to Dr. Weaver confirming the association's willingness to proceed with the disinterments. Initially, the HMA had resolved only to reclaim the bodies of those Virginia soldiers who remained at Gettysburg, but at some time during the winter of 1871–72 the women decided to remove the remains of all Confederates from the northern battlefield. With this agreed upon, the HMA women turned to engineer Charles Dimmock, who had designed the memorial pyramid in 1867, to visit Gettysburg and meet with Weaver in the spring of 1872.[50]

Upon his return, Dimmock reported to the HMA that approximately 500 identified and 2,000 unknown Confederate soldiers still rested on the battlefield. Dimmock had walked the entire battlefield and found the remains scattered in single graves as well as in mass trenches, many of which had been obliterated by farmers who had plowed and planted the land numerous times since the war. He reported on the "total want of feeling" displayed by many of the local farmers, some of whom demanded remuneration when bodies were found on their land. Dimmock made sure to convey to the Ladies—and to former Confederates in general—that Weaver was an exception to this general feeling in the North. He reminded them that Weaver was a "very competent and humane gentleman" and that, together with his father, had taken "great care and trouble" recording the location of Confederate graves. "But for them little would now be known concerning them," he believed. Pleased with Dimmock's testimony, the HMA requested that Weaver proceed with the disinterments, beginning first with the identifiable graves and then proceeding with as many unknowns as their funds could support.[51]

Forty-year-old Adeline D. Egerton of Baltimore served as the financial liaison between the HMA and Dr. Weaver. Beginning in the spring of 1872, the HMA's Elizabeth Brown was to forward funds to Brown, Lancaster & Company to Egerton's credit, at which point Egerton would send payment on to Weaver. Why Weaver and the HMA felt the need for such an arrangement remains unclear, but Egerton's devotion to the Confederacy was clear. Though a Marylander, Egerton had sympathized with the Confederates both during and after the war, focusing especially on the plight of prisoners of war, after one of her sons, a Confederate soldier, had been imprisoned by the Union. The wife of a Baltimore merchant, she was a member of a women's group that had helped supply destitute Confederate prisoners with clothes, money, and other provisions, often in exchange for jewelry crafted by the imprisoned soldiers. Following the war, she remained dedicated to aiding impoverished southerners as a member of the Soldiers' Relief Association, Southern Aid Society, and Southern Relief Association. No doubt her prominent role in the 1866 Baltimore Southern Relief Association Fair led the women of the HMA to name her an honorary member of their association that June. As a personal friend of Weaver's and an "honorary" representative of the HMA, Egerton appeared a natural choice for mediator between the two parties.[52]

After receiving an initial payment of $800 from Brown on April 7, 1872, the thirty-one-year-old Weaver began disinterments twelve days later. He labored continually during the warm spring days, identifying, collecting, and boxing the remains. "I am pushing the work with all my power," he wrote Egerton in late April, hoping to finish before the farmers began planting corn and thus avoiding any cause for resistance. "I fear that I will break down with the work," he continued. "I find it very hard on me. If I could have someone reliable to collect the bones I would be greatly relieved and the work would be greatly expedited," he explained. But identification was the most important and specialized aspect of his labor, requiring someone with "anatomical knowledge," and he preferred to do it all himself. Each morning, he headed to the fields with his crew before daybreak and did not return home for supper until well after dark. After eating, he would "arrange, in proper place and order, and label every remain or lot of remains." In all, he estimated that he worked between eighteen and twenty hours a day. Within just a few weeks, he had managed to exhume almost every body located near the General Hospital grounds and had moved on to the Second Corps Hospital, having collected a total nearing 200.[53]

On June 15, 1872, a boat from the Powhatan Steamship Company docked at Richmond's Rocketts wharf carrying the remains of 708 Confederate dead from Gettysburg. After lying in one of the wharf sheds for several days, the dead were ready for reinterment. At three o'clock on the afternoon of June 20, a detachment from the First Virginia Regiment assembled at the wharf to load the 279 boxes of remains in 15 wagons. Marking the mournful nature of the day, each of the wagons and several of the horses had been draped in black cloth, and two soldiers in reversed arms guarded each vehicle. With 400 men of the First Virginia Regiment leading the way, the cortege slowly wound along Main Street, "keeping time with the strains of funeral music," while most of the city's dignitaries, a fraternal organization called the Southern Cross Brotherhood, and more than 1,000 ex-Confederate soldiers trailed the procession. Among the more recognizable faces were those of Generals George E. Pickett, John D. Imboden, James H. Lane, and Patrick T. Moore, who marched along with their fellow veterans. The Gettysburg veterans in particular donned mourning badges of miniature battle flags with the words "Gettysburg, July 1863" printed on them; still others waved Confederate flags. Throngs of weeping spectators of all ages lined the city sidewalks, crowded into windows, or climbed to rooftops to watch the pageant, and a banner draped over the Arlington House porch simply read "They Died for Us."

After reaching Hollywood Cemetery, members of the First Virginia Regiment removed the remains from the vehicles, placing them on what had been consecrated as Gettysburg Hill. The regiment then drew up in a line, and the Reverend Dr. Hoge began the services by reminding thousands of mourners that God should be thanked for allowing that "our sons and brothers" had been returned from their "graves among strangers." The *Richmond Daily Dispatch* heralded the occasion as "the most solemn and imposing demonstration of respect to the dead ever witnessed in Richmond"—even rivaling previous Memorial Days in which more than 20,000 ex-Confederates had participated. Richmonders surely needed little reminder as to who had been behind such an imposing tribute to the war dead. Even so, the newspaper informed its readers that the reinterments and the memorial service that followed had been made possible "through the patriotic agency of the ladies of the Hollywood Memorial Association."[54]

Five more shipments between August 3, 1872, and October 11, 1873, brought the total to 2,935 reinterred bodies, 313 identified and 2,622 unknown, and the expenses to $9,536. But the HMA had been able to send payment for only one-third of the shipments. Even before the last three shipments arrived, HMA secretary Elizabeth Brown had written to Egerton, explaining that the women lacked the cash at the present time to pay Weaver. The Ladies had managed to send $3,180, but they had invested additional funds with R. H. Maury & Company—a firm that failed that year. Although the full payment had not been made, Brown assured Egerton that the money would be available sometime in 1873. But, she cautioned, because the funds were not currently accessible, perhaps Weaver should not continue with the disinterments. Whether it was a misunderstanding between the HMA and Weaver regarding funds or whether Weaver simply had abiding faith in the women because he had been paid in full by other LMAs remains unclear, but, by the fall of 1873, as the nation plunged into a severe depression, the HMA still owed Weaver $6,356.[55]

As with the Lee monument debate, the Gettysburg dead became a battleground between Richmond's ex-Confederate males and females. Even before the issues surrounding the debt issue arose, Fitzhugh Lee, nephew of Robert E. Lee, had considered invading the women's territory by taking on the direction of interments. He had written to Early just days before Hollywood's 1871 Memorial Day suggesting that the AANVA involve themselves in the retrieval of soldiers buried on "foreign" soil. Furthermore, he suggested that the remains be relocated to "our state cemetery," meaning Hollywood— by no means a "state" property. Certainly, he must have been aware of the HMA's project already well under way, given the close-knit networks of ex-Confederates within Richmond. But the AANVA was not the only veterans' group to take a position against the women. When the HMA had been unable to further compensate Weaver in the spring of 1873, Egerton contacted Colonel William C. Carrington of Richmond, an attorney, future mayor of the city, and a representative of the Southern Cross Brotherhood.[56]

The Order of the Southern Cross, or Southern Cross Brotherhood (SCB), had been founded in Chattanooga in the summer of 1863. Before the battle of Chickamauga, several officers came to Lieutenant General Leonidas Polk's headquarters proposing an institution within the army, both social and charitable, to serve as a military brotherhood. According to member Dr. Charles Todd Quintard, the group was "to foster patriotic sentiment, to strengthen the ties of army fellowship and at the same time to provide a fund, not only for the mutual benefit of its members, but for the relief of disabled soldiers and widows and orphans" of the Confederate cause. Generals Patrick Cleburne, John C. Brown, and St. John R. Liddell, along with Quintard, drafted a constitution, which was adopted on August 29, 1863, after which several "companies" organized immediately. Active military operations hampered the organization's growth, and it soon disappeared. By the summer of 1872, however, the SCB had resurfaced, at least in Virginia, composed entirely of ex-Confederate soldiers.[57]

If the SCB's goal in 1863 had been to provide for the welfare of soldiers and their families, by 1872, for unknown reasons, it had redefined the organization's primary objective to be the removal of the Gettysburg dead. In Petersburg, the SCB arranged to donate the proceeds from a celebration to assist in the "great pious labor" of removing "the ashes of the Confederate soldiers" from Gettysburg. On July 4, 1872, the SCB held a "grand demonstration" at the state's fairground in an effort to solicit funds for the same purpose. Meanwhile, the HMA continued to believe that it was exclusively responsible for the fund-raising and administrative components of the reinterments.[58]

When Carrington responded to Egerton's inquiry about the HMA debt in June 1873, he told her that his organization would immediately send $500 and would likely raise more funds in the near future. He informed Egerton of a "disagreement" between his association and the Hollywood women that prevented the two groups from working together, though he did not provide details. Having endured two years of Early and his group's attempts to manipulate and control them, the HMA was not inclined to permit yet another male association to usurp its work and refused to cede control to Carrington. Regardless of the dispute, Carrington reassured Egerton that he had spoken with Brown and believed that the HMA indeed had sufficient funds to finish removing the dead, but the money was currently tied up with Robert H. Maury & Company. "If your contractor will be able to wait a while he will be paid even if we raise no more," Carrington promised. He explained that the so-called Sabre clubs (or militia groups) of the South were mere soldiers, and "therefore we can hope for but little from them except parades and future service (if needed) in the field." In a clear class distinction, and subsequently gender implication, Carrington believed that the impoverished soldiers would not be capable of raising the money—as opposed to the elite and wealthy women of the HMA. Clearly the burden of paying for the reinterments should fall on the shoulders of those other than the common soldiers who had already served their failed nation.[59]

The fact that Egerton and Weaver turned to Richmond's men to help pay the debt must have angered the women of the HMA. Not only were they now embroiled in a dispute with two different men's associations (Lee Monument and SCB), but Carrington also had aligned himself with Egerton, an honorary member of the HMA since 1866, questioning the women's honor and ability to control their own projects. Four years later, having received no more payments from the women, Egerton enlisted the aid of Robert Stiles, a Confederate veteran and prominent Richmond attorney, as well as Judge J. H. C. Jones, to acquire the funds from the HMA.[60] But for all the Ladies' resentment toward the men's involvement, the debt remained.

In 1877, five years after the last shipment of Gettysburg remains had arrived at Rockett's wharf, the HMA women had still not paid the debt owed Weaver. Their attentions appeared to be elsewhere, perhaps on the Lee monument, or not focused on memorial work at all, and they failed to reply to Egerton's inquiries regarding their financial situation. "May I not hope that you will take some active steps in placing this matter in proper shape?" Egerton inquired in December 1878. Although she asked that the women take into account the embarrassment Weaver had suffered throughout the process, the HMA apparently made no attempt to rectify the situation. For nearly a decade, the Gettysburg debt would remain unresolved, and unpaid, as the women lost interest or found new outlets for their energies.[61]

The disputes over both the Lee monument and the Gettysburg dead may at first appear to be petty gender conflicts, but they had significant implications for the trajectory of the Lost Cause. First, the women of the LLMC set the standard by which women would continue to take the lead in commissioning and erecting memorials to the Confederacy, even after the organization of veterans groups. Richmond's equestrian sculpture of Lee was one of the South's most famous monuments to the Confederacy's most celebrated hero. The perseverance of the LLMC not only shaped the physical appearance of the statue, but more important, it also proved to the South that women were quite capable of honoring the Confederate past in extensive public memorials. Through the LMAs and eventually the United Daughters of the Confederacy (founded in 1894), white women would erect thousands of Confederate monuments in nearly every southern community, thereby altering the very landscape of the region. In fact, by the 1880s and 1890s, numerous men's associations eagerly turned to their female counterparts for help in completing monuments.[62] Without the Ladies, southern towns and cities might look very different today.

If the women had acquiesced to Early, the AANVA, and the SCB, the organizational structure of the Lost Cause likewise could have appeared very different in the late 1880s and 1890s. Had they agreed to serve as supporting organizations to the men's groups, the memorial associations might have disappeared. These women, like their northern counterparts in the Women's Relief Corps, could have simply acted as auxiliaries to the men's associations, directing their attention primarily on needy and destitute veterans. Like the northern veterans' association, the Grand Army of the Republic, the men might have focused exclusively on the military aspects of the war, thereby disappearing with the last veteran. Veterans alone might have failed to inculcate the next generation with the "Confederate spirit," through children's organizations and museums that became so central to the LMA mission during the final decade of the nineteenth century. Even more important, women's Confederate associations could have vanished entirely. Simply put, these gendered battles in the 1870s had enormous consequences for the endurance of Confederate traditions into the twentieth century.

At the same time that Richmond's memorial women struggled to retain their position within the Lost Cause, LMAs from Winchester to Lynchburg continued to experience a decline in membership.[63] Many factors contributed to this decline, including the completion of projects and the political and financial climate. Although officers occasionally met and the associations persisted with their annual Memorial Day celebrations, many of the rank-and-file LMA members simply lost interest in the memorial work once the reinterments and cemeteries had been finished.[64] The Depression of 1873 hampered both the LMAs' fund-raising powers and the women's ability to contribute dues. Simultaneously, the end of Reconstruction meant that it was no longer imperative that the Lost Cause be cast in an apolitical or feminine guise, and women thus lost much of the impetus behind their initial work.

Deaths and relocations of key LMA leaders likewise took a toll on the memorial associations. The HMA, for example, solemnly noted that "the death and removal from the city of some of its most efficient members" accounted for the "depressed" interest in the association. By the mid-1880s, several of the most active memorial women in the state had passed away, including the HMA's Mary Adams Randolph (1871), Mrs. George Gwathmey (by 1880), and Elizabeth H. Brown (by 1882); the Fredericksburg LMA's Helen Beale (1885) and Jane Ficklin (1886); and Petersburg LMA president Margaret Joynes (1884). Other prominent players moved from the area. Fredericksburg's Lizzie Alsop, for example, had married Henry Wynne and moved to Ohio. The Hollywood association would later note that "those who remained in spite of much to discourage them, struggled bravely to maintain the life of the association, but it was barely life, for the largest number to attend some of the meetings was six" and "at times it was impossible to secure any attendance." The LLMC likewise experienced the death or relocation of four of the five leading members by mid-decade. Only Lizzie Nicholas and Sarah Randolph remained active, the latter commuting from Maryland for LLMC meetings after accepting a position as principal of the Patapsco Institute near Ellicott Mills in 1879.[65]

Ironically, the diminishing popularity of LMAs among the state's women testified to the associations' success. Building on their wartime societies, participation in the memorial associations had increased southern white women's civic activity and introduced them to an array of alternative causes. The women who had dedicated so much time and energy to the LMAs did not simply cease to take part in women's associations once their cemeteries and monuments were complete; rather, they looked to other organizations in which they might put to use their new organizational skills and find companionship with like-minded women. The LMAs had thus served another purpose, as transitional organizations between wartime associations and the benevolent and suffrage movements of the late nineteenth century.[66]

Like their sisters both north and south, Virginia's middle- and upper-class women found new benevolent and club opportunities available to them during the 1870s and 1880s. Historians Lori D. Ginzberg and Suzanne Lebsock have both shown extensive evidence for antebellum societies in the North and Upper South, but the industrialization and urbanization that followed the Civil War accounted in large measure for the proliferation of female societies during the postwar years. Although two-thirds of adult women in the United States continued to live on farms and in that way contribute to the household economy, the increasing availability of factory-produced goods and poorly paid black and white household servants relieved more prosperous women (especially urban women) of their domestic responsibilities. These women busied themselves with a range of activities, including shopping and attending college, but many became involved in female voluntary associations.[67]

The largest number of organized women joined the church associations that had been the mainstay of women's activism since the antebellum period.[68] Women stayed busy organizing fairs and feasts for their congregations. An 1874 dinner in Petersburg was held to clear a church debt, and Richmond's women solicited donations for an organist at the Episcopal Church of the Savior. But in addition to religious societies, women enthusiastically established an array of secular societies, for their own improvement and for the betterment of their communities, which they began to call "clubs." Petersburg's women, including LMA members Mrs. R. G. Pegram and Mrs. Richard Bagby, assisted the local Agricultural Society in its fund-raising endeavors. Richmond's women chose from a variety of associations, such as the Women's Christian Temperance Union, the St. Paul's Orphan Asylum, the Ladies' Aid Society, and literary societies. And many women in towns throughout the Commonwealth joined the national Women's Christian Temperance Movement, organized in Virginia in 1883.[69]

Middle- and upper-class Virginia women also joined together to influence public policy when they organized the Women's Association for the Liquidation of the Virginia State Debt.[70] "The time has come," they claimed, "for us to encourage and aid our fathers, husbands, brothers, and sons in their earnest endeavor to meet the just and fair obligations of our beloved Commonwealth." In a lengthy appeal to the "Daughters of the State," the women demonstrated that they fully comprehended the economic and political consequences of the debt, detailing the amount of the principal, interest, and yearly payments necessary to retire the debt. But, they maintained, it was the duty of "all honorable and honest *men*" to fulfill their obligations. "While the women of the State might endeavor directly to raise a large amount of this balance by self-denial," they believed it "more honorable for the men to do it." Seeming to overlook the HMA's explicit failure to repay Weaver for the Gettysburg dead, the women lauded their own patriotism while shaming the men into action. Women might act as arbiters of male honor but seemed to apply no such critique to their own behavior.[71]

Regardless of their hypocritical stance on honor, women's involvement in the state debt issue demonstrated how very political Virginia's middle- and upper-class white women had become. Through their memorial work, women of the LMAs had sharpened the organizational and lobbying skills first learned through antebellum benevolent societies and wartime associations. By the late 1870s, the South's white women were actively engaged in policy making—and not ashamed to admit it. "It is said we have helped and encouraged our noble State in a darker hour than this," they claimed. "Shall we not, by the blessing of God, aid her now?" They employed the tactics of appeals and fundraising, honed so skillfully in the LMAs, to mobilize the state's "daughters." As they had done in their cemetery and monument projects, they sent appeals throughout the state to raise funds. They circulated a petition among the commonwealth's women asking the legislature to increase taxes, no doubt relying on the networks established by the memorial associations. Most important, however, the Women's Association for the Liquidation of the State Debt served as evidence of women's direct entry into partisan politics. LMAs had attempted to diffuse the political significance of Memorial Days in the 1860s and had functioned as quasi-bureaucratic agencies when they directed memorial projects, and these experiences had given them training of sorts in the male-dominated world of political wrangling. These women believed that their wartime record, combined with their postwar loyalty, gave them a legitimacy to enter such debates. As opposed to Progressive Era women who invoked maternalism to involve themselves in the state, ex-Confederate women reasoned that their wartime record and postwar loyalty gave them a certain amount of influence within partisan circles.[72]

The decline in LMA membership during the 1870s and 1880s, therefore, was not tied to the rise in male associations. The men certainly did not pull any of their members from the women's organizations, and no evidence exists to suggest that women became discouraged by the likes of Early and his comrades. Moreover, like the women's associations, the AANVA, the Southern Historical Society, the Lee Monument Association (Richmond), the Lee Memorial Association (Lexington), the SCB, and even the Union veteran association, the Grand Army of the Republic, all began to lose popular support in the late 1870s, as economic dislocation, increasing immigration, labor disputes, and political corruption captured the nation's attention.[73] For instance, the Southern Historical Society, which had moved its headquarters to Richmond in 1873 under the new leadership of Early, had begun to falter by 1880.[74] Dabney H. Maury's frequent letters to Early underscored the waning interest in the Southern Historical Society and its papers. Mired in debt, with meager membership rolls, the society found it difficult to achieve a quorum of executive members at annual board meetings. Some of the most prominent players in the organization, including William Preston Johnston, Charles Venable, and Judge George L. Christian, resigned, and others, such as George Munford and Archer Anderson, failed to attend meetings. Sadly, Maury reported, "I have noticed a loss of interest in war papers, and the subject of the war generally."[75]

If the men of the Southern Historical Society lamented a general decline of interest in all things Confederate during the late 1870s and early 1880s, the women of the LMAs could at least take pleasure in knowing that their efforts had been immensely successful on a number of levels. First, under their supervision, tens of thousands of southern soldiers had been buried in *national* Confederate cemeteries (including those removed from Gettysburg). Second, the LMAs had erected monuments in these cemeteries to serve as permanent reminders of the South's cause for generations to come. And finally, in a bittersweet twist, the Ladies had been so successful at mobilizing middle- and upper-class white southern women to join their efforts that they had depleted their own ranks as these same women found other worthy and engaging work through benevolent associations and female clubs.

By 1884, only Sarah Randolph and Lizzie Nicholas remained active in the LLMC, but attempts to consolidate the women's association with the governor's continued to stall. Two years later, Governor Fitzhugh Lee worked out a compromise association that included a new board of directors with representatives from the government and LLMC. With fund-raising nearing completion, the new association selected the women's initial choice of Mercié for sculptor. Jubal Early balked at the decision, describing Mercié's design as "General Lee on a 'bob tail horse,' looking like an English jockey" and implying that if it were erected he would rouse "the survivors of the 2d Corps" to demolish the statue. But the women had prevailed, and the statue's cornerstone was laid on a wet and soggy day in October 1887.[76]

The HMA's Gettysburg dead project, however, continued to be a source of

humiliation for the association, Richmond, and Virginia. When a new generation of women stepped forward to revitalize the memorial association in the
late 1880s, Weaver renewed his quest for payment, sparking yet another round
of fights and testing of the limits of women's memorial authority.

By the mid-1880s, at least a few prominent leaders of Virginia's LMAs had
secured women's leadership of Confederate traditions by resisting men's
efforts to control memorialization efforts. They had maintained a voice in the
Lee Monument effort and refused to surrender the Gettysburg project to the
SCB. Without these gendered battles, the landscape of the South would have
looked very different in the late 1880s and 1890s. Without women's refusal to
cede control, men might have dominated the public rituals of the Lost Cause.
Moreover, as the next chapter will explore, the LMAs and their efforts to preserve women's influence over public representations and memories of the
Confederate past had helped prepare the way for the high tide of Lost Cause
memorialization in the 1880s and 1890s.

The Old Spirit Is Not Dying Out

5

The Memorial Associations'
Renaissance, 1883–1893

Beginning in 1866, the white citizens of Richmond had welcomed the warm days of spring with their annual memorial tributes at the Hebrew, Oakwood, and Hollywood Cemeteries. Whether in grand processions with orations or more subdued occasions of merely laying flowers on the graves, each year Richmonders had looked to the city's Ladies' Memorial Associations (LMAS) for direction and instruction. But a strange thing happened in the spring of 1883. Although the Hollywood Memorial Association (HMA) had made plans to decorate the graves, a newly formed veterans' organization, the Lee Camp, took the liberty of inviting all Confederate veterans who might make the trip to Richmond as well as the Philadelphia chapter of the Grand Army of the Republic (GAR) to unite with them in the services at Hollywood Cemetery. Memorial Days had been the province of women since the war, and now men were attempting to co-opt the celebrations in their own name.[1]

The disputes with Early, the Association of the Army of Northern Virginia (AANVA), and the Southern Cross Brotherhood (SCB) during the 1870s had frustrated members of the HMA. But the Lee Camp's attempts to direct Memorial Day celebrations in 1883 eventually proved to be more than many of the women could bear. Refusing to be treated as mere ornaments on a day that they had inaugurated, in the spring of 1886 the HMA met to rejuvenate its association and take back authority over commemorations of the war dead. That year, in a carefully worded invitation, the women requested that the Lee Camp join them in a memorial service at Hollywood. The men were to be their guests, not vice versa. Asserting its leadership, the HMA directed the Lee Camp to take over some of the more mundane aspects, such as organizing the procession. But the Ladies, not the men, would direct the day's festivities. The HMA's experiences with the Ladies' Lee Monument Committee (LLMC) and the Gettysburg dead project had taught the members that they needed to dictate the terms of the cooperation. Ironically, with this reassertion on the part of the Ladies came a new era of gender cooperation between the women and the veterans associations.[2]

Contrary to historians' assertions that LMAs disappeared after Reconstruction, in the early-to-mid-1880s women across Virginia revitalized their organizations and redefined their message.[3] Reestablishing the gender division of labor in Confederate commemorations that had existed in the 1860s, the Ladies tentatively joined with aging veterans in the hope of passing on the Confederate traditions to future generations. The women continued with their early focus on cemeteries and Memorial Days, but more forward-looking groups, such as the HMA, adapted their strategies to the increasingly national culture of the late 1800s, electing to erect more centrally located monuments, establishing a museum to showcase relics of the Confederacy, and organizing "junior" associations to pass on the Confederate spirit. Despite this renewed spirit of cooperation between white southern men and women and the proliferation of LMA projects, the Ladies ultimately proved more resistant than their male counterparts to reconciliation with white northerners. As the nineteenth century came to a close, the LMAs, far from being obsolete, proved to be an integral part of the Confederate revival that swept through the region.

Just as spring was beginning to reveal itself in 1883, eleven women from the nearly defunct Petersburg LMA gathered to voice their frustrations to one another regarding the status of their organization. Without more aid, they recognized, the association would have to be permanently dissolved. Certainly, the "good women of Petersburg" would be roused by a call for support and join their efforts—just as they had done during the days of the war. If not, the group would "fall to pieces simply for the want of help and encouragement to keep it up." Determined not to endure such a fate and allow the work of their founding generation to be overlooked, the women launched a vigorous effort to recruit new members and bring back old members. They employed their social circles to solicit support, especially the myriad of women's organizations throughout the city to which many former Petersburg LMA members belonged. They encouraged their sisters and daughters to enlist and placed an advertisement in the local paper encouraging all of the city's "ladies" to assist them in their efforts.[4] Only three weeks after reorganizing their society, the Petersburg LMA had increased its membership from 11 to 45 members. Such interest and rapid growth led the women to "feel quite encouraged" about their revitalization. And Petersburg was not the only Virginia city that could declare renewed interest among the Ladies. In Richmond, the HMA showed a similar resilience; by the spring of 1890, it boasted that 196 women had been enrolled as members, although not all were annual subscribers.[5] Fredericksburg, on the other hand, elected to limit its membership to 20 women, perhaps in an effort to guarantee constant participation and to restrict its membership to the city's most elite families.[6]

As had been the case since the 1860s, Fredericksburg was not alone in its class bias. Like the earliest LMA members, Virginia's women who joined the revitalized organizations overwhelmingly represented the middle- and upper-class segments of their communities. But they also represented two different generations of Virginia women: the older generation born between 1830 and 1850 who had been members of the LMAs since the 1860s and the second, younger generation, born between 1850 and 1870. Although individual differences certainly existed, women of these two generations brought with them their life experiences that had shaped both their perceptions about the past and women's place in the present-day South.[7]

Most of the women who joined the LMAs in the 1880s made up the older generation, and demographically they closely resembled the founding generation of LMA members. Born during the 1830s and 1850s, they had experienced the war as young women. Like the LMA women of the 1860s, many had family members who served in the Confederate army or government, but most did not have relatives who had died in the war. A fair number of these women, especially the officers, had been active in the earlier memorial associations. In Fredericksburg, for example, at least nine of the twenty members had been active in the 1860s and 1870s; at least eleven of Hollywood's members had been active in the first decades of memorial work. All five of Winchester's founding members remained active by the 1880s, and at least nine of Petersburg's forty-five members had originally enrolled in the LMA during the 1860s. In fact, the percentage of 1880s members who participated in LMAs during the 1860s might be even higher if it were possible to find the rosters for every memorial association in the South, as many women moved during these years and perhaps transferred their membership from one association to another.

A closer examination of individual personalities reveals the motivations of this earliest generation of women. Known to her family as Belle, Isobel Lamont Stewart Bryan was born in 1847 to John Stewart and Mary Amanda Williamson Stewart at the family's home of Brook Hill in Henrico County just outside of Richmond. The daughter of a wealthy tobacco merchant, Belle had access to an extensive education, taking lessons at home from a Scottish governess. During the war, her father had established a hospital at Brock Hill, bringing young Belle into frequent contact with Confederate soldiers. Even the army's most preeminent leader, Robert E. Lee, visited the home at least once, and young Belle developed a deep admiration for the general. Following Appomattox, her mother appears to have joined the HMA in 1866. More than likely, given her own Confederate sympathies, Belle would have joined as well, had she not been visiting her father's family in Edinburgh, Scotland, between 1865 and 1866.[8]

In February 1871, Belle married Joseph Bryan, an attorney, Confederate veteran, and editor of the *Richmond Times*. They took up residence at Brook Hill, and between 1871 and 1882 she gave birth to six sons (five of whom survived to adulthood). As with many of her contemporaries, mothering was not Bryan's only focus; rather, she sought a more public role for herself, and she quickly took on the role of president for three different women's organizations. In 1887, she helped found the Richmond Women's Christian Association, charged with locating decent housing for women who worked in the city's factories and shops. The association nominated her for president in 1889, and she served in this capacity for a decade. Managing to find more time in her already tight schedule, she subsequently joined the Richmond Ice & Milk Mission and the Colonial Dames, and she ran the Belle Bryan Day Nursery. In 1890, Bryan took over as president of the Association for Preservation of Virginia Antiquities, whose purpose was to raise funds to purchase and restore the state's historical sites in an effort to correct the "misinterpretations of Virginia's glorious colonial past by historians from New England." Not content to preside over just one historically minded women's group, that same year Bryan was named president of the HMA.[9]

One hundred miles west of Richmond, Ruth Hairston Early's life closely resembled that of Belle Bryan. Daughter of Samuel and Henrian Cabell Early and niece of Jubal A. Early, Ruth was born at Charleston, Virginia, in 1849 and moved to Lynchburg in 1852. As a member of the slaveholding class, she, like Bryan, had been a privileged young woman. During the war, she attended the Lynchburg Female Seminary, where she studied Latin, English, and music. Because of a close bond with her Uncle Jubal, Early formed relationships with many of the Confederacy's leaders and their wives, including Varina Howell Davis. Early probably joined the city's numerous female clubs, such as the reading and musical associations, and was clearly a member of the Lynchburg LMA by 1887. A daughter of one of Lynchburg's most prominent families, she emulated Sarah Randolph by dedicating much of her time to writing histories of Virginia and the region. Her many works included such titles as *By Ways of Virginia History*, *The Early Family*, and *Campbell Chronicles and Family Sketches*. She also oversaw the publication of Jubal Early's small book *The Heritage of the South* (printed on Confederate gray paper and bound in gray cloth) and his memoirs. Like Bryan, she later joined other statewide and national women's associations, including the Poetry Society of Virginia, the Pocahontas Memorial Association, the Southern Industrial Educational Association, the Daughters of the American Revolution, the United Daughters of the Confederacy, and the International Anglo-Saxon Society.[10]

In addition to Bryan and Early's generation of LMA members, a younger group of women, born mainly between 1850 and 1870, joined the ranks of the reconstituted memorial associations in the mid-1880s. As historian Karen Cox has explained, those women born after 1850 "developed their perceptions about the Old South based on their parents' memories." They had come of age during Reconstruction, a period considered by many white southerners to have been one of "Yankee aggression" and "black betrayal" that they wished to forget. Rather than forsaking the defeated Confederacy, this generation of white southerners, even more so than their mothers and fathers, created and romanticized the "Old South." They had grown up hearing tales of beautiful plantations, faithful slaves, and heroic Confederate soldiers. They had heard countless stories of the "southern lady" and the Confederate woman, two role models that this generation of women wished to both celebrate and emulate.[11]

Lucy Dunbar Williams, Nannie Lightfoot, and Kate Pleasants Minor offer insights into this younger generation of LMA women, many of whom were the literal daughters of the founding generation. Lucy Dunbar Williams was born in 1850 to Phillip Williams II and Mary Dunbar Williams of Winchester. Her mother and aunt had been the cofounders of the Winchester LMA, so it seemed fitting that Lucy would follow in their footsteps, eventually becoming secretary of the association. Nannie Lightfoot, a member of the Petersburg LMA, was born in 1858 to physician John Herbert Claiborne and his wife, Sarah. Like Williams, her mother had been an active member of the LMA in the 1860s, although she, too, had passed away by the 1880s. Many of these young women, in their twenties and thirties when the LMAs reorganized, joined in the spirit of Confederate memorialization and to honor the "noble work" their mothers had initiated twenty years earlier.[12]

Like several of those in the older generation, many if not most of the younger women committed themselves to multiple women's organizations beyond the LMAs. Kate Pleasants Minor, corresponding secretary for the HMA, was born in 1857 to John Adair and Virginia Cary Pleasants, spending her entire life in Richmond. In addition to her work with the HMA, Minor originated the idea of a state board of charities and corrections, joined a group that was responsible for juvenile court and detention homes, enlisted in an elite Richmond intellectual circle known as the Saturday Afternoon Club, was a member of the Equal Suffrage League, served as a delegate to the Virginia and national Democratic conventions (1924), and acted as the serials librarian at the Virginia State Library from 1912 to 1925.[13] As Minor and her contemporaries suggest, unlike their grandmothers, the women of these two generations found greater civic opportunities open to them. And LMA work was one facet of club life for these "new" Virginia women.[14]

In fact, those LMA women active in the 1890s, regardless of their generation, might be called the "new women of the New South." Contrary to the image they hoped to present, they were clearly not imitations of the "southern lady" from bygone days. At the same time that they waxed nostalgic about the Confederate past, these LMA women participated in a wave of reform sweeping both the North and the South. These "new women" petitioned for property rights and age of consent and antiliquor laws; appealed for admission to state universities; advocated for school reform; and requested that women be appointed to boards of public institutions. Among their ranks, they could count authors and journalists, as well as social and political activists (such as Lucy Bagby, Sarah Randolph, Belle Bryan, and Janet Weaver Randolph). Most members also joined other female associations, including the Women's Christian Temperance Union, the Young Women's Christian Association, the Woman's Club of Richmond, and the Equal Suffrage League. Although the majority of LMA members never embraced the most progressive reform of the day, woman suffrage, their work in the LMAs (and other organizations) allowed them to achieve a greater public voice and influence than their mothers and grandmothers might ever have dreamed.[15]

Those who joined the LMAs in the 1880s and 1890s also differed from the earliest members in their goals. In the 1860s, cemetery work had served simultaneously as a necessity and a political response to the war's outcome. But twenty and thirty years later, as the war generation began to give way to children and grandchildren, the social and political climate dictated a change in the direction of the Lost Cause. In the mid-1880s, Virginians, along with the rest of the South, witnessed a period of renewed enthusiasm and concern for the Confederate past. Interest in soldiers' pensions, the death of Jefferson Davis, the beginnings of industrialization, integration into the national economy and mass culture, gender anxieties, and racial tensions all contributed to the development of a regional celebration that honored white southerners' self-sacrifice and honor. This Confederate revival helped facilitate a sense of white southern solidarity through veterans' associations, monuments, parades, and a new emphasis on the next generation, amid what many assumed was the decline of white southern civilization. As several other historians have argued, during these years reverence for the Lost Cause became a "tonic against the fear of social change" and an "escape to a mythic past."[16]

Southern race relations also may have occasioned a rise in nostalgia for the Lost Cause. This celebration of the Confederate past occurred within years of the formal end to Reconstruction in 1877, coinciding with a surge in white supremacy. The emergence of a black middle class, the movement of strangers along the region's railroads, the growth of towns, white women's suffrage activities, a new consumer culture, and political and economic conflicts of the era all led white southerners to disenfranchise black men, remove black officeholders, legally implement segregation in every possible venue, and lynch many black men who refused to play by the white rule book.[17] But it also prompted many middle-class white southerners to look to the past for affirmation. Building on a number of antebellum stereotypes, they exaggerated stories of plantation tranquility, honorable (white) men, southern belles, and happy slaves to legitimate a new racial and gender hierarchy. By imagining the interracial peace of the "Old South" and the "blackness of Reconstruction," southern whites rewrote their history to make their white supremacist laws seem not only natural, but necessary. As Grace Hale argues, this fictional narrative of the past "absolved white southerners of moral obligation to the freedpeople and blurred white class and gender differences while legitimating segregation as the only possible southern future."[18]

But two other factors also helped stimulate popular interest in the Lost Cause at the grassroots level. First, the generation of Confederate veterans and women who had experienced the war as young adults was now coming into its own, running businesses and rearing children. As such, these people had the financial resources and time to participate in such endeavors. Second, and related to the first, they desperately needed their offspring to understand their devotion to the Confederate cause even though it had failed. When asked, "Why are the old Confederates gathering together again? and what are they going to *get out of it*?" Thomas Munford reminded a crowd of Lynchburg veterans in the mid-1880s that the answer lay with the next generation: "To our children and their children's children, let it be our pride to teach them, as is done in every land where patriotism and self-sacrificing spirits are honored and esteemed, that the Confederates shed their blood for their Mother, Vir ginia, defending a cause she knew to be just and right."[19] But even more so than the veterans, the LMA women understood that passing along the Confederate tradition to future generations must be their primary goal.

Twenty years after the close of the war, parklike Confederate cemeteries continued to attract white southerners of every generation, providing a tranquil and contemplative setting for them to reflect on the heroic deeds of the war dead. Foreshadowing historians' claims that public spaces were powerful tools in shaping memory, LMAs recognized the symbolic role these settings possessed for both current and future generations and so continued to emphasize the aesthetic nature of these cities of the dead.[20] Like several of the LMAs, the Lynchburg society regretted that it could not tend to such duties alone and elected to hire someone to clean and clear the cemetery, on occasion requesting that salt be sprinkled on the walkways to prevent grass from growing. The Petersburg LMA erected a gothic arch over the entry to its memorial grounds and convinced the town council to donate money toward widening the road and building a new bridge in the cemetery. The Winchester Ladies directed their energies toward replacing the wooden grave markers with more permanent marble slabs. Reinterments continued as well. The Petersburg Ladies proposed reburying those Confederate soldiers whose remains lay along the Richmond and Petersburg Railroad in Blandford Cemetery, and in 1893 the Hollywood association succeeded in having Jefferson Davis's remains reinterred in its cemetery.[21]

The LMAs also spent a great deal of their efforts building monuments during these years. At their 1890 Memorial Day, the Petersburg Ladies dedicated a thirty-foot granite monument "surmounted by the figure of a Confederate soldier" of white bronze. The city's newspaper gushed that the LMA was "the pride of all our citizens, and justly so, because they have succeeded where others could see only failure and disappointment." The Fredericksburg LMA had "earnestly desired" to erect a monument since the spring of 1873; the city's residents were elated when the reorganized association finally fulfilled its goal in 1891. Although the Lynchburg LMA had dedicated a monument to the Confederate dead in its cemetery in 1869, during the spring of 1890 the women appointed a committee to erect another monument in the city to soldiers "who were killed in, or died in consequence of the late war," from the surrounding area. The Winchester LMA and their spin-off organizations, including the Virginia Shaft Association, continued to sponsor state monuments in their cemeteries, such as the Louisiana state monument, completed in 1896.[22]

Richmond, not surprisingly, erected even more magnificent monuments than it had in the 1860s or 1870s. By 1886, the disputes between Early and the

LLMC regarding the Lee monument had largely been resolved, and four years later the large equestrian statue was unveiled in a grand celebration along what would become Monument Avenue. People from all parts of the South traveled to Richmond, where they were greeted by miles of bunting, portraits of Washington and Lee, and thousands of waving Confederate and American flags. A parade of more than 20,000 participants marched west out of the city to bands playing "Dixie" and other southern tunes. Jubal Early, though denied his choice of sculptor, served as the master of ceremonies, and other former Confederate leaders such as Dabney H. Maury and Joseph E. Johnston joined in the revelry. Between 100,000 and 150,000 people participated in the festivities, most likely the largest crowd to gather for a Confederate celebration to that point. The success of the monument and ceremonies that accompanied its unveiling provided evidence that cooperation between the veterans' and women's groups could indeed produce the grandest of Confederate tributes.[23]

So it came as no surprise that when a group of veterans suggested erecting a monument in Richmond to the common soldiers and sailors of the Confederacy they invited the cooperation of the city's LMAs. Recognizing the HMA's ability to raise money, in the spring of 1891 the men asked the association to organize a bazaar to aid their project. Initially, the Ladies declined, noting that many "pressing calls" on their association made it impossible for them to undertake "so grave a responsibility," although they would "most cheerfully assist any other organization of ladies who would assume the responsibility." But the men persisted in their appeals to the women. Wilfred Emory Cutshaw, a member of both the HMA advisory committee and the Soldiers' and Sailors' Monument Association, reminded the women that the men of the Monument Association had always been their "most zealous friends" and urged that the HMA should undertake "to *lead* an enterprise to which all the Veteran associations will pledge their cordial support to raise the necessary funds to complete the monument." Clearly, Cutshaw and the veterans admired the HMA's ability to garner popular support—and to lead such a venture. The women finally agreed, eventually providing almost half of the $35,000 necessary to erect a column supporting a bronze figure of the common soldier located on Libby Hill.[24]

As these examples indicate, the pace, subject matter, and placement of LMA-, or veteran-, sponsored monuments changed during the 1880s. Gaines Foster has pointed out that between 1865 and 1885, ex-Confederates erected approximately 70 percent of their monuments in cemeteries. These monuments typically reflected some aspect of funeral design—obelisks, urns, or pyramids, as in the case of the HMA memorial. Cemetery monuments, though, "attested to the belief that, however noble, the cause had failed." By the late 1880s, the number of communities erecting monuments had increased. Most frequently, these tributes to the Confederacy found themselves integrated into public spaces, along city streets or on courthouse lawns, and funeral designs gave way to monuments featuring the Confederate soldier. But why the emphasis on monuments?[25]

Those who sponsored public monuments intended them to be fixed, to need no interpretation. In fact, one southern woman explained that memorials represented "in permanent physical form the historical truth and spiritual and political ideals we would perpetuate." Monuments were meant to provide historical closure—as Kirk Savage has pointed out, "to mold a landscape of collective memory, to conserve what is worth remembering and discard the rest." But monuments were about much more than the past. As Fitzhugh Brundage has demonstrated, they were also symbols of power. Public monuments allowed white southerners in the 1880s and 1890s to rewrite history from a Confederate or Lost Cause perspective; that is, the memorials intentionally ignored the issue of slavery, focusing instead on "honor, courage, duty, states' rights, and northern aggression." Monuments to the common soldier allowed the war generation to etch their devotion to the cause in stone, but they also stood as reminders of the southern social order and heroic Confederate cause to subsequent generations. At the dedication of the Soldiers' and Sailors' Monument in 1894, for example, Rev. Dr. Moses Hoge suggested that monuments acted as a history lesson for those who could not read, especially children. "Books are occasionally opened," but "monuments are seen every day," he noted. Ladies and veterans alike understood that monuments served as daily reminders of white southerners' Confederate past.[26]

The reburial of the Gettysburg dead had caused considerable conflict among the Hollywood Ladies and men's groups in the 1870s, but when the issue resurfaced nearly twenty years later the women turned to like-minded men for assistance. In an effort to both demonstrate their commitment to working with the men and solicit formal support, the women of the HMA created an official male advisory board in the spring of 1890. Although the Ladies made it clear that they would determine the conditions of male-female cooperation, the renewed debate over paying the Gettysburg reburial project debt made it increasingly apparent that a new era of gender cooperation had arrived among Virginia's Lost Cause advocates.

Upon hearing of the HMA's success (actually, the LLMC's success) in the

Lee monument endeavor, in the spring of 1889 Dr. Rufus Weaver renewed his efforts to claim the money owed him by the Ladies. Infuriated that the women had managed to collect the funds to erect an enormous statue even as they had failed to pay more than $6,000 owed him for the Gettysburg reinterments, he vowed to collect the money. Again turning to Adeline Egerton for her assistance, he calculated that with interest the HMA now owed him approximately $12,000. He reminded the honorary HMA member that she had claimed that the debt was one of "sacred honor" and therefore must be repaid. Recognizing the dense network of Confederate women's organizations and their obvious fund-raising abilities, he suggested to Egerton that perhaps *all* of the LMAs of the South be asked to pay the HMA's balance. After all, he noted, there were "hundreds of Confederate dead from the different states among those buried in Hollywood from the battle of Gettysburg." Surely the Hollywood women could convince their like-minded memorial sisters to provide assistance.[27]

But another year passed without any response from the Ladies. Although male intervention had not been successful in the 1870s, Weaver recognized that this was a new era of gender cooperation and encouraged Egerton to take the matter up with some of Virginia's most influential men, namely Dr. Hunter Maguire and Governor Fitzhugh Lee. There is no evidence that Egerton contacted the two men or that these men in turn addressed the Ladies. But if Governor Lee knew of the matter, surely he must have spoken to his wife, Ellen, an HMA member, about the impending uproar. Egerton did, however, contact HMA male advisory member Robert Stiles, requesting that he convey this "unpleasant piece of information to the HMA."[28]

At least eleven members of the HMA had been active participants when the Gettysburg reburial project began, but when Stiles finally approached the Ladies in mid-May 1890, they all claimed complete surprise. "It was like thunder in a clear sky," corresponding secretary Kate Pleasants Minor recalled; "no single member of the association knew anything about the matter." To protect itself against a potential lawsuit, the HMA pointed out in April 1890 that the 1866 association had never been chartered and therefore was not legally liable for the debt. Furthermore, the HMA leadership failed to disclose the issue to the association at large for several months until, they claimed, it could be thoroughly investigated. They reported to members that they had no recollection of the affair and that all records from that period had been lost (which may account for the fact that no minutes exist between 1868 and 1886). Fortunately, or perhaps unfortunately for the HMA, Weaver and Egerton had kept copies of all correspondences regarding the project and therefore had a viable claim against the association.[29]

By the following spring, the Ladies still had failed to act. At a meeting in early May 1891, the subject of Weaver's claim again came up, but all agreed to table the matter until after the annual Memorial Day celebration later that month. In November, when the association met to discuss the claim, the recording secretary noted that, "as usual, this was the cause of much debate," and the women referred the matter to their newly created male advisory board. A few days before Christmas, Weaver arrived at the Richmond Times building to meet with the male advisory board, most of whom were husbands of HMA members. After hearing Weaver's case, the men were fully persuaded that the association had a "strong moral obligation" to pay off as much of the debt as it could afford. They subsequently recommended that the Ladies secure an accountant to review the books of R. H. Maury & Company to determine the amount that might be reclaimed from their investments in the 1870s.[30]

An attorney hired by the association to examine the R. H. Maury & Company books estimated that the HMA might be able to claim $3,618 that was due them, but this was far less than the Ladies had expected. Even if they managed to claim the entire amount from Maury & Company, they would remain nearly $3,000 short of what they owed Weaver. Although they had rebuffed efforts by the SCB to assist and had ignored Weaver's suggestion that all the LMAs in the South be enlisted to repay the debt, the HMA was willing to appeal to the state legislature for an appropriation. After all, the women had been acting on behalf of the state when they undertook the initial reburial of Confederate soldiers in 1866. Asserting that the HMA was still under the control of the Ladies, the HMA rejected the male advisory board's objection to requesting the appropriation. Belle Bryan asked the women to employ their lobbying skills through their well-connected social and political networks, calling on the entire association to interview members of the legislature and leaving "no means untried" to secure the appropriation. Their efforts paid off. Within a month, Weaver acknowledged the receipt of $3,000 paid by the state of Virginia.[31]

Having sent the state funds, the HMA believed it was soon to be free of the tiresome debate so that the members might focus their attention on other more immediate issues, such as the proposed Soldiers' and Sailors' Monument on Libby Hill. But still Weaver had not released the HMA from debt. In a tersely written letter dated April 14, 1892, Minor demanded that Weaver give her formal statement of receipt of $3,000 and "of your acceptance of that and the Maury claim as full satisfaction for your claim against our Association." The Ladies would not, however, feel compelled to provide the interest. It was "beyond [their] utmost endeavors" to provide an additional $6,000,

Minor noted, and they "could not morally be held responsible for the delay in payment of a debt of whose existence [they] had *all* been ignorant." Weaver, distrustful of the Ladies' word, politely declined. Even with the appropriation from the state, he refused to capitulate until he had proof that the Maury estate would yield the $3,356 necessary to satisfy the original debt. "When I learn that the Maury estate will yield any adequate percentage of the *original* debt to warrant my so doing," he wrote, "I will without complaint release *all claim for interest* although I have suffered *seriously* by long waiting for the principal."[32] In May, the HMA announced that it had "arranged" for the full payment. The Ladies insisted that the debt had been settled, and it was time for them to get back to their business of organizing a bazaar for the Libby Hill monument.[33]

Throughout the fall of 1892, the Ladies devoted their energy and attention to the upcoming bazaar, choosing to believe that they had settled the Weaver debt or secretly hoping that he would go away (as he had so many years earlier). But the following February, Weaver was knocking on their door once again, still waiting for $3,356 of the principal. A second lawyer hired by the HMA to review the Maury & Company books had uncovered $1,347.93 deposited to the credit of the Gettysburg fund, but Weaver still had not seen one penny from the account. Nevertheless, many HMA members insisted that the issue had been legally settled and thus that the newly discovered money be put to some other use. After bitter wrangling within the group, however, Lora Ellyson succeeded in convincing the association to send the funds to Weaver. She, for one, believed that the women were honor bound to "pay Dr. Weaver as near his twelve thousand [the principal plus interest] as possible." By spring 1893, it appears that Weaver had finally received approximately $2,235 from the Maury & Company account; still, more than $1,120 of the principal had not been settled.[34]

Almost ten years later, Weaver again wrote to the HMA. During those years, he informed the group, he had been waiting and hoping most patiently for the final payment, as he had done for the twenty years prior to their assumption of the debt. He inquired as the prospects of receiving the payment for the balance of $1,196.34.[35] Minor fired back a terse letter reminding Weaver that he had "formally relinquished all claim for interest" and that the HMA had never intended "any payment beyond what the Maury estate would make." Again, she demanded a release from all claims. It appears as if Weaver finally gave up on the HMA, writing to Egerton that he had every reason to believe the association would pay "every copper of the *original* debt." He had believed that the debt was one of honor, "so sacred, that any individual or organization should blush for shame one would think to permit it to go unpaid." Perhaps alluding to the Commonwealth's perception of itself as a noble state, Weaver claimed that he could not fathom that as "*Virginians*" they would shirk on such a debt of honor. But the HMA did just that. It never did repay the entire principal, much less the interest owed to Weaver.[36]

Although the women of the HMA had succeeded at organizing Hollywood Cemetery, compiling a register of the dead, and erecting a grand monument to the soldiers, they had not succeeded in upholding their end of the bargain with Weaver. For all their rhetoric about honor and loyalty, their actions failed to live up to their words. Even as they praised the heroics of the past, they had little patience for backward-looking individuals such as Weaver; he only impeded their progress. In the end, they used their knowledge of the law by claiming that the original HMA had not been chartered and, therefore, they were not legally liable for the debt. Weaver's claim may have continued to serve as a source of embarrassment for the women, but the HMA was more interested in keeping control over the Lost Cause's direction than worrying about a debt that they considered paid. With all its interest in remembering the past, the revitalized HMA was not inclined to remember its own history; but it was disposed to work more closely with ex-Confederate men and their organizations.[37]

At the same time that LMAS across the state were experiencing a renaissance of sorts, veterans in Virginia and other states of the former Confederacy began to organize their own associations. The AANVA and the Southern Historical Society continued to experience financial difficulties and a lack of interest, but in April 1883, a group of Richmond veterans agreed to form an independent, grassroots association, calling themselves the Lee Camp of Confederate Veterans.[38] Taking their cue from the capital, other camps soon organized throughout the Commonwealth, including the Matthew F. Maury Camp (Fredericksburg, 1883), the A. P. Hill Camp (Petersburg, c. 1887), the Turner Ashby Camp (Winchester, 1891), and the Garland-Rhodes Camp (Lynchburg, c. 1894).[39] Their primary goals were twofold: to perpetuate the memories of their fallen comrades and to "minister as far as practicable to the wants of those who were permanently disabled in the service."[40]

But it was the national spirit of reconciliation extolling the battlefield experience of both Union and Confederate veterans that most influenced the men's organizations. As the centennial of the American Revolution approached, some northerners and southerners began to participate in joint Blue-Gray reunions, as soldiers on both sides acknowledged the commonalities of camp life and experiences of battle. One of the earliest examples of this spirit occurred when the Federal commander at the Ash Barracks in Nashville invited Governor James D. Porter Jr., an ex-Confederate officer, to review his troops in April 1875. The "novelty of the scene" apparently attracted between 5,000 and 8,000 spectators. The city of Boston likewise invited military organizations in South Carolina, Virginia, Maryland, New York, and other states to attend the festivities at Bunker Hill to celebrate the "era of good feeling between the sections." That same year, a GAR post in Chicago invited all Confederate soldiers to join in its celebration of "patriots" rather than "traitors and rebels." In 1881, a New Jersey GAR post and Knights of Templars from Boston and Providence made a trip to Hollywood Cemetery and placed a wreath on the city's Jackson statue. The following year, ex-Confederates from Richmond visited the New Jersey post, and in 1887 Union and Confederate veterans met for the first reunion at Gettysburg. During these years, veterans from both sides would meet at no less than nineteen formal Blue-Gray reunions.[41]

Choosing to avoid the "animosities" of the war and embrace sectional reconciliation, the Lee Camp participated in activities with the GAR within a month of its organization, including a reception held for a Pennsylvania GAR post visiting Richmond on May 5 and Memorial Day services at the national cemetery later that month. Much to the chagrin of Jubal Early, the Lee Camp members even solicited aid from northerners for a Confederate veterans' home in Richmond; the Joint Committee of Conference, made up of GAR and ex-Confederates in New York and chaired by former Confederate general John B. Gordon, agreed to assist the Lee Camp by endorsing a series of fundraisers. This Blue-Gray cooperation was a marvelous success—the veterans' home opened its doors only two years later.[42]

This era of cooperation extended not only to the veterans who had once been the battlefield enemies of the Confederate veterans but also to LMAS. Despite the tensions that had mounted between the LLMC and Jubal Early's AANVA, the LMAS appeared open to cooperation with male veterans' associations by the mid-1880s. Several factors played a role in this shift from gender strife to cooperation. First, the undeniable success of the Lee monument (finally erected in 1890) prompted men and women to appreciate the contributions of the opposite sex. Second, in looking through their founding documents, the LMAS were reminded of the productive relationship they had had with men in the 1860s. But the two most significant reasons for this era of cooperation were the reinstatement (in the case of Memorial Days) and the recognition of a gendered division of memorial labor and the marital/familial alliances among the LMAs and the new veterans' associations.

The problems between Early's group and the women had arisen largely because the men of the AANVA had attempted to usurp women's roles as monument builders. But with the decline of the AANVA, the growth of more veterans' associations, and the reorganization of LMAs in the 1880s, men and women seemed to agree that specific tasks belonged to each sex. The women would concentrate on perpetuating Memorial Days, organizing fund-raising endeavors, tending to the cemeteries, and encouraging the next generation to remember the Confederate past. Men would organize reunions (both with other Confederates and with Union veterans). Even though the Lee monument had initially served as a dividing force, the men and women recognized that collaboration would ensure that memorials could be erected that were far more impressive than those either sex could build on its own and so elected to jointly pursue projects such as the Soldiers' and Sailors' Monument.[43] By respecting the goals of the other group, both the Ladies and the veterans could avoid the disputes that had frustrated their efforts in the 1870s.

As is so often the case, this cooperative relationship also developed because of personal alliances, whether through marriage or kinship, between the veterans and the Ladies. In Winchester, several of the Ladies were related to men in the Turner Ashby Camp of Confederate Veterans, including both the wife (Emilie Gray Williams) and sister (Lucy Dunbar Williams) of Confederate Veterans camp commander John J. Williams.[44] At least eighteen of the forty-six Petersburg Ladies (or 39 percent) had husbands, sons, or fathers who were members of the A. P. Hill Camp of Confederate Veterans, including the president and vice president. At least fourteen of the Hollywood Ladies in 1890 were married to or daughters of prominent members of the Lee Camp, including leaders such as Janet Henderson Randolph, Kate Pleasants Minor, Emma Christian, and Lora Ellyson.

Unlike Early and the LLMC, then, the LMAs had personal and private ties to the leadership of the veterans' camps. These marital alliances proved remarkably helpful in generating support for Confederate memorial activities, as the men and women championed each other's causes. No doubt there was many a night when the HMA's Lora Ellyson and her husband, J. Taylor Ellyson, chairman of the Democratic state committee and Lee Camp member, discussed the business of their respective organizations over dinner. And as had been the case in 1860s, the men willingly lent their business and political connections to support the Ladies in their endeavors. This arrangement allowed the women's associations to retain their independence and status while securing backing from the men.[45]

In several instances, women agreed to align themselves more formally with the men as auxiliary associations; however, these groups never received the following that memorial associations garnered. After much debate over inducting "honorary" female members or electing "daughters" of the camp, women in Winchester joined forces with the Turner Ashby Camp of Confederate Veterans in 1893 to organize a Ladies' Auxiliary for the express purpose of raising funds and coordinating social activities for the camp and soldiers' homes. In addition to the more "traditional" roles played by auxiliaries, Winchester's women also took on the task of preserving the deeds of the South's heroic women and "aid[ing] the time honored Ladies' Memorial Association." Moreover, the veterans recognized the special skills, such as fund-raising, that women brought to their organizations. The Turner Ashby Camp duly noted that the women should serve as a body "to whom the Confederate Veterans may go for council to aid in matters belonging especially to their skill and experience."[46]

The Lee Camp Auxiliary officially formed in 1888, although women had played at least a symbolic role in the camp since its inception. Taking a cue from the earliest LMAs, the Lee Camp named Mildred and Mary Lee (daughters of Robert E. Lee), along with Mary Anna Jackson (widow of Stonewall Jackson) and her daughter, honorary members of its camp in 1884. That same year, a group of women had volunteered to conduct a bazaar to raise the inaugural funds for the Lee Camp soldiers' home. Two years later, James McGraw proposed a committee to "get the wives and daughters of the Confederate soldiers to organize themselves as an auxiliary corps." For some unknown reason, the proposal failed to pass. A notation in the margins of the camp's minutes simply noted that it "was never appointed." Still, the veterans relied on the women: they requested that some unnamed group of females embroider a flag for the camp and asked that they sponsor an entertainment for the benefit of the soldiers' home.[47]

In the summer of 1888, the camp finally reported the organization of a ladies' auxiliary, to be temporarily chaired by Mrs. A. L. Phillips. These women, however, played a fairly marginal role, occasionally granting relief to a distressed family but never managing to generate much enthusiasm. By the spring of 1891, the women's association could not even garner a quorum to conduct business and issued a call to reorganize. Even with appeals in the newspapers, no one responded. Colonel A. L. Phillips, husband of the auxiliary's president, threw up his hands in frustration, reporting to the camp that "he did not know how he could reorganize the Ladies Auxiliary Corps." The men continued to press the issue, perhaps feeling competition with other camps, such as Petersburg, that had managed to solicit at least a modicum of female cooperation. That fall, the Lee Camp made one last effort, disbanding the old auxiliary and reorganizing it under the direction of Mrs. James W. White, wife of the camp's former commander.[48]

By January 1892, the Ladies' Auxiliary claimed forty-six active and six contributing members. But this was a far cry from the nearly 200 reported members of the HMA, and Mrs. White again appealed to the veterans to "induce their wives and daughters to join the camp." Still, there was little interest. Only three members of the Ladies' Auxiliary appear to have been members of the HMA; but at least fourteen members of the HMA were wives or daughters of Lee Camp members. In Winchester, the women who joined the auxiliary came directly from the Winchester LMA. Why then, did the Lee Camp Auxiliary struggle to fill its ranks? More than likely, the HMA simply remained a more popular organization among women, especially as it shifted its attention to the creation of a Confederate museum. Class, too, probably played a role in the diverse constituencies of the competing organizations; as historians of Confederate Veterans have pointed out, most members came from the working class. For example, 30 percent of the Lee Camp represented the lower classes, in contrast to the LMAs that drew heavily from the upper middle class and the elite. As had been the case in the 1860s, women most likely to join the LMAs had the time and financial resources that allowed them to do so.[49]

Northern women likewise took up the banner of Civil War commemoration in auxiliaries of the GAR under the name of the Women's Relief Corps (WRC) in 1883, representing northern women's first organized foray into Civil War commemorations (in a stark contrast to their southern sisters, who had led the Confederate memorial movement since the 1860s).[50] That year, GAR commander Paul Vandervoort approached a group of Massachusetts women, noting that the men needed a national organization of women to assist the aging veterans, "since federal assistance and state infrastructure were grossly inadequate for dealing with the tens of thousands of veterans." Within months, twenty-six different women's associations from sixteen states joined under the banner of the WRC at a national convention in Denver. Like the Confederate auxiliaries, the WRC sought to relieve the sufferings of disabled veterans and their families, to assist in the preservation of veterans' documents and records, and "to teach patriotism and the duties of citizenship, the true history of our country, and the love and honor of our flag." Historian Nina Silber has observed that the association was defined by its relationship to the GAR. The corps' rules demanded that each WRC be attached to a specific GAR post and adopt the name of the post with which it was affiliated. According to Silber, "The organization's raison d'être kept them tied to an ideology of female submissiveness."[51]

Although the historical record leaves no direct evidence, it is possible that the Confederate Veterans modeled their auxiliaries after the WRC. Perhaps the United Confederate Veterans looked north and saw Union veterans enjoying the support of the region's women—without the conflict that had previously raged between the Confederate veterans and the LMAs. Regardless of the inspiration for Confederate auxiliaries, it is clear that both Union and Confederate groups shared at least one key element: both the GAR and the United Confederate Veterans identified women's participation as an extension rather than modification of existing gender roles. As historian Cecilia O'Leary has pointed out, "The creation of women's 'auxiliaries' allowed men to maintain the exclusive character of their fraternal orders by designating separate and subordinate affiliations for women. Auxiliaries, in turn, provided public women with an avenue for reconciling aspirations for autonomy and masculine acceptance."[52]

Historians John Coski and Amy Feely argue that Confederate auxiliaries differed from the LMAs in that they "dedicated themselves not to the memory of the dead, but to the welfare of the 'living monuments' among them." Although it is true that auxiliary women primarily focused on supporting destitute veterans (and in some cases their children and widows), LMA women, too, aided the impoverished soldiers. In Lynchburg, for example, the Ladies appealed to Confederate sympathies on Memorial Day to collect funds for a soldiers' home. The Oakwood Memorial Association (OMA) offered assistance to several Confederate widows, often working directly with the Lee Camp to identify individuals. Petersburg's LMA likewise contributed to the soldiers' welfare, even when the soldiers were not locals, sending $115 from its meager budget to a disabled veteran, his wife, and children in Cumberland County in 1888. Eventually, the Petersburg LMA became an auxiliary to the A. P. Hill Camp of Confederate Veterans for the purpose of "assisting in caring for the destitute widows and orphans," as did the Winchester LMA. But regardless of their efforts on behalf of the "living monuments," LMA women were not simply throwbacks to an era of mourning and bereavement. They, too, concentrated on the living in their efforts to instruct future generations about their past. Moreover, as the Lee Camp Auxiliary clearly indicates, many women simply avoided acting in supporting roles when they could control their own affairs through memorial associations.[53]

The most substantial difference between women who served in auxiliaries and those who joined LMAs seems to be the desire for autonomy. And those women, such as in Petersburg and Winchester, who served both in independent LMAs and in auxiliaries found an even more productive compromise position. They could simultaneously lay claim to the veterans' support and remain an independent organization. Like Sarah Randolph and her contemporaries during the Lee monument disputes, women of the LMAs had learned that cooperation with men could be useful, but they adamantly refused to cede control of their movement to male organizations. Because they believed they had inaugurated the Lost Cause through Memorial Days and Confederate cemeteries, they sought to retain their place in the pantheon of Confederate memory. They would not agree to serve merely as secondary participants.

By the mid-1880s, communities throughout Virginia and the South recognized both Confederate and National (as it came to be called) Memorial Days. Although they dubbed National Memorial Day "Decoration Day," Winchester's municipal figures strongly encouraged the townspeople to participate in the 1884 festivities under the auspices of the Union Cornet Band. "We trust these ceremonies will be attended by a large number of our people, thereby giving evidence of the patent fact visible all around us that all bitterness engendered by the struggle of twenty years ago has entirely effaced," they remarked. The following year, the paper noted that the day was of "interesting character and largely attended." A procession of townsmen, veterans, and boys (not girls) bearing garlands and evergreens wound through the town and to the Federal Cemetery, where the LMA had wreathed the graves with flowers. In the spirit of reconciliation, the day's orator, Captain Joseph A. Nulton of the Winchester Light Infantry, encouraged those present to convey the true meaning of the war to the next generation. As with the LMAs, both Confederate and Union veterans understood that these annual visits were meant to secure a legacy of bravery, patriotism, and honor for their children.[54]

Perhaps because of these common goals, the Lee Camp, in 1885, suggested merging Confederate and National Memorial Days throughout Virginia. In Richmond this should not have met with much resistance, considering that the GAR had selected May 30, the day traditionally celebrated by the HMA, to honor the fallen soldiers from both sides. The OMA, for example, agreed to celebrate both May 10 (their traditional day) and May 30, after receiving a letter from the Lee Camp. The Petersburg LMA also agreed to the change, even though the women "regret[ted] giving up the day [June 9] so sacred to us." But the joint May 30 celebrations elicited little participation. "None of the military companies were present as had been promised and the number of persons present was by far smaller than in former years," the OMA reported. The change for the Ladies "proved to be a failure," and they returned their celebrations to the "original day" the following year. The OMA women had refused to omit their day altogether, but by 1887 each of Richmond's memorial and veteran associations, both Union and Confederate, had agreed to decorate the graves of all soldiers on May 30. The Petersburg LMA gave the joint Memorial Day one more year before returning to the June 9th celebration in 1889. Winchester, Lynchburg, and Fredericksburg, however, continued to ignore the veterans' plea altogether, opting to recognize only the Confederate dead on their individual days. Although women of the LMAs did not appear to resist the celebration of National Memorial Day, they adamantly refused to give up their own memorial celebrations and the independence those days provided.[55]

But this road to reconciliation was not nearly as effortless and natural as some historians have suggested—especially when it came to the women.[56] Former Confederate women were often more hesitant to embrace reconciliation than their male counterparts, sometimes resisting it altogether. In Winchester, it was the women who continued to vent antagonism against the "Yankees." A large delegation of Federal veterans who had participated in Sheridan's 1864 Valley Campaign and their families gathered in the city's Federal cemetery, only yards away from the Confederate burial ground, to dedicate several monuments to the fallen comrades in the late summer of 1883. The veterans had been given a warm and public welcome by much of the community, including the Friendship Band, the Sarah Zane Band, the mayor, and the city council. But, according to one local historian, not all the town's citizens were so accepting of the reunion. The Union veterans, it seems, generated "considerable opposition," especially among the "female element."[57]

Many LMA women became embittered with the emphasis placed on National Memorial Day—a day many white southerners referred to as a "Negro holiday."[58] But what irritated southern white women most was the apparent decline in popularity of Confederate commemorations. In 1885, a member of the Oakwood association wrote to the *Richmond Dispatch* denouncing the lack of enthusiasm for Confederate Memorial Days. "On national memorial-day the national cemeteries East, West, North, and South will be alive with flowers. . . . Why can our people not do as much for the brave boys who fell in a cause none the less just because it was impracticable?" she asked. "It cannot harm the living or promote disloyal sentiment to show this much respect to the honored dead," she concluded. Evidence from the years surrounding the member's complaint suggests that Confederate Memorial Days were in fact not experiencing a decline in participation. Rather, it appears that the Ladies were reacting to the growing popularity of the Federal memorial celebration. Debates concerning Confederate and Union symbols also plagued the groups. For instance, in 1889, an intense discussion ensued within the HMA when Lucy Webb suggested decorating the speaker's stand with two small U.S. flags. It remains unclear whether the women decided to use the flags, but the dispute indicates how tenuous reconciliationist spirit remained.[59]

In other instances, the women proved to be even more embittered toward the North. Although Jefferson Davis had not been well liked in many Confederate circles during the war, his subsequent imprisonment and support for the Lost Cause had made him immensely popular. Davis died in December 1889 while visiting New Orleans, and calls for a memorial to the former president rang out immediately in the South. But northerners did not share white southerners' fondness for Davis. Citizens of Albany, New York, had condemned white southerners in 1886 for applauding Davis, denouncing the South "as untrue to the Union." Perhaps it was this animosity that engendered a defensive posture among certain LMA women when it came to the ex-president. In the spring of 1893, OMA member Ella Smith moved that a vote of thanks be tendered an HMA member "for her prompt refusal to accept any amount offered by Northern Capitalists for the Jeff Davis Monument." Only donations from southerners were to be accepted for such a project.[60]

Even more telling was the failure of southern white women to clasp hands over the bloody chasm, as it was called among veterans, when it came to northern women's organizations. While the Confederate Veterans and GAR managed to overlook their wartime differences through Blue-Gray reunions, the LMAs never replicated this relationship with their northern counterparts, the Women's Relief Corps. This might seem to be a product of the militaristic nature of veterans' reunions. But what makes this lack of Blue-Gray women's affiliation significant is that northern and southern white women were uniting through other nonsectional benevolent and reform societies, including the Women's Christian Temperance Union, the Young Women's Christian Association, and the General Federation of Women's Clubs, to name but three.[61]

Although Union and Confederate women could have united to celebrate Memorial Days and aid needy veterans, the primary goals of the LMAs simply did not mesh with those of their northern sisters. Union and Confederate veterans might find common ground in their battlefield heroics, but women of both sides continued to show their devotion to their separate causes primarily by honoring their own dead. As historian John Neff has argued, honoring the Civil War dead proved an obstacle to national reunion rather than a solution to regional divisions. Although many women North and South could certainly agree that alcohol was poisonous to society, the war remained another issue entirely. On Memorial Days, northerners and southerners took to the cemeteries to "interpret their dead, their separate causes, and their separate nationalisms," thus heightening a sense of sectional animosity. Ironically, focusing on the dead allowed the living to keep the flames of sectionalism alive and burning. How, then, could southern white women actively pursue their primary mission of honoring the Confederate past and instilling a "southern" sense of pride in their youth if they joined forces with northern women?[62]

Through their antipathy toward National Memorial Day and northern donors and their failure to create cross-regional bonds with northern women over the memory of the war, southern white women expressed their aversion to the increasing Blue-Gray amity. Perhaps this helps explain why so few joined the ranks of the Lee Camp Auxiliary. Regardless, their behavior indicates that reunion was not as quick or smooth as many historians have suggested.[63] Veterans could perhaps meet again on the battlefield and celebrate one another's bravery, courage, and other masculine qualities, but former Confederate women clung to their devotion on the home front, loyalty to their men, and abhorrence of Yankees as emblems of their part in the war. For them, this was the war. The emotions and activities they had experienced throughout the war hardly ended in 1865 or 1877. Their war continued. Without the fraternal bonds of soldiering, women felt compelled to emphasize their allegiance to the Confederate cause as their distinct contribution to the war effort.

There were two other reasons that southern white women remained on the periphery of reconciliationist sentiment. The first was tied to the notion that had fueled the LMAS' work since the beginning: women simply were not viewed by men as political beings. If southern white women had not been a threat to sectional reunion in the 1860s when they encouraged rituals to perpetuate the memory of the Confederacy, then why should men, North or South, think any differently of women's position in the 1890s? An increasing number of women were demanding the vote through the National Woman's Suffrage Association, but they had yet to achieve their goals of electoral participation and political recognition by mainstream America. Reconciliation would occur on the political landscape of legislative halls and former battlefields, but not in the spaces occupied by women. Even as southern white men might celebrate the sacrifices and devotion of "their ladies," reunion remained a political prerogative of white men. Whether or not southern white women supported reunion simply did not matter to most American men, North or South.

The second motivation for southern white women to resist reconciliation reflected the origins of the Ladies. Because women were not thought of as political, they *could* continue to espouse Confederate rhetoric and sympathy even as their male counterparts could not. White southern men and women had recognized this in the 1860s and continued to do so three decades later. Celebrating Confederate Memorial Day (as a day independent of National Memorial Day) and restoring the White House of the Confederacy would allow former Confederates and their descendants to hold on to a separate "southern" identity that had been forged through secession, war, and, ultimately, the Lost Cause. Defining the past became a powerful weapon for ex-Confederates to define who was—and by extension who was not—a "legitimate" southerner. Through their memorial activities, interpretations of the past, and other public celebrations of the Confederacy, LMAs encouraged their communities to demonstrate pride in their southern heritage (meaning "white") in an effort to quell the political, social, and cultural changes unleashed by the war, emancipation, and industrializing society around them. Moreover, retaining a separate southern identity implied that northern (that is, federal) intervention in southern race relations was not necessary. By allowing the Ladies to emphasize a heroic past of the Confederacy free from the issue of slavery, white southerners were able to white-out black interpretations of the past and also to exclude African Americans from public spaces and positions of power—without the interference of outsiders to the region. In short, gender excluded women from the national dialogue on reunion just as it continued to provide white southerners a source of power over regional politics and race relations.[64]

Of all the work undertaken by LMAs in the last two decades of the century, none was more explicit in its emphasis on future generations than that of the Hollywood association. This goal manifested itself in the HMA's two primary objectives between 1890 and 1894, the establishment of "junior" associations to encourage Confederate sympathy among the South's youth and the preservation of the White House of the Confederacy. W. Fitzhugh Brundage points out that in the late nineteenth century "white women acquired expertise and influence through what is now called public history" by expanding the concept of volunteerism to include matters of history. He documents an "explosion" of white women's organizations in the mid-1890s, including the Association for the Preservation of Virginia Antiquities, Daughters of the American Revolution, Colonial Dames, Daughters of the Pilgrims, Daughters of the War of 1812, Order of the First Families of Virginia, and, eventually, the United Daughters of the Confederacy. By "preserving" the past and teaching the "true history" of the South, white women sought to counter the negative and condescending stereotypes of the region and instill regional pride in coming generations.[65]

Like women, children had played important symbolic roles in Memorial Day celebrations and veterans' events since the 1860s. But in the early 1890s, several associations had spearheaded the establishment of "junior" associations: Oakwood in 1891, Hollywood the following year, and Winchester a few years later. Within a month of formation, the HMA celebrated the popularity of their endeavor, claiming that more than 200 youths from the capital city had flocked to their organization. The goals of the junior associations differed little from those of the adults; they were to aid in the caring of graves, participate in Memorial Days, assist in the collection and preservation of memorials to the Confederacy, and, as the Winchester Juniors proclaimed, "go forward and try and fill [the LMA seniors'] places." Clearly, the ambition of the senior members of the LMAS was to secure their own legacy as much as that of the Confederate soldiers they honored.[66]

In 1892, the HMA invited all "persons," regardless of class or claims to Confederate heritage or loyalty (a condition for joining the WRC), to join its newly formed junior association. Interestingly, the women did not restrict the membership to youth alone; the constitution and bylaws clearly admitted anyone ten years or older willing to pay the dues. (Originally, married persons were to be excluded, but this condition was soon abandoned.) Although the HMA clearly intended the Juniors to serve as an auxiliary organization filled by any person who wished to further their cause, sons and daughters of the HMA born primarily in the late 1870s (therefore teenagers) made up the group. The HMA Juniors did, however, include one specific membership restriction—only white persons would be allowed.[67]

Although there is no evidence that any African American or mixed-race woman applied for membership with the Juniors, the association may have been reacting to a heated debate within the northern-based WRC. From its establishment in 1883, the national WRC had welcomed black women who had been loyal to the Union into their folds. But during the 1890s, northern white women loyal to the Union cause began moving south, where they launched local WRCs. Fearing they might be ostracized by their neighbors, many demanded a whites-only clause and began efforts to segregate WRC chapters.

"There can never be in our day," one white southern WRC member contended, "a Department of white and colored Corps working harmoniously together." According to historian Cecilia O'Leary, the attitude of northern members revealed an array of opinions: a minority of white and black members who had been abolitionists defended a membership policy of equality; others hoped to build an alliance with southern black women, thus suggesting the paternalism that inspired northern white women to venture south to act as schoolteachers during Reconstruction. Together, these two factions of northern members sought to protect the rights of black women within the organization. They stood by this policy throughout the 1890s, but eventually they gave into de facto segregation, and in 1900 the national convention finally agreed to racially divide the Maryland and Kentucky departments so as not to antagonize the white southern membership. But such questions were not relevant to the majority of LMAS. Even as the southern chapters of the WRC implemented segregationist policies in the waning years of the century, most members of the LMAS simply assumed white supremacy and therefore found little cause to explicitly address the issue.[68]

Like race, gender also became an issue in the Juniors. The HMA had originally considered forming one group for girls and another for boys, but after little debate the women consented to establishing a single association. Nevertheless, a clear gender division existed even within the youth group. At Memorial Day celebrations, the HMA instructed the boys to wear gray caps, as their veteran ancestors had done, and the girls to wear badges. The HMA arranged for a "military man" to instruct the boys in a drilling company and offered to raise funds for equipment and uniforms so that the "HMA cadets" might be an independent organization. Likewise, in 1892 the Sons of Confederate Veterans invited the boys to join in the Memorial Day parade while the girls assisted the Ladies in decorating the cemetery. Although both boys and girls formed committees and served as officers, young women filled the majority of offices and always held the most prestigious position of president. Moreover, it was especially significant that women's groups, not veterans, established youth organizations. The HMA sought to frame its youth organization in the same manner in which they envisioned the Lost Cause as a whole: males directed their attention toward a more martial and fraternal interpretation of war; women honored the patriotism of the fallen soldiers at Memorial Days and dictated the direction of the movement.[69]

Above all, the LMAS' insistence on junior associations demonstrates both their adaptability to the times and their forward-looking nature. They repeatedly extolled the virtues of their "young people," who demonstrated that "the old spirit is not dying out." For these women of the 1890s, most of whom had come of age either during the war or during Reconstruction, teaching their children and grandchildren to honor the Confederacy was more than mere sentimentalism. "When we have passed away," the HMA remarked, "they will still cherish the memorial of the heroes who died for liberty, truth, and duty." In what Karen Cox has called "Confederate motherhood," LMA women looked beyond their traditional realm of Memorial Days and cemeteries when they sought to indoctrinate the future generations with a romanticized and sanitized version of the past. They realized that the next generation did not carry the same emotional and personal ties to the war as those who had lived through it, so it became their burden to modify celebrations of the Confederacy into terms that the current generation could best understand.[70]

The landscape of the South had changed substantially since the senior HMA members' childhoods: emancipation, Union occupation, political and economic conflicts, the first signs of state-sanctioned segregation in the 1880s and 1890s, and the increasingly public role of women.[71] LMA women desperately wanted their children—and all southern white children for that matter—to appreciate what the Confederate soldiers had fought for (namely honor and defense of their homes) and also to comprehend what white southerners had endured since the war. In a world of racial uncertainty, LMA women believed it necessary to promulgate the southern, that is, "white," view of the war—that Confederates had fought to preserve states' rights rather than slavery. If veterans insisted upon celebrating the bravery and honor of soldiers on both sides of the field, the women understood that the perpetuation of their identity as both southerner and American depended on their success at transmitting cultural ideas to the next generation.

Junior associations targeted only a select group of young white southerners. But the Ladies also wanted an outlet that spoke to a broader audience, thus launching the HMA's efforts to save the White House of the Confederacy. In late fall of 1889, the Richmond city council announced its plans to demolish the former White House, also known as the Davis Mansion. The home, built in 1818 and remodeled substantially in the 1850s, had served as the residence of several wealthy Richmonders prior to the war. In 1861, it had been sold to the city for use as the executive mansion of the Confederacy. After the war, the former executive mansion served as the headquarters for Federal commanders overseeing Reconstruction until 1870; subsequently, it served as the Central Public School. During those years, souvenir hunters had scavenged for relics, removing upholstery and drapery trimmings. And, as the

Ladies pointed out, "the constant tread of little feet did almost as much damage." By the late 1880s, the house had fallen into such a degraded state that the city council, though dominated by Confederate veterans, agreed to raze the structure and replace it with a more modern school building.[72]

The HMA's new direction in the late 1880s reflected national patterns of women's activism and Civil War commemoration, but the Davis Mansion project was in large part due to the leadership of president Belle Bryan. One of the most vocal opponents of demolition was Joseph Bryan, Bryan's husband and editor of the *Richmond Times*. With her husband's endorsement, Belle Bryan proposed that the HMA undertake the project of rescuing the Davis Mansion and converting it into a regional Confederate museum so that all future generations might know "the true history of the war and the principles for which these soldiers laid down their lives." In mid-March 1890, she used her position as HMA president to elicit support from the OMA, the Hebrew Memorial Association, and all the veterans' organizations of the city. With this united support, the HMA petitioned the city council for a deed to the mansion, to be used as a "Memorial Hall and Museum of Confederate relics."[73]

Mayor James Taylor Ellyson, Confederate veteran and husband of HMA member Lora H. Ellyson, readily endorsed the plan. But an unforeseen technicality discovered by a city attorney revealed that the council could not deed the building to a memorial association. Bryan, ever the deft leader, found a loophole in the law. She met with representatives from the HMA, the Virginia Historical Society, and the Southern Historical Society to discuss the possibility of creating a "Southern Memorial Literary Society" that would "conform to the city charter" and allow for the transfer of property to an association dedicated to educational or literary pursuits. HMA members thus agreed to create an auxiliary society, to be called the Confederate Memorial Literary Society (CMLS), and on May 31, 1890, they signed the charter. On January 5, 1891, the city council formally voted to transfer the deed of the property to the HMA as soon as another schoolhouse could be provided.[74]

Unlike the LLMC, which had technically been an arm of the HMA, the CMLS was, in theory, a separate and independent association. The HMA would continue to organize Memorial Day and maintain the soldiers' section of Hollywood Cemetery; the CMLS would deal exclusively with the Davis Mansion. The actual organization and operation of the two associations, however, remained unclear and complicated. Initially, the groups shared both a membership base and leadership—the CMLS electing to appoint the same officers as the HMA, with an addition of a board of directors. But within the CMLS's first year, debates arose regarding fund-raising. "This led to an animated dis-

OFFICERS OF THE CONFEDERATE MEMORIAL LITERARY SOCIETY.

Officers of the Confederate Memorial Literary Society, 1896. (Courtesy Museum of the Confederacy, Richmond, Virginia, copy photography by Katherine Wetzel)

cussion as to whether the HMA and CMLS should be kept two separate organizations with different issues and management," the secretary reported. The question remained unresolved after a vote to table it for future discussion, and thus the two groups continued to operate jointly. By 1892, Bryan insisted that it would be "wiser to have separate officers for the [CMLS] in addition to its Board of Directors." Not surprisingly, Bryan remained president of both groups. Moreover, the CMLS agreed that in order to prevent a "loss of interest" in the HMA, only HMA members would be eligible to join the more popular CMLS.[75]

The CMLS believed that its most important function was to preserve the Confederate legacy for future generations. "The glory, the hardships, the heroism of the war are a noble heritage for our children," they declared. The museum, therefore, would be "a greater monument than the entire wealth of the North or of England could produce." In order to "keep green such memories, and to commemorate such virtues," it was imperative to acquire and preserve both the executive mansion and "sacred relics of those glorious days." The museum would serve as a living monument to the Confederacy. Marble figures that watched over cemeteries and city squares might stand as silent reminders of the lives lost in battle, but a museum, and more precisely relics, encouraged visitors to reconstruct the meaning of the past from objects. Cemeteries and monuments offered symbols of courage and heroism, but artifacts provided more tangible means of remembering (for some) or imagining (for others) the Confederate cause. For many white southerners, these relics served as physical manifestations of the cause. Items such as a last ration of coffee or tattered uniforms testified to the hardships of war, while officers' accoutrements heralded the virtues of Confederate leaders. Other objects, like samples of homemade cloth, a flag of the 18th Virginia Regiment sewn by women, or a silk flag made from Mrs. A. P. Hill's bridal gown given to the 13th Virginia Regiment, reinforced the integral role women played on the home front and in support of the battlefield.[76]

Indeed, it was significant that the Ladies wished to establish their museum in the former White House of the Confederacy. Even though Reconstruction had long ended and calls of treason had abated years before, the CMLS women chose to house their collections in the very halls where the Confederate government had operated. They elected to showcase their relics in rooms where councils of war had been held, policies discussed, and campaigns mapped. They sought to preserve what Governor Charles O'Ferrall called the home of "the Chief Magistrate of the new American republic, founded upon the eternal principles of right and justice." This was not the mere sentimentalism that had been attributed to cemeteries and Memorial Day services. These women were consciously extolling the virtues, and in their words, "constitutional liberty," of the Confederate nation.[77]

As with Memorial Days and Confederate cemeteries, the CMLS members never intended the museum to be merely a local attraction. Rather, they believed that all white southerners would find motivation, inspiration, and patriotism by participating in the organization of their museum, and they therefore solicited items from the entire region in yet another circular. They used the traditional method of sending the appeal to prominent newspapers throughout the former Confederacy, but, just as soldiers' aid societies and the earliest LMAs had done, they also relied on the extensive social networks of their elite members. Mary Maury Werth, for example, distributed every one of the 200 circulars allotted to her while vacationing at White Sulphur Springs, West Virginia. "I could have given away 500 through my friends," she reported to the HMA.

Even before the CMLS had gained title to the Davis Mansion, individuals from throughout the South had begun to send relics. Following the death of Joseph E. Johnston, his nephew, George Ben Johnston, sent a sword, battle flag, and saddle the general had used in the Mexican War. Other items included the key to Davis's prison cell at Fort Monroe, a soldier's pocket Bible, two table-spoons of coffee ration from Company E of the 4th Virginia Regiment, and items from the Confederate commerce raider *Shenandoah*. More "curious" donations included a brooch carved from the hoof of Turner Ashby's horse and a bit from Robert E. Lee's horse Traveller. A substantial museum collection was beginning to develop.[78]

But the museum was not to simply consist of random rooms filled with relics. Rather, Belle Bryan envisioned an organizational structure that reflected the regional identity of the entire South. The CMLS leadership included the traditional officers found among most LMAS (president, vice presidents, recording secretary, corresponding secretary, and treasurer), but the association also appointed regents and vice regents to represent each state that had supported the Confederacy. According to historians Coski and Feely, these women were "appointed primarily to win prestige and influence for the museum throughout the South" and included many of the region's most prominent women. Varina and Winnie Davis, widow and daughter of Jefferson Davis, served as regents, as did the daughters of Robert E. Lee and Wade Hampton. The vice regents, however, were to be selected from those Richmond women who had contributed significantly to the 1893 bazaar—a reward of sorts for dedication to the cause. Their primary duties consisted of serving as liaisons to the room's regent and overseeing the collections within their respective state rooms.[79]

This combination of regents and vice regents ensured the CMLS center stage and control over the most well-known Confederate museum project. Other cities had initiated their own Confederate museums, such as New Orleans's Confederate Memorial Hall, dedicated in 1891. But, unlike the CMLS, the New Orleans project had been under the direction of Louisiana veterans (not women), and most of its relics came from those groups. The Richmond women, however, were determined not to be merely a local institution and worked diligently at making it the "paramount Confederate museum." Through its system of state rooms and regents and its regionwide relic collection, the CMLS became the central executive agency for a southern, not merely Richmond or Virginian, museum. Much in the way that LMAS had served as bureaucratic agencies when they organized cemeteries in the days following the war, the CMLS anointed itself as the chief association to deal with the Confederate relics and employ contacts (that is, regents) throughout the South to legitimate its claim.[80]

Before the CMLS could place its wealth of Confederate treasures in the museum, major renovations would be necessary to repair nearly thirty years of neglect. One of the most important of these restoration projects was fire-proofing. To raise the funds for this undertaking, the CMLS chose to sponsor a bazaar the following spring. The women expected the 1893 bazaar to be no less grand than the one in 1867, but there would be two important differences. First, the bazaar, like the museum, would be organized by state. Each of the thirteen states that had contributed to the Confederate war effort would be represented by a table bearing its name, shield, and colors and containing souvenirs unique to that state. For example, North Carolina would have tobacco products for sale; Florida would offer flowers, fruits, soaps, and perfumes. The Lady, or "chair," in charge of each table was to be native-born or a descendant of that state (or, at the very least, allied by marriage). Every "man, woman, and child" in the South was asked to donate items for sale, including "articles, money, Confederate relics, etc."[81]

Second, although the 1867 bazaar had been strictly under the authority of the HMA, the CMLS wanted the 1893 affair to represent a collective southern effort. As recent Memorial Days had demonstrated, LMAs and veterans' associations had begun to work together to increase the popularity of their causes. Therefore, the women asked every Richmond Confederate organization to participate, including the OMA, the Hebrew Memorial Association, the Ladies' Auxiliary of the Lee Camp, the city's veterans' associations, and the Soldiers' and Sailors' Monumental Association. And, of course, the women's associations elected themselves officers of the Memorial Bazaar Committee.[82]

Given the spirit of cooperation that had existed between male and female groups for several years, it was surprising when a dispute arose between the 1st Virginia Volunteers and the CMLS. Apparently, the women had asked to use the Volunteers' headquarters for the bazaar. Although the commanding officer had granted the CMLS permission to use the space, the grounds and building committees had denied the women access in early February 1893. These committees had voted no in "regard for the discipline, efficiency, and rights of the Regiment," deciding that it was "injurious to the discipline and efficiency of the Regiment to be turn[ed] out of the armory for any period." The committees contended that giving up the armory for "fairs and bazaars" for such a length of time (one month) was "a bad precedent." But the prestige and political clout of the CMLS ultimately prevailed. These women clearly carried more influence than the regiment did within both Richmond and the region, and the commander wished not to alienate them or their prominent husbands. He subsequently insisted that the regiment did not lack sympathy with the goals of the bazaar, nor did it lack "a proper chivalrous respect for the ladies who have generously and patriotically undertaken it." Indeed, the men would be happy to oblige. "We assure the ladies of our respect, admiration, and support . . . and we withdraw all opposition," he reported.[83]

Ultimately, the bazaar proved to be a great success, free from any conflict or controversy. The CMLS raised more than $30,000, which was split evenly between the museum project and the Soldiers' and Sailors' Monument. The following year proved to be a busy one for Confederate memorialists in the city. In May, the Soldiers' and Sailors' Monument was dedicated not far from Oakwood Cemetery with as much pomp as had accompanied the Lee monument dedication four years earlier. Several days later, on June 3, 1894, the eighty-sixth anniversary of Jefferson Davis's birth, the city of Richmond formally transferred the Davis Mansion to the CMLS. The women of the HMA could thus claim responsibility for, or at least extensive involvement in, the capital city's four most recognized and popular symbols of the Confederacy: the pyramid in Hollywood Cemetery, the Lee monument, the Soldiers' and Sailors' Monument, and the White House of the Confederacy. Their mark on the landscape of the city was undeniable.[84]

Even if they did not call for sectional reunion with the same zeal as veterans, by the mid-1890s Virginia's LMAs could count themselves among the oldest and most successful Confederate memorial organizations in the region. They had endured the postwar changes of Reconstruction, Redemption, and the beginnings of Jim Crow. Not only had they endured—they had managed to adapt to the changing political and social circumstances while maintaining their position as the inventors of Confederate traditions. Groups such as the HMA had learned a valuable lesson from the LLMC: In order to sustain enthusiasm for the memorial association they must remain independent. But simultaneously they had found ways to cooperate (again) with men. Most important, they had discovered means by which to inspire and inform the next generation about the Confederate past. The LMAs in Virginia and throughout the South had remained independent organizations since their inception. But the long-standing ties among the groups would prove invaluable in the coming decade as the Ladies struggled to retain their position in the Lost Cause in the face of a challenge from another group of Confederate women.

Lest We Forget

6

United Daughters and
Confederated Ladies,
1894–1915

In 1894, a new Confederate women's organization, the United Daughters of the Confederacy (UDC or Daughters), entered the memorial scene. The birth and overwhelming success of the Daughters in many ways served as a testament to the triumph of the Ladies' Memorial Associations (LMAS). Their decades-long work had provided the conditions and opportunity for the UDC to take up the banner of Confederate patriotism, and initially memorial women rejoiced that their efforts to instill reverence for the Lost Cause had succeeded so well. But it soon became clear that the Daughters intended to take over both the Ladies' objectives and associations. As if challenges from the Daughters were not enough, Richmond's Confederate Memorial Literary Society (CMLS), yet again, had to contend with the attempts of veterans to dictate the direction of the Lost Cause during debates over the Battle Abbey.

Throughout the 1890s and into the twentieth century, women of the LMAS refused to surrender their pivotal role in Confederate traditions. They reinvigorated their organizations through new projects, such as Petersburg's Blandford Church and Richmond's Confederate Museum, and united their disparate efforts under the Confederated Southern Memorial Association. The Ladies were not "elbowed aside" by the veterans. They did not immediately give way to the Daughters in the 1890s. Neither did LMAS cease to exist. Instead, they held fast, determined not to yield their influence over Lost Cause commemorations. They continued to sponsor Memorial Days, tend Confederate graves, erect memorials to the Cause, and tell their story of the Confederate past to younger generations. By the fiftieth anniversary of Appomattox in 1915, however, the Ladies' numbers and influence had been greatly reduced as the immensely popular Daughters took center stage. Although the LMAS had been responsible for setting in motion many of the Lost Cause traditions, they became increasingly invisible as the more modern organizational techniques of the Daughters continued to generate appeal in the new century.[1]

On September 10, 1894, a group of women gathered in Nashville, Tennessee, for the purpose of organizing a "federation of all Southern Women's Auxiliary, Memorial, and Soldiers' Aid Societies," with the authority to charter chapters and divisions in all parts of the United States. The Daughters, as they called themselves, listed five primary objectives for their new organization: memorial, historical, benevolent, educational, and social. But they directed most of their efforts toward raising funds for Confederate monuments, sponsoring Memorial Day parades and activities, and maintaining Confederate museums and relic collections—all duties that the LMAs already performed.[2]

The UDC's national leadership recognized that it was not pathbreaking in its objectives and wanted to respect the women of the LMAs. Eliza Nutt Parsley, a member of the national constitution committee from Wilmington, North Carolina, warned that "we will probably meet with some opposition on the part of the older ladies from a sentiment in regard to the original organization." Writing to UDC cofounder Anna Raines in 1894, Parsley commented that the Daughters should respect the LMAs because they had been the first to organize and erect monuments and had initiated memorial celebrations to the Confederate cause while the South "was under martial law" and "carpetbag rule." Parsley's efforts to charter a UDC chapter included plans "to retain the Memorial Association." UDC historian Mildred Rutherford likewise suggested that the relationship between the LMAs and the UDC "should be that of 'mothers' and 'daughters,' for without the memorial associations, there would be no Daughters."[3] In short, the UDC recognized that the Ladies had paved the way for this next generation of southern white women to achieve their own lofty goals.[4]

The UDC grew rapidly in membership and influence; during its first year alone, 20 chapters were chartered, and within six years that number had swelled to 412 chapters and nearly 17,000 members. By 1900, it could claim more than 20,000 members. Like those in other states, Virginia's UDC chapters grew rapidly. Lynchburg's Old Dominion chapter, for example, began with 15 members in the summer of 1896 but had increased its ranks to 65 within three months. Fredericksburg's UDC eventually claimed more than 200 names on its roll, and the Richmond chapter counted more than 500 members within six years of organizing.[5] By 1897, UDC chapters had been established in Lynchburg, Fredericksburg, Richmond, Petersburg, and Winchester—with Lynchburg serving as the home base for two chapters. Three years later, the number of UDC chapters in Virginia alone reached 57, representing more than 3,200 women.[6]

The LMAs helped ensure the early success of the Daughters by providing a natural constituency.[7] Kate Mason Rowland, corresponding secretary for the UDC in 1896 and 1897, frequently contacted prominent women throughout the South, especially LMA members, urging their cooperation in establishing Daughters chapters. The UDC recognized not only that members of the memorial associations brought years of experience in Confederate memorialization, but also that their status within their respective communities lent weight and prestige to the newly formed UDC chapters. Most of Virginia's LMA women retained their membership in the Ladies but also heeded the Daughters' call to initiate or join their local chapters. Almost every member of the Winchester LMA (which had changed its name to the Stonewall Memorial Association) joined the UDC, including Nannie Boyd, Mary Clayton Kurtz, and Lucy Fitzhugh Kurtz. Other Virginia memorial women followed their example, including Ruth Early and Mollie Early (Lynchburg); Nannie Seddon Barney, Virginia Knox, and Betty Churchill Lacy (Fredericksburg); Bessie Callender, Ida Baxter, and Lucy McIlwaine (Petersburg); May Baughman, Isabel Maury, and Janet Randolph (Hollywood).[8]

But even allowing for the overlap in LMA/UDC membership does not explain why women flocked to the Daughters in such unprecedented numbers while the Ladies had struggled to retain members for several decades. Karen Cox, in the most thorough history of the Daughters, argues that women were attracted to the UDC for two primary reasons: social status and their desire to vindicate the Confederate generation. She contends that most of the women joined "out of a real sense of duty and obligation to honor the Confederate generation and to instill the values of those men and women among future generations of white southerners."[9] But women of the memorial associations had been motivated by these same desires for more than three decades. Perhaps something more concrete, more practical, spurred interest in the Daughters.

The Daughters may have gained such widespread popularity because they appeared to be a more youthful association. Most of the LMA women had been born between 1830 and 1850 (thus experiencing the war as adults). But, according to Cox's research, most of the women who joined the Daughters between 1894 and 1919 were born after 1850—and like the second generation of LMA women, their lives had been largely shaped by their experiences as children or young adults during Reconstruction. Even though a fair number

of this generation joined the LMAS, many young southern white women may
have thought of the Ladies as older associations filled with aging women that
simply did not correspond with their images of themselves as youthful and
modern.[10]

More important than the actual age of the members was the perception
that the Daughters had a more contemporary and broader social purpose than
the LMAS, who, in some peoples' eyes, merely cared for Confederate graves.
According to the UDC's founding documents, it sought "to fulfill the duties of
sacred charity to the survivors of the war and those dependent upon them . . .
to perpetuate the memory of our Confederate heroes and the glorious cause
for which they fought" and "to endeavor to have used in all Southern schools
only such histories as are just and true." As UDC historian Mildred Rutherford
once remarked, "The memorial women honor the memory of the dead—the
Daughters honor the living." But as evidence from the Hollywood Memorial
Association (HMA) and other memorial associations makes abundantly clear,
Virginia's LMAS, at least, were not merely interested in looking to the past;
they, too, sought to disseminate Confederate memory to future generations
and, in some cases, provide aid to needy veterans and their families. In fact,
they had been pursuing such goals years before the UDC had been organized
(and before many of the members had even been born).[11]

Despite the reality of the situation, many southern white women in the
1890s wanted to join a vibrant and active female association because doing so
provided a popular social outlet for middle-class women. Women's associations had been growing for several decades, but the last decade of the century
witnessed a surge in the sheer number of organizations and the coalescing of
these associations into national unions. Beginning in the North and Midwest
but quickly spreading throughout the nation, in the 1880s groups of women
had begun to organize societies devoted to literature, art, scientific culture, and
general self-improvement. In 1890, representatives from sixty-one women's
groups met in New York City to coordinate their activities, agreeing to form
the General Federation of Women's Clubs. Four years later, the same year the
Daughters initiated their association, fourteen of Richmond's most active and
educated women gathered in the West Franklin Street home of Jane Crawford
Looney Lewis to organize the Woman's Club of Richmond.[12]

Women looked around them and saw their sisters, mothers, neighbors, and
church acquaintances flocking to join their local woman's clubs or national associations such as the Daughters of the American Revolution, Women's Christian Temperance Union, Colonial Dames, and a host of other benevolent and
literary societies and simply wanted to be part of that larger community of

club women.[13] In fact, most of Virginia's UDC chapters formed in towns or cities where no LMA existed, suggesting that many Daughters' primary motivation to join was based on the desire to affiliate with other women who felt passionate about a common issue.[14] By joining the Daughters, women expanded their communities to include not just like-minded women from their own neighborhoods, cities, and state but also those from across the region and nation.

At the same time that the women's club movement was gaining national popularity, the South was immersed in a new round of racial conflict. White southerners had mobilized efforts to roll back the tide of Republican-sponsored civil rights legislation before Reconstruction ever came to a close, largely through secret societies like the Ku Klux Klan. But by the late 1880s, a new generation of white southerners, those who had come of age after emancipation, took up the banner of white supremacy in an effort to remove black officeholders, disenfranchise African American men, forestall black economic advancement, and institute state-sanctioned segregation. In 1890, Mississippi became the first state to disenfranchise African Americans by a constitutional convention. Five years later, Louisiana and South Carolina were preparing to follow Mississippi's lead—it seemed that every southern state was likely to follow suit. Equally as significant was segregation. Much of the South had already been segregated by race since emancipation through a combination of social practice and laws. This, however, was not enough for many white southerners. Increasingly, they called for all railroads to be segregated by race, and, by 1895, every state of the former Confederacy except Virginia and North Carolina required that passenger cars be segregated.[15] Where disenfranchisement and segregation efforts proved inadequate measures to keep southern blacks in their subservient position, white southerners turned to the extra-legal method of lynching.[16]

In this atmosphere, middle- and upper-class southern white women involved themselves in contemporary political and social issues of their day by celebrating their Confederate (that is, white) heritage. As the self-appointed guardians of southern and Confederate history, many white women born during or after Reconstruction used the Daughters to commemorate the traditional privileges of race, gender, and class by casting them as "natural" parts of the region's history. Just as the Ladies had provided a platform for ex-Confederates to condemn federal policies at Memorial Day celebrations during Reconstruction, in the 1890s members of the Daughters looked to the region's past as a means to shape race and gender relations in the New South. UDC historian Mildred Rutherford, for one, firmly believed that African Americans needed to behave as faithful "servants" if the New South was ever to approximate the Old (and supposedly racially harmonious) South the Daughters sought to venerate. As historian Fitzhugh Brundage has argued, members of the Daughters offered solutions grounded in the region's past by "extolling the memory of slavery as a golden age of race relations when love and 'familial' duty bound the races together."[17]

The Daughters promoted this sanitized image of slavery through published accounts recalling devoted family slaves and through several efforts to erect a national monument to so-called faithful slaves, but their most visible (and perhaps most successful) efforts were campaigns targeting the South's white children.[18] During the 1890s, numerous women's organizations, including the Daughters of the American Revolution, the Women's Relief Corps (WRC), the UDC, and LMAs, embarked on a crusade to win over the hearts and minds of the next generation. The Ladies were busy restoring the White House of the Confederacy while the Daughters of the American Revolution had dedicated itself to the memory of the Revolution through monument building and an emphasis on patriotism. The WRC, likewise, took up the banner of patriotic campaigns aimed at children. The organization supported efforts to have the American flag flown over every school, petitioned the federal and state governments for laws prohibiting desecration of the flag, and encouraged a daily pledge of allegiance in schools.[19]

All of these efforts were benign enough in the Daughters' eyes, but the WRC exceeded acceptable limits when together with the Grand Army of the Republic (GAR) it began agitating for the "proper" history of the Civil War to be taught in the nation's public schools. Fearing that schoolchildren might not be taught the "true history" of slavery and the Civil War, Daughters chapters closely monitored and censored textbooks (frequently published by northern presses) used in the region's burgeoning public school system. The UDC insisted that any texts used must conform to the tenets of the Lost Cause: secession was provoked by a constitutional dispute; Confederate soldiers fought admirably and honorably against insurmountable odds; and the South fought for self-government, not slavery. This last principle became a focal point for the Daughters and like-minded white southerners.

Susan Pendleton Lee, daughter of a Confederate general, wife of Robert E. Lee's second cousin, and native Virginian, offered one of the most popular texts among the Daughters. In *A School History of the United States*, Lee argued that southern people knew that "the evils connected with [slavery] were less than those of any other system of labor. Hundreds of thousands of African savages had been Christianized under its influence—The kindest relations existed between the slaves and their owners. . . . [The slaves] were better off than any other menial class in the world." Finally, should anyone doubt the text's position on contemporary race relations, she declared that the Ku Klux Klan had been necessary "for self-protection against . . . outrages committed by misguided negroes." By 1904, Mrs. W. C. H. Merchant could triumphantly claim that "owing to the efforts and influence of the United Daughters" schools in every southern state had adopted books such as Lee's that supported the Lost Cause.[20]

Overwhelmingly, the Daughters' strident efforts to shore up white supremacy by focusing on the Confederate past, whether through textbooks or otherwise, seemed to have been avoided by the Ladies. Even though the LMAs were clearly for whites only and had espoused the "faithful slave" myth since 1866, they appear to have avoided commentary on the New South's so-called Negro problem in the 1880s and 1890s.[21] In fact, the only documented instance of the Virginia Ladies commenting on race appears as a matter-of-fact statement in the HMA Junior association's records declaring that the association was limited to whites only. Perhaps as members of the generation coming of age in the 1890s, the Juniors felt compelled to follow the legal and social precedents of their fellow segregationists. It does not seem like coincidence that the Juniors reiterated their position that "all white persons, over 10 years of age, shall be eligible for membership" when revising their constitution in 1897—just a year after the U.S. Supreme Court's support of state-sanctioned segregation in *Plessy v. Ferguson*.[22]

The fact that the Daughters were much more explicit in their defense of states' rights and white supremacy than their predecessors may have eliminated the need for LMAs to do so. Moreover, numerous women were members of both organizations, perhaps allowing them to satisfy their need for vocal white supremacy by aligning with the Daughters. This is not to suggest that the Ladies were opposed to the sentiments held by the Daughters, merely that LMAs did not see activism on the part of white supremacy as part of their mission. Nevertheless, living in an era of mounting racial tension and violence, many southern white women might simply have felt more inclined to join the UDC than the Ladies.

Emphasis on class may also help explain the overwhelming number of Daughters as compared to Ladies. In short, class served to restrict the membership pool of the Ladies much more than that of the Daughters. According to Cox, UDC members were of the social elite, married to merchants, lawyers, judges, and members of state legislatures. But Cox only examines the UDC leadership, arguing that they were representative of the vast majority of members. Even without a statistical survey of every UDC chapter, the sheer number of members suggests that they could not have all been from elite families. In fact, historian Grace Hale argues that middle-class white southerners dominated the UDC around the turn of the century. Evidence from Virginia supports this claim, confirming that although the UDC leadership of the state may have reflected an elite bias, most of the rank-and-file members were not of the same social background as most LMA members.[23]

Ironically, it was the Daughters rather than the LMAs who were more rigid in their eligibility requirements and who consciously constructed an image of themselves as elite women. With the exception of the Fredericksburg LMA, memorial associations only required that individuals pay monthly or annual dues to claim membership. The UDC reflected a broader trend toward hereditary groups that emerged in 1890 with the Daughters of the American Revolution, in which members had to prove the family lineage that connected them with the Revolution. As historian Cecilia O'Leary has pointed out, hereditary membership allowed groups like the Daughters of the American Revolution to thwart the fluidity of social boundaries at the turn of the century; by relying on an objective membership standard, such groups could dismiss charges of exclusivity while maintaining their middle- and upper-class bias.[24]

The UDC followed suit, believing that the organization could command respect by excluding not only lower-class "undesirables" but also another unwelcome group of potential members: northern women who had married southern men after the war. The WRC had welcomed all women loyal to the Union cause, including those southern women who had married Confederate soldiers, as long as the "lady had remained loyal, notwithstanding the influence of her husband." But the Daughters were much more intent on retaining their regional identity, regardless of declarations of devotion to the Confederate cause. Membership in the UDC was therefore reserved for women who could prove to be the descendants of male or female Confederate ancestors (the Daughters claimed that Confederate women shared in the same "dangers, sufferings, and privations" as their male counterparts). Moreover, many chapters reserved the right to refuse any potential member who was "not personally acceptable to the chapter." As cofounder Anna Raines noted, voluntary associations were not "compelled to receive as a member one who is morally or otherwise objectionable." Despite these seemingly restrictive measures, women flocked to join the ranks of this memorial army.[25]

Many of the earliest UDC members were also leaders within the memorial associations, thereby providing a natural alliance between the organizations. Janet Henderson Weaver Randolph, for example, proved to be an invaluable member of both the HMA (as well as the CMLS) and the Richmond UDC. Described by one writer as the "best-known and most-loved woman in the South" shortly before her death in 1927, Randolph devoted much of her adult life to memorializing the Confederacy. Born in 1848 at the family estate of "Cleiland" near Warrenton, Virginia, she was the eldest child of Richard Arrel Weaver and Janet Cleiland Horner. She spent the war years in Warrenton, which was frequently behind Federal lines. With her mother, sister Margaret, and the family slaves, she claimed to have helped nurse sick and wounded soldiers from both the Confederate and Union armies. She later maintained that her dedication to memorial work began during the war, as she and other women of Warrenton placed makeshift wooden markers on the graves of Confederate soldiers buried there after the battle of Second Manassas. Her wartime experiences and the Confederate defeat forever altered her life and determined the causes she would pursue. In July 1865, she wrote to a friend: "That at last we should submit to the hated Yankees, the very thought makes my blood run cold. But it cannot be that their lives have been given up for nothing, and a day of reckoning must come although it may be far distant."[26]

In 1880, the woman once dubbed "Mrs. Normous Randolph" by a school-child because of her large stature moved to the capital city when she married Confederate veteran and businessman Norman Vincent Randolph.[27] It was there that she earnestly pursued Confederate memorial work, first chairing the Tennessee table at the April 1893 bazaar, then joining the HMA and the HMA Juniors, serving as an officer in the Lee Camp Ladies' Auxiliary, and becoming vice regent of the Confederate Museum's Tennessee Room in February 1896.[28] Randolph also committed herself to other avenues of social activism, including the Young Women's Christian Association, the Negro Community House, and the Virginia Bureau of Vocations for Women. She was particularly active in the campaign to create a "co-ordinate college" for women at the University of Virginia. But for thirty-one years, Randolph's primary devotion was to Richmond's UDC chapter, which she founded in January 1896.[29]

During her tenure as chapter president (1896–1927), she encouraged Richmond's Daughters to avoid excessive "sentimentalism" and focus on how they might improve their society. She used her position in the Daughters to address not only Confederate memorial and historical issues, but also issues relating to the relief of Confederate widows. Like most members of the HMA and the CMLS, she discouraged the United Confederate Veterans and the Sons of Confederate Veterans from building a monument to Confederate women, believing that the Confederate Museum served in its own right as a monument to southern womanhood and women's devotion to "the Cause." She urged the

UDC to contribute more liberally to the museum and encouraged the Virginia division to pass a resolution in 1907 pledging at least one dollar annually from each chapter. In her dual role as UDC chapter president and vice regent of the Tennessee Room, she worked diligently at eliciting support for the museum from beyond the Commonwealth, eventually securing funding from the Tennessee legislature to endow the room completely. Above all, Randolph committed her life to honoring the "true" history of the Confederacy—a cause embraced equally by the LMAs and the UDC.[30]

Ruth Hairston Early of Lynchburg likewise exemplified the ties between the LMAs and Daughters. She had been a member of the Lynchburg LMA since at least 1887 and probably joined the Lucy Mina Otey Chapter of the UDC in 1895 (her sister Mollie served as the group's second vice president). Although her motivation remains unknown, Early issued a call in the spring of 1896 in the local newspaper for a second UDC chapter in the city, eventually named the Old Dominion Chapter. The following year, the Daughters elected her president of the chapter, a post she held several times during her life. Like Randolph, Early's primary interests included caring for needy Confederate veterans and widows, collecting and preserving Confederate relics, and perpetuating the memory of Confederate heroes.[31]

Because of the leadership of women like Randolph and Early, LMAs across the Commonwealth appeared eager to cooperate with the Daughters. The Lynchburg LMA first invited the Otey Chapter of Daughters to unite with them in their 1896 Memorial Day services. The following year, both the Otey and the Old Dominion Chapters joined the Lynchburg LMA, and their "cordial cooperation was very generously given."[32] Daughters from across the state assisted the vice regent of the Virginia Room with her duties collecting relics at the White House of the Confederacy. When the HMA asked the legislature in 1900 to assume financial responsibility for the state's Confederate cemeteries, the Ladies requested every UDC chapter in the state to use its influence with representatives from its district. Emily Hendree Park, regent of the Georgia Room and a UDC officer, urged every state division of the Daughters to support the museum and lobby its legislatures for funds.[33] The involvement of UDC chapters at memorial celebrations, monument unveilings, and any other activities under the auspices of the LMAs seemingly heightened the influence of the memorial women.

The Daughters also benefited from their ties to the memorial associations. Many of the LMA members joined the younger association and provided invaluable support for the Daughters' projects.[34] For example, when the Virginia UDC divisions (both the 1st Virginia and the Grand Division) nominated

Richmond as the location for the 1899 national convention, they asked the state's LMAs to unite with them. The CMLS and the HMA agreed to take up the banner, sending out more than 180 letters to UDC chapters across the South urging them to vote for their capital city. But the LMAs did not stop at lobbying for the city. After Richmond had been secured as the site, the CMLS and HMA invited every memorial association in the South to send delegates to the November meeting. Even though the CMLS experienced its own financial difficulties, the association annually donated a small sum to the Daughters. The LMAs likewise offered to sponsor a concert for the benefit of the Daughters' monument to Jefferson Davis in Richmond. And in 1902, the CMLS agreed to assist the Philadelphia-based Dabney H. Maury Chapter of the UDC when it was "forbidden by the fanatical prejudice of northern men, to rear a monument to the Confederate dead" buried in the City of Brotherly Love. With the HMA, the CMLS warmly offered a spot in the Soldiers' Section of Hollywood Cemetery for the monument.[35]

But even with this spirit of cooperation, the LMAs sought to distinguish themselves from the Daughters and refused to cede too much influence to the younger organization. Just prior to the HMA's 1902 memorial festivities, for example, the Ladies demanded that the UDC use the term "Memorial Day" rather than "Decoration Day." Since at least the 1870s, LMAs across the state and region had systematically employed the term "Memorial Day" (even though it often caused confusion with the national holiday), and they refused to allow the UDC to alter their language or diminish the significance of the Ladies' annual tribute. UDC historian Mildred Rutherford supported the LMAs' claims to dictate all aspects of Memorial Day. She held that they had every right and privilege to conduct those exercises as they saw fit, "just as it is the right and privilege of the UDC to bestow crosses of honor on the deserving veterans." Even more indicative of a potential turf war was the HMA's message to the Daughters to "back-off" regarding the Gettysburg dead issue. In May 1902, Janet Randolph reported to the HMA that appeals had been made to numerous UDC chapters to compensate Weaver for the funds still due him. Led by Mary Crenshaw, the HMA furiously responded that "all [UDC] associations be requested to have nothing to do with that matter, as it is entirely between the HMA and Dr. Weaver."[36]

The Confederate Museum likewise proved a source of friction between the two groups. The CMLS women depended on the assistance of the Daughters, but they were simultaneously wary of allowing them too much control. For example, when Lora Ellyson suggested allowing the Daughters to select State Room regents in 1899, most of the society's members protested the idea. The discussion provoked such an acrimonious response that the motion was withdrawn. Ella Darcy Dibrell, regent for the Texas Room, informed CMLS president Lizzie Cary Daniels that although she believed the Daughters should take an active interest in the museum, only society members should have the authority to fill regent vacancies. "We must not let state U.D.C. politics invade the Museum," she warned.[37] The LMAS might welcome the Daughters' aid in their Memorial Day celebrations and expect support for the Confederate Museum, but they drew clear boundaries that the new generation of women was warned not to cross.

Despite a mostly amicable and productive relationship between the LMAS and the Daughters, the memorial women worried that their work might be eclipsed by the UDC's powerful reach and so sought ways to strengthen their organizations in the late 1890s. Although the LMAS across the state and region had demonstrated a remarkable degree of cooperation with each other since their beginnings in the 1860s, the organization of the UDC prompted even more collaboration among the memorial associations. In Richmond, the HMA, the Oakwood Memorial Association (OMA), and the Hebrew Memorial Association had been gathering together to celebrate each group's Memorial Day since 1886, but after the emergence of the Daughters these memorial associations began to work together more closely by forming committees for joint projects. For example, in May 1896, representatives from each of the three associations met "to organize ladies of the whole city for the purpose of assisting the [Confederate Veterans] Camps in the necessary preparation for the Confederate reunion to be held in Richmond on June 30 and July 1, 2."[38]

LMAS across the South felt threatened as the Daughters continued to gain popularity while their own societies struggled to maintain their memberships. In the spring of 1900, Julia A. Garside of the Southern Memorial Association of Fayetteville, Arkansas, issued a call for all LMAS to unite in one body to be called the Confederated Southern Memorial Association (CSMA). Delegates from thirteen LMAS from all parts of the South arrived in Louisville, Kentucky, on May 30 to discuss the possibility of merging their associations. The site and date had been chosen because the annual meeting of the United Confederate Veterans was to be held at the same time, thereby—hopefully—attracting a fair number of Ladies who might accompany their husbands. Virginia, home of several of the oldest LMAS, was well represented, with delegates from Hollywood, Junior Hollywood, the CMLS, Petersburg, Oakwood, and Front Royal attending the inaugural meeting.[39]

The newly organized CSMA devoted its first meeting to crafting a consti-tution and bylaws, creating committees, and electing officers, including Katie Behan of New Orleans as president. In keeping with the objectives of the LMAS since the 1860s, the association would seek to collect relics and preserve the history of the Confederacy, instill in the minds of children "a proper venera-tion for the spirit and glory that animated" the South's soldiers, and continue to direct Memorial Day services. Like in the UDC, the women agreed that a vice president at large be elected from every state represented in the associa-tion (Mrs. D. C. Richardson of the Oakwood association was elected as vice president from Virginia), with other associations to elect vice presidents to represent their states as they entered. Emblematic of their mission to sear the memory of the Confederacy into every southern heart, the women selected as their motto "Lest We Forget." In the spirit of a confederation, the CSMA declared that no individual work of any LMA would be interfered with by the association and no joining association would be required to assume, except on a voluntary basis, any new work. Most important, "each association [would be] recognized as a free agent to continue its parent work, and devote itself exclusively, if it so desires, to its own local work." Unlike the Daughters, there was to be no hierarchy, only an available network for support.[40]

Founding members of the CSMA also realized that it was imperative that they gain the endorsement of the United Confederate Veterans. Although de-termined to control their own organization, they recognized that men's po-litical and economic support over the years had in many ways contributed to the success of the memorial associations. The new association believed that if it could have representatives attend the annual United Confederate Veterans meetings and gain the backing and cooperation of these men, they would be even more successful in their endeavors. The delegates, sensing the urgency of time, immediately began drafting a memorial to be read at the veterans' meeting the next day.[41]

"Throughout the south are scattered memorial associations, who have not relinquished their original organization . . . some of which were formed as far back as 1865," began Charles Coffin of Arkansas, speaking on behalf of the CSMA. In a comment intended to distinguish it from the Daughters, the CSMA claimed to bring the United Confederate Veterans a "more tangible demon-stration of work done than any other organized body of southern people, men or women. . . . We are not willing to lose our identity as memorial associa-tions, nor to merge ourselves into the younger organizations, 'The Daughters of the Confederacy.'" Further pointing to the differences between their orga-nization and the UDC, the CSMA leaders identified themselves as veterans,

"veterans as much as the gray, battle scarred old soldiers, though we bided at home." Women of the memorial associations, those of the war generation, they claimed, were equally devout Confederates and therefore should be seen as partners in the traditions of the Lost Cause, even more so than their off-spring, the Daughters. When Coffin finished reading the remarks, the old veterans jumped to their feet in deafening applause, likely recounting among themselves the privations, courage, and endurance of southern women during "those trying times of war." Noting that the csma was composed of organizations that antedated the work of the United Confederate Veterans, the men fully endorsed the confederation.[42]

In light of the csma's statement to the veterans, it seems almost unnecessary to speculate on why the memorial associations desired to join a confederation. Clearly they wanted to maintain their independence and receive what they deemed to be the appropriate recognition for their years of hard work. But as always, practical matters were never far behind. The Lynchburg association, for instance, cited "fuller organization and cooperation" as its chief reason for joining in 1902. The Petersburg lma likewise sought to employ the csma as a regional platform to solicit support. The association had recently embarked on a project to restore Blandford Church as a Confederate Memorial Chapel, and its representatives asked that each Confederate Veteran camp and memorial association donate three dollars toward the venture. Always present in their minds was "the best method of securing help from each state in restoring Blandford Church," and for years they would renew their requests for aid at the annual meeting of the csma. With its new organizational structure, the csma, like the Daughters, could potentially reach supporters (and wallets) in every corner of the South.[43]

According to the annual reports of the csma, it was succeeding marvelously in its primary goals of uniting the associations, infusing new life into local lmas, and reviving Confederate work in general. By its second annual convention in 1901, the confederation had more than doubled, with twenty-eight associations represented, and by 1903 that number had grown to fifty-five.[44] But reports from Mrs. Shelton Chieves, vice president for Virginia, in 1905 suggested that the confederation had not produced nearly the response its founders had hoped for. "It is with regret that I come to you to-day with a very unsatisfactory report of work accomplished," she began. Although she had written countless letters to members of memorial associations and endeavored to "arouse their dying enthusiasm," it had proved to be "a difficult task, to prevail upon those women who were identified with the sad days of anxiety and sorrow, to hold their Association together." The Lynchburg association, for example, had decided to withdraw from the confederation in the summer of 1903, determining that "continued membership was costly and unnecessary." Even so, CSMA corresponding secretary Sue H. Walker refused to acknowledge that memorial associations simply were not interested—or found little use for the union, instead arguing that "many more would have joined us, but for their inability to do so, having merged into the younger organization the Daughters of the Confederacy."[45]

Despite the frequent not-so-flattering references to the Daughters, Walker insisted that the confederation would not "conflict or interfere in any way with the U.D.C." She maintained that even though the organizations remained separate, "both are working for the same sacred cause." The Davis monument endeavor proved that assertion, as did the opening reception the CSMA received each year from the Daughters in the hosting city of their annual convention. For their part, the UDC tried to appease the memorial women by applauding their work and dedication to the Cause.[46]

The "older women," as they liked to call themselves, continued to reminisce about their role in the 1860s and insist that they stood between "a calamitous past and an uncertain future, in determined protest against the blackness of calumny and the leveling power of time." In a testament to the continuity between the earliest LMAs and the CSMA sixty years later, the two priorities of the confederation remained Memorial Days and care of the Confederate graves. Recalling an attempt by Richmond's Lee Camp in the 1890s to establish a single Memorial Day for the entire South, CSMA president Katie Behan suggested that all the associations celebrate Jefferson Davis's birthday on June 3 as "Southern Memorial Day." When this failed to occur (not surprisingly in a group dedicated to protecting each association's individuality), she urged the LMAs to give details of their individual Memorial Day celebrations in their annual reports, send quarterly reports to their local newspapers, and write articles for the *Confederate Veteran* every three months in order to give the public "some idea of the work being done by the Memorial Associations" and "increase the interest of the younger generation."[47]

Despite the growing numbers and presence of the UDC, it seemed unnecessary for the Ladies to remind their respective communities that Memorial Day activities remained under their dominion. Even as the services took on a more martial tone with the increased presence of the Confederate veterans, newspapers from Winchester to Lynchburg heralded the days' events as the province of women. The Petersburg paper, for example, noted that "ever since the close of the civil war the ninth of June has been observed as memorial day when appropriate memorial exercises are held under the auspices of the Ladies Memorial Association." The CSMA need not worry that the Ladies would cede their influence over Memorial Days.[48]

Tending to the graves of Confederate soldiers buried on northern soil and erecting granite shafts in their memory also occupied much of the CSMA's time. Most famously, the association embroiled itself in the conflict regarding the creation of a Confederate section in Arlington National Cemetery on the grounds of Robert E. Lee's former home. In an 1898 speech, President William McKinley pledged to care for the graves of all soldiers in Arlington, and former Confederates immediately began lobbying Congress to improve the approximately 136 rebel graves scattered throughout the cemetery "intermingled with federal soldiers—both white and black." The Ladies, however, strongly objected to such a plan. Under the influence of Janet Randolph, the CSMA, together with the HMA and the Richmond chapter of the UDC, demanded that the bodies be reinterred in Hollywood Cemetery so as to protect the graves from desecration by the GAR. Repeatedly, the CSMA appealed to its member associations, requesting them to claim the dead of their states, and President Katie Behan traveled to Washington to meet with the secretary of war. "We may not succeed in this particular instance," Behan noted, "but my dear sisters, we have the proud satisfaction of knowing that we have been, and are to-day, and will be forever true to the pledge we took more than thirty years ago." Despite the CSMA's intense efforts, in 1901 the War Department adopted resolutions for the reburials in Arlington. Having lost this battle, the CSMA counterattacked by insisting that the federal government agree to assume the obligation of tending to the graves of approximately 30,000 Confederate soldiers who had died in northern prison camps and hospitals. Congress finally passed the legislation in 1906, sanctifying the Ladies' "labor of love" as a governmental responsibility.[49]

Never a group to avoid controversy, the CSMA found other contentious issues with which to involve itself. The association inaugurated movements to place pictures of Jefferson Davis in every southern classroom and have his name restored to the Cabin John Bridge in Washington, D.C. In 1913, it passed a resolution requesting Congress to issue a return on the cotton tax. Perhaps most surprising, at first glance, was its effort to change the words to the South's unofficial anthem, "Dixie." When the *Montgomery Advertiser* asked, "What is the matter with the old words to Dixie?" the women of the association offered a sharp reply. "The words are unworthy of the air" because they had been composed for a "negro minstrel performance." While the tune became popular during the war, the memorial women contended that "the words are nothing but doggerel and negro dialect. Some do not even rhyme."

Since the CSMA wanted schoolchildren to sing the song, they thought it only fitting that the words be changed to something more solemn that reflected the seriousness of the war rather than the light-hearted nature of a minstrel show. Venerating Confederate soldiers might be their mantra, but CSMA women clearly understood their power to shape young *white* southern minds regarding proper race relations in the early twentieth century.[50]

But neither these stirring debates nor the LMAS' "traditional" Memorial Day activities would be enough to shore up interest and participation. In order to continue to attract members to their struggling associations, the CSMA and its memorial associations would have to differentiate themselves from the Daughters through projects both novel and grand.

As evidenced in Mrs. Shelton Chieves's comments before the CSMA in 1905, the Petersburg LMA had struggled for decades to maintain its popularity and appeal among the community's upper-class women. When a chapter of the UDC was formed in the city, the Petersburg LMA again solicited support for its own organization, whose membership had by 1899 dwindled to fifteen. Within a week of placing an ad in the local paper, attendance at the Ladies' meetings had doubled to thirty and in two weeks numbered forty-three. At one such meeting, a member suggested transforming the abandoned Blandford Church (around which the association had interred more than 30,000 Confederate soldiers) into a nonsectarian mortuary chapel for every southern state. Perhaps the fact that the HMA and its auxiliary, the CMLS, were busy establishing a Confederate Museum in Richmond, replete with relics from every southern state, sparked the notion of a shrine in memory of all Confederates. Or maybe the member had read about a proposal in 1867 to establish a memorial church in Memphis with mural tablets to honor the Confederate dead, inscribed with the names of associations throughout the South that contributed. Whatever the inspiration, the women of the LMA believed Petersburg to be just as sacred to the South as Richmond or Memphis. The city had witnessed the Confederates' last stand, and more Confederate soldiers were interred on its hillsides than at any other spot in the South. The Petersburg LMA thought that restoring Blandford might induce the South's sons and daughters to make annual pilgrimages to this shrine. "A melancholy pride will fill their hearts for duty well performed to those who fought for constitutional liberty and law," the women claimed.[51]

Such a grand project had the added benefit of generating local and regional support for their cause. The Petersburg LMA promptly contacted Confederate Veteran member James Quicke Sr., requesting that he devise the best means of bringing it to the attention of the different Confederate Associations. Quicke wrote a proposal embodying the Petersburg LMA's plans for Blandford Church and presented it at the annual meeting of the Grand Camp of Confederate Veterans in Charleston, South Carolina, on May 10, 1899. Recognizing the regional breadth of the Confederate Veterans, the Ladies hoped that the men's influence would "contribute toward making it a memorial to our Heroes, buried around this old church."[52]

Built as an Anglican church in 1735 but abandoned by 1803, Blandford had been donated to the city of Petersburg by John Grammer in 1819. Left unattended, the church had begun to crumble, and by 1868 one citizen remarked that it had "gone much to decay: the walls of . . . brick are standing, the roof in part gone, moss and ivy covering the ravages of time." Because the chapel was the focal point for the Confederate Cemetery on nearby Memorial Hill, the Petersburg LMA's first priority was to restore the chapel to its original plan. The most ambitious of the proposals for the church was the installation of stained glass windows to be dedicated to the memory of the soldiers from different Confederate states buried in the cemetery. Within nine months, the Ladies had decided to employ the services of Louis Comfort Tiffany, the celebrated stained glass artist, to design "a perfect memorial" for the dead.[53]

In order to increase support for the restoration of the church across the South, the A. P. Hill Camp of Confederate Veterans volunteered to assist the Petersburg LMA in preparing and distributing circulars asking for contributions to the Blandford Memorial Fund. By October 1900, more than 8,000 circulars had been printed, and donations from individuals throughout the nation—not merely the South—began flooding the memorial association. The first contribution, one dollar, came from Mrs. E. J. Mead of Topeka, Kansas; other early donations arrived from cities in Virginia, including Waynesboro and Bowling Green. The Washington Artillery of New Orleans provided the Petersburg LMA with an enormous boost when its members expressed their desire to "be granted the privilege of furnishing a window." The Ladies reported that "letters from persons in several states" expressed "great interest in the work of restoring 'Old Blandford Church' and also showing that they still cherish loving memories of the Lost Cause that should always be dear to Southern hearts." If the women of Petersburg lacked enthusiasm for the LMA, the Ladies found solace that other white southerners still relished their "heroic past."[54] Finally, after a petition from the Petersburg LMA, in January 1901 the City of Petersburg delegated authority to the LMA to convert the old church into a mortuary chapel and a Confederate memorial.

Perhaps if the town council and veterans' camp supported the project, be-

Blandford Church was built in 1735 and abandoned by 1803. In 1899, the Petersburg Ladies embarked on an effort to transform the deteriorating building into a nonsectarian shrine in memory of all Confederates. (Courtesy Library of Virginia)

lieved the memorial women, other such local organizations might also lend their assistance to the endeavor. Despite the Petersburg LMA's desire to remain an independent organization, in 1901 the Ladies formally invited the local UDC chapter, as well as the national organization, to cooperate in raising funds to restore the church. The UDC accepted, and the Petersburg chapter promptly donated $100. Nonetheless, the LMA made a concerted effort to remind Petersburg and the nation that they remained distinct from the UDC, especially after the October 1903 edition of the *Women's Home Companion* credited the Daughters for the restoration of Blandford Church. Mrs. W. C. Badger, a member of both the Petersburg LMA and the Petersburg UDC, pointed out the error at a memorial association meeting, clearly disturbed that the Daughters should be praised for directing a project so near and dear to the memorial women's hearts.[55]

Throughout 1902, the Petersburg Ladies, CSMA, UDC, Confederate Veterans, state legislatures, and individuals across the South continued to raise money for the church. To avoid disputes among the donors over the design of each memorial window, the Petersburg LMA requested that Tiffany choose a subject and theme that would unify all the windows—twelve compass windows, two smaller rectangular windows, and one lunette. After sending a representative in early 1903 to survey the church, Tiffany decided on the Gothic Revival style of the late nineteenth century. He designed the eleven first-floor compass windows to feature either an evangelist or an apostle. Above each saint, he inserted a medallion to designate the window's donor. Below the figures, each donor would be able to choose a memorial verse. The four smaller windows would complement the larger windows.[56] Because each state would be responsible for raising the $385 needed for its window, Tiffany's associate suggested that the Ladies assign a member to work with each state until the necessary funds were in place.

By mid-1903, individuals and associations from Virginia, Missouri, and Louisiana (represented by the Washington Artillery) had collected the funds for their respective windows. The following Memorial Day, June 1904, the Petersburg LMA dedicated the first three windows and consecrated Blandford as a Confederate Memorial Chapel. Described by the local paper as the most important celebration "yet held under the auspices of the Ladies Memorial Association," the day attracted thousands of spectators from across the region and honored guests such as Katie Behan, president of the CSMA, and Stonewall Jackson's granddaughter, Julia Jackson Christian. Following an address by Judge George Christian of Richmond that praised the Army of Northern Virginia and noted that Virginia did not go to war to defend the right of secession, the Ladies unveiled the three windows and a marble tablet dedicated by the UDC. After the unveiling exercises, a chorus of "Our Southland" brought the ceremonies to a close. According to the *Petersburg Daily Index-Appeal*, the Ladies were wiser than they realized, as "this chapel will be not only a memorial to the dead, but it is also an honor to the living."[57]

Six years later, on June 3, 1910, the 102nd anniversary of the birth of Confederate president Jefferson Davis, the Petersburg LMA dedicated eleven more windows (several of which had already been installed in the chapel). The North Carolina window had been placed in the church in 1907. The following year, Tiffany completed the Alabama, Mississippi, Tennessee, Florida, Texas, and Missouri compass windows, along with three smaller windows representing Arkansas, Maryland, and the Ladies' Memorial Association. In 1910, the South Carolina window and Tiffany's personal donation, a "Cross of Jewels," were installed. Finally, thirteen years after the Ladies first discussed restoring Blandford Church as a memorial shrine, the project was officially concluded on November 13, 1912, with the dedication of the Georgia window. By transforming the old Blandford Church into a Confederate chapel, the Ladies had appealed to a national memory of the war dead that invoked an otherworld-

Created by Tiffany Studios and installed in 1907, this window representing North Carolina in Blandford Church depicts the apostle St. Bartholomew. (Courtesy Library of Virginia)

liness—an eternal life for the martyrs of the Lost Cause. Like many defenders of the Confederacy, they moved beyond death to celebrate the triumphs of not only their ancestors, but also of themselves. They had created an enduring landmark, a shrine to the Confederate dead, to be forever associated with the Ladies' Memorial Associations.[58]

At one o'clock in the afternoon on a sunny winter day in 1896, the doors to the White House of the Confederacy, now the Confederate Museum, finally opened. The choice of February 22 was no coincidence; the women had selected the date to correspond with George Washington's birthday, as well as with the inauguration of the Confederacy's first and only president exactly thirty-four years earlier.[59] The CMLS officers, led by president Belle Bryan, greeted thousands of visitors in what had been the central parlor of the executive mansion (now called the "Solid South" Room) while other members served refreshments in the former state dining room. The rooms would eventually be filled with relics and Confederate records; however, because of the throngs of spectators streaming through the building, the rooms remained sparse, "decorated only with appropriately colored bunting, festoons, flags, flowers, palm leaves, and occasional portraits on mantels and walls." In introducing the day's orator, Governor O'Ferrall reminded his audience of the southern soldiers' "courage and daring, chivalry and bravery." But, he hastened to add, "as grand as the South was in her sons, she was grander still in her daughters; as sublime as she was in her men, she was sublimer still in her women." For several more minutes, he continued lauding the sacrifices and devotion of Confederate women, before finally introducing the day's official speaker, General Bradley T. Johnson. The opening day had been a triumph, as thousands of museumgoers packed the mansion until nearly midnight. The CMLS could not have been more delighted with its success.[60]

Even though the women needed more relics to fill their rooms, in the weeks after its opening the museum proved to be instantly popular, welcoming 6,026 visitors in a mere 12 months. In June 1896, the Confederate Veterans held their annual reunion in the city and gathered at the former executive mansion for the first time since 1865. State and local government officials and their wives, visitors to the city, and schoolchildren all poured into the new museum, anxious for a close examination of some of the Confederacy's most precious artifacts. The HMA and its sister society, the CMLS, had succeeded in ensuring that future generations would not forget the Confederacy or its White House. Moreover, they proved to themselves that even with the rising popularity of the Daughters, the work of the memorial associations would not be overlooked.[61]

Following the museum's dedication in 1896, the CMLS embarked on an even more ambitious agenda. The group urged all the railroads in the state to mark the battlefields through which their respective lines passed so that tourists might learn about the war as they traveled along the rails. Not only did all of the railroads agree to comply, but Major E. D. Myers of the Richmond, Fredericksburg, and Potomac Railroad donated one acre of land on the Fredericksburg battlefield to the CMLS on which he erected a pyramid modeled after the ninety-foot structure in Hollywood Cemetery.[62] The Chesapeake and Ohio Railroad followed suit, consenting to designate "in a substantial manner" the Williamsburg battlefield and the "outer fortifications of the city which were never broken." The CMLS also looked beyond the railroads to make their mark. In 1900, the association received permission from the Virginia legislature to place a placard on "any and all buildings or other property, belonging to the Commonwealth, that were used for the purposes of or associated with the war between the states." Even after thirty-five years, the LMA continued to act on behalf of the state when it came to Confederate issues. And in 1904 the association undertook a project that closely resembled efforts of the UDC when it announced a prize of ten dollars in gold to the grammar school student who wrote the best paper on a Confederate subject. Like their counterparts, the Ladies believed that such essay contests, along with the railroad and building markers, would offer a "proper education of the younger generation . . . awakening their greater interest in Confederate history."[63]

The women of the CMLS and HMA more directly returned to their 1860s' role as lobbyist when they pressured the Virginia legislature to provide an annual appropriation for upkeep of the state's thirty-four Confederate cemeteries. In November 1900, the women sent an appeal to every LMA and UDC chapter in Virginia asking for assistance in this effort. Associations from Winchester, Manassas, Blacksburg, Culpepper, Leesburg, Petersburg, and numerous other localities agreed to petition their delegates and state senators. Employing the maternalist language that had become so popular among women's lobbying efforts on behalf of children and working women, in 1902 the Ladies convinced the General Assembly to provide annual contributions to these national Confederate cemeteries based on the number of interments. As one of the largest burial grounds, for example, Hollywood was to receive $500 annually. The significance of these state appropriations should not be discounted. After more than thirty years, the women of the LMAs had not forsaken their identity as political lobbyist on behalf of the defunct Confederacy; rather, they had confirmed that their role as caregivers to the Confederate dead had been a state function. Just as women's voluntary associations throughout the nation were helping to expand the role of the state to include obligations of welfare to veterans, widows, and children, the Ladies were likewise pushing the state to assume new responsibilities in the realm of historic preservation. The LMAS failed to take up the banner of suffrage, but they nevertheless succeeded in crafting a new relationship between themselves and the state, as well as a new relationship between the state and the larger populace—for generations to come.[64]

Even with these other efforts to remind future generations about the Confederacy's past, the museum remained the CMLS's most precious goal and dearest achievement. Other white southerners, including men, also recognized the significance of the museum and the pivotal role women played in memorializing the Confederacy. Speaking at the museum dedication, Confederate veteran and Virginia governor Charles T. O'Ferrall asked the visitors, "Why is it we are here?" The answer, he proclaimed, "is ready upon every tongue, Southern women's love for the memories of a generation ago; Southern women's devotion to the cause which, though enveloped in a cloud of defeat, yet circled in a blaze of glory, has called us from our firesides and businesses to this spot." He reminded the crowd that rather than veterans and generals, "the daughters and granddaughters" of the Confederacy's devoted women were responsible for "dedicating this structure as a depository of Confederate cards and relics."[65]

When wealthy Confederate veteran Charles Broadway Rouss of New York (but originally of Winchester) proposed donating $100,000 for the creation of a "Battle Abbey" or repository to collect the records and relics of the "Southern Cause" in 1894, the women of the CMLS felt confident that their museum would be an appropriate site for this Memorial Hall. Mary Maury Werth viewed Rouss's proposal as "fulfilling and perpetuating the very objects for which the CMLS was established" and urged fellow members to "secure the valuable cooperation & assistance of so zealous a Confederate as Mr. Rouss." The Lee Camp, including many husbands of CMLS members, concurred. It sent a delegation to address Rouss on behalf of the women, touting them as an "organization to which the patriotic trust might worthily be committed" and noting that the society already possessed "the finest and most extensive collection of Confederate relics ever made."[66]

Rouss initially remained cautious of pledging his Battle Abbey to any locality, confiding to several veterans' associations that he considered the

Confederate Museum a distinctly local institution and that he desired to create one that would be "national in character." Representatives from other cities, including Atlanta, Nashville, Memphis, Vicksburg, Washington, and New Orleans, fueled his reservations and suggested that their communities offered better sites for the repository. No doubt hearing of Rouss's hesitancy, CMLS corresponding secretary Lizzie Cary Daniel declared that the Confederate Museum was "more than a local institution. The society was started in February 1890, [four years prior to Rouss's appeal] with exactly the design and scope of what has later become so well-known as the 'Battle Abbey of the South.'" She admitted that the society may have fallen short of making known "its aim and its success" but reminded the veterans that the museum's grounds, "now in such beautiful order," could be secured free of cost. Invigorated by Daniel's words and feeling confident that they would win Rouss's approval, the society voted in February 1896 to raze the outbuildings associated with the Confederate White House in an effort to clear a space for the Battle Abbey. To sweeten the appeal, the CMLS subsequently offered a contribution of $50,000 toward the project. The existence of the Ladies' museum and cash indeed proved significant when Richmond was selected as the site for the Memorial Hall and its administrative body, the Confederate Memorial Association (CMA), in 1898.[67]

With the city (and presumably the location) selected, leaders of the CMLS believed that they would have a significant degree of control, if not full administrative authority, over the CMA. J. Taylor Ellyson, Richmond businessman, chairman of the Democratic state committee, husband of CMLS member Lora Hotchkiss Ellyson, and CMA member, guaranteed the women that the Memorial Hall would not threaten their museum. He informed them that the CMA unanimously wished to place the Abbey under their management, "as it would be impolitic to have two such organizations in one city." Janet Randolph took Ellyson at his word, later demanding that he fulfill his promise and relinquish control of the Battle Abbey to the museum. But skeptics abounded. Writing to Lynchburg's Ruth Early in 1896, Dabney H. Maury expressed "no respect for the scheme nor for the promoters of it," although he understood the Richmond women's desired to build "a grander museum" than in any other state. Varina Davis, too, opposed "the scheme." Attending a meeting of the CMLS in the spring of 1898, she claimed that it would "never be built if the Southern women understood the object of it." Perhaps, like Joseph Bryan, she had a glimmering of the gender disputes that would follow. For his part, Bryan warned the CMLS that trouble was sure to arise, because members of the CMA would come seeking relics in possession of the museum.[68]

Although these skeptics apparently had every reason to be cautious, fissures that developed between the women of the CMLS and the all-male CMA initially had little to do with the collections. Instead, the bitterness revolved around the location for the Memorial Hall. Many members of the CMA complained that the site adjacent to the Confederate Museum was simply too steep to accommodate the building they envisioned. But they realized that if they did not secure a lot within the city by the time of the Confederate Veterans' reunion in 1909, Richmond might lose its bid as host city. As the CMLS continued to advocate the lot beside the White House of the Confederacy, many of the men expressed reluctance for the Battle Abbey to be incorporated either physically or organizationally into the women's museum. The Lee Camp, for instance, railed against placing it near the Confederate White House and wanted it placed in the West End, close to the city's famed Monument Avenue. Yet some men continued to acknowledge that the women had successfully developed and managed the museum and therefore "might give the same protecting care and wise administration to the other building." Dr. James P. Smith, for example, considered it of "absolute importance" that the proposed building be placed close enough to the Confederate White House so as "to gain the help and support of the women now in charge of that institution."[69]

Some men recognized the vital role the CMLS women played in the conservation and preservation of Confederate memory, even as others wanted their own more masculine hand in the project. J. Taylor Ellyson, by this time lieutenant governor of Virginia and president of the CMA, claimed that he wished to remain neutral as to the location; however, he reminded the Lee Camp that it had been the CMLS women who "pushed to conclusion the move to insure the erection of the Abbey in Richmond" with their donation of $50,000. Despite his attempts at compromise, it quickly became apparent to the women where his loyalties lay. One can only imagine the many intensely silent dinners in the Ellyson household as J. Taylor and Lora sat in uncomfortable silence— she on the side of the CMLS and he trying to find some precarious middle ground between the two associations.[70]

In May 1909, the CMA unanimously voted to erect the Battle Abbey close to Monument Avenue because the men believed the area was "fast becoming the new Confederate section of the city."[71] In an almost antagonizing fashion, the CMA thanked the CMLS for their hard work, promising to work in conjunction with the women in future endeavors. "How could this be possible," Janet Randolph fired back, "with these buildings in entire[ly] different sections of the City." J. Taylor Ellyson simply did not respond. Infuriated with the men's betrayal, Randolph introduced a formal resolution specifying that the CMLS would have no other dealings with the Battle Abbey. Virginia Robinson concurred. When a researcher mailed a question regarding the CMA to the CMLS, Robinson responded that "the so-called 'Battle Abbey' is a distinct organization from this one . . . entirely composed of gentlemen." The CMLS, she proudly announced, was "woman's work."[72]

As in the case of the Ladies' Lee Monument Committee twenty years earlier, the women once again had to defend their position as the preservers of Confederate memory. After so many years of dedication to "the cause," men were asking for their assistance, using the Confederate Museum as a lobbying point, and then attempting to shove them aside.

The wrangling over the location finally came to an end, when on March 25, 1910, Governor William Hodge Mann wrote to Lieutenant Governor Ellyson, formally conveying the six acres for the Battle Abbey near Monument Avenue and adjacent to the Lee Camp Soldiers' Home. While many members of the CMLS, including Randolph and Robinson, continued to fume at the decision, Belle Bryan found some sense of solace as she and her husband had long feared the CMA might encroach on the women's independence. Rumors that the Battle Abbey would seek to acquire the museum's collections did not end with appropriation of the site. The CMLS thus agreed to take Bryan's warning seriously and issued a statement "contradict[ing] all rumors to the contrary." In November 1910, the society adopted a resolution stating that "the Confederate Museum is the work of women and a monument to the women of the South and can never pass from the care of the CMLS as chartered May 1890." They would not cede the fruits of their labors. Should anyone care to ask, they remained in control of the Confederate Museum.[73]

By 1915, the women of Virginia's LMAs and their counterparts across the South could look back on nearly fifty years of work and proudly proclaim that they had been responsible for much of the current southern landscape. Beginning immediately after Appomattox, they had initiated and directed efforts to create national Confederate cemeteries. They had instigated Memorial Days under the guise of feminine mourning, thereby providing a forum for Confederate veterans to insist in the earliest days of Reconstruction that their cause had been just. Memorial associations had raised countless monuments to the Confederate dead in communities throughout Virginia and the South and had fended off efforts by veterans to assume control of such projects. In Richmond alone, a city dotted with stone tributes to the Confederacy, LMAs could claim at least partial responsibility for the city's three most significant monuments—the pyramid in Hollywood, the Lee Monument, and the Soldiers' and Sailors' Monument. They had saved the White House of the Confederacy from demolition and transformed it into a national Confederate museum that would inculcate generations of white southerners with the Lost Cause message. In Petersburg, they had created a national Confederate shrine replete with stained glass windows designed by one of the country's premier artists. And, perhaps most ironically, the LMAS could count among their successes the birth of the Daughters.

It is very likely that even without the establishment of the UDC, the memorial associations might have faded from the picture by the early twentieth century. The Ladies' projects of cemetery establishment and monument building were losing momentum, and the women themselves were reaching the ends of their lives. In fact, the Daughters had proved to be a rallying call for the older generation of LMAS, prompting many of them to reinvigorate their societies and seek new, more ambitious projects like the Confederate Museum and the Blandford Church.

Yet memorial associations could not compete with the Daughters' ever-increasing numbers or national organizational structure. The memorial associations had established informal connections among their members and had united in cooperation through the CSMA, but they had failed to attract significant numbers of associations, incorporate new chapters, or even to revitalize the membership of their independent associations. The Daughters, conversely, drew members from throughout the state, region, and in some cases, other regions of the nation, making sure to distribute their state and national offices geographically so as to reach the broadest possible base. Their membership continued to grow at a rapid pace, reaching 80,000 by 1912, while the LMAS' rolls steadily declined.[74]

For more than six decades, the LMAS had worked tirelessly to promote a positive memory of the Confederacy and to cultivate white southern solidarity. By the first decades of the twentieth century, however, the UDC simply proved to be a much more attractive organization than the LMAS for thousands of southern white women. But even as the Ladies gradually took a back seat to the Daughters, it was clear that their legacy would endure for generations to come.

Epilogue

A Mixed Legacy

*It is almost impossible for our young people of today
to believe that in 1890, when the charter was secured
[for the Confederate Museum], this splendid memorial to
the men of the sixties emanated from the brains of a band
of women, and has been carried on by women ever since.*
—SALLY ARCHER ANDERSON, CMLS PRESIDENT,
1926

One hundred and forty years after the close of the
Civil War, reminders of the Confederacy can be seen and in many ways felt
in nearly every southern community. Rare is the southern town or city that
cannot boast of a Confederate cemetery or, at the very least, a marble statue
dedicated to its Confederate soldiers standing guard over the town square or
courthouse lawn. Along with these physical reminders of the South's history,
numerous southern communities continue to observe many of the traditions
put in place by the Ladies' Memorial Associations (LMAS) in the 1860s. Celebrations of Confederate Memorial Days persist in a manner reminiscent of
the earliest celebrations, replete with floral offerings, Confederate battle flags,
patriotic dirges such as "Dixie," and speakers lauding the bravery and sacrifice of southern soldiers. In nearly every instance, however, LMAS no longer
care for the cemeteries nor do they direct the rituals. In their place, members
of the United Daughters of the Confederacy (UDC) or Sons of Confederate
Veterans have stepped forward to prolong the traditions. Even as their legacy
continues, the Ladies have largely been forgotten with the passage of time.

Beginning with their decline in the early twentieth century, LMAS have re-
ceded from the southern landscape, leaving only three known associations
in Virginia, those in Fredericksburg, Petersburg, and New Market. The reasons and means by which these three managed to sustain themselves over
the years—when others did not—are unclear. Nevertheless, the LMAS in these

locales remain dedicated to many of the same projects and goals as their predecessors of the last century: maintaining cemeteries, providing information to soldiers' descendants regarding grave locations, and sponsoring Memorial Day celebrations. Still other LMAS have transformed their associations since the early 1900s. In Lynchburg, for example, a small but devoted group of women persisted as the caretakers of the Confederate section of the Old City Cemetery until 1993, when the group took on the much larger civilian section. While the organization—known today as the "Southern Memorial Association"—retains its role as custodian of the burial ground, its biracial membership of eighteen men and women stands as a stark contrast to the LMA's 1866 composition.[1]

Richmond's Hollywood association, too, has evolved since its Reconstruction era origins.[2] The Hollywood Memorial Association ceased to exist sometime in the mid-twentieth century, but its auxiliary group, the Confederate Memorial Literary Society (CMLS), continues to operate the museum, attracting at its height, more than 88,000 annual visitors. In 1969, it altered its direction, revising its organizational structure, constructing a new museum to house its ever-growing collections, restoring the White House, and changing the name from the Confederate Museum to the Museum of the Confederacy. The state room arrangement became obsolete, and the board eliminated the regent system in the 1980s. In 1991, the men's advisory board abolished itself, and the society's board elected its first male and black members, effectively ending a century of leadership by white women.[3]

Along with the change in organizational structure came a new focus in the museum's interpretation of the Civil War and Confederacy. During the 1980s, the museum featured one of the first examinations of southern social history in its exhibit, "The People of the Confederacy," and provided a chronological framework in "The Confederate Years"—context that had been absent in its early years. With the support of the National Endowment for the Humanities, in 1991, the museum unveiled a new and pathbreaking exhibit entitled "Before Freedom Came: African American Life in the Antebellum South." The institution founded to glorify the white South had evolved into one that provided a glimpse into the harsh realities of life for southern blacks. Although the museum no longer admits schoolchildren free of charge, it remains committed to educating the next generation and even has programs designed to supplement Standards of Learning exams given in Virginia's public schools.[4]

Today, a dwindling number of visitors and encroachment by Virginia Commonwealth University's medical campus and hospital jeopardize the fate of the Museum of the Confederacy. The three-quarter-acre museum site is already surrounded by immense hospital and university buildings to the south and west and might soon be further obscured by a sixteen-story hospital wing to the east. According to executive director Waite Rawls, the difficulty in finding the institution has resulted in the decline in the number of visitors by a third during the last decade. That, in turn, has led to financial woes. As of February 2007, the museum was considering relocating its collection of Civil War artifacts, the largest in the world, to Lexington, Virginia (although the adjacent White House would remain in Richmond). Moreover, museum officials have indicated that they will likely drop the word "Confederacy" from its name. A recent survey conducted by the museum indicated that the word "Confederacy" carries "enormous, intransigent, and negative intellectual baggage with many. For them, Confederacy, and by association, the Museum of the Confederacy, now symbolizes racism." Rawls has noted that changing the name would be more in tune with the organization's repositioning during the past thirty years to become "more of a modern education institution and less of a memorial . . . to the Confederacy." The CMLS has thus moved beyond the sectional feelings that motivated its founding, while remaining dedicated to the objectives of educating future generations about the South in the Civil War—even when the message has become less than flattering, if not antithetical, to its founding mission. One can only imagine what Belle Bryan and her colleagues would think of the museum's evolution.[5]

From the inaugural Memorial Days in 1866 to the contemporary issues surrounding the Museum of the Confederacy, LMAs offer historians a complex and mixed legacy. In many respects the Ladies should be heralded as independent, politically engaged, and community-oriented women. Even though many historians have not appreciated the Ladies' importance in part because they were tied to the Confederate tradition rather than Progressive reforms, LMAs add to our understanding of the national pattern of women's activism in the latter half of the nineteenth century. Just like their northern counterparts, women of the LMAs were part of the national women's club movement, Progressive Era reform, and women's political mobilization.

But regionally contextualizing the meaning of women's political activism makes the Ladies more, not less, central to understanding the broader narrative of women's history. The Ladies had proven to be instrumental in the development of southern white women's organizations, providing a transition between the localized benevolent societies of the antebellum period and the women's club movement of the late nineteenth century. Instead of joining the movement for women's rights, thousands of southern white women found the ostensibly apolitical memorial associations an acceptable avenue for entry into the public theater. In short, the LMAs had been good for southern white women because the associations gave those who were not comfortable in the women's rights movement and other female political venues an alternative public outlet. Moreover, there are parallels to be drawn between southern white and black women's political engagement if we broaden our view to include groups such as the Ladies. For example, both the LMAs and southern African American women sometimes found that their gender protected them.[6] Such does not make light of the inherent differences of experience imposed by race; rather, it suggests that by shifting our lens of analysis we might find alternative meanings of political power exercised by southern women, both white and black.

But the Ladies also have another less laudable legacy to bear. As a relatively small but powerful group of upper- and middle-class white women, the LMAs succeeded in crafting enduring memories and celebrations of the Confederacy that remain with us today. In recent years, debates regarding the Confederate past have surfaced throughout Virginia and the greater South. In 2003, the National Park Service's decision to erect a statue at Richmond's Tredegar Ironworks commemorating Abraham Lincoln's 1865 visit to the Confederate capital ignited a firestorm of protest among local heritage groups. Many supporters of the sculpture touted its reconciliatory theme, but countless others launched an internet petition and staged protests at the dedication. Still other debates about the southern past raged on a more national level. In Maryland, a Sons of Confederate Veterans member filed a lawsuit seeking to allow the Confederate battle flag to fly at Point Lookout National Cemetery in honor of the 3,300 Confederate prisoners of war who died at the camp. More widely known disputes arose when groups such as the National Association for the Advancement of Colored People called for the removal of the Confederate battle flag from the state flags of Georgia and Mississippi and demanded that the battle flag cease to be flown over the statehouses of South Carolina and Alabama. As the flag debate has revealed, it is not only the symbols of rebellion that remain. The issues surrounding them continue to loom—disputes over the Confederacy's military and political leaders, its heritage associations such as the Sons and Daughters of the Confederacy, and, most pointedly, arguments over whether or not slavery was a catalyst for the Civil War.[7]

All of this can be traced in part back to the LMAs. Without these devoted and persistent women, the rituals and symbols associated with the defeated Confederacy might have been swept away by the victorious federal government in the wake of Appomattox. Protected by their gender, white women were able to escape charges of treason during Reconstruction and construct an expression of Confederate sympathy that did not threaten Republicans, Union veterans, the northern populace, and ultimately, reconciliation. In the immediate aftermath of the Civil War, the Ladies initiated the symbols and conditions for the endurance of Confederates' devotion to their nation, even as it ceased to exist and federal forces occupied the South. The Virginia associations alone could claim responsibility for the reinterments of nearly 28 percent of Confederate soldiers, the creation of six *national* Confederate cemeteries, the establishment of the Museum of the Confederacy, assistance with the erection of Richmond's Robert E. Lee and Soldiers' and Sailors' Monuments, and the transformation of Petersburg's Blandford Church into a Confederate shrine.

The Ladies thus succeeded in creating memorial tributes and traditions that intensified existing emotional attachment to the Confederate cause. But, more important, they had created a landscape of permanent symbols that could not simply be lowered as with the battle flag. Through their endeavors, the LMAs had likewise seeded the ground for the more popular, more well-known, and more controversial organizations, including the UDC, the Sons of Confederate Veterans, and even the League of the South. Consciously or not, Lost Cause sentiments fostered by the Ladies in the mid-to-late-nineteenth century laid the foundation for many of the racial and social tensions over Confederate memory that continue to haunt the South today.

In 1926, CMLS president Sally Archer Anderson proudly reminded her fellow memorialists that the legacy of the men in gray had emanated "from the brains of a band of women." For good or ill, she could not have been more correct. Even if future generations would forget their contributions with the passing of time, the women of the Ladies' Memorial Associations had been in large part responsible for the making of the Lost Cause.[8]

Appendix

TABLE A.1. Confederate Burials in LMA Cemeteries from Five Virginia Communities

Cemetery	Number of Confederates Buried in Cemetery
Fredericksburg	>3,300
Hebrew (Richmond)	30
Hollywood (Richmond)	>18,000
Lynchburg	2,701
Oakwood (Richmond)	>16,000
Blandford (Petersburg)	>30,000
Stonewall (Winchester)	2,489
Total	>72,520
% of total Confederates killed (out of 260,000)	27.89

TABLE A.2. Number of LMA Members in Five Virginia Communities, 1860s

Name and/or Location of LMA	Minimum Number of Members between 1866 and 1870
Fredericksburg	56
Hebrew (Richmond)	60
Hollywood (Richmond)	105
Lynchburg	45
Oakwood (Richmond)	217
Petersburg	63
Winchester	65
Total number of members	611

Note: Data includes the number of women only. Male advisors and/or officers were not counted. These numbers are approximate, as the number of women fluctuated over the months and not all new members were listed in a systematic fashion in the organizations' records.

Notes

UDC	United Daughters of the Confederacy
UVA	Alderman Library, University of Virginia, Charlottesville, Va.
VHS	Virginia Historical Society, Richmond, Va.
W&M	Earl Gregg Swem Library, College of William and Mary, Williamsburg, Va.
WLMA	Winchester Ladies' Memorial Association
WRC	Women's Relief Corps

INTRODUCTION

1   CSMA, *History of the Confederated Memorial Associations*, 282–88.

2   On the memory of the Civil War and the Lost Cause, see Brundage, *Southern Past*; Coski, *Confederate Battle Flag*; Neff, *Honoring the Civil War Dead*; Fahs and Waugh, *Memory of the Civil War*; Blair, *Cities of the Dead*; Cox, *Dixie's Daughters*; Bishir, "A Strong Force of Ladies," 3–26; Goldfield, *Still Fighting the Civil War*; Bonner, *Colors and Blood*; Blight, *Race and Reunion*; Gallagher and Nolan, *Myth of the Lost Cause*, 1–34; O'Leary, *To Die For*, 122–23; Hale, *Making Whiteness*, 47–49, 79–80; Savage, *Standing Soldiers*; Brundage, "White Women," 115–39; Parrott, "Love Makes Memory Eternal," 219–38; Foster, *Ghosts*; Wilson, *Baptized in Blood*; Woodward, *Strange Career of Jim Crow*; Osterweis, *Myth of the Lost Cause*; and Woodward, *Origins*.

3   For example, Gaines M. Foster claims that most white southerners were hesitant to cele-brate the Confederate past in the years between 1865 and the mid-1880s, in part because he fails to recognize the significance of women's earliest roles in memorial associations. W. Fitzhugh Brundage, too, suggests that the 1860s and 1870s were marked by "little organized interest in the past," because he discounts the importance of LMAs. Even those few historians who take seriously the role of the LMAs see these women's associa-tions as either temporary (lasting only through the 1870s or "giving way" to the UDC in the 1890s) or largely irrelevant because they were merely concerned with "memori-alization." (Foster, *Ghosts*, 36–62; Brundage, "White Women," 115.) Blight, in *Race and Reunion*, fails to acknowledge that the LMAs played a significant role in the Lost Cause (see especially 258). The exceptions to this trend in the historiography are Blair, *Cities of the Dead*; Neff, *Honoring the Civil War Dead*; and Fahs and Waugh, *Memory of the Civil War*. In his account, Blair acknowledges the political significance of the LMAs. (Blair, *Cities of the Dead*, 61–65, 78–97, 131, 189–91, 203–4.) John Neff likewise notes that "honoring the war's soldier dead always possessed a political dimension" and further acknowledges that "the duty of commemoration fell in the South to those whom society considered politically irrelevant—women." (Neff, *Honoring the Civil War Dead*, 146.) This account, however, is the first book-length study of LMAs to date. Historians who have dealt with the LMAs in articles or chapters include Whites, *Civil War as a Crisis in Gender*, 160–98; Bishir, "A Strong Force of Ladies," 3–26; Censer, *Reconstruction*, 191–203, 206, 218, 275–78; and Coski and Feely, "A Monument to Southern Womanhood," 130–63.

4   *Richmond Dispatch*, May 31, 1887; *Southern Opinion*, June 15, 1867, June 6, 1868; Robert E. Lee to Miss Ida Dodge, May 11, 1866, Lee Letterbook, Lee Family Papers, VHS; *New York Times*, June 5, 1868; *Petersburg Daily Index-Appeal*, June 11, 1901. Stith Bolling (1835–

1916) enlisted as a sergeant in the Lunenberg Light Dragoons (Company G of the 9th Regiment, Virginia Cavalry) in 1861. Eventually he rose to the rank of acting assistant adjunct general. After the war, he refused to surrender with the remainder of the Army of Northern Virginia and attempted to join General Joseph E. Johnston in North Carolina. He surrendered, however, on April 15, 1865. After the war, the governor appointed him brigadier general of the militia, and he served as commander of the Petersburg A. P. Hill Camp of Confederate Veterans and subsequently as major general of the Virginia Division. (Gunter, "Stith Bolling," in Kneebone et al., *Dictionary of Virginia Biography* 1: 71–72.)

5 Like many other historians of the Lost Cause, I elected to end the study between 1914 and 1915. These years marked the fiftieth anniversary of the war and also the commencement of World War I. At this point, reconciliation had been firmly established between white people of the North and South, and beginning at this time Memorial Days no longer exclusively celebrated Civil War soldiers. (Blair, *Cities of the Dead*, 6–7; Blight, *Race and Reunion*, 6–30, 381–97; Foster, *Ghosts*, 163–98.)

6 Cox argues that the UDC aspired to "transform military defeat into a political and cultural victory, where states' rights and white supremacy remained intact." I am arguing, however, that their predecessors, the LMAs, had already established this transformation by the time of the UDC's organization in 1894. (Cox, *Dixie's Daughters*, 1.)

7 See, for example, Foster, *Ghosts*, 36–62; Brundage, "White Women," 115; and Blight, *Race and Reunion*, 258.

8 I have discussed the cyclical nature of Lost Cause memory in further detail in "To Honor Her Noble Sons," 256–69.

9 Blair, *Cities of the Dead*; Blight, *Race and Reunion*; Neff, *Honoring the Civil War Dead*; Fahs and Waugh, *Memory of the Civil War*; Brundage, *Southern Past*, 2–7.

10 Anne Firor Scott, *Southern Lady*.

11 For argument that the Civil War served as a watershed for middle- and upper-class southern white women, see Schultz, *Women at the Front*, 3, 6; Censer, *Reconstruction*; Ryan, *Women in Public*, 142, 156; and Scott, *Natural Allies*, 79. For scholars who disagree with Scott's findings, see Lebsock, *Free Women*; Rable, *Civil Wars*; Whites, *Civil War as a Crisis in Gender*; and Faust, *Mothers of Invention*.

12 Judith Ann Giesberg has argued similarly that the U.S. Sanitary Commission "served as an interim structure . . . between the localized feminine activism of the first half of the century and the mass women's movements of the late nineteenth and twentieth centuries." (Giesberg, *Civil War Sisterhood*, 11.)

13 Baker, "Domestication of Politics," 620–47; Ginzberg, *Women and the Work of Benevolence*, 68–69; Kierner, *Beyond the Household*, 180–211; Varon, *We Mean to Be Counted*, 1–9. For further definitions of women and politics, see also Skocpol, *Protecting Soldiers*; Ryan, *Women in Public*; Edwards, *Angels in the Machinery*; and Allgor, *Parlor Politics*.

14 Censer, *Reconstruction*, 188; Varon, *We Mean to Be Counted*, 124, 171; Scott, *Southern Lady*, 102.

15 For historians who argue that gender patterns returned in large part to their antebellum status, see Whites, *Civil War as a Crisis in Gender*, 132–98; Faust, *Mothers of Invention*, 248–54; and Rable, *Civil Wars*, 228.

16 For the argument that LMAs were dedicated to the "reconstruction of southern white

men," see Whites, "Stand by Your Man," 133–49; Whites, *Civil War as a Crisis in Gender*, 160–98; Cox, *Dixie's Daughters*, 9–10; and Piehler, *Remembering War the American Way*, 63. For argument that LMAs were more interested in patriotic endeavors, see Censer, *Reconstruction*, 202.

17 This number is based on the LMAs that joined the CSMA in 1900 as well as other documented associations in Virginia. The CSMA, discussed in chapter 6, collected histories from each of the LMAs that joined the association and published them in a collection in 1904. (CSMA, *History of the Confederate Memorial Associations*.)

18 Virginia undeniably sent the most men to war of any Confederate state. According to the Confederate Service Records, Virginia sent 214,476 men; followed by Georgia, 181,033; Tennessee, 141,728; North Carolina, 137,527; and Mississippi, 127,069. Gary W. Gallagher and Robert K. Krick suggest that one-third of the total for each state should be deducted to account for duplicate records for individual men. According to Krick, "The infantry-to-cavalry syndrome, abetted by the imbecilic spring 1862 conscription plus bounty/elections legislation, accounts for the majority of that." That brings the estimated total of men who fought from Virginia to 142,984. (Krick, *Smoothbore Volley*, 243–44.)

19 *Southern Opinion*, August 29, 1868; CSMA, *History of the Confederate Memorial Associations*.

20 For list of burial numbers by cemetery, see Table A.1 in the Appendix.

21 For more discussion of Winchester, see Mahon, *Winchester Divided*, vii–ix; Morton, *Story of Winchester*, 145; and Quarles, *Occupied Winchester*, iii.

22 For more detailed analysis of Fredericksburg, see Blair, "Barbarians at Fredericksburg's Gate," 142–70; Harcourt, "Civil War and Social Change," 5–13; Rable, *Fredericksburg! Fredericksburg!*; Quinn, *History of the City of Fredericksburg*; and Goolrick, *Historic Fredericksburg*.

23 Henderson, *Petersburg in the Civil War*, 1–20, 136–43; Hartzell, "Exploration of Freedom," 134–56; Davidson, *Cullings from the Confederacy*, 10.

24 For more information on Lynchburg during the Civil War, see Morris and Foutz, *Lynchburg in the Civil War*, 1–56; Civil War Hospitals in Lynchburg, accessed through the internet, <http://www.gravegarden.org/hospitals.htm>; Tripp, *Yankee Town*; Christian, *Lynchburg and Its People*; and Moore and Baber, *Behind the Old Brick Wall*. The battle of Lynchburg occurred on June 18, 1864. General David Hunter commanded 19,000 Union troops, and General Jubal A. Early, later a resident of Lynchburg, commanded 16,000 Confederate troops. After a daylong assault, Early realized that Hunter had begun retreating and ordered an immediate pursuit. Early pressed Hunter past Salem, Virginia, where the Union forces slipped into the mountains of West Virginia. Casualties in the battle were minimal: Hunter lost approximately 250 killed, wounded, or captured; Confederate losses were far fewer.

25 For discussion of antebellum and wartime Richmond, see Green, *Chimborazo*, 46–47; Putnam, *Richmond during the War*, xvii; Chesson, *Richmond after the War*, 3–23; Mitchell, *Hollywood Cemetery*, 47; Jones, *Ladies of Richmond*; Woodward and Muhlenfeld, *Private Mary Chesnut*; and Woodward, *Mary Chesnut's Civil War*.

26 Clark, *Defining Moments*; Blight, *Race and Reunion*; Blair, *Cities of the Dead*; Savage, *Standing Soldiers*; Clark, "Celebrating Freedom," 107–32; Van Zelm, "Virginia Women."

27 There is an extensive literature on white supremacy. For some insightful examples, see

Gilmore, *Gender and Jim Crow*; Kantrowitz, *Ben Tillman*; Ayers, *Promise*; Hale, *Making Whiteness*; Cox, *Dixie's Daughters*, 4–5, 13–15, 121–28; and Lebsock, *Murder in Virginia*.

28 For the most complete work on men's organizations, see Foster, *Ghosts*; Blight, *Race and Reunion*; and Gallagher and Nolan, *Myth of the Lost Cause*.

29 The minutes for the Winchester LMA have not been located, but the records for an associated group, the Stonewall Cemetery Records, have provided sufficient evidence of the WLMA's work. These records can be found at the HRL.

CHAPTER ONE

1 Suzanne Lebsock, "Foreword," ix–xii. Not all of Virginia's white women supported the Confederacy, though most did. For examples of Virginia women who felt intense loyalty to the Union, see Mahon, *Winchester Divided*; Quarles, *Occupied Winchester*; and Katherine Couse, Letter to unidentified recipients, May 4–20, 1864, Accession #10441, UVA. Northern women, too, participated in the war effort in many of the same ways as southern women, that is, through soldiers' aid societies, as nurses, and as spies. See Seidman, "We Were Enlisted for the War," 59–80.

2 Lizzie Alsop Diary, June 6, July 2, July 14, 1862, Wynne Family Papers, VHS. Lizzie's mother, Sara Alsop, was a directress of the Fredericksburg Relief Association. Lizzie's diary suggests that she and her sister participated in the association when they were home from boarding school in Richmond. For discussion of Confederate women's hostility to the United States flag, see Bonner, *Colors and Blood*, 163–64.

3 Historian Elizabeth Varon argues that women entered the public sphere through claims of feminine benevolent moral duty. (Varon, *We Mean to Be Counted*, 139–54.) For argument that southern women did not develop substantial benevolent associations or networks until after the Civil War, see Friedman, *Enclosed Garden*.

4 Parmelee, *Confederate Diary of Betty Herndon Maury*. This is a very rare book, and I used the edition held at UVA. Adelaide Clopton to Nannie Clopton, July 9, 1862, Southern Women's Collection, MOC.

5 O'Leary, *To Die For*, 71–74; Kerber, *No Constitutional Right to Be Ladies*, 8–13, 21–22, 28–29, 82, 146, 236, 241–42, 299, 308. Jeanie Attie argues that in the North a distinct version of female patriotism developed that "placed economic voluntarism at the heart of women's participation in the defense of the nation." (Attie, "Warwork and the Crisis of Domesticity in the North," 251.) Evidence from southern white women suggests that the economic and social conditions of the South did not allow for such a clear-cut distinction.

6 Putnam, *Richmond during the War*, 39–40; McDonald, *A Woman's Civil War*, 17.

7 Christian, *Lynchburg and Its People*, 194, 198, 214; Tripp, *Yankee Town*, 122; *Lynchburg Daily Virginian*, April 19, 22, May 2, 1861; Lucy Wood quoted in Faust, Glymph, and Rable, "A Woman's War: Southern Women in the Civil War," 5.

8 Minutes of the Washington Street Ladies' Association, Campbell Papers, W&M; Lebsock, *Free Women*, 245–46; Bessie Callender, "Personal Recollections of the Civil War," PETE. The sewing societies that have been identified in Petersburg include the Market Street M.E. Church, the Tabb Street Presbyterian, the High Street M.E. Church, the Washington Street M.E. Church, the High Street Church (not M.E.), and another un-

named church society. For discussion of Petersburg's antebellum female associations and networks, see Lebsock, *Free Women*, 195–236.

9   Rable, *Civil Wars*, 139; Ladies' Ridge Benevolent Society Record Book, MOC; *Richmond Whig*, May 16, June 20, 1861; Bell, "Female Benevolence," 24; Lucy Bagby, "Chronicle," Bagby Family Papers, VHS.

10 Jones, *Ladies of Richmond*, 183; Woodward, *Mary Chesnut's Civil War*, 119, 155–56. Mary Elizabeth (Adams) Pope Randolph ran a fashionable salon with her husband, George, grandson of Thomas Jefferson. After George Randolph resigned as secretary of war on November 15, 1862, the family remained in Richmond while he organized volunteers for its defense. In the fall of 1864, the family moved to Europe, due to his health.

11 Harcourt, "Civil War and Social Change," 18.

12 *Lynchburg Virginian*, April 2, 1862.

13 Sallie R. Munford to Charles Ellis Munford, June 21, 1861, Munford-Ellis Family Papers, DU; Abby Manly Gwathmey to parents, April 29, 1861, Southern Women's Collection, MOC; Parmelee, *Confederate Diary of Betty Herndon Maury*, June 26, 1861; Lucy Muse Walton Fletcher Diary, May 22, 1864, DU.

14 *Lynchburg Daily Virginian*, April 20, May 2, 1861, September 21, 1861; *Richmond Enquirer*, August 23, 1861; *Richmond Whig*, clipping from April or May 1861, Clipping File, MOC.

15 *Richmond Whig*, July 22, 1861; *Southern Opinion*, October 12, 1867 (emphasis added).

16 For women who disguised themselves as male soldiers, see Leonard, *All the Daring of a Soldier*.

17 For discussion of Confederates comparing themselves to the Revolutionaries of 1776, see Thomas, *Confederacy as a Revolutionary Experience*; Mitchell, *Civil War Soldiers*; and McPherson, *What They Fought For*.

18 *Richmond Whig*, clipping from April or May 1861, Clipping File, MOC.

19 *Fredericksburg News*, April 25, 1861. Historian Elizabeth Varon argues that during the antebellum period Virginia's elite white women entered the public sphere through their claims of benevolent moral duty. She notes that through their political action, they shaped sectional tensions. (Varon, *We Mean to Be Counted*, 2.) For discussion of women's participation in the nonimportation movement during the American Revolution, see Breen, *Marketplace of Revolution*, 230–36.

20 Parmelee, *Confederate Diary of Betty Herndon Maury*, August 16, 21, 1861; "Meeting of the Ladies of Fredericksburg," microfilm collection, MOC; Cannon, *Flags of the Confederacy*, 14. The names available for each organization suggest that at least the leadership of the two Fredericksburg associations was distinct. For further discussion of Confederate women's efforts to design flags, see Bonner, *Colors and Blood*, 46–47.

21 Faust, *Mothers of Invention*, 28–29. Her terminology suggests that soldiers' aid societies, Fredericksburg's flag committee, and other like-minded organizations failed to provide a political context.

22 Cynthia B. T. Coleman to "friend," March 25, 1862, Tucker-Coleman Papers, W&M. Women in Richmond were not the only Virginians to propose a gunboat. On March 25, 1862, Cynthia B. T. Coleman of Williamsburg suggested a similar "scheme emanating from some of the patriotic ladies of this old city." Like Richmond's women, she proposed raising a fund through concerts, suppers, and subscriptions to furnish a gunboat.

She believed that cities across the state should form auxiliary organizations that would remit their collections to the "Parent Society," in Williamsburg.

23 Ladies' Defense and Aid Association Papers, MOC.

24 *Richmond Whig*, April 1, 12, 22, 1862; *Charleston Mercury*, March 14, 1861. During the war, at least two ships were named *Lady Davis*. Along with the Richmond ship, the first war vessel put afloat by South Carolina since the Revolutionary War was also named *Lady Davis*.

25 Coski, *Capital Navy*, 82–83; Ladies' Defense and Aid Association Papers, MOC; *Lynchburg Virginian*, March 27, 29, 1862; Harriette Branham Diary, April 11, 1862, DU; Parmelee, *Confederate Diary of Betty Herndon Maury*, April 30, 1862. Martha Maury was Captain Matthew Fontaine Maury's niece. Richmond's *Lady Davis* became the CSS *Virginia II* before she was ever sailed. She was launched in June 1863 and finally completed and commissioned in May 1864.

26 Ryan, *Women in Public*, 142; Faust, *Mothers of Invention*, 28–29; Harriette Branham Diary, April 11, 1862, DU; *Lynchburg Virginian*, April 2, 1862; Cynthia B. T. Coleman to "friend," March 25, 1862, Tucker-Coleman Papers, W&M (emphasis added). For additional argument that women resented men for not protecting them, see Rable, *Civil Wars*, 73–90.

27 Friedman, *Enclosed Garden*, xi–xvi, 98. For additional argument that southern white women did not develop networks or a female consciousness prior to the war, see also Fox-Genovese, *Within the Plantation Household*; and Edwards, *Scarlett*, 27. For historians who argue that white southern women organized benevolent associations prior to the American Civil War, see Lebsock, *Free Women*, 195–236; Varon, *We Mean to Be Counted*, 10–70.

28 Parmelee, *Confederate Diary of Betty Herndon Maury*, July 20, 27, 1862.

29 Woodward, *Mary Chesnut's Civil War*, 119; Woodward and Muhlenfeld, *Private Mary Chesnut*, 125–26.

30 *Lynchburg Virginian*, October 4, 1861; Parmelee, *Confederate Diary of Betty Herndon Maury*, August 16, 21, 1861; "Meeting of the Ladies of Fredericksburg," microfilm collection, MOC; *Richmond Whig*, June 26, 1861.

31 Rachel Filene Seidman estimates that thousands of northern women formed as many as 20,000 ladies' aid societies during the war. She notes that some of these associations formed immediately after the attack on Fort Sumter. "Others were drummed up later by agents of the United States Sanitary Commission." The organization was under the direction of men such as Henry W. Bellows, D.D., and Frederick Law Olmsted, but many northern women filled the ranks of the Sanitary Commission. (Seidman, "We Were Enlisted for the War," 61–63.) For more detailed analysis of the U.S. Sanitary Commission, see Giesberg, *Civil War Sisterhood*.

32 General Order No. 4, Daniel Ruggles Collection, DU; *Richmond Whig*, April 3, 1863.

33 *Richmond Whig*, June 21, July 4, August 7, 9, 1861. In addition to gathering supplies, the association also organized a committee to engage competent nurses for the local camps and hospitals.

34 Greenville Ladies' Association Minutes, DU; Woodward, *Mary Chesnut's Civil War*, 119; Jones, *Ladies of Richmond*, 131–32; Ballou, "Hospital Medicine in Richmond," 26–27; *Richmond Whig*, June 21, July 4, 1861, August 7, 9, 1861. It is difficult to determine if

the Soldiers' Aid Society of Virginia and the Richmond Ladies' Association, headed by Mary Randolph, ever merged into one organization. According to the Greenville Ladies' Association, these women received a circular from the Soldiers' Aid Society but sent provisions to Mary Randolph of the Richmond Ladies' Association.

35 Jane E. Schultz argues that "the most significant wartime labor in which women directly engaged military life was hospital and relief work."(Schultz, *Women at the Front*, 2–3.)

36 Lucy Mina Otey, born in 1801, was the wife of city leader Captain John M. Otey. Prior to the war, she served as president of the Ann Norvell Orphan Asylum of Lynchburg, which had been founded by her mother. She also participated in the local Dorcas Society. During the war, she remained in Lynchburg with one niece, while her seven sons and husband joined the ranks of the Confederate army. At the end of the war, only four sons survived. Her only daughter, Lucy, married Captain John Stewart Walker of Richmond, who died at Malvern Hill. ("Mrs. Lucy Mina Otey," *Southern Literary Messenger* 1 [July 1895]: 15–16.)

37 Moore and Baber, *Behind the Old Brick Wall*, 25; *Lynchburg News*, March 6, 1960; Tripp, *Yankee Town*, 122, 141; "Lynchburg Hospital Association," Irvine, Saunders, Davis, and Watts Families Papers, UVA; *Lynchburg Daily Virginian*, August 29, September 30, October 4, 1861, May 7, 31, 1862. By August 29, 1861, the Ladies announced that they were prepared to have the cooking performed at the hospital, although donations would still be accepted. Believing that their class status prevented them from performing the more laborious tasks, the matrons—some of the city's most prominent women—supervised nurses paid through charitable subscriptions. The upper-class women daily visited the hospital to bring food and drink, distribute tracts, and write letters; the nurses prepared food, changed bandages, and provided general aid to the surgeons.

38 Blair, *Virginia's Private War*, 96–97. Attitudes about women's work in hospitals met with mixed reactions from Confederate men. Many appreciated women's maternal touch in the wards. The surgeon who inspected Maria Clopton's hospital in 1862 believed that patients were most comfortable and happy in hospitals where women had general management of the nursing. During the spring of 1862, a soldier from Company I, 11th Virginia Volunteers, wrote a Lynchburg newspaper, praising the women's efforts. "Too much cannot be said of this institution, and of the untiring energy and perseverance of its officers," wrote the volunteer. Commending Lucy Otey personally, he wished that all the Commonwealth's women were as loyal to the cause of liberty as she and that all the hospitals were conducted under such principles. But other men felt quite strongly that women did not belong in such an indelicate atmosphere. Phoebe Pember, a nurse at Chimborazo, encountered resistance to her presence upon arriving at the Richmond hospital. The women of Lynchburg had been prompted in part to organize their own hospital after a sentinel denied Lucy Otey entrance to the hospital where she had been volunteering. He claimed that Dr. William Otway Owen, Lynchburg resident and chief surgeon of all the city's military hospitals, had ordered that "no more women or flies were to be admitted." Otey, a well-connected woman who had entertained Robert E. Lee in her home, went directly to Richmond to speak with her personal friend, President Davis. The president granted her carte blanche to conduct her hospital as she deemed fit and appointed Dr. Thomas L. Walker as surgeon in charge. Owen, however, continued his efforts to close the Ladies' Hospital. (Report of Clopton Hospital Surgeon to Surgeon

General S. P. Moore, September 15, 1862, Clopton Records, Hospital Collection, MOC; *Lynchburg Virginian*, April 9, 1862; Faust, *Mothers of Invention*, 98; Pember, *Southern Woman's Story*, 3; Tripp, *Yankee Town*, 122–23; "Lynchburg Hospital Association," Irvine, Saunders, Davis, and Watts Families Papers, UVA; *Lynchburg News*, March 6, 1960; Morris and Foutz, *Lynchburg in the Civil War*, 15, 17, 19, 21–23, 29, 36, 55.)

39 Mrs. William B. Lightfoot, "Biographical Sketch of Sally Tompkins," Hospital Collection, MOC; Faust, *Mothers of Invention*, 94; Woodward and Muhlenfeld, *Private Mary Chesnut*, 118, 137–40; Woodward, *Mary Chesnut's Civil War*, 143, 530. With the help of her sister, Ellen, Mary Jones, Martha Carter, various other elite women, and four family slaves, Tompkins cared for more than 1,300 soldiers during the war. She achieved considerable notoriety within the city largely because of her low mortality rate, so much so that Mary Chesnut dubbed her the Florence Nightingale of the South. Chesnut later referred to Lucy Mason Webb as "our Florence Nightingale," as well. Sally Tompkins was born in Poplar Grove, Mathews County, to Christopher and Maria Booth Patterson Tompkins in 1833. She appears to be the only woman ever commissioned by the Confederate States of America (although some claim that Lucy Otey of Lynchburg was commissioned).

40 Clopton Hospital officially opened on May 28, 1862, under the direction of Captain Israel Warner. Twelve to fifteen women initially nursed soldiers in two homes, until they split. One group went with Mrs. Joseph Jackson, and the other remained with Maria Clopton. (Clopton Records, Hospital Collection, MOC.)

41 Clopton Records, Hospital Collection, MOC. Of the 565 patients treated by the fall of 1862, there were 98 furloughs, 11 deaths, and 4 discharged from service. Despite its success, officials closed the hospital in October 1862 and offered Maria Clopton a position as matron of her own ward at Winder Hospital in the city's West End. The surgeon's report noted the difficulty in obtaining "intelligent nurses for the wages paid by the Confederacy." For more discussion of the nursing shortage, see Faust, *Mothers of Invention*, 95–97; and Rable, *Civil Wars*, 121–28.

42 Woodward, *Mary Chesnut's Civil War*, 416, 439, 474–75; Jones, *Ladies of Richmond*, 71–72, 97–98. Confederate officials recognized the success of female-run hospitals, and in September 1862 Congress passed legislation that created positions for women in the military hospitals. Specifically, the law designated that each hospital allow matrons, assistant matrons, and nurses, as needed by surgeons. Matrons were responsible for procuring provisions, overseeing housekeeping, and administering food and medicine when necessary; nurses performed the more grueling tasks of assisting with surgeries and changing bandages. These women were not merely volunteers but were to be paid a monthly salary, ranging from twenty-five dollars to forty dollars, along with lodging and rations. Congress justified its decision to fill jobs traditionally reserved for invalid soldiers and slaves with women by invoking the feminine notion of maternal caregiving. As Drew Faust has pointed out, the Hospital Act represented a significant statement regarding the changing relationship between the state and its female citizens. (Faust, *Mothers of Invention*, 97–98; U.S. War Department, *War of the Rebellion: Official Records*, ser. 4, vol. 2, pt. 199–200.)

43 Janet Henderson Weaver Randolph was a key member in the HMA, the CMLS, the UDC, and Lee Camp Ladies' Auxiliary. See chapters 5 and 6.

44 Mrs. J. S. Kennedy to Janet Cleiland Weaver, August 28, 1861, Randolph Family Papers, VHS; Kate Kern Letters, October 1864 through May 1865, LOV. For the argument that church and family were the most important (if not exclusive) ties among southern white women, see Friedman, *Enclosed Garden*, 3–20.

45 Ash, *When the Yankees Came*, 44–45, 60–61, 73. Ash notes that as the war went on and more citizens gave in to pressures to take oaths, breaking oaths was increasingly common.

46 Delauter, *Winchester in the Civil War*, 25, 48; Mahon, *Winchester Divided*, 77–78; McGuire, *Diary of a Southern Refugee*, October 2, 1861, 66–67; Sarah Ann Alsop to Lizzie and Nannie Alsop, May 29–31, 1864, Wynne Family Papers, VHS.

47 Emily Aylett to Alice and Etta Aylett, July 27, 1864, Aylett Family Papers, VHS; Lucy Muse Walton Fletcher Diary, June 7, 1864, DU; Pember, *Southern Woman's Story*, xv.

48 Campbell, *When Sherman Marched North*, 4, 12–13, 15, 71–74, 91–98, 101–4.

49 For the argument that most Confederate women lost faith in the war effort, see Faust, *Mothers of Invention*, 234–47; and Rable, *Civil Wars*, 73–90. For the argument that most Confederate women did not abandon nationalistic feelings, see Campbell, *When Sherman Marched North*; and Gallagher, *Confederate War*, especially 75–80.

50 See especially Faust, *Mothers of Invention*, 238–47.

51 Lucy W. Otey to Colonel Lyle Charles, March 8, 1864, quoted in Gallagher, *Confederate War*, 4–5; Maria Smith Peeks Diary, June 6, 1864, Marrow Family Papers, VHS; Lucy Muse Walton Fletcher Diary, April 14, 1864, DU; Kate Mason Rowland Diary, January 23, 1865, Kate Mason Rowland Papers, MOC; Lucy Bagby, "Chronicle," Bagby Family Papers, VHS; Lizzie Alsop Diary, February 17, March 3 (emphasis in original), 1865, Wynne Family Papers, VHS.

52 *Richmond Whig*, February 3, 1863; Christian, *Lynchburg and Its People*, 214–15; Dr. John Herbert Claiborne to Sarah Joseph Alston Claiborne, May 14, 1864, UVA; Harcourt, "Civil War and Social Change," 29; *Richmond Daily Examiner*, March 25, 1865; Murrell, "Two Armies," 79; Bessie Callender, "Personal Recollections of the Civil War," PETE. At least one instance of women refusing to aid the Confederacy has been documented. The women of Richmond's Monumental Episcopal Church refused to sew socks for soldiers during the spring of 1865. But evidence also exists for the continuation of soldiers' aid societies outside of Virginia. For example, the women of Milton, North Carolina, continued to send supplies to Richmond hospitals in the summer of 1864, and the Greenville South Carolina Ladies' Association met through April 1865. (Greenville Ladies' Association Minutes, DU; *Richmond Whig*, June 2, 1864.) According to Diana Bell, the war's effect on women's societies varied by region. Her research indicates that women who were cut off from supplies, such as those in South Carolina, were less likely to continue benevolent work than those in other regions. (Bell, "Female Benevolence," 44.) For the argument that "soldiers' aid became another of the Confederacy's glorious failures," see Rable, *Civil Wars*, 142.

53 Gallagher, *Confederate War*, 65, 73; Rubin, *A Shattered Nation*, 2–7, 117, 234–39; Campbell, *When Sherman Marched North*, 12–13, 15, 71–74, 91–98, 101–4; Faust, *Creation of Confederate Nationalism*; Beringer et al., *Why the South Lost the Civil War*; Foster, *Ghosts*, 36–62; Neff, *Honoring the Civil War Dead*, 10–12; Brundage, "White Women,"

115. Gallagher demonstrates that white women were as likely as their male counterparts to exhibit such intense passion for the Confederacy. Arguments for and against Confederate nationalism abound. Emory Thomas argues that nationalism flowed from the formation of national institutions such as the Confederate government or state-sponsored industries. When these institutions failed to be maintained, nationalism floundered. Conversely, Drew Faust contends that common elements in the culture of the South, namely religion, provided the foundation for nationalism. Elites such as government officials and the clergy used these features of Southern distinctiveness to construct a national identity. Beringer, Hattaway, Jones, and Still understand nationalism to be an ideology based on perceived southern distinctiveness that proved fragile and insecure from its inception. They situate Confederate "cohesiveness" in southern churches, slavery, and states' rights but conclude that only slavery truly separated the sections. The authors argue that when white southerners' allegiance to slavery failed, they lacked any ground for distinctiveness. For an excellent discussion of northern nationalism and the role of citizens' voluntary organizations fostering nationalism, see Lawson, *Patriot Fires*.

54 For discussion of mourning rituals during the nineteenth century, see Loughridge and Campbell, *Women in Mourning*; and Douglas, *Feminization of American Culture*, 200–226. Douglas argues that mourning rituals were a source of authority for women and ministers, thereby widening their spheres of influence. For detailed discussion of how the Civil War affected mourning and notions of death for the common soldier, see Faust, "Civil War Soldier and the Art of Dying," 3–38.

55 Faust, *Riddle of Death*, 21; Loughridge and Campbell, *Women in Mourning*, 14–15; Lycurgus Washington Caldwell to Susan Emiline Jeffords Caldwell, September 27, 1864, in Welton, *"My Heart Is So Rebellious,"* 239; Lizzie Alsop Diary, March 18, 1863, Wynne Family Papers, VHS; McDonald, *A Woman's Civil War*, 49–50.

56 Lucy Muse Fletcher Diary, June 7, 1864, DU; Mary E. Rambant Morrison Memoir, 1832–1904, written in 1902, VHS; John Herbert Claiborne to wife, June 12, 1864, UVA; K. C. C. to Sallie Munford, February 13, 1863, Munford-Ellis Family Papers, DU.

57 Mitchell, *Hollywood Cemetery*, 47–48. Constance Cary Harrison is also quoted in Mitchell, *Hollywood Cemetery*, 48.

58 For a discussion of death during wartime, see Laderman, *Sacred Remains*; Rable, *Fredericksburg! Fredericksburg!*, 277–78, 288–300, 315–16, 320–21, 358, 395–96; and Neff, *Honoring the Civil War Dead*, 16–65.

59 Faust, *Riddle of Death*, 11–12; Kate Sperry Diary, April 3, 1862, HRL; Mitchell, *Hollywood*, 47–60.

60 Reed, "On My Way Rejoicing," 56.

61 Woodward, *Mary Chesnut's Civil War*, 439, 474–75; Pember, *Southern Woman's Story*, xiii; Kate Sperry Diary, June 12, 1863, HRL; Kate Mason Rowland Diary, May 21, 1862, Kate Mason Rowland Papers, MOC. Her mother, Lucy Mason Webb, was a member of the Hollywood Memorial Association.

62 "Burial of Latané: A Touching Incident of the Civil War Recalled," *SHSP* 24: 192–94; "Burial of Latané," newspaper clipping, Women's Collection, MOC; *Richmond Whig*, September 25, 1862; Faust, *Mothers of Invention*, 188–89; Neff, *Honoring the Civil War Dead*, 150–52.

63 Mahon, *Winchester Divided*, 46; unknown to Nannie, June 11, 1862, Lucas-Ashley Papers, DU. Turner Ashby died at the rank of colonel but was posthumously awarded the rank of general.

64 Mahon, *Winchester Divided*, 89; Putnam, *Richmond during the War*, 222–25; *Lynchburg Daily Virginian*, May 13, 14, 1863; Cooke, *Stonewall Jackson*, 446–49.

65 Delauter, *Winchester in the Civil War*, 15–16; Mahon, *Winchester Divided*, 89–90; Quarles, *Occupied Winchester*, 16–19.

66 *Richmond Enquirer*, June 11, 1864; Faust, *Riddle of Death*, 12–13, 18; Kate Sperry Diary, March 17, 1862, HRL; John Coski, "Janet Henderson Weaver Randolph," unpublished article, MOC.

67 *Lynchburg Daily Virginian*, May 19, 1863.

68 Mary E. Rambant Morrison Memoir, 1832–1904, written in 1902, VHS; Mary Burrows Fontaine letter, April 30, May 3, 1865, Southern Women's Collection, MOC; Diary of Mrs. William A. Simmons, April 2, 1865, Southern Women's Collection, MOC; Pickett, *Pickett and His Men*, 2–3. For more description of Confederate evacuation and Union occupation of Richmond, see Chesson, *Richmond after the War*, 57–84.

69 Mary Cabell Diary, April 4, 7, 8, 1865, Early Family Papers, VHS.

CHAPTER TWO

1 CSMA, *History of the Confederate Memorial Associations*, 275–318; Morton, *Story of Winchester*, 247; unidentified newspaper clipping, Winchester Confederate Memorial Day, Memorial Collection, MOC. Throughout the late nineteenth and early twentieth centuries, representatives from LMAs across the South debated which group had been the first to organize. My research suggests that Winchester was at least the first LMA in Virginia, if not in the South. In addition, these same groups disputed who first celebrated Memorial Day. Alternatively, David Blight has shown that one of the first Decoration Days occurred in South Carolina under the direction of black men and women on May 1, 1865. For more on this debate, see Blight, *Race and Reunion*, 68–71; and Mildred Rutherford Scrapbook Collection, MOC.

2 Brundage, "White Women," 115–39; Chesson, *Richmond after the War*, 204–10. Brundage argues that memorial organizations in the 1860s and 1870s were too scattered and their membership too small to constitute a concerted effort to honor the Confederacy. Likewise, Michael B. Chesson contends that "in the 1860s and 1870s Richmonders had been too poor and too busy recovering from the war and Reconstruction to celebrate their Confederate experience."

3 See Foster, *Ghosts*, for the argument that in the 1870s the Lost Cause movement was lead by veterans and members of the officer corps, primarily from Virginia. He contends that their antinorthern tone and elitist attitude discouraged most white southerners from joining. For an argument similar to the author's, see Bishir, "A Strong Force of Ladies," 3–23.

4 Putnam, *Richmond during the War*, 389; Lucy Muse Walton Fletcher Diary, April 12, 1865, DU; Swint, *Dear Ones at Home*; Letter from Lucy Chase, May 17, 1865, 274. I have followed Elizabeth Varon's lead in referring to Putnam as Brock in the text. Brock published her memoir in 1867 under the guise of "A Richmond Lady." She married

Richard F. Putnam in 1882; subsequent editions of her book carry the name of Sallie Brock Putnam. I have elected to refer to her as Putnam in the notes. (Varon, *Southern Lady*, 273n2.)

5 Foster, *Ghosts*, 15; George W. Munford to Mrs. Elizabeth T. Munford, April 28, 1865, Munford-Ellis Family Papers, DU. For extensive discussion of Confederate reaction to the end of the war, see Rubin, *A Shattered Nation*, 117–38, 219–20.

6 Silber, *Romance of Reunion*, 26–29. Silber has demonstrated that many northern men believed that southern white women displayed an intense attachment to the Confederacy and hostility to the federal government beyond that of southern men. Believing that gender behavior was indicative of "civilization," white northerners quickly pointed out that these southern white women were lacking in proper Victorian manners.

7 Lizzie Alsop Diary, April 12, 1865, Wynne Family Collection, VHS; Mary Cabell Diary, April 11, 1865, Early Family Papers, VHS; Isabel Maury to Mollie Maury (later Mary Maury Werth), January 1, 1866, Isabel Maury Papers, MOC. New Year's was traditionally a day for hiring out slaves for the forthcoming year in the South; thus parties were a rare occurrence.

8 As William Blair has pointed out, slaveholding women were often the most virulent in expressing their opinions regarding emancipation. (Blair, *Virginia's Private War*, 135.)

9 Lucy Muse Walton Fletcher Diary, April 12, 1865, DU; Emmy Wellford to brother, Phil, April 20, 1865, John Rutherfoord Papers, DU; Mrs. Charles Ellis Sr., April 1865, Munford-Ellis Family Papers, DU; Emmie Sublett to Emilie, April 29, 1865, Southern Women's Collection, MOC; "Recollections of Isabel Maury," Isabel Maury Papers, MOC.

10 Mildred Rutherford Scrapbook Collection, vol. 41, MOC; *Lynchburg News*, January 15, 1866; *Lynchburg Daily Virginian*, April 20, 1866; Christian, *Lynchburg and Its People*, 241; Rable, *Civil Wars*, 236; *Richmond Times*, April 13, 1866.

11 *Richmond Times*, December 4, 1865; Morton, *Story of Winchester*, 247–48; CSMA, *History of the Confederated Memorial Associations*, 316.

12 Even as early as April 1866, northerners were beginning to question the notion of an impoverished South. On April 9, 1866, the *New York Times* commented on this issue only a year after the war: "If one were to listen to the tales by people of this section [the South], or to read their newspapers about the scarcity of money, the natural impression would be that business is stagnant, and there is no capital actively employed here. To disprove such an inference it is only necessary to walk through the 'burn district' of Richmond and see the immense improvements now progressing. Somebody has money, and that money will soon find its way into the pockets of the masses. . . . The fact of the matter is, the South, at least this section, is not so badly off as we have been made to believe."

13 Rable, *Civil Wars*, 240–64; *Ladies Memorial Association of Montgomery, Alabama, 1860–1870*, Pamphlet Collection, MOC; Stonewall Cemetery Records, HRL; Morton, *Story of Winchester*, 248; CSMA, *History of the Confederated Memorial Associations*, 316; "Circular and Address of the Monumental Association of the Stonewall Cemetery," c. 1867, VHS; *Richmond Times*, December 4, 1865.

14 In one such example, a writer for the *New York Times*, on June 20, 1865, noted: "The number of soldiers buried around and near Petersburg since active operations began there a year ago, must be very great. Shall these graves be given over to the plow and wagon wheel, the trampling of animals and the feet of passer-by? What shall be done

must be done quickly. Ought there not to be a National Cemetery at Petersburgh [*sic*]?" Civilian organizers were likewise involved in the establishment of cemeteries for Union soldiers, such as at Antietam. For an excellent discussion of this, see Neff, *Honoring the Civil War Dead*, 108–11.

15 *New York Observer and Chronicle*, July 13, August 31, 1865; *New York Times*, July 4, 1865; Neff, *Honoring the Civil War Dead*, 127–28; Faust, "Dread Void of Uncertainty," 7–32.

16 On April 13, 1866, Congress passed an act to "preserve from desecration the graves of the soldiers of the United States that fell in battle or died of disease in the field and in hospital during the war of rebellion." On February 22, 1867, Congress passed legislation that formally linked these resting places under the National Cemetery System. (Neff, *Honoring the Civil War Dead*, 131.)

17 *New York Daily News*, April 5, October 12, 1866; Quarles, *Occupied Winchester*, 130; Morton, *Story of Winchester*, 249–50; Faust, *Riddle of Death*, 17–18; Blair, *Cities of the Dead*, 52–53; Neff, *Honoring the Civil War Dead*, 125–67; Blight, *Race and Reunion*, 68–70.

18 As Neff points out, "No Confederates who died while under arms opposing the Union were interred in any of the national cemeteries. Only those who died in Union custody—while prisoner of war or in Union hospitals—were interred in the grounds that eventually became part of that system." There were cases, however, where "smaller Confederate plots or individual graves were contained within the walled national cemetery, although almost always relegated to a separate corner of the field." (Neff, *Honoring the Civil War Dead*, 132.)

19 Calkins, "History of Poplar Grove National Cemetery," 44; Blair, *Cities of the Dead*, 53, *Richmond Daily Examiner*, May 5, 1866; *Advocate of Peace*, May/June 1866, APS Online, p. 70; *New York Times*, November 18, 1866.

20 For discussion of Union burial practices and exclusion of Confederates from national cemeteries, see Neff, *Honoring the Civil War Dead*, 112–29.

21 Blair, *Cities of the Dead*, 52–54; Faust, *Riddle of Death*, 18.

22 *Lynchburg News*, March 30, April 5, 1866; *Richmond Dispatch*, March 26, 1866; Blair, *Cities of the Dead*, 35–42; Clark, *Defining Moments*, 25, 54.

23 The minor event of the day occurred when a single gunshot was fired into the crowd, but the perpetrator was immediately arrested and no one was struck by the shot. Two weeks later, however, violence erupted in Norfolk, Virginia, when the city's black residents held a procession in honor of the civil rights bill. Two white people were killed and several were wounded; one black youth was bayoneted in the stomach and several more were injured. (Van Zelm, "Virginia Women," 75; *Lynchburg News*, April 5, 1866; *Richmond Times*, April 18, 1866; Blair, *Cities of the Dead*, 35–42; Clark, *Defining Moments*, 54.)

24 For a discussion of the social, economic, and political uncertainty that followed the war, see Ash, *A Year in the South*.

25 *Lynchburg News*, March 30, 1866.

26 Oakwood is the only LMA in this study to have systematically recorded all the names of its members in the 1860s. Historian Susan Barber has postulated that Hollywood was the largest Richmond organization, although little concrete evidence remains to substantiate or refute her claim. (Barber, "Sisters of the Capital," 389–90.) Oakwood Cemetery had been established in 1854 on a sixty-acre parcel of land east of the city for St. John's Burying Ground, as Shockoe Cemetery became increasingly full. The city council

authorized the burial of Confederate soldiers in Oakwood in August 1861, and by late 1862 thousands had been buried there, often in shallow graves. At the war's end, more than 16,000 soldiers, including many Union soldiers who had died at Libby Prison, had been interred in Oakwood. Union dead were reinterred in one of the six national cemeteries established in the area. Most of the Union dead from Oakwood were reburied in the Richmond National Cemetery off Williamsburg Road, which opened in the fall of 1866. (*Richmond State*, December 15, 1894.) Racial hostilities flared in the summer of 1866 when U.S. soldiers, African Americans, and representatives of the Freedmen's Bureau forced their way into Oakwood Cemetery to bury black patients from Howard's Grove near the Confederate dead. The city council immediately called on the commanding general and secured his promise that all future interments of blacks would be in an unoccupied section of pine barrens separated from the white section by a creek. (Chesson, *Richmond after the War*, 102.)

27 The April 25, 1866, edition of the *Lynchburg Daily Virginian* issued a call by "several ladies" to meet, take into consideration, "and adopt the most speedy and effective measures for inclosing the graves of the Confederate soldiers" buried in the city. The newspaper followed the announcement with an endorsement of the proposal, noting that the thousands of graves were exposed to the elements and that this was "a shame, and a reflection on the people of Lynchburg." The next day, the paper noted that "every lady ought to be glad to do something toward an object which appeals so warmly in their sympathies and to humanity."

28 PLMA Minutes, May 6, 1866, LOV; FLMA Minutes, LOV; "To the Israelites of the South," broadside, June 5, 1866, BAMA. By the end of 1866, the PLMA claimed more than 200 members. (Presidents Report, PLMA Minutes, December 5, 1866, LOV.) Limited evidence exists to suggest that two other Ladies' Memorial Associations were organized in Richmond during the spring of 1866. According to Susan Barber, ten women from Shockoe Hill Cemetery signed an undated letter requesting funds from the Richmond Common Council for their cemetery. In June 1866, a group from Manchester had approximately twenty-four members. (Barber, "Sisters of the Capital," 386.)

29 Hollywood Cemetery Company was organized in 1847 and formally dedicated in 1849, as Shockoe Hill and other municipal and private cemeteries began to fill. Designed by architect John Notman, Hollywood was constructed as part of the rural cemetery movement of the mid-1800s. The cemetery began to achieve its high social status when President James Monroe was reburied there in July 1858. As at Oakwood, during the Civil War soldiers were buried in the cemetery. By August 1861, almost 100 interments had occurred in the two acres that the Hollywood Company had donated for the burial of Confederate soldiers. By the time the HMA finished their work, more than 18,000 Confederate soldiers had been buried in the cemetery. Colonel Thomas A. Ellis likewise was in distress regarding the financial situation of Hollywood, and he published an appeal for donations. Ellis's notice led to an anonymous letter to the paper suggesting that he ask the women of Richmond for help. For more information on the history of Hollywood Cemetery, see Mitchell, *Hollywood Cemetery*.

30 HMA Minutes, MOC; Mitchell, *Hollywood Cemetery*, 64; *Lynchburg Daily Virginian*, April 20, 1866. According to the HMA's history, discussions about a memorial organization first occurred during the winter of 1865–66 between Rev. Charles D. Minnegerode

and Captain Frank W. Dawson, who met in Mrs. Charles G. Barney's parlor. Mrs. Barney overheard their discussion and told many friends about their suggestion that a day should be put aside to honor the dead. This account, however, did not surface until 1896 and therefore appears somewhat unreliable. (HMA, *Our Confederate Dead*.) The assumption that HMA members might have been members of the postwar Ladies' Soldiers Aid Society is due to the connection of Rev. William H. Christian. Christian served as the agent for the LSAS, and his wife was a member of the HMA.

31 *Lynchburg Daily Virginian*, April 25, 1866; "A Leaf from the Past: From the Records of the Ladies' Memorial Association of Fredericksburg, VA," pamphlet, CRRL; "Confederate Memorial Days: Fredericksburg, Virginia, 1866–1985," CRRL, 1.

32 *Lynchburg Daily Virginian*, April 28, May 8, 1866; *Lynchburg News*, May 8, 1866; FLMA Minutes, June 1, 1866, LOV.

33 OMA Minutes, May 12–24, 1866, MOC; HMA Minutes, May 14–27, 1866, MOC; *Richmond Times*, May 25, 1866.

34 FLMA Minutes, June 15, 21, 26, 1866, LOV. Giesberg notes that northern women of the U.S. Sanitary Commission faced a similar dilemma. (Giesberg, *Civil War Sisterhood*, 7.)

35 PLMA Minutes, June 1866, LOV; Skocpol, *Protecting Soldiers*, 311–524; Ladies Memorial Association Broadside, December 1866, Papers of Eugene Davis, UVA.

36 HMA Minutes, MOC; FLMA Minutes, August 1866, LOV; Robert E. Lee to C. R. Bishop of Petersburg, May 5, Lee to Mrs. William Coulling of Richmond, May 5, Lee to Miss Ida Dodge of Lynchburg, May 11, Lee to Mr. William Beyers of Richmond, June 2, 1866, Lee Letterbook, VHS. Lee's response confirms Gaines Foster's assertion that Lee's role in the Lost Cause was often ambivalent. Though seemingly contradictory, Lee approved of Lost Cause books by Jubal Early and Robert L. Dabney, but he also "did avoid and sometimes discourage memorial ceremonies, monument campaigns, and other Confederate activities." Interestingly, while the women's organizations in Virginia were busy raising money to support their efforts, Lee believed that neither the students at Washington College nor the Shenandoah Valley residents could afford to donate funds to a proposed monument to Jackson in 1866. (Foster, *Ghosts*, 50–51; Robert E. Lee to Mr. William Beyers, June 2, 1866, Lee Letterbook, VHS.)

37 LMAs were not the first groups of southern white women to rely on circulars. In December 1852, Ann Pamela Cunningham issued a plea to the "Ladies of the South" in the *Charleston Mercury* calling for a movement to save Mount Vernon, home of President George Washington. The association foreshadowed and perhaps inspired the work of post–Civil War memorial associations with its emphasis on the South. In 1853, Cunningham appealed to the "Ladies of the South" to help save the home out of a "sense of national, and above all, Southern honor." In 1856, the Virginia legislature issued a charter for the Mount Vernon Ladies Association, the group that eventually saved the home. (Ribblet, "From Mount Vernon to Charlotte County," 3–14; Piehler, *Remembering War the American Way*, 30–32.)

38 *Ladies Memorial Association of Montgomery, Alabama, 1860–1870*, Pamphlet Collection, MOC; "To the Women of the South," HMA broadside, 1866, VHS.

39 These data are based on the author's membership databases for each LMA in this study. A total of 493 women have been identified within the seven LMAs. By the fall of 1868, at least twenty-six such societies were actively establishing cemeteries and arranging

memorial days throughout the state. *Southern Opinion*, August 29, 1868; CSMA, *History of the Confederated Memorial Associations.*

40 *Fredericksburg Ledger*, June 5, 1866; PLMA Minutes, May 6, 1866, LOV; FLMA Minutes, May 24, 1866, LOV. In almost every case, the women distinguished between active members, those who enjoyed the privilege of voting, and honorary members, who may or may not have resided within the community.

41 In Petersburg, this group of elite men represented 11 percent of the white population prior to the war. Within this upper class of approximately 2,000, the highest levels of office and power were held by fewer than 100 men. (Henderson, *Petersburg in the Civil War*, 1–21.) The OMA probably had a slightly less elite membership than its Richmond sister, the HMA. Surveys of both groups, including work done by historian Susan Barber, suggests that the OMA members came from a slightly less affluent section of the city, that is, Church and Union Hills. Likewise, Richmond residents buried in Hollywood and Oakwood Cemeteries appear to have come from different social classes. Michael B. Chesson notes that Hollywood "became both socially and symbolically the most important of Richmond's postwar cemeteries," but whites "who could not afford lots elsewhere were buried in Oakwood." (Barber, "Sisters of the Capital," 389–90; OMA Minutes, MOC; HMA Minutes, MOC; Chesson, *Richmond after the War*, 18; 1880 U.S. Census Records.)

42 A survey of several LMA presidents offers a brief indicator of the members' social standings. HMA president Nancy MacFarland's husband, William H. MacFarland, had been a prominent railroad president and banker prior to the war. He served in 1865 as the president of the city council and later as the head of Planters National Bank. Dr. John H. Wallace, husband of FLMA president Mary Wallace, had been president of the local Farmer's Bank and owned a substantial country home in Stafford County, "Liberty Hall." The husband of Lynchburg's LMA president, Susan Bocock, Henry F. Bocock, was a prominent town attorney. PLMA president Margaret Joynes's husband held the esteemed position of judge. Mary Williams, of the WLMA, was the wife of Philip Williams II, a Commonwealth attorney and state delegate before the war, who continued his law practice after Appomattox. (Chesson, *Richmond after the War*, 21, 63, 95; Wallace, *Two Chapters of a Life*, 9; 1880 U.S. Census Records; Quarles, *Some Worthy Lives*, 245–46.)

43 Lebsock, *Free Women*, 246; Inventory of the Ruffin and Meade Family Papers, <http://www.lib.unc.edu/mss/inv/r/Ruffin_and_Meade_Family>; PLMA Minutes, June 6, 1866, LOV.

44 Wallace, *Two Chapters of a Life*, 8–9; 1880 U.S. Census Records; FLMA Minutes, LOV.

45 Ladies' Defense and Aid Association, MOC; HMA Minutes, MOC; OMA Minutes, MOC.

46 Ladies' Defense and Aid Association, MOC; HMA Minutes, MOC.

47 Mrs. N. V. Randolph, "Recollections of My Mother, 1861–1865," MOC; "Confederate Memorial Day," Memorial Collection, MOC; CSMA, *History of the Confederated Memorial Associations*, 315; James A. Benson to Nora Davidson, July 25, 1862, MOC.

48 "Mrs. Lucy Mina Otey," *Southern Literary Messenger* 1 (July 1895): 15–19; Moore and Baber, *Behind the Old Brick Wall*, 25–26.

49 Goolrick, *Historic Fredericksburg*, 41–47; Civil War Damage Inventories of Fredericks-

burg, Office of Clerk of Court of Fredericksburg, transcribed by Kristen Benedetto, Fredericksburg Area Museum, April 1989 (transcript at MOC); *Richmond Whig*, April 10, 11, 12, 1865. Following the battle of Fredericksburg, word spread quickly throughout the Confederacy describing the wanton destruction. People from across the South, but primarily from Virginia, sent donations to aid in the city's recovery. By February 1863, donations totaled roughly $170,000. (Blair, "Barbarians at Fredericksburg's Gate," 156–59.)

50 For discussion of the ways in which white southern families struggled to maintain class status in the wake of the Civil War, see Morsman, "Big House after Slavery," chapter 2. For an extended discussion of southern ladies, see Scott, *Southern Lady*; Fox-Genovese, *Within the Plantation Household*; Clinton, *Plantation Mistress*; and Bynum, *Unruly Women*.

51 Rubin, *A Shattered Nation*, 2–7, 117, 234–39; Campbell, *When Sherman Marched North*, 91–98, 101–4; Neff, *Honoring the Civil War Dead*, 10–12. Although Rubin acknowledges that LMAs and women's involvement in memorialization served as one factor in sustaining a sense of Confederate nationalism or (white) southern identity in the postwar period, she does not see it as the primary cause.

52 *Richmond Whig*, June 26, 1861; OMA Minutes, MOC; *Lynchburg Daily Virginian*, April 25–27, 1866.

53 The Hebrew Memorial Association also used a circular to gain support from the South's Jewish population. On June 5, 1866, Rachel Levy, the association's corresponding secretary, issued an appeal to the "Israelites of the South." Noting the formation of both Oakwood and Hollywood, the Hebrew Ladies' organized for the express purpose of caring for the graves of Jewish soldiers, "which, of course, would not be embraced in the work of either of the first named Societies." They intended to mound and turf each Hebrew grave in their own private cemetery and then place on each of them a simple headstone with an inscription. "In order, however, to successfully accomplish our object, we need some pecuniary assistance," they noted. The LMA claimed that because their community was already heavily taxed, they could not fund all of the work: "We make this appeal for aid, well knowing that as Israelites and true patriots, they will not refuse to assist [us]." The Hebrew Ladies concluded that "while as Israelites we mourn the untimely loss of our loved ones, it will be a grateful reflection that they suffered not their country to call in vain." ("To the Israelites of the South," Hebrew Cemetery Records, BAMA.)

54 FLMA Minutes, May 24, 1866, LOV; Quinn, *History of the City of Fredericksburg*, 186–87. Other anonymous donations contributed during the summer and fall of 1866 ranged from five dollars to one hundred dollars. (FLMA Minutes, June 28, July 26, September 6, October, 1866, LOV.) As soon as a central site for a cemetery had been secured in Petersburg, the PLMA prepared a circular appealing to the legislatures of all the southern states requesting aid from the people of the South for the cemetery, which then held nearly 4,000 soldiers. Likewise, the women in Montgomery noted that during the spring of 1866 they received appeals not only from Winchester, Fredericksburg, and Richmond, but also from Franklin, Perryville, and "other places where great battles were fought." (*Montgomery Mail*, March 18, 1866.)

55 "To the Women of the South," HMA broadside, 1866, VHS; "Appeal of the Ladies Memorial Association for Confederate Dead interred at Oakwood Cemetery," Memorial Col-

lection, MOC; Hartzell, "Exploration of Freedom," 134–36; *Petersburg Index*, March 30, 1867; PLMA Minutes, LOV; FLMA Minutes, May 24, June 28, July 26, September 6, October, 1866, LOV.

56 Quarles, *Some Worthy Lives*, 42–43, 245–46; Delauter, *Winchester in the Civil War*, 20, 40, 62, 66–67, 80; Morris and Foutz, *Lynchburg in the Civil War*, 8, 35; The Political Graveyard, <http://politicalgraveyard.com>. Quarles suggests that Williams did join the Confederacy, but Delauter offers a more convincing case that he did not.

57 1880 U.S. Census Records; Krick, *Fredericksburg Artillery*, 78, 89, 102; OMA Minutes, May 1, 1866, "Constitution," MOC; PLMA Minutes, LOV. The conclusion is based on data drawn from extensive research on the members of each LMA surveyed in this project. Evidence from Virginia contradicts LeeAnn Whites's findings for Georgia and Alabama. She argues that the pattern of officeholding frequently represented the extent of maternal loss. For example, presidents might have been those members who lost the most sons, while vice presidents had just one unclaimed son. (Whites, "Stand by Your Man," 137.)

58 For a detailed listing of the number of burials in each cemetery, see Table A.1 in the Appendix.

59 The observance by Davidson's schoolchildren is often heralded as the first Memorial Day in the South and is frequently cited as the inspiration for the national Memorial Day. (Davidson, *Cullings from the Confederacy*, 155–60.)

60 *Petersburg Index*, June 11, 1867, June 10, 1868; *Richmond Times*, May 11, 1866.

61 Pryor, *Reminiscences of Peace and War*, 407; *New York Times*, June 17, 1866; PLMA Minutes, June 6, 1866, LOV.

62 *Lynchburg Daily Virginian*, May 10, 1866 (emphasis in original). As early as twelve months after Lee's surrender, white southerners were already employing the rhetoric of what would come to be the primary tenets of the "Lost Cause" by the 1890s. The Lynchburg paper argued that Confederate armies had fought well—as had the Union—and, therefore, both sides should honor the other's dead. In fact, the author noted that "the southern people would indeed deserve eternal dishonor were they to fail in paying all becoming consideration to their illustrious dead."

63 *Ladies Memorial Association of Montgomery, Alabama, 1860–1870*, Pamphlet Collection, MOC; *New York Times*, May 21, June 18, July 2, 1866; "A Woman in Washington," *Independent*, May 31, 1866, APS Online, 1; Williams quoted in Neff, *Honoring the Civil War Dead*, 146. The southern newspaper referred to in this quotation is the *Montgomery Mail*, May 20, 1866. The *Chicago Tribune* is quoted in the *New York Times*. For argument that white northerners saw southern white women as more hostile than southern white men to the Union and attached to the Confederacy, see Silber, *Romance of Reunion*, 13–27.

64 Dubois, *Feminism and Suffrage*; Gallman, *America's Joan of Arc*.

65 *New York Times*, May 21, 1866; *Lynchburg Daily Virginian*, April 28, May 14, 1866. The *Richmond Whig* is quoted in the *New York Times*.

66 During the war, Confederate women had been charged with treason. But an assumption existed among former Confederates by April 1886 that because the war was over, women could no longer be considered a threat to national security.

67 PLMA Minutes, May 6, 1866, LOV; Neff, *Honoring the Civil War Dead*, 146.

68 HMA Minutes, May 3, 1866, MOC; *Winchester Times*, October 31, 1866; R. E. Colston, "Address of R. E. Colston," *SHSP* 21 (1893): 38–49 (originally delivered at Wilmington, N.C., May 10, 1870).

69 For discussion of the religious nature of the Lost Cause, see Wilson, *Baptized in Blood*.

70 "Call for the First Anniversary of the American Equal Rights Association," http://rs6. loc.gov/learn/features/timeline/civilwar/freedmen/mott.html; Dubois, *Feminism and Suffrage*, 63; *Richmond Times*, May 11, 1866; Eighty-Eighth Anniversary of the OMA Program, May 8, 1954, RICH. A second observance also occurred in Richmond on May 10, 1866. On that day, the Richmond Light Infantry Blues celebrated its 73rd anniversary by making a pilgrimage to the shrines of its dead in Hollywood Cemetery. Unlike the Memorial Day celebrations, women had little to do with this affair, and it was more militaristic in tone. In his study of the political meanings of Memorial Days, William Blair notes that the Richmond Light Infantry's blatant military tone was one of the key elements that "forced the Cities of the Dead to become public spaces dominated by women's groups and with minimal symbolic representation of living Confederate veterans." (Blair, *Cities of the Dead*, 55–65.) Although I agree with Blair that the celebrations of 1866 led Union officials to crack down on Memorial Day celebrations in 1867 (see chapter 3), I believe this would have been the case with or without the Light Infantry's demonstration. Moreover, men clearly recognized the crucial role women played in 1866, well before the 1867 curtailing of Memorial Days.

71 *New York Daily News*, June 1, 1866. About 10,000 graves outside the cemetery remained to be cleared.

72 *Richmond Times*, April 27, May 31, June 1, 1866; Blair, *Cities of the Dead*, 59–61.

73 *Winchester Times*, June 13, 1866.

74 Ibid. Before the war, Uriel Wright had been a prominent St. Louis lawyer who had defended a free black (Charles Lyons) who had been apprehended in St. Louis for not carrying a license. Wright argued that the law was illegal because it was inconsistent with the U.S. Constitution. When the southern states seceded in 1860 and 1861, he was a staunch Unionist, but he later changed his stance after witnessing a massacre of St. Louis citizens by Union soldiers. By the winter of 1862–63, he had joined the Confederate war effort as a staff officer. (The Camp Jackson Incident, <http://www.nps.gov/jeff/Gazettes/CJackson.htm>.)

75 Ibid. For discussion of antebellum southern white women and politics, see Varon, *We Mean to Be Counted*, 71–168.

76 Rubin, *A Shattered Nation*, 208, 218–29. I have taken slight liberty with Rubin's use of the phrase "political ventriloquism." While she in fact argues that ex-Confederate men allowed women to speak for them, to "express their bitterness toward the conquering Yankees," her example of ventriloquism refers to newspaper columns written in the voice of women. She argues that publishing these columns allowed ex-Confederates of both sexes to publicly critique the Union government and Union soldiers without fear of reprisal. She further argues, however, that in these columns "women were also being told to cease their political activities and return to the work of reconstructing hearth and home." (Quote, 219–20.)

77 On June 6, 1862, Ashby died during a Federal assault on the rear of a Confederate column retreating to Port Republic. Ashby was born in Fauquier County, and his connec-

tion to Winchester was due only to his cavalry's defense of the town through the first two years of war. Following his death, the military buried him in an elaborate funeral at Charlottesville's University Cemetery. (Unknown woman [probably mother] in Charlottesville, Va., to "Nannie" [Anne Virginia Lucas], who is probably in South Carolina, June 11, 1862, Lucas-Ashley Papers, DU; Blair, *Cities of the Dead*, 90–94.)

78   Rev. James Battle Averitt was married to Mary Williams, daughter of Philip Williams II and Mary Dunbar Williams, cofounder of the WLMA. More than likely, his wife was a member of the WLMA as well. Joseph Holmes Sherrard was an honorary member of the WLMA and served on the committee to superintend removals. (Stonewall Cemetery Records, HRL; J. H. Sherrard to Mary Moncure, August, 22, 1866, Ashby Family Papers, VHS.)

79   Averitt, *Memoirs of General Turner Ashby*, 243–55; Stonewall Cemetery Records, HRL; *Winchester Times*, October 31, 1866.

80   The *Winchester Times*, October 31, 1866, estimated that 10,000 people attended the ceremony, but the *New York Times*, October 29, 1866, estimated that 4,000 to 5,000 people participated.

81   *Winchester Times*, October 31, 1866.

82   Ibid.; Blair, *Cities of the Dead*, 90–94; Delauter, *Winchester in the Civil War*, 95–96; *New York Times*, October 29, 1866. Northerners and the Republican government could tolerate only so much praise for the defeated South. Captain Brown, commander of the occupying Union forces in Winchester, must have been enraged at the political tone of the dedication. A *New York Times* reporter, however, noted that Wise's influence "over the mind of Virginia is not dangerous to the Union or new regime." Rather than focusing on Wise's statements about the Lost Cause, the reporter wrote that Wise had "impressed upon the youth of the state the dignity and necessity of labor." (*New York Times*, October 29, 1866.)

83   *Richmond Times*, May 31, June 1, 1866; *New York Daily News*, June 1, 1866; Mitchell, *Hollywood Cemetery*, 70; Letter of "Genie," Lewis Leigh Collection, Book 19, at U.S. Army Military History Institute, Carlisle Barracks, Pa., May 29, 1866; *New York Times*, October 29, 1866. Richmond papers noted that several freedmen took part in activities—many decorating the graves of their former masters—and that five black waiters from the city's lavish Spotswood Hotel, who had each subscribed one dollar to the HMA and had worked on the Soldiers' Section, also contributed flowers for the event (the historical record does not disclose the motives of these black men).

84   When the Federals saw a small group of citizens approaching their camp that afternoon, the Union soldiers gathered around the flagstaff, brandishing their weapons, and twenty armed cavalrymen arrived ready to defend their flag. No confrontation erupted, as the citizens claimed only to be looking for a local troublemaker. But the incident revealed the deep tensions surrounding the Confederate spirit still very evident in town. (Delauter, *Winchester in the Civil War*, 95–96.)

85   Blair, *Cities of the Dead*, 94. Blair concurs that "southern men knew how important the women's associations were for keeping alive the memory of the Confederacy and for allowing a form of political commentary."

CHAPTER THREE

1   *Winchester Journal,* April 13, June 29, July 27, 1866; *New York Times,* June 5, 1868. The *Winchester Journal* was a Unionist newspaper and frequently reprinted articles from other like-minded northern newspapers.

2   *Lynchburg Virginian,* May 1, 1867; Smith, "Virginia during Reconstruction," 440. For the most complete study of the Reconstruction Act, see Foner, *Reconstruction,* 271–80. Anne Rubin also notes that "Reconstruction under Andrew Johnson had been less punitive than white Southerners . . . had expected"; however, she also argues that "whites took advantage of his leniency to reassert their vision of racial supremacy." (Rubin, *A Shattered Nation,* 4.) For a more thorough examination of Richmond during this period, see Chesson, *Richmond after the War,* 96–104. The final tipping point for Union tolerance of Confederate memorial activities may have been the elaborate reburial of Confederate general Albert Sidney Johnston. Johnston's body was removed from New Orleans in the winter of 1867, accompanied by former generals P. G. T. Beauregard, Braxton Bragg, and John Bell Hood, and taken to Galveston, Texas. (*New York Times,* January 24, 1867.)

3   *Lynchburg Daily Virginian,* April 20, 1866. During the war, Pierpont, a pro-Union man, headed the "restored" government of Virginia in Alexandria. Lincoln recognized this "shadow state government," which controlled only a small part of northern Virginia. In May 1865, President Johnson nullified Confederate authority in the state and recognized Pierpont as the legitimate governor.

4   Tripp, *Yankee Town,* 171–72; Chesson, *Richmond after the War,* 87–96; Blair, *Cities of the Dead,* 43.

5   For detailed discussion of Schofield's tenure as commander in Virginia, see McDonough, *Schofield.* For information about racial tensions within Richmond during Congressional Reconstruction, see Chesson, *Richmond after the War,* 96–104. At the state's constitutional convention, for example, 24 of the 105 delegates, or roughly one-third of the Republican majority, were black.

6   According to Michael Chesson, following the incident, Schofield met with company officials and agreed to integrate four of the six cars. Two cars were reserved for white women, their children, and black nurses; the other four cars were open to anyone. Newspapers, however, reported that the agreement was a fraud, as white men were allowed to ride in the ladies' car. By November 1867, after securing the right to ride in some of the streetcars, apparently few black residents did so. By 1870, ten of the twelve streetcars ran with white balls on their roofs, indicating "whites only." (Chesson, *Richmond after the War,* 102–3.)

7   Ibid., 103–4; Tripp, *Yankee Town,* 172–73.

8   Tripp, *Yankee Town,* 172–73.

9   Maria Louisa Carrington to Susan Taylor, February 6, 1866, Saunders Family Papers, VHS, quoted in Censer, *Reconstruction,* 188; Lizzie Alsop Diary, March 1, 1867, Wynne Family Papers, VHS; Maria Louisa Wacker Fleet to Alexander Frederick Fleet, June 7, 1867, in Fleet, *Green Mount after the War,* 274.

10   *Southern Opinion,* June 15, 26, 1867.

11   Blair, *Cities of the Dead,* 62–63; Neff, *Honoring the Civil War Dead,* 150; CSMA, *History of the Confederated Memorial Associations,* 233.

12   During the spring of 1866, northern newspapers frequently reported on the occurrence of Confederate Memorial Days. See, for example, *New York Times*, May 16, July 13, 1866. Neff states that the extent of restrictions placed on memorial activities is difficult to assess, possibly because "they had been communicated by military officers through means other than formal orders, for example, through intimidation." (Neff, *Honoring the Civil War Dead*, 153.)

13   "A Leaf from the Past: From the Records of the Ladies' Memorial Association of Fredericksburg, Va.," pamphlet, CRRL; "Confederate Memorial Days: Fredericksburg, Virginia, 1866–1985," CRRL; OMA Minutes, April 30, 1867, MOC; *Richmond Times*, June 1, 1867; *Richmond Whig*, June 1, 1867; *Richmond Dispatch*, June 1, 1867; *New York Times*, June 3, 1867; Henry Clay Brock Diary, May 30, 1867, VHS; Blair, *Cities of the Dead*, 64; *Lynchburg Virginian*, May 1, 11, 1867. Pollard was later allowed to give his talk.

14   James H. Gardner to Mary Gardner Florence, June 1, 1867, James Henry Gardner Papers, VHS; *Lynchburg Virginian*, May 1, 11, 1867; Blair, *Cities of the Dead*, 64.

15   *Fredericksburg Ledger*, June 18, 1869; Hodge, "Confederate Memorial Days," 4, probably taken from the *Fredericksburg Harold*, June 14, 1869; *Winchester News*, June 11, 1869; *Southern Opinion*, May 16, 30, 1868; *Petersburg Index*, June 10, 1868; PLMA Minutes, June 13, 1868; LOV; *Lynchburg Virginian*; May 11, 1868, May 11, 1869; *Richmond Daily Dispatch*, May 30, 1868; *Southern Opinion*, May 23, June 13, 1868. The PLMA appears to have initially celebrated two different Memorial Days in their city. They decorated the graves at the Bethel burial grounds, also referred to as the fairgrounds, on May 16, and there was a June 9 celebration in Blandford Cemetery. Once the bodies from Bethel had been reinterred in Blandford, the PLMA sponsored only June 9.

16   *Winchester Times*, June 13, 1866; *Fredericksburg Ledger*, May 24, 1870. Recognizing the implications of lauding a black presence at memorial ceremonies, at least one northern newspaper went to great lengths to downplay the number of freedmen attending Confederate celebrations, suggesting instead that most African Americans elected to attend Union festivities rather than those of their former masters. (*New York Times*, June 3, 1867; June 5, 1868.)

17   *Richmond Times*, April 19, 1866; *Lynchburg Virginian*, May 3, 1867; *New York Times*, June 2, 1866. For discussion of the "faithful slave" image, see Hale, *Making Whiteness*, 51–70; Foster, *Ghosts*, 140–57; and Savage, *Standing Soldiers*, 155–62.

18   *Lynchburg Virginian*, May 3, 1867; Tripp, *Yankee Town*, 247–49.

19   Johnson, "Colors of Social Welfare," 170.

20   PLMA Minutes, May 30, 1867, LOV; *Petersburg Index*, May 12, 14, 1869; *Lynchburg Virginian*, May 6, 11, 1869. The railroads included the Virginia and Tennessee, Southside Railroad, and the Norfolk and Petersburg.

21   The origins of the national (Federal) Memorial Day are highly disputed. Some accounts argue that commemoration began at Gettysburg in May 1864; General John B. Murray claimed that he began the practice in Waterloo, New York, on May 27, 1866; still others contend that John Logan's wife witnessed such activities in Petersburg and suggested that northern soldiers implement the practice for their own fallen. For more discussion of the origins of Memorial Day, see Neff, *Honoring the Civil War Dead*, 136–41.

22   Blight, *Race and Reunion*, 71; Blair, *Cities of the Dead*, 69–76; Neff, *Honoring the Civil War Dead*, 137; McConnell, *Glorious Contentment*, 16, 183–84. According to Blight, ob-

servance of Federal Memorial Day grew in 1869 to 336 cities and towns in 31 states. He notes that, in 1873, New York's legislature designated May 30 a legal holiday, and by the end of the century, every northern state had followed suit.

23 *Richmond Daily Dispatch*, May 15, June 1, 1868; *Southern Opinion*, May 30, June 6, 1868.

24 The Philadelphia *Sunday Dispatch* quoted in *Southern Opinion*, June 6, 1868; *New York Times*, June 5, 1868.

25 *Richmond Daily Dispatch*, May 15, June 1, 1868.

26 To the contrary, William Blair argues that Union Decoration Days "contained features that made them distinctive." For example, he cites the fact that these ceremonies took place in conquered territory, drew together various regions on one common day of commemoration (as opposed to the variety of dates in the South), and "had the stamp of authority of the government." (Blair, *Cities of the Dead*, 70.)

27 *New York Times*, June 5, 1868.

28 *Richmond Daily Dispatch*, May 31, 1869; *Winchester Journal*, June 5, 1868, May 28, 1869; *New York Times*, August 18, 1866; Blight, *Race and Reunion*, 71; Blair, *Cities of the Dead*, 69; McConnell, *Glorious Contentment*, 183–85, 218–19. Blight claims that in both the North and the South, "women carried the primary responsibility of gathering flowers and mobilizing people . . . for Decoration Day ceremonies." But evidence from Virginia, as well as Stuart McConnell's study of the GAR, suggests that men were the primary impetus behind Union Memorial Days. Cecilia O'Leary concurs, noting that there were patriotic women's associations in the North as early as 1866, but they were excluded from the masculine culture of the GAR until 1883. (O'Leary, *To Die For*, 75.)

29 For discussion of northern women and children in supporting roles at Union Memorial Days, see Silber, *Romance of Reunion*, 59.

30 Clark, *Defining Moments*, 56–94.

31 Ibid., 82.

32 *Petersburg Daily Express*, June 15, 1868.

33 *Fredericksburg Ledger*, June 18, 1869; *Lynchburg Virginian*, May 11, 1869; *Petersburg Index*, June 10, 1868; *Petersburg Daily Express*, June 15, 1868.

34 Blair, *Cities of the Dead*, 97. Blair concurs that men accepted a secondary role to or, at the least, partnership with women in commemorative events during Reconstruction. He argues that "the fact that these rituals had originated through women's organizations became enormously helpful later when the movement toward reconciliation fondly remembered only the gentle hand that decorated the graves instead of rituals that helped forge a consensus on resistance during difficult political times."

35 OMA Minutes, Constitution, May 1, 1866, MOC; HMA Minutes, May 14, 1866, MOC; FLMA Minutes, Constitution, August 9, 1866, LOV; PLMA Minutes, May 30, 1866, LOV. Fredericksburg proved to be an exception to the rule of female-only officers. Dr. Francis P. Wellford served as the association's treasurer from May 1866 through the mid-1870s. Treasurer, however, was the only office open to men.

36 Foster, *Ghosts*, 38; FLMA Minutes, June 15, 1866, LOV; HMA Minutes, MOC; OMA Minutes, MOC; PLMA Minutes, May 7, 1868, LOV. FLMA's male advisory members in 1866 included J. Horace Lacy, Captain C. T. Goolrick, Dr. Francis P. Wellford, C. W. Braxton, and Edwin Carter. According to historian Jane Censer, some Georgia and Carolina LMAs turned over their business dealings to men. (Censer, *Reconstruction*, 197.)

37 FLMA Minutes, LOV; *Lynchburg Daily News*, January 15, 1866; PLMA Minutes, LOV.

38 FLMA Minutes, May 3, 1867, LOV. The men of the cemetery committee included Dr. Francis P. Wellford (also treasurer for the FLMA), J. Horace Lacy, and C. W. Braxton.

39 "A Leaf from the Past: From the Records of the Ladies' Memorial Association of Fredericksburg, Va.," pamphlet, CRRL.

40 OMA Minutes, May 12, 1866, MOC; Munford, "The Jewel's of Virginia"; Greene, *J. Horace Lacy*, 21; Major J. Horace Lacy commission, L-541, Metal Case 3, MOC; HMA Minutes, June 18, 1866, MOC. By 1870, Dabney H. Maury had relocated to New Orleans for a business venture. His signature appeared first on the impressive roster of ex-Confederate generals. Thirty-nine former Confederate officers signed the endorsement of Lacy. Lacy apparently owned a plantation in Louisiana, which allowed him to reside in the state while he collected money for the FLMA.

41 Lynchburg LMA broadside, 1867, UVA; HMA Minutes, December 11, 1866, MOC.

42 HMA Minutes, December 11, 1866, MOC; OMA Minutes January 15, 1867, MOC.

43 HMA Minutes, MOC; PLMA Minutes, May 7, June 13, 1868, LOV; *Lynchburg Virginian*, May 29, 1866.

44 Morton, *Story of Winchester*, 247–48; CSMA, *History of the Confederated Memorial Associations*, 316.

45 Stonewall Cemetery Records, HRL; "Circular and Address of the Monumental Association of the Stonewall Cemetery," 1870, UVA; CSMA, *History of the Confederated Memorial Associations*, 317; Delauter, *Winchester in the Civil War*, 94; The officers of the Monumental Association included Judge Joseph H. Sherrard, president; Governor F. W. M. Holliday, vice president; Captain George W. Kurtz, vice president; Mary Williams, vice president; Eleanor Boyd, vice president; Captain Lewis N. Huck, treasurer; Albert Baker, secretary; Lieutenant E. Holmes Boyd, executive committee; Colonel William R. Denny, executive committee; Major Holmes Conrad, executive committee; and Lieutenant H. K. Pritchard, executive committee. Of the nine male members, six appear to have had female relatives active in the WLMA.

46 Evidence regarding northern white women's mid-nineteenth-century associations suggests some cases of men and women working jointly together. For example, men and women sometimes served together as members of abolitionist societies, but women usually were merely auxiliaries. In 1833, after being denied the right to vote or sign the Declaration of Sentiments and Purposes of the American Anti-Slavery Society (which she had helped design), Lucretia Mott formed the Female Anti-Slavery Society. Soon thereafter, exclusively female antislavery societies began to form across the North and West, many in locales where male-dominated societies already admitted women to their meetings. On male and female abolitionists, see Scott, *Natural Allies*, 45–50. Numerous cases of male-female organizations suggest that in mixed-sex groups, men held executive control. For example, Judith Giesberg's work on the U.S. Sanitary Commission reveals that men controlled the executive board but women usually controlled the twelve regional branches that administered an extensive network of 7,000 affiliated women's soldiers' aid societies. (Giesberg, *Civil War Sisterhood*, 5.)

47 *Winchester News*, June 11, 1869; "Circular and Address of the Monumental Association of the Stonewall Cemetery," 1870, UVA.

48   *Petersburg Index*, June 10, 1868; PLMA Minutes, December 5, 1866, LOV; Censer, *Recon-*
     struction, 196.

49   PLMA Minutes, May 30, 1866, June 13, 1868, LOV.

50   Foster, *Ghosts*, 38; *Petersburg Index*, June 7, 1867, June 15, 1868; *Petersburg Daily Express*,
     January 19, 1869; PLMA Minutes, December 5, 1866, July 29, 1867, LOV.

51   Lebsock, *Free Women*, 226–31. Lebsock notes that mixed-sex organizations led to two
     new rituals of female deference in the late 1850s: women increasingly used their hus-
     bands' names rather than their own given names (for example, "M. W. Campbell" be-
     came "Mrs. John W. Campbell"), and the question of female public speaking was settled
     in the negative.

52   *Southern Opinion*, July 27, 1867, May 16, 1868 (emphasis added). The *Southern Opinion*
     was published between June 16, 1867, and May 1, 1869. Owned and operated by Pollard
     until his assassination in December 1868, which was precipitated by an article he printed
     on November 21, 1868, the paper changed hands twice in its last five months of publica-
     tion. Messrs. W. D. Chesterman and Company bought the paper in December 1868 but
     sold it to D. S. Hardwick and Company in March 1869. J. Marshall Hanna, editor under
     Hardwick's ownership, chose to terminate the paper in May 1869, citing that its mission
     had been fulfilled.

53   *Southern Opinion*, June 15, 1867. For those readers who might not have comprehended
     the symbolism of the sketch, Pollard explained its significance in the first edition.

54   Ibid., August 24, September 14, December 21, 1867, April 11, May 2, 9, 16, 23, 30, 1868.
     Anne Rubin interprets Pollard's intentions differently. Citing an incident in which the
     Ladies of King George's County, Virginia, hired a Connecticut firm to create a monu-
     ment, the *Southern Opinion* expressed its regret that the Ladies should obtain a monu-
     ment from "living Yankees!" Rubin argues that Pollard used the opportunity to "subtly
     patronize women, implying that they were perhaps ill-equipped to make business deci-
     sions." (Rubin, *A Shattered Nation*, 239.) After reading the entire run of the newspaper,
     the incident cited by Rubin is the only example I have been able to document of Pollard
     criticizing the Ladies.

55   For the argument that LMAs were dedicated to the "reconstruction of southern white
     men," see Whites, "Stand by Your Man," 133–49; Whites, *Civil War as a Crisis in Gender*;
     Faust, *Mothers of Invention*, 252; Cox, *Dixie's Daughters*, 9–10; Brundage, *Southern Past*,
     26–27; Blair, *Cities of the Dead*, 85; Goldfield, *Still Fighting the Civil War*, 96–103; Piehler,
     Remembering War the American Way, 63; and Rubin, *A Shattered Nation*, 208–9, 234–39.
     For the argument that LMAs were more interested in patriotic endeavors, see Censer,
     Reconstruction, 202. Had the PLMA simply intended to reassure southern white men
     that they were no less masculine from having lost the war, the women would not have
     publicly ridiculed the Gentlemen's Association for its failure to help or its lack of patrio-
     tism.

56   On southern postwar gender relations, see Whites, *Civil War as a Crisis in Gender*;
     Bardaglio, *Reconstructing the Household*; Edwards, *Gendered Strife and Confusion*; and
     Edwards, *Scarlett*, 117–86.

57   Scott and Censer argue for the Civil War as a watershed for southern white women.
     (Scott, *Southern Lady*; Censer, *Reconstruction*.) Rable, Faust, and Whites argue for

changes in southern gender roles during the war; however, they believe that the postwar period marked a retrenchment in such practices. (Rable, *Civil Wars*; Faust, *Mothers of Invention*; Whites, *Civil War as a Crisis in Gender*.)

58 PLMA Minutes, December 5, 1866, July 29, September 4, November 1867, January 1868, LOV; *Southern Opinion*, November 16, 1867 (emphasis in original).

59 PLMA Minutes, July 11, July 18, October 12, 16, December 5, 1866, LOV; CSMA, *History of the Confederate Memorial Associations*, 288–90; FLMA Minutes, May 11, June 28, July 26, September 6, October 11, 25, 1866, LOV; Skocpol, *Protecting Soldiers*, 373–524.

60 PLMA Minutes, December 5, 1866, LOV. In September 1868, Major Robert T. Harper of Alabama traveled to Fredericksburg to place a stone and proper inscription on his brother's grave. When he arrived at Salem Church, where he had been told his brother rested, he found that the grave appeared to have been emptied and then partly refilled. After inquiring at a neighbor's home, he learned that, indeed, the FLMA had supervised the removal and reinterment of his brother and hundreds of other Confederate soldiers into a lot adjoining the city cemetery. (Statement written by Major Robert T. Harper, June 1890, FRSP.)

61 T. B. Shepherd to Mary Williams, April 17, 1866, Williams Family Papers, HRL; Mr. Woodward to Nancy MacFarland, December 18, 1869, MacFarland Papers, VHS; Mitchell, *Hollywood Cemetery*, 74. In the North, families frequently wrote letters to Clara Barton regarding the whereabouts of prisoners of war. But unlike her southern counterparts, Barton could rely on the federal government for assistance. Although Barton also aided in the reburial of dead from Andersonville, the notorious Confederate prisoner of war camp, the military, not northern women, was the impetus behind most soldiers' reinterments. (Oates, *A Woman of Valor*, 291–336; Pryor, *Clara Barton*, 136–48.)

62 See, for example, Foster, *Ghosts*, 38–54.

63 By 1867, the women were beginning efforts to "bring home" their communities' fallen brethren. After organizing formal Confederate cemeteries, both the FLMA and the PLMA embarked on a plan for the accomplishment of "one of the most imperious duties of our association." Each association appointed a committee to determine a list of those native sons who still lay buried on distant battlefields, "away from their loved homes," and then to retrieve the soldiers' bodies. In keeping with the spirit of patriotism evident on Memorial Days, railroad officials agreed to provide free transportation of soldiers' bodies. On occasion, these retrievals were made at the appeal of a family member—as in the case of James K. Witherspoon, whose father requested that he be removed from a farm in Culpeper to the Fredericksburg cemetery. Petersburg, however, was one of the most active groups in returning soldiers home during the 1860s. By the PLMA's June 12, 1867, meeting, six bodies had been brought home, and another had been forwarded to the family in South Carolina. Efforts to recover dead from Gettysburg and Antietam will be discussed in chapter 4. (FLMA Minutes, August 8, 1866, LOV; PLMA Minutes, March 9, 1867, April 3, 1867, June 12, 1867, June 13, 1868, LOV.) LMAs in other locales employed similar methods, including the Raleigh, North Carolina, Memorial Association. (Bishir, "A Strong Force of Ladies," 6–7.)

64 PLMA Minutes, May 6, 1866, LOV.

65 Gallagher, *Confederate War*, 8–12, 163.

66 Blair, *Cities of the Dead*, 50–52. On April 29, 1865, President Johnson lifted restrictions on trade in the former Confederacy, but, as Bill Blair points out, he specified "gray uniforms and cloth" as an exception.

67 Neff, *Honoring the Civil War Dead*, 134.

68 *Southern Opinion*, August 29, September 12, 1868.

69 "Appeal of the Ladies' Memorial Association for the Confederate Dead Interred at Oakwood Cemetery," 1866, MOC; OMA Minutes, January 15, April 2, 1867, September 1868, MOC. Louisville sent one hundred dollars to the PLMA in July 1866. There is no indication that the HMA received contributions from state legislatures during the 1860s. The process of asking state legislatures to fund cemeteries occurred in the northern states as well—although women were not involved in these efforts. In August 1866, Maryland's General Assembly passed an act incorporating a National Cemetery Association for Antietam Battlefield. The state legislature subsequently appropriated $7,000 for the project and requested that other states do likewise. West Virginia, Maine, Rhode Island, Pennsylvania, Minnesota, New Jersey, and Massachusetts all sent contributions totaling over $15,000. (*New York Times*, August 18, 1866.)

70 *Winchester Times*, March 13, 1867; Smith, "Virginia during Reconstruction," 17. Smith notes that ninety-five of the ninety-six House members were "old time Whigs." The Senate had a similar makeup. Despite the legislature's reluctance to support Confederate projects, it did vote in March 1867 to protect Confederate cemeteries from destruction.

71 Skocpol, *Protecting Soldiers*, 3, 20–21, 50–51; Odem, *Delinquent Daughters*, 8–37. Maternalist legislation includes laws enacted to restrict women's hours of employment or minimum-wage laws and special safety regulations for women. Skocpol argues that "such labor laws were premised on the idea that women workers needed extraordinary protection as actual or potential mothers."

72 HMA Minutes, June 10, 1867, MOC; Thomas H. Ellis to Mrs. C. S. Barney, May 18, 1866, HMA Correspondence Files, MOC.

73 HMA Executive Committee to Managers, February 1867, Correspondence Files, MOC; Mitchell, *Hollywood Cemetery*, 72.

74 Mitchell, *Hollywood Cemetery*, 72–73; Coski and Feely, "A Monument to Southern Womanhood," 130–63; *Richmond Whig*, May 1, 2, 7, 13, 1867; *Richmond Times*, May 1, 1867.

75 Imogen Lyons to Sallie Lyons Taliaferro, Richmond, May 2, 1867, William Booth Taliaferro Papers, W&M; *Richmond Whig*, May 13, 1867. Lyons was particularly galled with General Schofield because of a recent order in which he had designated two of the city's streetcars for "ladies and children," which was to include both "'colored' ladies and children as well as white."

76 Piehler, *Remembering War the American Way*, 30–32. The Washington Monument was built in two phases, in 1848–56 and in 1876–84.

77 Piehler, *Remembering War the American Way*, 3; Kammen, *Mystic Chords*, 55. Kammen points out that debates over private-versus-state money often surrounded the erection of antebellum monuments, due to the "democratic ethos" of a people's republic: "If people wished to commemorate an anniversary, celebrate a battle, or save a historic site, they would have to take the initiative."

78 Varon, *We Mean to Be Counted*, 88–93. Although women from Boston and Vermont

contributed to the Henry Clay monument, the primary impetus and organization for the monument occurred within the South. The Clay monument remained in Richmond's Capitol Square until 1930, when it was moved to the Old Hall of the Virginia House of Delegates. Virginia's white women also formed the Mount Vernon Ladies' Association in 1854 to help restore and protect the home of George Washington. A discussion of this group was omitted from this chapter because, although it might be considered a memorial group, it did not erect a monument as such. For more discussion of the Mount Vernon Ladies' Association, see Varon, *We Mean to Be Counted*, 124–36.

79 Piehler, *Remembering War the American Way*, 61.

80 Mitchell, *Hollywood Cemetery*, 71; *Richmond Times*, April 26, June 1, 1866; HMA Minutes, June 10, 1867, MOC; Foster, *Ghosts*, 40–41; *Richmond Daily Dispatch*, May 11, 1868; Foster, *Ghosts*, 59. Although men formed the basis of the Stuart Memorial Association, they relied on the HMA for assistance. As historian Gaines Foster has pointed out, most of the earliest monuments incorporated themes of bereavement and therefore appeared best suited for placement in cemeteries. More than 90 percent of early memorials (1860s–80s) had some funeral aspect in either design or placement. For example, most monuments were a rendition of a classical obelisk, often with an urn or drape on them. (Foster, *Ghosts*, 40–41.)

81 Charles Dimmock to Mrs. Dr. Batton, June 28, 1867, Charles Dimmock Papers, VHS; Mitchell, *Hollywood Cemetery*, 73; HMA Minutes, June 10, 1867, MOC. Like most early Confederate monument efforts, the HMA believed that the most natural and obvious location for a memorial was within the cemetery. In fact, no other site was even suggested.

82 Mitchell, *Hollywood Cemetery*, 73–74.

83 FLMA Minutes, LOV; PLMA Minutes, LOV; *Lynchburg Virginian*, May 7, 1868, May 11, 1869; Moore and Baber, *Behind the Old Brick Wall*, 26–27. The LLMA corresponded with the HMA regarding the Hollywood monument in the spring of 1869; the correspondence no longer appears to exist.

84 OMA Minutes, September, October 18, 1868, January, April 19, 1869, April 4, May 24, 1871, May 10, 1872, MOC.

85 Brundage, *Southern Past*, 6.

86 Ginzberg, *Women and the Work of Benevolence*, 80–88. For antebellum women and petitions to the government, see also Scott, *Natural Allies*, 45, 48, 50–52, 73; and Lebsock, *Free Women*, 196.

87 For examples of Confederate women's wartime appeals to the government, see Faust, *Mothers of Invention*, 162–63, 193–94; and Rable, *Civil Wars*, 74–75.

88 See, for example, "Appeal of the Ladies' Memorial Association for the Confederate Dead Interred at Oakwood Cemetery," 1866, MOC.

89 The Fifteenth Amendment, which guaranteed that the right of citizens to vote "shall not be denied or abridged by the United States or by any State on account of race, color, or previous condition of servitude," was ratified in 1870. The amendment, however, ignored women, even though many had contributed to the abolitionist movement. Ultimately, the amendment caused a split in the woman's movement. Those who supported suffrage but opposed the amendment because it excluded women, such as Susan B. Anthony and Elizabeth Cady Stanton, formed the National Woman Suffrage Association. Those who

supported the amendment as it was and believed that they should focus on suffrage in the states, such as Lucy Stone and Alice Stone Blackwell, formed the American Woman Suffrage Association.

90 *Winchester Times*, June 23, 1880. Although this article did not appear until 1880, it is representative of sentiment among the five communities in the 1870s as well. It was selected because of its vivid quotes.

91 *Richmond Times*, April 13, 1866.

92 OMA Minutes, MOC; FLMA Minutes, LOV; PLMA Minutes, January 16, 1869, LOV.

93 *Richmond Daily Dispatch*, May 5, 1868; Ida L. Dodge to Carrie Warwick, May 15, 1869, LLMA Collection, JML. Oakwood continued to meet on a monthly basis through 1872, when it too met only once or twice a year to plan for Memorial Day. (OMA Minutes, MOC.) No minutes remain for the WLMA, so it is impossible to determine the frequency of meetings. More than likely, however, it too met less often. The HMA's minutes ended abruptly in the spring of 1868, but other evidence, including newspaper accounts and correspondences, suggests that the women of this association remained active in other venues, such as the Ladies' Lee Monument Association and the Gettysburg dead project, to be discussed in the next chapter.

94 "Appeal of the Ladies' Memorial Association for the Confederate Dead Interred at Oakwood Cemetery," 1866, MOC. The estimated number of Confederate graves in Oakwood had dropped from 16,000 in 1866 to 14,000 by the spring of 1868. It is possible the number was reduced when Union officials removed the bodies of Federal soldiers from the cemetery.

95 *Richmond Daily Dispatch*, May 5, 9, 11, 30, 1868, May 11, 1869.

96 Twenty-six Confederate generals are now buried in Hollywood Cemetery. Confederate generals killed in battle and interred in Hollywood during the war included James Jay Archer, Richard Brooke Garnett, David Rumph Jones, John Pegram, John Caldwell Calhoun Sanders, William Edwin Starke, and J. E. B. Stuart. Additional generals were buried in Hollywood after the war: Joseph R. Anderson, Robert H. Chilton, Philip St. George Cocke, Raleigh E. Colston, John R. Cooke, Henry Heth, Eppa Hunton, John D. Imboden, Edward Johnson, Samuel Jones, Fitzhugh Lee, Thomas M. Logan, George E. Pickett, William "Extra Billy" Smith, Isaac Munroe St. John, Walter H. Stevens, William R. Terry, R. Lindsay Walker, and Henry A. Wise. Several other generals were interred in Hollywood before being reburied elsewhere, including Lewis Addison Armistead, Archibald Gracie Jr., John Gregg, John Hunt Morgan, Elisha Franklin ("Bull") Paxton, and Leroy Augustus Stafford. (Owen and Owen, *Generals at Rest*, 262–78.) According to Mary H. Mitchell, Lieutenant General Ambrose Powell Hill was buried in Hollywood for twenty-four years, from 1867 to 1891, before his remains were reinterred outside of Richmond, where his former soldiers erected a monument in his honor. (Mitchell, *Hollywood*, 60–62.)

97 Dabney H. Maury, "Southern Historical Society: Its Origins and History," *SHSP* 18: 349–65; Foster, *Ghosts*, 50–51. State vice presidents included Robert E. Lee, Wade Hampton, D. H. Hill, and John C. Breckinridge. Foster notes that two other male Confederate organizations formed in 1869: the Confederate Survivors' Association of South Carolina and the Confederate Relief and Historical Association of Memphis. He argues that both

of these societies operated locally and quickly disappeared. The SHS, on the other hand, eventually became vital to the Lost Cause.

98 Foster, *Ghosts*, 50–51; Maury, "Southern Historical Society."

99 *New York Times*, January 26, 28, 1870. See chapter 4 for discussion of the Lee Monument controversy.

CHAPTER FOUR

1 *Richmond Daily Dispatch*, October 13, 14, 1870; *Petersburg Index*, October 14, 15, 1870; *Staunton Spectator*, October 18, 1870; Connelly, *Marble Man*, 11–12; Thomas, *Robert E. Lee*, 412–15. The collector of customs refused to lower the flags to half-mast. The *Richmond Daily Dispatch* (reprinted in the *Petersburg Index*) noted that this was "in striking contrast with that of the proprietor of the Union (colored) Hotel, who half-masted his flag from daybreak to sunset."

2 *Richmond Daily Dispatch*, October 13, 14, 1870; *Petersburg Index*, October 14, 15, 1870; Lizzie Alsop Diary, October 14, 1870, Wynne Family Papers, VHS; PLMA Minutes, n.d., LOV; Connelly, *Marble Man*, 28; *Lynchburg Virginian*, quoted in *Richmond Daily Dispatch*, October 14, 1870.

3 *Petersburg Index*, October 14, 1870; *Richmond Daily Dispatch*, October 15, 1870.

4 *Richmond Daily Dispatch*, October 14, 1870.

5 For discussion of Lee's death stimulating renewed interest in the Confederate past, see Foster, *Ghosts*, 57.

6 The executive committee of the Lee Memorial Association was composed primarily of former officers from the Army of Northern Virginia, representing locales from across the state, including William N. Pendleton, William Preston Johnston, William Allan, F. W. M. Holliday, John S. Mosby, Robert Stiles, Bradley T. Johnson, and Charles S. Venable. Gaines Foster argues that male Confederate societies did not organize during Lee's lifetime "not only because of his potential opposition but because they would not and could not usurp his leadership." (*Richmond Daily Dispatch*, October 20, 1870; Foster, *Ghosts*, 51.)

7 *Richmond Daily Dispatch*, October 13, 14, 20, 1870; *Petersburg Index*, October 14, 1870; Foster, *Ghosts*, 52.

8 *Richmond Daily Dispatch*, October 21, 25, 1870; "Monument to General Robert E. Lee: History of the Movement for Its Erection," *SHSP* 17: 185–205; October 19, 1870, Lee Monument Association Records, LOV. The officers of the LLMC were Nancy MacFarland, president; Mary Adams Randolph, Henrietta Watkins Lyons, and E. H. (Mrs. William) Brown, vice presidents; Elizabeth Byrd Nicholas, treasurer; and Sarah Nicholas Randolph, secretary.

9 *ANB* 18: 136–37. Randolph's other more popular works included a piece on Martha Jefferson Randolph in Mrs. Wister's *Famous Women of the Revolution* (1876) and *Life of Stonewall Jackson* (1876). Her uncle, George Wythe Randolph, had served as the secretary of war for the Confederacy, and her aunt, Mary Randolph, was the president of the Richmond Ladies' Association during the war. Karen Cox incorrectly identifies Sarah Randolph as Janet Randolph. (Cox, *Dixie's Daughters*, 13.)

10 *Richmond Daily Dispatch*, October 21, 25, 1870 (emphasis added). Four days later, the HMA added nine more men to its list of gentlemen.

11 Osborne, *Jubal*, xiii, 6–9, 18–21, 34–52, 390, 402–13. Historians Gary W. Gallagher and Gaines Foster have demonstrated that, although Early's efforts in controlling the public memory of the war were very persuasive, many white southerners refused to embrace his more elitist and nostalgic views. (Gallagher, *Lee and His Generals*, 200–202; Foster, *Ghosts*, 60–61.) Early refused to take the amnesty oath to the U.S. government; however, he returned to the country after President Andrew Johnson issued an unconditional amnesty that ultimately pardoned all combatants against the United States during the war.

12 Jubal A. Early to General William N. Pendleton, October 24, 1870, William N. Pendleton Papers, SHC; J. A. Early, October 24, 1870, printed in *Richmond Daily Dispatch*, October 26, 1870.

13 Apparently, Bradley T. Johnson and several of his fellow officers in the Army of Northern Virginia had been contemplating a veterans' organization just prior to Lee's death. In a letter dated October 25, 1870, Johnson asked Early to serve as the president of the AANVA. Johnson and his comrades had been planning the association for "some months" and had considered Lee for the presidency. But with Lee's passing, Johnson asked Early to take on the role. The group would serve to "preserve our old friendship, to collect materials for the history of the Army, and to cherish the names and fame of our dead comrades." Johnson suggested that Early might fuse his desire for a Lee monument association with this veterans' group. (Bradley T. Johnson to Jubal A. Early, October 25, 1870, Jubal A. Early Papers, LC.)

14 *Richmond Daily Dispatch*, October 24, 28, 1870, November 4, 1870; J. A. Early, October 24, 1870, printed in *Richmond Daily Dispatch*, October 26, 1870; Jubal A. Early to Dabney H. Maury, December 14, 1870, item #50, *Goodspeed's Catalogue 592* (Boston: Goodspeed's Book Shop, n.d.), 11; Connelly, *Marble Man*, 42–47. Kirk Savage argues that "Jubal Early's group sought contributions only from the veterans who had actually fought under Lee's command." Early certainly only wanted to include members from this "band of brothers," but he was more than open to receiving contributions from any source willing to donate, evident in later attempts by the group to canvass the entire South. (Savage, *Standing Soldiers*, 136.)

15 Osborne, *Jubal*, 440–41; Foster, *Ghosts*, 52–53. Early was elected president of the temporary Lee Monument Association, but later in the meeting the group elected Jefferson Davis as the permanent president.

16 Jubal A. Early to Dabney H. Maury, December 14, 1870, item #50, *Goodspeed's Catalogue 592* (Boston: Goodspeed's Book Shop, n.d.), 11; "To the Survivors of the Army and Navy of the Confederate States and to all the admirers of the Character of the late General Robert E. Lee, wherever they may reside," November 1870, Lee Monument Association Records, LOV; *Richmond Daily Dispatch*, November 15, 1870; *New York Times*, October 28, 1870; Connelly, *Marble Man*, 43–45. For discussion of the Lee Monument Association (Early) and Lee Memorial Association (Lexington group), see Foster, *Ghosts*, 52–53, 88–89, 98, 100–103; and Osborne, *Jubal*, 442–43.

17 *Richmond Daily Dispatch*, November 15, 1870; Sarah N. Randolph to General Jubal A. Early, Richmond, March 13, 1871, Lee Monument Association Records, LOV.

18 Connelly, *Marble Man*, 45; Circular, "Monument to General Lee," October 19, 1870, Lee Monument Association Records, LOV; *Richmond Daily Dispatch*, November 8, 1870; "To the Survivors of the Army and Navy of the Confederate States and to All the Admirers of the Character of the Late General Robert E. Lee, Wherever They May Reside," November 1870, Lee Monument Association Records, LOV.

19 *Richmond Daily Dispatch*, November 8, 1870; Osborne, *Jubal*, 443–44; Jubal A. Early to Governor F. W. W. Holliday, March 11, 1878, Lee Monument Association Records, LOV.

20 Sarah N. Randolph to General Jubal A. Early, Richmond, March 13, 1871, Lee Monument Association Records, LOV.

21 Ibid.

22 Ibid.; "To the Survivors of the Army and Navy of the Confederate States and to All the Admirers of the Character of the Late General Robert E. Lee, Wherever They May Reside," November 1870, Lee Monument Association Records, LOV; Moore had collected $3,000 to $4,000 on his tour, which was not included in the LLMC's estimate of $7,000 on hand.

23 Jubal A. Early to the Editor of the *Galveston News*, March 17, 1871, copy in Lee Monument Association Records, LOV; newspaper clipping from the *Richmond Times*, undated, but probably 1880, Jubal Early Papers, LC. As of April 29, 1871, Moore still had not seen Early's retraction. (Sarah N. Randolph to General Jubal A. Early, April 29, 1871, Lee Monument Association Records, LOV; Connelly, *Marble Man*, 45; Osborne, *Jubal*, 443–44.)

24 Younger, *Governors of Virginia*, 112; *Shepherdstown Register*, August 30, 1873; Fitzhugh Lee to Jubal A. Early, March 15, 1872, Jubal A. Early Papers, LC; Jubal A. Early to Miss Emma Cameron, March 7, 1880, UVA; Osborne, *Jubal*, 73; Jubal A. Early to Hon. W. F. Slemons, May 22, 1878, Tucker Family Papers, SHC.

25 For details on the battle of Lynchburg, see Osborne, *Jubal*, 254–60; and Blair, *Virginia's Private War*, 119.

26 LLMA Minutes, April 6, 1869, JML; Charlottesville *Weekly Chronicle*, June 9, 1871; *New York Times*, May 30, 1871.

27 Lynchburg Ladies' Memorial Association broadside, 1867, UVA; HMA Minutes, December 11, 1866, MOC; *Valley Virginian*, October 17, 1866; Nannie Seddon Barney to General Early, December 4, [1870s], Jubal A. Early Papers, LC; *New York Times*, January 22, 1872; *Shepherdstown Register*, August 30, 1873; *New York Times*, October 28, 1874.

28 Wyatt-Brown, *Honor and Violence*, 27–29. For more discussion of manhood/masculinity among both Union and Confederate soldiers during and after the Civil War, see McPherson, *For Cause and Comrades*, 6, 13, 25–31, 76–78; Berry, *All That Makes a Man*, 9–10, 171–73; Mitchell, *Civil War Soldiers*, 17–18, 42; Foster, *Ghosts*; Whites, *Civil War as a Crisis in Gender*, 160–224; Bardaglio, *Reconstructing the Household*, 129–36; and Edwards, *Gendered Strife and Confusion*, 111–19.

29 Jubal A. Early, Lynchburg, Va., October 24, 1870, reprinted in the *New York Times*, October 28, 1870; "To the Survivors of the Army and Navy of the Confederate States and to All the Admirers of the Character of the Late General Robert E. Lee Wherever They May Reside," November 1870, Lee Monument Association Records, LOV; *Winchester Times*, June 7, 1889, Jubal A. Early Papers, LC. Gary W. Gallagher asserts that Early "found only

honor in the Confederate performance against daunting odds." (Gallagher, *Lee and His Generals*, 208.)

30 Gallagher, *Lee and His Generals*, 199.

31 On the postwar careers of Confederate generals, see Hesseltine, *Confederate Leaders*. For a discussion of Early's influence over the Lost Cause, see Gallagher, *Lee and His Generals*, 199–226; Foster, *Ghosts*, 47–62; Connelly, *Marble Man*, 43–61; and Osborne, *Jubal*, 429–53. Early easily dismissed James Longstreet as a leader of the Lost Cause due to his affiliation with the Republican Party.

32 Quote from Foster, *Ghosts*, 60–61. Although Foster claims that Early and the AANVA ultimately were not successful in mobilizing the entire South in the way the UCV would do in the 1880s and 1890s, this does not diminish the nature of the gender battles that took place in Virginia between 1870 and the mid-1880s.

33 Papers included with a letter from Jubal A. Early to Governor F. W. W. Holliday, March 11, 1878, Treasurer's Office Inventory, Lee Monument Association Collection, LOV; Osborne, *Jubal*, 443.

34 This is a similar pattern to what had occurred with antebellum southern women's associations. (Lebsock, *Free Women*, 228–31; Kierner, *Beyond the Household*, 202.)

35 Minutes of the Lee Monument Association, September 28, October 30, 1875, Lee Monument Association Records, LOV; "Monument to General Robert E. Lee, Part 1," *Southern*, January–December 1889, APS Online, 187.

36 Savage, *Standing Soldiers*, 137; *New York Times*, January 9, 1878; Bassett French to Mayor of Mobile, Alabama, December 18, 1875, and circular (n.p., n.d.), both in Walthall Papers, Mississippi Department of State Archives, quoted in Connelly, *Marble Man*, 46; Minutes of the Lee Monument Association, September 28, 1875, February 2, 1877, to May 4, 1877, Lee Monument Association Records, LOV; Samuel Bassett French Letterbooks, MOC.

37 Kirk Savage claims that "the issue of art was so pivotal for the women's committee that it led to a painful public breach between the women and the governor's association." While I agree that this dispute was by far the most public and tense of the debates between the men and the women, tensions had been present since 1870, as the previous portion of this chapter demonstrates. (Savage, *Standing Soldiers*, 140.)

38 The LLMC's focus on art and culture stemmed from its desire to recast the South as a civilized place. Fitzhugh Brundage argues that women monopolized the fields of history and public culture in the 1880s and 1890s in part so that they could claim for themselves "the work of recording and narrating the progress of civilization." He demonstrates that southern white women, in particular, turned to historical work such as monument building "as an antidote to the pejorative and dismissive portraits of the region and its past propagated by nonsoutherners." (Brundage, "White Women," 119–21.) For a discussion of women, gender, and civilization, see also Bederman, *Manliness and Civilization*.

39 Ladies' Lee Monument Committee to his Excellency the Governor of Virginia and the members of the Lee Monument Association, Richmond, March 3, 1877, Minutes of the Lee Monument Association, February 2, 1877, to May 4, 1877, Lee Monument Association Records, LOV; Osborne, *Jubal*, 451; Foster, *Ghosts*, 98–100. For more detail on the various design competitions and frustrations, see Savage, *Standing Soldiers*, 138–47.

40 The New Orleans monument to Lee was dedicated on February 22, 1884. According to Gaines Foster, fund-raising efforts (independent of those in Virginia) had begun in 1870 but had not proved successful until the end of the decade. As opposed to the recumbent statue of Lee at Washington and Lee College, the New Orleans statue featured the general standing on the top of a pillar. (Foster, *Ghosts*, 91–92.)

41 For discussion of controversy over segregating Union and Confederate dead at Antietam National Cemetery, see Neff, *Honoring the Civil War Dead*, 116–24.

42 *Republican Vindicator*, December 15, 1865; *Valley Virginian*, February 14, 1866.

43 *Charleston Mercury*, quoted in the *Southern Opinion*, July 6, 13, 1867; *Valley Virginian*, February 1866.

44 *Southern Opinion*, September 21, 1867, October 10, 1868.

45 *Southern Opinion*, June 29, July 13, August 10, 17, 1867, June 28, 1868. The *Southern Opinion* subsequently took it upon itself to send a special correspondent, "Pilgrim," to Gettysburg to discern the "truth" about the Confederate dead, although no reports from Pilgrim appear to have been published. A later report from a Georgia paper, reprinted in the *Opinion*, however, noted that some citizens of Gettysburg had proposed gathering the remains of the Southern soldiers and interring them in a "decent" locality. According to the paper, Pennsylvania authorities forbade this reinterment, threatening "severe punishment" to "the movers in the matter."

46 *Southern Opinion*, June 29, 1867; Censer, *Reconstruction*, 193.

47 Mitchell, *Hollywood Cemetery*, 84–85; Neff, *Honoring the Civil War Dead*, 156–57. In 1870, Rufus Weaver had just finished medical school in Philadelphia and had accepted a teaching position at Hahnemann Hospital and Medical College. Mitchell speculates that Rufus had probably assisted his father in the 1863 interments. She argues that he was perhaps the only person knowledgeable about the specific location of Confederate graves.

48 Mary W. Barney to Mrs. E. C. (Kate Pleasants) Minor, November 30, 1891, HMA Collection, MOC.

49 *New York Evangelist*, October 21, 1869, APS Online; *Richmond Daily Dispatch*, October 20, 1870, May 17, 18, 1871; Mitchell, *Hollywood Cemetery*, 85.

50 Elizabeth H. Brown to Rufus Weaver, November 8, 1871, Charles Dimmock to Rufus Weaver, February 10, 1872, HMA Collection, MOC; Mitchell, *Hollywood Cemetery*, 85–86.

51 *Richmond Daily Dispatch*, April 19, 1872; Mitchell, *Hollywood Cemetery*, 86; *Lynchburg Virginian*, April 19, 1872; Mrs. E. H. Brown memo, April 20, 1872, HMA Collection, MOC.

52 Adeline Egerton to Rufus Weaver, April 20, 1872, HMA Collection, MOC; Elizabeth H. Brown to Adeline Egerton, September 14, 1871, HMA Collection, MOC; Adeline Egerton Papers, LOV.

53 Charles Dimmock to Rufus Weaver, May 15, 1872, HMA Collection, MOC; Elizabeth H. Brown to Rufus Weaver, April 7, 1872, HMA Collection, MOC; Rufus Weaver to Ada Egerton, undated (probably April 1872), Rufus Weaver to Robert Stiles, March 8, 1892, HMA Collection, MOC.

54 *Richmond Daily Dispatch*, June 21, 1872; Reardon, *Pickett's Charge in History*, 79–80.

The remains of an additional eighty-one Confederate soldiers who had been buried at Arlington arrived in Richmond that May and were subsequently interred in Hollywood prior to Memorial Day. (Mitchell, *Hollywood Cemetery*, 87.)

55 List of Gettysburg Dead Shipments, HMA Collection, MOC; Mrs. Elizabeth H. Brown to Ada Egerton, May 23, 1873, Ada Egerton to Mrs. Brown, December 23, 1878, HMA Collection, MOC; Mitchell, *Hollywood Cemetery*, 91. There are numerous discrepancies in the accounts of the amounts sent and received by Weaver. My estimations are based on a thorough comparison of both the HMA's and Weaver's accounts. For discussion of the Panic of 1873, see Foner, *Reconstruction*, 512–63.

56 Fitzhugh Lee to Jubal A. Early, May 6, 1871, Jubal A. Early Papers, LC; Chesson, *Richmond after the War*, 189; Colonel W. C. Carrington to Mrs. Ada L. Egerton, June 17, 1873, HMA Collection, MOC.

57 Elliot, *Doctor Quintard*, 81–82; constitution of the Comrades of the Southern Cross, adopted August 28, 1863, <http://docsouth.unc.edu/comrades/comrades.html>; *Petersburg Index*, July 2, 1872. Membership in the Southern Cross required that one was "a commissioned officer or enlisted soldier in the Confederate States service, a free white male over eighteen years of age, intelligent in his military duties and of known patriotism and integrity." Quintard notes that despite the demise of the Southern Cross, the "Confederate Veterans' Organization subsequently embodied some of the features which it was intended that the Comrades of the Southern Cross should possess."

58 *New York Times*, July 5, 9, 1872; *Petersburg Index*, July 2, 1872.

59 Colonel William C. Carrington to Mrs. Ada L. Egerton, June 17, 1873, HMA Collection, MOC. Carrington went on to inform Egerton that he believed funds could be appropriated from the various legislatures of the South.

60 Robert Stiles to Mrs. A. Egerton, March 26, 1874, Ada Egerton to Elizabeth H. Brown, December 23, 1878, HMA Collection, MOC. A year after Carrington's 1873 letter to Egerton, the feud between the HMA and the SCB continued.

61 Ada Egerton to Elizabeth H. Brown, December 23, 1878, HMA Collection, MOC. Mitchell argues: "Their major objective achieved, the women who belonged to the Hollywood association lost interest in the organization, which slowly began to disintegrate as enthusiasm waned and members died or moved out of town." (Mitchell, *Hollywood Cemetery*, 91–92.)

62 For essays on women's role in monument building, see Mills and Simpson, *Monuments to the Lost Cause*.

63 See chapter 3 for the initial decrease in 1868 and 1869.

64 For a case study, see author's "To Honor Her Noble Sons." For evidence of interest in the Confederate cause waning among women in Raleigh, North Carolina, see Censer, *Reconstruction*, 200.

65 HMA Minutes, May 4, 1891, MOC; *ANB* 18: 136–37; "Monument to General Robert E. Lee: History of the Movement for Its Erection," *SHSP* 17: 185–205. For additional demographic information, see membership databases for each LMA in author's possession.

66 Judith A. Giesberg argues that, for northern white women, the U.S. Sanitary Commission "served as an interim structure . . . between the localized feminine activism of the first half of the century and the mass women's movements of the late nineteenth and twentieth centuries." (Giesberg, *Civil War Sisterhood*, 11.)

67　Ginzberg, *Women and the Work of Benevolence*, 5, 11–98; Lebsock, *Free Women*, 195–236; Censer, *Reconstruction*, 153–206; Scott, *Natural Allies*, 79–81. Ginzberg argues that the rhetoric of benevolence changed after the Civil War. Antebellum activists used language suggesting that "virtue was more pronounced in women than in men and that this virtue could be the force behind a moral transformation of society at large." By the 1870s and 1880s, however, activists referred less to "a mission of moral regeneration" and more to the responsibility of controlling the poor and vagrant. It should be noted, however, that Ginzberg only examines northern women's associations.

68　Scott, *Natural Allies*, 79–81; Friedman, *Enclosed Garden*, 3–20.

69　*Richmond Daily Dispatch*, May 4, 1883; *Petersburg Index and Appeal*, September 15, 1874; *Petersburg Index*, October 13, 1870; Lebsock, *Share of Honour*, 108; Scott, *Natural Allies*, 93–140; Censer, *Reconstruction*, 153–206; Barber, "Anxious Care and Constant Struggle," 120–37. For more about women's postwar public activities, see also Scott, *Southern Lady*. The national Women's Christian Temperance Union organized after a meeting of temperance-minded women at Lake Chautauqua, New York, in 1874.

70　Beginning in the late 1870s, questions regarding repayment of the state debt ushered in the Readjuster Movement. Conservative Democrats insisted on paying off all public debts from the war era in order to preserve the state's honor, but the Readjusters wanted to scale down, or "readjust," the state debt. This biracial party consisted of black and white Republicans and "rebellious Conservatives" (the party name used by the Democrats in Virginia from 1868 to 1883). In addition to the repudiation of the debt, Readjusters supported the expansion of public schooling and economic development that served ordinary people of both races. For a detailed examination of the Readjuster period in Virginia, see Jane Dailey, "Limits of Liberalism," 88–114; Henderson, *Gilded Age City*, iii; Hartzell, "Exploration of Freedom," 154; Osborne, *Jubal*, 415–16, 467; Younger, *Governors of Virginia*, 63–64, 84–91, 99–101, 104–7; Foner, *Reconstruction*, 592, 604; and Censer, *Reconstruction*, 188–89. According to historian David Blight, "The 'Readjuster' movement in Southern politics brought another form of rejection to the Lost Cause." The Readjuster Party held power in Virginia from 1879 to 1883, gaining control of the governor's mansion, the legislature, and six of ten seats in Congress and sending William Mahone to the U.S. Senate. By the mid-1880s, Democrats' appeals to white supremacy swept the party out of office. (Blight, *Race and Reunion*, 293.)

71　*Winchester News*, July 5, September 20, 1878 (emphasis added). According to Wyatt-Brown, southern white women were critical to men's honor. He notes that "a male's moral bearing resided not in him alone, but also in his women's standing." That is, men were expected to defend their female dependents against outside attacks and women were to uphold their chastity, since it reflected on their men. (Wyatt-Brown, *Honor and Violence*, 35–38.) There appears to have been an effort by pro-Funder men (those who wanted to pay off the debt) to organize like-minded women. In March 1878, a Warrenton newspaper reported on the meeting of women who had initiated a movement for the payment of the debt, although the paper failed to report any subsequent meetings of the association. (Censer, *Reconstruction*, 189.)

72　*Winchester News*, July 5, September 20, 1878. For a discussion of maternalism and politics, see Baker, "Domestication of Politics," 620–47; and Skocpol, *Protecting Soldiers*, 50–53, 480–539. Although a full membership list has not been discovered, it appears that at least one member of the Women's Association for the Liquidation of the State Debt executive committee, Mrs. Andrew Pizzini, was a member of the HMA in the 1860s. (HMA Minutes, MOC; *Winchester News*, September 20, 1878.) For a discussion of women's symbolic role in antebellum politics, see Varon, *We Mean to Be Counted*, 1–11.

73 Foster, *Ghosts*, 61; Silber, *Romance of Reunion*, 61. Gaines Foster has demonstrated that the male organizations in Virginia, including the AANVA, the Lee Monument Association, the Lee Memorial Association, and the SHS, "failed to gain widespread support." He estimates that the AANVA probably never had more than 200 members, and the SHS attracted only 1,560 subscribers during its height in 1876. Foster suggests several reasons for the failure of the men. First, he cites "confusion, if not corruption," as a factor in the low membership and fund-raising campaigns. Second, he cites the "contentious personalities" of Early and Pendleton (Lee Memorial Association) as detrimental to their success. Finally, he suggests that the "aristocratic bias" of the groups discouraged popular support. Although these regional-level groups faltered, the period between the mid-1870s and mid-1880s witnessed the establishment of numerous regimental veterans' associations. For instance, the *Lynchburg Daily Virginian* reported on reunions of the 3rd Georgia, Mahone's Old Brigade, and Mosby's 43rd Battalion of Cavalry in a period of four weeks in 1875. (*Lynchburg Daily Virginian*, April 13, May 12, and May 17, 1875.) The last documented account of the SCB appears to have been in the spring of 1875, when the members escorted Valentine's recumbent statue of Lee to Lexington. (*Petersburg Index and Appeal*, April 14, 1875.) Stuart McConnell points out that the GAR was "virtually moribund" by 1872, due to a "general desire to forget war that is common to most postbellum periods." He notes that, with reorganization, the GAR began to revive in the late 1870s. (McConnell, *Glorious Contentment*, xiv, 20, 33.)

74 Early became vice president of the SHS for Virginia following Lee's death. At a meeting in White Sulphur Springs, West Virginia, in May 1873, the society elected Early as its president. He subsequently appointed an all-Virginian executive committee chaired by Dabney H. Maury (who had returned from New Orleans to Richmond). In 1876, the organization began publication of the *SHSP*. The SHS supported both the Lee Monument (Richmond) and the Lee Memorial (Lexington) associations. For more details on the SHS, see Foster, *Ghosts*, 50–54, 90–95; Connelly, *Marble Man*, 41–45, 72–73, 82; and Osborne, *Jubal*, 431–40, 448.

75 Dabney H. Maury to Jubal A. Early, October 30, December 31, 1880, May 13, 1883, January 30, November 1, 1884, Jubal Early Papers, LC. Although the SHS appeared to rally in 1883 when it emerged from its debt, a year later it was on the downslide again. As vacancies and resignations continued to increase, Maury suggested selling its papers to raise money.

76 "Monument to General Robert E. Lee: History of the Movement for Its Erection," *SHSP* 17: 185–205; Connelly, *Marble Man*, 45. Early quoted in Foster, *Ghosts*, 98–100; Savage, *Standing Soldiers*, 146–50.

CHAPTER FIVE

1 Lee Camp, Minutes, May 17, 1883, June 7, 1884, VHS; *Richmond Daily Dispatch*, May 23, 24, 1883. As if this incursion into the Ladies' sphere was not enough, the following year

the Lee Camp proposed an even more direct assault on women's domain when it suggested securing "appropriate headboards" for the graves of the Gettysburg dead.

2 HMA Minutes, May 16, 1887, May 11, 1888, May 4, 1889, MOC. It appears that the HMA never ceased to exist entirely during the 1880s. For example, in 1883, the association expressed its desire to plaster the Soldiers' Monument (pyramid) in Hollywood Cemetery so that it might become covered with vines. (*Richmond Daily Dispatch*, May 5, 1883.)

3 For historians who argue that LMAs were temporary, see Foster, *Ghosts*, 36–62; Brundage, "White Women," 115; and Mills and Simpson, *Monuments to the Lost Cause*, xvi.

4 *Petersburg Daily Index-Appeal*, April 12, 1883. There is no direct correlation to reorganization dates among the associations; Lynchburg was the first to reconvene in 1880, followed by Oakwood in 1882. In May 1886, several Richmond women met at the home of Lucy Mason Webb to revive the HMA. The PLMA followed suit in 1883. Winchester alone, with its ties to the Stonewall Monumental Association that was open to both sexes, remained active from 1865 well into the 1890s. (LLMA Minutes, JML; PLMA Minutes, LOV; OMA Minutes, MOC; HMA Minutes, MOC; Henderson, *Gilded Age City*, 258–59; *Petersburg Daily Index-Appeal*, April 27, 1883; Mitchell, *Hollywood Cemetery*, 102.) A survey of the *Winchester Times* from 1865 through the mid-1880s provides evidence that the WLMA remained active the entire period, although its leadership changed with the passing of Mary Williams sometime before 1879.

5 PLMA Minutes, April 26, May 3, 10, 17, July 5, 1883, LOV; HMA Minutes, May 4, 1891, "1890 Annual Report," MOC.

6 FLMA Minutes, April 18, 1893, LOV.

7 On a generational approach to understanding southern white women, see Censer, *Reconstruction*, 5–6n9. Like Censer, I see the Civil War as a formative experience, though I do not believe that these women would have defined themselves as part of a particular generation.

8 Betsy Brinson, "Bryan, Isobel Lamont Stewart," in Kneebone et al., *Dictionary of Virginia Biography* 1: 347–49; Coski and Feely, "A Monument to Southern Womanhood," 139.

9 Brinson, "Bryan, Isobel Lamont Stewart," 347–49; Belle Bryan to Cousin Parke (Lucy Parke Chamberlayne Bagby), July 10, September 10, 17, 1889, Bagby Family Papers, VHS; *New York Times*, September 12, 1910.

10 "Memorial Services Held for Miss Ruth H. Early," Mary Cabell to Eva, February 20, 1864, Evelyn Russell Early to Mother, May 16, 1887, Varina Howell Davis to Ruth H. Early, March 2, 1890, miscellaneous certificates, Early Family Papers, VHS; Halsey, *Historic and Heroic Lynchburg*, 73–74.

11 Cox, *Dixie's Daughters*, 37; Woodward, *Origins*, 154–55; Hale, *Making Whiteness*, 47–49; Foster, *Ghosts*, 3–10; Daniel, *Lost Revolutions*, 26; Censer, *Reconstruction*, 6.

12 Quarles, *Some Worthy Lives*, 246; *Petersburg Daily Index-Appeal*, April 12, 1883.

13 "Mrs. Minor and the Library," undated clipping, *Richmond News Leader*, Clipping File, MOC; Treadway, *Women of the Mark*, 6.

14 Censer argues that some women of the youngest generation, such as Ellen Glasgow, found Confederate memorial activities to be oppressive "and criticized them for holding the South back from the modern world." (Censer, *Reconstruction*, 275–76.)

15 For a discussion of "New Women," see Scott, *Southern Lady*, 106–231; Ayers, *Promise*,

316–17; and Censer, *Reconstruction*. For more specific discussion of southern white women and the suffrage movement, see Wheeler, *New Women*.

16 Foster, *Ghosts*, 79–87; Blight, *Race and Reunion*, 255–99 (quote, 266); Ayers, *Promise*, 310–38; Skocpol, *Protecting Soldiers*, 102–51; Currey, "Virtuous Soldier," 133–39. Blight defines the 1880s and beyond as the "reconciliationist phase" of the Lost Cause.

17 Lebsock, *Murder in Virginia*, 17, 61–64, 145, 306; Ayers, *Promise*.

18 Hale, *Making Whiteness*, 43–84; Blight, *Race and Reunion*, 6–30. Blight notes that this was a myth the white North seemed increasingly willing to believe, making reconciliation on the basis of a *white* memory of the Civil War possible.

19 Speech of Thomas T. Munford to Confederate Veterans at Lynchburg, c. 1884, Munford-Ellis Family Papers, DU (emphasis in original).

20 See for example, Brundage, *Southern Past*, 6–7.

21 LLMA Minutes, May 22, 1885, JML; PLMA Minutes, August 8, December 2, 1883, June 28, 1884, December 1892, LOV. Not all of the cemetery interest came from within the LMAs. The OMA's dedication, or at least investment, in its cemetery appears to have been questioned by the Richmond City Council Committee on Cemeteries. In April 1887, the committee asked to remove all the wooden boards marking the ranges, sections, and graves of the Confederate dead in Oakwood, as the rapid decay of the headboards prevented the committee from beautifying the grounds. The OMA initially denied the city's request but eventually consented so long as the engineer drew detailed maps showing each grave. (OMA Minutes, April 1887 meeting, fall 1887 meeting, MOC.) Jefferson Davis had died on December 6, 1889, and his body had originally been laid to rest in a vault in New Orleans's Metairie Cemetery. As early as March 1890, however, the HMA requested that Varina Davis reinter her husband's remains in Richmond. Originally, the Ladies wished to place his remains in a crypt within the White House of the Confederacy, but Varina Davis declined this idea. The former statesman was finally laid to rest in Hollywood Cemetery on May 31, 1893. (HMA Minutes, March, April 19, 1890, May 4, October 31, November 13, 1891, May 9, 1893, MOC.) For more on Davis's reinterment, see Fariello, "Personalizing the Political," 16–32.

22 PLMA Minutes, February 2, 1889, LOV; *Richmond Dispatch*, June 8, 10, 1890; *New York Times*, June 10, 1890; FLMA Minutes, May 1873, n.d., 1873, LOV; *Fredericksburg Star*, May 2, June 13, 1891; LLMA Minutes, May 11, 1890, JML; Morton, *Story of Winchester*, 249–50.

23 Foster, *Ghosts*, 100–101; Blight, *Race and Reunion*, 267–69; Savage, *Standing Soldiers*, 150–51.

24 HMA Minutes, November 13, 1891, January 19, 1892, MOC; Kernodle, *Guide Book of the City of Richmond*, 82.

25 Foster, *Ghosts*, 40–42, 44, 128–30, 158, 168, 273; Savage, *Standing Soldiers*, 162; Currey, "Virtuous Soldier," 135; Piehler, *Remembering War the American Way*, 64–65. Foster estimates that more than 60 percent of the monuments built between 1886 and 1899 featured a Confederate soldier.

26 Savage, *Standing Soldiers*, 4, 162–208; Brundage, "Woman's Hand and Heart," 66; Mills and Simpson, *Monuments to the Lost Cause*, xv–xxx; Brundage, *Southern Past*, 6–7; Hoge quoted in Foster, *Ghosts*, 129. Kirk Savage argues that "the modern soldier monument arose to perform a more complex cultural task, not merely to assuage the

collective grief of a nation but to rehabilitate and modernize the seminal figure of the citizen-soldier." (Savage, *Standing Soldiers*, 167.) Grace Elizabeth Hale notes that erecting monuments provided the war generation's offspring with a "lesser but still arguably heroic role of memorialists." (Hale, *Making Whiteness*, 242.) Edward L. Ayers also points out that Confederate statues served as monuments "to the thoroughly commercialized present." (Ayers, *Promise*, 334–35.)

27 Rufus Weaver to Mrs. Egerton, April 26, 1889, Rufus Weaver to Mrs. Egerton, April 10, 1890, Rufus Weaver to Mrs. Egerton, April 11, 1890, Robert Stiles to Mrs. Maxwell Clark, June 2, 1890, HMA Collection, MOC.

28 Rufus Weaver to Mrs. Egerton, April 10, 1890, Rufus Weaver to Mrs. Egerton, April 11, 1890, Robert Stiles to Mrs. Maxwell Clark, June 2, 1890, HMA Collection, MOC.

29 HMA Minutes, April 9, August 4, 1890, MOC; Kate Pleasants Minor to Rufus Weaver, April 14, 1892, HMA Collection, MOC.

30 HMA Minutes, May 9, November 13, 1891, January 19, 1892, MOC; HMA Advisory Board to HMA, December 21, 1891, HMA Collection, MOC. Members of the Advisory Board included Joseph Bryan, E. C. Minor, Robert Stiles, Jonathan B. Purcell, and W. E. Cutshaw. Unlike the Winchester and Fredericksburg LMAs, the HMA did not appoint a male advisory board until May 1890 as it embarked on the White House of the Confederacy project.

31 HMA Minutes, February 2, April 12, 1892, HMA Collection, MOC; Rufus B. Weaver to Morton Marye, auditor of public accounts of Virginia, March 28, 1892, HMA Collection, MOC.

32 Kate Pleasants Minor to Rufus Weaver, April 14, 1892 (emphasis in original), Rufus Weaver to Kate Pleasants Minor, April 18, 1892 (emphasis in original), HMA Collection, MOC.

33 HMA Minutes, April 23, 1892, "1892 Annual Report (May)," February 7, 1893, MOC.

34 HMA Minutes, February 7, May 3, 1893, HMA Collection, MOC; Kate Pleasants Minor to Rufus Weaver, April 13, 1893, Rufus Weaver to Kate Pleasants Minor, April 18, 1893, HMA Collection, MOC.

35 The records for debt payment do not add up correctly. According to the receipts sent by Weaver, the Ladies owed him approximately $1,121 as of the spring of 1893 (not including any interest). He claimed they owed him $1,196.34. Although these numbers do not match, the records clearly indicate that the HMA owed him at least $1,100, which it never paid.

36 Rufus Weaver to Kate Pleasants Minor, December 28, 1901, Kate Pleasants Minor to Rufus Weaver, January 18, 1902, Rufus Weaver to Mrs. Egerton, January 31, 1902, HMA Collection, MOC (emphasis in original). In 1919, the issue resurfaced for the HMA, but it appears to have been quickly dropped; Mary Maury Werth informed Janet Randolph that it was impossible to examine all of the papers regarding the matter. (Mary Maury Werth to Mrs. Randolph, April 15, 1919, HMA Collection, MOC.)

37 HMA Minutes, April 12, 1892, MOC.

38 Lee Camp Minutes, April 3, 27, 1883, VHS. Foster notes that "exactly why they chose to organize a new society rather than work through the AANVA remains unclear. Perhaps they did so because veterans of units other than the Army of Northern Virginia could not join the AANVA or because the older group showed no interest in a soldiers' home."

Nevertheless, the Lee Camp had a different membership base and "expressed a view of the past rather different from that of the AANVA." The AANVA's membership base was primarily upper class; the Lee Camp reflected a split between the working class and the middle class. (Foster, *Ghosts*, 93.) In keeping with a military structure, the Lee Camp desired to establish a statewide association by organizing similar associations in towns across Virginia. The following year, the camp created a "committee on charters and subordinate camps," and a second camp organized in the city within a year. During the remaining years of the 1880s, Confederate veterans held reunions with increasing frequency throughout the South, and in 1887 the Lee Camp finally achieved its goal of a statewide confederation. At least two other states followed suit (Tennessee and Georgia). But a handful of veterans, led primarily by a group in Louisiana, pursued the idea of a regional Confederate veterans' association. In February 1889, a committee of veterans in New Orleans called for a meeting to establish such an organization. That June, veterans from Louisiana, Tennessee, and Mississippi met in the Crescent City, where they adopted a constitution and chose a name, the United Confederate Veterans (UCV). The Lee Camp joined the UCV the following year; by 1892, 188 camps had joined; by 1896, 850 camps claimed membership.

39 Foster, *Ghosts*, 104–8; Turner Ashby Camp No. 22, Minutes, September 28, 1891, HRL; Quinn, *History of the City of Fredericksburg*, 191. The death of former Confederate president Jefferson Davis on December 6, 1889, probably stirred interest in the Lost Cause as well. But it would be misguided to attribute the revival of memorial associations simply to the Lee Camp or the UCV, as the timing simply does not coincide. For example, the Lynchburg, Oakwood, and Petersburg associations had already reconstituted themselves by the time the Lee Camp initiated activities.

40 The emphasis on needy veterans reflected evolving national trends in distributive public policy. Although Union veterans had received pensions for service-related injuries since the war, in the mid-1880s the GAR began lobbying Congress to improve benefits. Confederate veterans were ineligible for federal pensions. But in the late 1880s and 1890s, the Democratic governments of the former Confederate states instituted pensions for service-connected disabilities and "truly indigent veterans or widows"; in 1888, Virginia granted the first pensions to veterans and the widows. The Lee Camp, organized prior to the state's support, believed one of its priorities should be to improve the living conditions of the aging and often disabled soldiers by establishing a home for Confederate veterans.

41 *Lynchburg Daily Virginian*, April 19, May 19, 20, 1875. For discussion of reunions and reconciliation, see Blight, *Race and Reunion*; Foster, *Ghosts*; and Silber, *Romance of Reunion*. Although all three historians highlight reconciliation in this period, they acknowledge that such reunions did not indicate an end to sectional hostilities. The first official Blue-Gray reunion appears to have been held on July 21, 1881, when the Captain Colwell Post of the GAR of Carlisle, Pennsylvania, traveled to Luray, Virginia, to meet with ex-Confederates from the Luray (or Page) Valley. (George L. Kilmer, "A Note of Peace," *Century Illustrated Magazine (1881–1906)* 36 (July 1888), APS Online, 440.)

42 Foster, *Ghosts*, 88–103; Lee Camp Minutes, April 27, May 28, 1883, VHS.

43 Beginning in the early 1890s, many veterans' organizations suggested building monuments to the "Women of the Sixties." In fact, Richmond's Pickett Camp of Confederate

Veterans suggested in 1894 that "the place for such a monument . . . should be side by side of the Confederate soldier on Libby Hill. It is not well for a man to be alone, nor woman either." ("Women of the South," *SHSP* 22: 54–63.) Between 1912 and 1926, veterans across the South erected seven state monuments to the women. For more discussion of these monuments, see Mills, "Gratitude and Gender Wars," 183–200.

44 Quarles, *Some Worthy Lives*, 245–48.

45 "Roster and Historical Sketch of A. P. Hill Camp C.V. No. 6. Va.," UVA; Lee Monument Unveiling Committee Assignments, Lee Camp Collection, VHS; HMA Minutes, MOC; Lee Camp Minutes, May 28, 1886, VHS.

46 "98th Anniversary of the Turner Ashby Chapter No. 54, UDC," November 11, 1995, HRL; Turner Ashby Camp, No. 22, Minutes, June 6, August, 26, 1892, December 11, 1893, HRL.

47 Coski and Feely, "A Monument to Southern Womanhood," 137; Lee Camp Minutes, May 9, 23, July 18, 1884, September 3, 1886, February 11, April 8, 1887, VHS. Jefferson Davis's wife and daughter were not elected honorary members of the Lee Camp until 1886.

48 Lee Camp Minutes, June 22, 1888, May 16, 1890, March 13, April 25, May 1, October 16, 23, 1891, VHS.

49 Lee Camp Minutes, January 1, 1892, VHS; "98th Anniversary of the Turner Ashby Chapter No. 54, UDC," November 11, 1995, HRL; Foster, *Ghosts*, 93. The women who were members of both the Lee Camp Auxiliary and the HMA include Minnie Baughman, Mrs. Alfred Courtney, and Janet Randolph.

50 O'Leary notes that between 1866 and 1883 "patriotic women" of the North joined relief corps, but there do not appear to have been memorial associations like the LMAs. (O'Leary, *To Die For*, 75.)

51 McConnell, *Glorious Contentment*, 218; O'Leary, *To Die For*, 70–76; Women's Relief Corps Michigan, <http://www.mifamilyhistory.org/civilwar/wrc/default.asp.>; Silber, *Daughters of the Union*, 273. Evidence exists of WRCs in the South. For example, Tampa, Florida, claimed WRC #5. There appears to be some debate as to when the WRC officially became an auxiliary of the GAR. McConnell points to 1881, but O'Leary argues for 1883. O'Leary, Silber, and Lawson all agree that the WRC's focus on soldierly valor minimized the long-term recognition of women's wartime roles. (Lawson, *Patriot Fires*, 183.)

52 O'Leary, *To Die For*, 76.

53 Coski and Feely, "A Monument to Southern Womanhood," 137; LLMA Minutes, May 15, 1884, May 9, 1887, JML; OMA Minutes, October 2, 1891, MOC; PLMA Minutes, March 12, 1888, March 7, 1892, LOV. The OMA subsequently decided to abandon the work for widows, requesting instead that the Lee Camp appoint a committee to do the work. (OMA Minutes, March 3, 1892, MOC.) The veteran from Cumberland County had written to Mr. C. F. Collier of Petersburg, requesting aid for himself, his wife, and his children.

54 *Winchester Times*, May 21, 1884, June 3, 10, 1885.

55 OMA Minutes, May 1885, MOC; LLMA Minutes, April 24, May 1, 15, 1885, JML; PLMA Minutes, June 9, 1885, LOV; *Richmond Dispatch*, May 29, 1887; PLMA Minutes, May 2, 1887, March 16, 1888, April 5, 1889, LOV.

56 For historians who have emphasized reunion and reconciliation, see Buck, *Road to Re-*

union; Silber, *Romance of Reunion*; and Blight, *Race and Reunion*. For discussion of the complexities of reconciliation, see Neff, *Honoring the Civil War Dead*.

57 Morton, *Story of Winchester*, 250; Delauter, *Winchester in the Civil War*, 97. That same year, the Union Cornet Band had assisted in decorating the Stonewall Cemetery on June 6 and then had proceeded across the street to "play a solemn dirge" and place flowers on the Union graves. (*Winchester News*, June 8, 1883.)

58 Blair, *Cities of the Dead*, 22.

59 *Richmond Daily Dispatch*, May 11, 1883, May 10, 1885, May 11, 1886; HMA Minutes, May 4, 1889, MOC. The 1883 account of Oakwood's Memorial Day observed that "attendance . . . was quite as large as in former years, and more than the last two or three." A reporter for the *Richmond Daily Dispatch* estimated that in 1886 "there were more present than on any similar occasion since the foundation of the monument was laid." Evidence from the *Petersburg Daily Index-Appeal* during the mid-1880s confirms that thousands of people continued to gather at Blandford Cemetery for the PLMA's memorial exercises.

60 Brundage, "Woman's Hand and Heart," 73; Blight, *Race and Reunion*, 266; *Richmond Dispatch*, June 1, 1886; OMA Minutes, May 2, 1893, MOC. The official Jefferson Davis monument campaign, led by members of the UCV, began in 1896. But by 1899 the members had been unable to secure enough funds, and they turned over the project to the UDC. The monument was unveiled in 1907.

61 For more on Blue-Gray reunions, see Foster, *Ghosts*, 67–68.

62 Neff, *Honoring the Civil War Dead*, 12.

63 Blight, *Race and Reunion*, 98–139; Foster, *Ghosts*, 51, 63–94, 152–56, 184–86; Kammen, *Mystic Chords*, 102.

64 For historians who have argued that historical memory was tied to power relations, see Brundage, *Southern Past*; Neff, *Honoring the Civil War Dead*; Hale, *Making Whiteness*; Blight, *Race and Reunion*.

65 Brundage, "White Women," 115–39; Brundage, *Southern Past*, 12–54.

66 OMA Minutes, June 8, 1891, MOC; HMA Minutes, May 3, 9, 26, 1892, MOC. HMA Junior Minutes, May 4, 1894, MOC; clipping dated January 30, 1899, in United Daughters of the Confederacy collection, Minutes, 1895–1899, HRL.

67 HMA Junior Minutes, Constitution and Bylaws, drafted May 4, 1894, MOC.

68 O'Leary, *To Die For*, 82–90 (quote, 83); Silber, *Daughters of the Union*, 270–72.

69 HMA Minutes, May 9, 1892, MOC; HMA Junior Minutes, May 12, 26, June 3, November 5, 19, 1892, MOC. Young men did serve as treasurer of the HMA Juniors, much like the earliest LMAs. (HMA Junior Minutes, May 7, 1892, MOC.)

70 HMA Minutes, May 3, 1893, MOC. For a discussion of "Confederate motherhood" under the UDC, see Cox, *Dixie's Daughters*, chapter 7.

71 On this "deep uncertainty of life" in the 1890s, see Hale, *Making Whiteness*, 43–49; and Foster, *Ghosts*, 3–10.

72 "The Confederate Museum," *Virginia Pamphlets*, vol. 23, UVA; Collier, *White House of the Confederacy*, 7–29; Coski and Feely, "A Monument to Southern Womanhood," 139. The home was originally built by John R. Brockenbrough and his wife, Gabriella Harvie Randolph Brockenbrough, in 1818. They occupied it until 1844, when they sold the home to James M. Morson. Within a year, Morson sold the home to his sister-in-law, Sally Bruce, who later married James Seddon. They owned the house until 1857, when it was

bought by Lewis Crenshaw. After Virginia seceded and Richmond was named capital of the Confederacy, Crenshaw sold the home to the Confederate government for $42,894.97.

73 Coski and Feely, "A Monument to Southern Womanhood," 140; HMA Minutes, March 18, April 9, 1890, MOC; William H. Palmer (member of the Old 1st Virginia Infantry Association) to Mrs. E. C. Minor, March 26, 1890, HMA Collection, MOC; Bazaar Records, Box II-8, MOC.

74 HMA Minutes, May 15, 22, 26, 1890, May 4, 1891, MOC; CMLS Minutes, May 26, 1890, MOC; Coski and Feely, "A Monument to Southern Womanhood," 140–41. The charter declared that the CMLS's purpose was to "establish in the city of Richmond . . . a Confederate Memorial Literary Society or Association to collect and receive, by gift, purchase, or otherwise all books and other literary productions pertaining to the late war between the States, and of those engaged therein; all works of art or science, all battle-flags, relics . . . to preserve and keep the same for the use of the said society and the public." Belle and Joseph Bryan preferred to use the term "Southern." They believed the scope would appear wider, but when put to a vote, "Confederate" prevailed.

75 HMA Minutes, April 8, 1891, June 3, 1892, MOC; CMLS Minutes, May 26, 1891, June 3, 1892, MOC; Coski and Feely, "A Monument to Southern Womanhood," 140–41. An example of cooperation between the two associations is their agreement to divide the proceeds of an excursion in April 1891. HMA members could become CMLS members by paying fifty cents per year.

76 Relic Circular, c. fall 1891, HMA Collection, MOC; George H. B. Burton to Mrs. Hotchkiss, c. 1893, Bazaar Records, Box II-8, MOC; Report of Relic Committee, May 24, 1892, CMLS Committee Reports, MOC; Coski and Feely, "A Monument to Southern Womanhood," 147.

77 Address of Governor Charles O'Ferrall quoted in the *Richmond Dispatch*, February 22, 1896; Mrs. James R. Werth to Colonel J. Bell Bigger, Keeper of the Books of Virginia, Capitol, February 21, 1896, reprinted in the *Richmond Dispatch*, February 22, 1896.

78 Mrs. James R. Werth to HMA, October 27, 1891, HMA Collection, MOC; HMA Minutes, May 4, 9, 16, June 16, November 13, 1891, MOC; *Mexico* (Mississippi) *Ledger*, January 1893 clipping, Lizzie Cary Daniel Papers, MOC; Report of Relic Committee, May 24, 1892, CMLS Committee Reports, MOC; Coski and Feely, "A Monument to Southern Womanhood," 146–47.

79 Coski and Feely, "A Monument to Southern Womanhood," 144; CMLS Minutes, June 15, 1892, March 28, 1898, MOC.

80 Coski and Feely, "A Monument to Southern Womanhood," 147; Foster, *Ghosts*, 116.

81 HMA Minutes, June 15, November 15, 30, 1892, MOC; 1893 Bazaar Records and Florida Department of Memorial Bazaar circular, Box II-8, MOC; Coski and Feely, "A Monument to Southern Womanhood," 144.

82 HMA Minutes, November 15, 30, 1892, MOC. The officers of the Memorial Bazaar were as follows: Belle Bryan, representing the HMA, 1st vice president; Mrs. Albert Mayo, representing the OMA, 2nd vice president; Janet Randolph, representing the Ladies' Auxiliary of the Lee Camp, 3rd vice president; and Mrs. F. S. Myers, representing the Hebrew Memorial Association, 4th vice president. Perhaps these offices suggest a hierarchy among the Richmond women's Confederate associations.

83 1st Regiment Virginia Volunteers, Richmond, February 15, 1893, to Mrs. Hotchkiss, president of Memorial Bazaar, Bazaar Records, MOC.

84 Coski and Feely, "A Monument to Southern Womanhood," 140–44.

CHAPTER SIX

1 For historians who see the LMAs as giving way to veterans' associations or the Daughters by the 1890s, see Foster, *Ghosts*, 36–62; Cox, *Dixie's Daughters*, 2; Censer, *Reconstruction*, 201–2. Censer notes that in the late 1880s and 1890s, LMAs were "simply elbowed aside" by the more martial interpretation of the war of the veterans. Blight, on the other hand, fails to acknowledge that the LMAs played a significant role in the Lost Cause. (Blight, *Race and Reunion*, 258.) For historians who mark 1914 or 1915 as the decline of the Lost Cause era, see Blair, *Cities of the Dead*, 6–7; Blight, *Race and Reunion*, 6–30, 381–97; and Foster, *Ghosts*, 163–98. Edward L. Ayers marks the peak years of the Lost Cause as between 1885 and 1912. (*Promise*, 335.) These years also marked the beginning of World War I, a point at which reconciliation had been firmly established between whites of the North and South and when Memorial Days no longer solely celebrated Civil War soldiers.

2 Quoted in Cox, *Dixie's Daughters*, 16–21; Poppenheim, *History of the United Daughters of the Confederacy*, 8; and O'Leary, *To Die For*, 82. The UDC may have simply been emulating the organizational structure of the northern WRC, which had a three-tiered organization, with national office, state departments, and local corps.

3 Quoted in Cox, *Dixie's Daughters*, 21–22; Mildred Rutherford Scrapbook Collection, vol. 41, "Origins of the Ladies Memorial Associations," MOC. Raines concurred that the LMAs deserved reverence but maintained that memorial association women could also join the ranks of the Daughters, "unless of course they are not [eligible]."

4 Cox agrees that the Ladies paved the way for the Daughters. (*Dixie's Daughters*, 16, 26, 50.)

5 Quinn, *History of the City of Fredericksburg*, 323; "Old Dominion Chapter, United Daughters of the Confederacy," c. 1938, VHS; UDC, *Minutes of the Seventh Annual Meeting (1900)*, 9–37; Richmond Chapter UDC Minutes, January 18, 1902, MOC. The minutes of the UDC's annual meetings were all published by Foster and Webb in the year following the meeting.

6 The organization dates for UDC chapters in these five cities are as follows: Lynchburg's Otey Chapter, July 5, 1895; Richmond, January 1896; Fredericksburg, February 28, 1896; Lynchburg's Old Dominion Chapter, July 9, 1896; Winchester, November 1897; Petersburg, by November 1897.

7 For women in Fredericksburg, motivation to join the UDC may have sprung from the exclusionary policies of the FLMA. As chapter 5 noted, when the FLMA reorganized in 1893, it restricted its membership to twenty members. Although many of the FLMA members, including both the president and the vice president (Nannie Seddon Barney and Betty Churchill Lacy), joined the UDC chapter, most of the 200 Daughters had not been invited to join the ranks of the memorial association and so sought out their own organization. (FLMA Minutes, April 18, 1893, LOV; Quinn, *History of the City of Fredericksburg*, 323.)

8   Cox, *Dixie's Daughters*, 30; UDC, *Minutes of the Fourth Annual Meeting (1897)*, 116–36, VHS; Lucy Dunbar Williams, secretary, Stonewall Memorial Association, Winchester, to Mrs. Minor, December 18, 1900, HMA Collection, MOC. A cursory examination of the UDC members listed for Virginia chapters in 1897 suggests that most if not all of the LMA women in the state joined the ranks of the Daughters.

9   Cox, *Dixie's Daughters*, 32. Fitzhugh Brundage supports Cox's argument that class status motivated southern white women to join clubs and hereditary associations such as the UDC and Daughters of the American Revolution. (Brundage, *Southern Past*, 36.)

10 Cox, *Dixie's Daughters*, 34–39. Thus, those women who were most likely to join the Daughters more closely resembled the second generation of LMA women rather than the founders, at least in terms of life experience.

11 Constitution of the United Daughters of the Confederacy, 1903, LOV, cited in Parrott, "Love Makes Memory Eternal," 219–39; Mildred Rutherford Scrapbook Collection, vol. 41, MOC.

12 Sklar, "Florence Kelly," 327–39; Treadway, *Women of the Mark*, 3–13. By 1897, more than 500 associations had joined this umbrella association to address issues of good government and civil service reform. Among those present at the Woman's Club of Richmond inaugural meeting were at least four who had connections to the HMA or CMLS: Virginia Robinson, Jane Rutherfoord, Mary Maben Lyons, and Emeline Tabb Wellford.

13 *Richmond Times*, May 30, 1895. The Virginia Federation of Women's Clubs did not form until 1907. (Lebsock, *Share of Honour*, 110.) In Richmond alone in the mid-1890s, women joined the ranks of the Virginia Home for the Incurables, the Magdalene Home for Prostitutes, the Richmond Humane Society, the Baptist Home for Aged Women, and the Richmond Women's Club, among others.

14 Of the forty-seven UDC chapters in Virginia in 1897, only thirteen were located in cities that had LMAs. In other words, 72 percent of Virginia's UDC chapters that year were not located in communities where women might have had the opportunity to join an LMA. (UDC, *Minutes of the Fourth Annual Meeting [1897]*, 116–36, VHS.)

15 On the era of segregation, see Lebsock, *Murder in Virginia*, 13–19, 59–65, 149; Ayers, *Promise*, 132–59; Woodward, *Strange Career of Jim Crow*; Hale, *Making Whiteness*; Gilmore, *Gender and Jim Crow*; and Kantrowitz, *Ben Tillman*.

16 According to Suzanne Lebsock, lynchings were not as common in Virginia as in other southern states; however, they were equally intense and the numbers appeared to be escalating in the late 1880s. She notes that "three lynchings [occurred] in Virginia in 1888, seven in 1889, nine in 1892, and, in 1893, twelve." (Lebsock, *Murder in Virginia*, 62.)

17 Brundage, "White Women," 115–39 (quote, 127); Hale, *Making Whiteness*, 61–62, 86; Cox, *Dixie's Daughters*, 2, 13–15, 39, 84–87, 121–28, 138–40.

18 For more discussion on efforts of the UDC to raise a monument to so-called faithful slaves, see Janney, "Written in Stone," 117–41.

19 O'Leary, *To Die For*, 79–80, 97–100; Silber, *Daughters of the Union*, 269–70.

20 McPherson, "The Long-Legged Yankee Lies," 64–93 (Lee quote, 69); Cox, *Dixie's Daughters*, 121, 123–27. Merchant quoted in Brundage, *Southern Past*, 46. Southern African Americans also turned to their public school systems to nurture black historical memory. Responding to the efforts of groups such as the UDC, the National Association

of Colored Women, founded in 1896, attempted to counter the message of white supremacy and white historical memory found in many school textbooks. (Brundage, *Southern Past*, 140, 147–48.)

21 According to Marjorie Spruill Wheeler, white southerners employed the term "Negro problem" to connote "the enfranchisement after the Civil War of several million African Americans considered by whites to be ignorant, purchasable, and unfit for political participation." (Wheeler, *New Women*, 101.)

22 HMA Junior Minutes, May 25, 1897, MOC.

23 Cox, *Dixie's Daughters*, 5; Hale, *Making Whiteness*, 53; Foster, *Ghosts*, 171. Foster argues that the UDC drew its membership primarily from the middle class and the upper class.

24 O'Leary, *To Die For*, 78–80. O'Leary notes that hereditary groups proved especially popular in the late nineteenth century; by 1895, twenty-four such groups had formed, including the Sons of the American Revolution and the UDC. See also Brundage, *Southern Past*, 24, 36.

25 Silber, *Daughters of the Union*, 271; Report of the President-General, UDC, *Minutes of the Eighteenth Annual Meeting, (1911)*, 98–99; Report of the President-General, UDC, *Minutes of the Nineteenth Annual Meeting, (1912)*, 95; Cox, *Dixie's Daughters*, 24, 31. Cox points out that the extraordinary growth of the UDC alarmed many of its leaders, who then recommended restrictions on membership.

26 Mrs. N. V. Randolph, "Recollections of My Mother, 1861–1865," MOC; Douglas S. Freeman, "Mrs. Norman Randolph Remembered," *Richmond Quarterly* 7 (Summer 1984): 46–48; *Richmond Times-Dispatch*, April 27, 1924; *Richmond News Leader*, October 28, 1927; John Coski, "Janet Henderson Weaver Randolph," unpublished article, MOC; Janet H. Weaver to Miss Jenkins, July 12, 1865, MOC. According to John Coski, Federal troops allegedly used the headboards erected by the Warrenton women for their campfires.

27 Both Randolph's father and husband served in the Confederate army. Her father enlisted as a private in the Warrenton Rifles, 17th Virginia Infantry, in April 1861, but died of typhoid in May 1862. Her husband, Norman Vincent Randolph, enlisted in the 24th Battalion Virginia Cavalry at the age of fifteen and later transferred to Mosby's Rangers, 43rd Battalion. Although he was wounded at Upperville in 1863, Randolph returned to action with Mosby's men. After the war, he made his living as a businessman, including stints as president of the Richmond Paper Box Company and Virginia State Insurance and vice president of James Taylor Ellyson's Old Dominion Savings and Loans. He was a member of the R. E. Lee Camp No. 1, UCV, and served on the board of trustees for the Lee Camp Soldiers' Home. (John Coski, "Janet Henderson Weaver Randolph," unpublished article, MOC.)

28 Other Confederate organizations that Randolph took part in as board member included the Stonewall Jackson, Matthew Fontaine Maury, and the (abortive) Fitzhugh Lee Monument associations. She also served as the chairman of the central committee for the Jefferson Davis Monument Association. (John Coski, "Janet Henderson Weaver Randolph," unpublished article, MOC.)

29 Mrs. N. V. Randolph, "Recollections of My Mother, 1861–1865," MOC; Douglas S. Freeman, "Mrs. Norman Randolph Remembered," *Richmond Quarterly* 7 (Summer 1984):

46–48; *Richmond Times-Dispatch*, April 27, 1924; *Richmond News Leader*, October 28, 1927; John Coski, "Janet Henderson Weaver Randolph," unpublished article, MOC; *Minutes of the Virginia Division, UDC*, 1912: 74, MOC. Coski points out that the UDC appears to have been the most important organization to her; her tombstone at Shockoe Cemetery reads: "Founder of the Richmond Chapter / UDC 1896 / And its president / Until Her Death." There is no mention of the HMA or the CMLS. Although she was asked several times to consider serving as president of the Virginia Division or as president-general of the General Convention, she never served as either (though she was named honorary president of both).

30   John Coski, "Janet Henderson Weaver Randolph," unpublished article, MOC.

31   "Old Dominion Chapter, United Daughters of the Confederacy," Early Family Papers, VHS; "Memorial Services Held for Miss Ruth H. Early, January 30, 1928," Early Family Papers, VHS.

32   LLMA Minutes, April 30, 1896, April 28, 1897, JML.

33   "History of the Virginia Division United Daughters of the Confederacy, 1895–1967," compiled by Mrs. Cabell Smith, Miss Sarah B. Graham, and Miss Alice Whitley Jones, MOC; Richmond Chapter UDC Minutes, January 18, 1902, MOC; HMA Minutes, March 30, 1900, MOC; Coski and Feely, "A Monument to Southern Womanhood," 154; "To the United Daughters of the Confederacy," Resolution of Mrs. R. E. Park, Regent for the State of Georgia, November 1899, MOC.

34   According to Coski and Feely, as well as the author's own research, most of the early CMLS/HMA leaders were also members of the UDC. (Coski and Feely, "A Monument to Southern Womanhood," 154.)

35   CMLS Minutes, May 25, November 30, 1898, January 25, 1899, MOC; CMLS Committee Reports File, 1898 report of the corresponding secretary, Lydia P. Purcell, 1900 Annual Report, 1902 Annual Report, MOC; Cox, *Dixie's Daughters*, 49–50, 52–53, 57; HMA Minutes, May 9, June 6, October 30, 1900, March 14, 1901, MOC.

36   HMA Minutes, May 3, 1902, MOC; Mildred Rutherford Scrapbook Collection, vol. 41, "Origins of the Ladies Memorial Associations," MOC.

37   CMLS Minutes, January 16, 1900, MOC; Ella Darcy Dibrell to Lizzie Cary Daniel, c. August 1911, Lizzie Cary Daniel Papers, MOC; Coski and Feely, "A Monument to Southern Womanhood," 155.

38   HMA Minutes, May 8, 1896, MOC.

39   Other charter members included the Southern Memorial Association of Fayetteville, Arkansas; Ladies Confederate Memorial Association of New Orleans; Ladies Memorial Association of Knoxville, Tennessee; Ladies Memorial and Literary Association of Springfield, Missouri; Ladies Confederate Memorial Association of Fort Mills, South Carolina; Ladies Confederate Association of Memphis, Tennessee; and Ladies Confederate Association of Gainesville, Alabama. (*Minutes of the CSMA*, May 1900, UVA.)

40   "A Confederation of Southern Memorial Associations," *SHSP* 28: 377–84; *Minutes of the CSMA*, May 1900, UVA.

41   Ibid.; "The Confederated Southern Memorial Association—It's [*sic*] Origin and Purpose," c. 1920, Janet Randolph Papers, Box II-4, MOC.

42   *Minutes of the CSMA*, May 1900, UVA (emphasis added); CSMA, *History of the CSMA*,

37, 291; "Confederated Southern Memorial Associations," *Confederate Veteran* 9 (1901): 15.

43 *Minutes of the CSMA*, May 1900, May 1901, May 1904; LLMA Minutes, April 21, 1902, JML; PLMA Minutes, May 21, 1900, LOV.

44 By 1901, the CSMA reported that several "distinguished Southern women" had been elected honorary members of the body, including Mrs. Jefferson Davis, Mrs. Stonewall Jackson, Mrs. D. H. Hill, Misses Mary and Mildred Lee, and Mrs. Frances Kirby-Smith Wade. ("Confederated Southern Memorial Associations," *Confederate Veteran* 9 (1901): 368.

45 *Minutes of the CSMA*, May 1901, May 1902, May 1903, May 1904, May 1905, May 1907, UVA; LLMA Minutes, June 23, 1903, JML; Sixth Annual Convention of the CSMA, 1905, Mildred Rutherford Scrapbook Collection, vol. 41, "Origins of the Ladies Memorial Associations," MOC. By 1907, the number of associations that had joined the CSMA had reached fifty-seven, including all of the associations from Richmond, Petersburg, Winchester, Lynchburg, and Fredericksburg.

46 *Minutes of the CSMA*, May 1902, May 1903, May 1904, May 1907, May 1908, UVA. The FLMA joined the CSMA sometime between January and May 1907. For unknown reasons, the association had voted unanimously to "dismiss the subject" of joining the CSMA, on January 9, 1907, but subsequently agreed to attend the annual CSMA meeting in Richmond that May. (FLMA Minutes, January 9, May 13, 1907, LOV.)

47 *Minutes of the CSMA*, May 1901, May 1902, May 1903, May 1904, UVA. Desiring to preserve both the individuality and the identity of the LMAs, the confederation resolved to compile the histories of each memorial association in a book form that could then be sold for the benefit of the Jefferson Davis Monument. The book was completed in 1904 and sold for $1.35 (including delivery).

48 *Petersburg Daily Index-Appeal*, June 9, 1901. Some historians have cited the more martial spirit of Memorial Days as an indication that the LMAs were yielding their influence over commemorations to the veterans. See, for example, Censer, *Reconstruction*, 206.

49 "Confederate Dead in the North," *Confederate Veteran* 9 (1901): 196–98; *New York Times*, May 2, 1901; Blair, *Cities of the Dead*, 171–208; *Minutes of the CSMA*, May 1901, 1904. The CSMA proposed erecting granite shafts at national cemeteries in Philadelphia, Pennsylvania; Elmira, New York; Point Lookout, Maryland; and Finns Point, New Jersey. McKinley approved the reburial act in June 1900, and the first ceremonies to dedicate the section were held in May 1903 (which now included 264 graves, after the removal of graves from the Soldiers' Home). The CSMA, together with the UDC and other Confederate groups, succeeded in having a memorial erected to the Confederate dead at Arlington in 1914.

50 Mildred Rutherford Scrapbook Collection, vol. 41, "Origins of the Ladies Memorial Associations," MOC; "Confederated Southern Memorial Associations," *Confederate Veteran* 11 (1903).

51 PLMA Minutes, May 1, 17, 1899, LOV; CSMA, *History of the Confederated Memorial Associations*, 290–92. Honorary members for the Memphis project included Mrs. Jefferson Davis, Mrs. Robert E. Lee, Miss Augusta Evans, and Mrs. Nathan B. Forrest. (*Petersburg Daily Index-Appeal*, January 26, 1867.)

52 PLMA Minutes, May 1, 17, 1899, LOV.

53 Charles Campbell quoted in Briggs, *Compass Windows of Old Blandford Church*, 2; Nichols, *A Sketch of Old Blandford Church*, 7.

54 PLMA Minutes, October 12, November 16, 1900, LOV.

55 Ibid., February 14, 1901, November 19, 1903, LOV. According to the membership list of the *Fourth Annual Meeting, (1897)*, 125, Mrs. W. C. Badger was a member of the UDC as well.

56 Briggs, *Compass Windows of Old Blandford Church*, 4–8.

57 PLMA Minutes, June 16, 1904, LOV; *Petersburg Daily Index-Appeal*, June 9, 10, 1904. In 1901, *Daily Index-Appeal* began printing accounts of the Memorial Day activities on the front and back pages, rather than hiding them within the local announcements.

58 Nichols, *A Sketch of Old Blandford Church*, 4–10.

59 Jefferson Davis was inaugurated February 22, 1862 (the anniversary of George Washington's birth), in Richmond's Capitol Square as the president of the Confederate States of America. Davis had been elected in November 1861. Since April 1861, he had served as president of the provisional Confederate government.

60 *Richmond Dispatch*, February 23, 1896; *New York Times*, December 14, 1895.

61 *Richmond Dispatch*, February 23, 1896; Coski and Feely, "A Monument to Southern Womanhood," 131; CMLS Committee Files, clipping from the *Richmond Times*, c. December 1897, MOC.

62 CMLS Minutes, April 30, June 3, October 15, 1897, January 28, 1898, MOC; "Pyramids in Fredericksburg," Off the Beaten Path, Vol. 3, <http://www.simplyfredericksburg. com/printpage.php.>. Apparently, the CMLS had originally proposed erecting wooden signs, but the Richmond, Fredericksburg, and Potomac Railroad rejected this idea on the grounds that it looked too much like advertising. In 1898, the railroad moved seventeen tons of Virginia granite to construct the pyramid, which ironically became known as Meade's Pyramid, after Union General George G. Meade. It should be noted that the railroad did not approach the FLMA for reasons unknown, although one might speculate that the CMLS simply had more appeal and pull than the twenty women who composed the Fredericksburg association.

63 CMLS Minutes, April 30, June 3, October 15, 1897, January 28, 1898, MOC; CMLS Committee Files, clipping from the *Richmond Times*, c. December 1897, 1900 Report of Committee to Locate and Mark Confederate Sites and Fortifications, 1904 Report to the CSMA, MOC.

64 HMA appeal to all Virginia towns and cities with Confederate cemeteries, November 1900, HMA Collection, MOC; Lucy Dunbar Williams, Secretary, Stonewall Memorial Association, Winchester, to Mrs. Minor, December 18, 1900, HMA Collection, MOC; Richmond Chapter UDC Minutes, January 18, 1902, MOC; Virginia Senate Bill No. 94, Janet Randolph Papers, Box II-4, MOC. On maternalist legislation, see Skocpol, *Protecting Soldiers*, 3, 20–21, 50–51; and Odem, *Delinquent Daughters*, 8–37. Some years later, the HMA requested that the General Assembly make an appropriation of $8,000 to trustees named by the HMA (members of the association), who would make a contract with the Hollywood Cemetery Company to ensure the upkeep of the graves. By doing so, the Ladies claimed that the cost to the state would be substantially lowered. The Blandford Cemetery in Petersburg did not request funds from the state because the city government took responsibility for the maintenance. In 1930, however, the Vir-

ginia General Assembly appropriated money from the state treasury to aid Confederate memorial associations "in caring for the cemeteries and graves of the Confederate soldiers and sailors buried in the cemeteries . . . specified, and in erecting and caring for markers and monuments to the memory of said soldiers and sailors." (1930 Virginia Acts, chapter 439, 94.) For more on the connection between women's memorial efforts and state-sponsored historic preservation efforts, see Brundage, *Southern Past*, 49–54, 105–37.

65   O'Ferrall's speech quoted in *Richmond Dispatch*, February 23, 1896; Coski and Feely, "A Monument to Southern Womanhood," 131–32; Minor T. Weisger, "Charles T. O'Ferrall, 'Gray Eagle' from the Valley," in Younger, *Governors of Virginia*, 142.

66   "A National Repository for the Records and Relics of the Southern Cause, Proposed by Charles Broadway Rouss, of New York," *SHSP* 22: 387–89; Mary Maury Werth quoted in Coski and Feely, "A Monument to Southern Womanhood," 147–49; Hall, "Virginia Historical Society," 100–105; Rasmussen, "Planning a Temple to the Lost Cause," 163–82; Foster, *Ghosts*, 116. Ramussen points out that the idea for this "Temple to the Lost Cause" coincided with efforts to erect the Grant Monument (popularly known as Grant's Tomb). According to Ramussen, "Rouss watched as the sum of $600,000 was raised for the project by popular subscription and as ground was broken in 1891. Three years later—and three years before the monument was completed—this former Virginian sent a letter to various camps of Confederate veterans, calling for a Confederate Memorial Association (CMA) that would honor Grant's former opponents."

67   Rouss quoted in Coski and Feely, "A Monument to Southern Womanhood," 147–49; Ramussen, "Planning a Temple to the Lost Cause," 166; CMLS Minutes, February 4, June 5, 1896, MOC; "The Work of the CMLS," c. 1896, Lizzie Cary Daniel Papers, MOC (emphasis in original); Battle Abbey Files, MOC; *Richmond Times-Dispatch*, January 23, 1909.

68   Gay, "James Hoge Tyler: Rebellious Regular," 151, 153; Battle Abbey Files of John Coski, MOC; Ramussen, "Planning a Temple to the Lost Cause," 169; Coski and Feely, "A Monument to Southern Womanhood," 147–49; Ellyson Scrapbook, CMA Papers, VHS; John Coski, "Janet Henderson Weaver Randolph," unpublished article, MOC; D. H. Maury (Richmond) to Ruth Early, February 10, 1896, Early Family Papers, VHS; CMLS Minutes, April 18, December 27, 1898, MOC.

69   *Richmond Times-Dispatch*, January 23, February 28, 1909; Ramussen, "Planning a Temple to the Lost Cause," 169; Coski and Feely, "A Monument to Southern Womanhood," 157–59;

70   *Richmond Times-Dispatch*, January 23, February 28, 1909; CMA Records, VHS.

71   The original site for the Battle Abbey was to be on the property of a Mr. Branch on the southeast corner of Monument and Boulevard. After that site fell through in 1909, the CMA continued to pursue land in the West End and found a site on Monument Avenue and Franklin Street. The city initiated condemnation hearings because some of the residents refused to sell their properties. Finally, the Lee Camp offered the land adjacent to the Soldiers' Home.

72   *Richmond Times-Dispatch*, July 22, 1898, May 20, 1909; Ramussen, "Planning a Temple to the Lost Cause," 169; Virginia Robinson quoted in John Coski, "Janet Henderson Weaver Randolph," unpublished article, MOC; Janet Randolph to J. Taylor Ellyson, July

20, 1909, CMA Records, VHS. Robinson did note that the CMLS had a board made up of men.

73 CMLS Minutes, November 30, 1910, MOC; Hall, "Virginia Historical Society," 101; Coski and Feely, "A Monument to Southern Womanhood," 158–59. The 1910 proclamation was very similar to an 1896 statement by the CMLS: "The Confederate Museum is our conception, and its organization owes its success to the HMA. Our first care was for the graves of those whose very silence is their highest claim to our consideration. Let this still be the first. Men are already full of the historical importance of our Museum. If we should today abandon it, they would shoulder the burden, for they recognize its value as a factor in this busy practical life of ours; but if we women abandon the soldiers' graves, who will care for them? We have ever realized that the privilege of keeping green the memories of our dead is a sacred trust. It is also essential to the very existence of the sentiment of which the museum is an exponent." (Signed by Kate Pleasants Minor, HMA annual meeting, 1896, HMA correspondence, MOC.)

74 *Minutes of the Third Annual Convention of the First Virginia Division of the United Daughters of the Confederacy*, 1897, MOC; Cox, *Dixie's Daughters*, 50.

EPILOGUE

1 Conversation with Ted Delany, August 24, 2006.

2 The last documented meeting of the HMA was on May 11, 1934. The dates for the Hebrew and Winchester associations remain unknown. The Oakwood association was still conducting Memorial Day services as late as May 1954. (HMA Minutes, May 11, 1934, MOC; Eighty-eighth Anniversary of the Oakwood Memorial Association Program, May 8, 1954, RICH.)

3 Coski, "A Century of Collecting," 11, 22–24; Unpublished Visitation Statistics, courtesy of John M. Coski, March 10, 2005, MOC; MOC, <http://www.moc.org/edbring.htm>. During the 1920s and 1940s, it attracted more than 10,000 visitors a year. The number of visitors continued to grow each year, reaching an annual high of 88,000 in the early 1990s, before beginning to decline. In the fiscal year that ended in June 2004, the number had dropped to 54,000—the first time in a quarter of a century that the visits had fallen below 60,000. (*Daily Progress* [Charlottesville, Va.], February 3, 2005.)

4 Coski, "A Century of Collecting," 11, 24–22; *Richmond Times-Dispatch*, October 9, 2004; *Daily Progress* (Charlottesville, Va.), February 3, 2005.

5 *Richmond Times-Dispatch*, February 20, 2007.

6 For example, just as Glenda Gilmore has shown that southern middle-class black women likewise stepped forward to fulfill a political role when black men were pushed aside by disenfranchisement in 1900, the Ladies also stepped forward when many ex-Confederate men were disenfranchised during Reconstruction. (Gilmore, *Gender and Jim Crow*; Foner, *Reconstruction*.)

7 Brundage, *Southern Past*, 2–3, 15; "We Say No to the Proposed Lincoln Statue in Richmond," <http://www.petitiononline.com/noabe/petition.html>, accessed August 16, 2006; Fahs and Waugh, *Memory of the Civil War*, 1; Coski, *Confederate Battle Flag*; Bonner, *Colors and Blood*, 1–7.

8 President's Report, in *Year Book, 1926, of the Confederate Memorial Literary Society*, 7.

Bibliography

PRIMARY SOURCES

Manuscripts

Alderman Library, University of Virginia, Charlottesville
    Letters of John Herbert Claiborne
    Katherine Couse Correspondence
    Papers of Eugene Davis
    Irvine, Saunders, Davis, and Watts Families Papers
    Minutes of the Confederated Southern Memorial Association
Beth Ahabah Museum and Archives, Richmond, Va.
    Hebrew Cemetery Records
Central Rappahannock Regional Library, Fredericksburg, Va.
    Hodge, Robert, ed., "Confederate Memorial Days: Fredericksburg, Virginia, 1866–1985"
    "A Leaf from the Past: From the Records of the Ladies' Memorial Association of
        Fredericksburg, VA"
Earl Gregg Swem Library, College of William and Mary, Williamsburg, Va.
    Campbell Papers
    William Booth Taliaferro Papers
    Tucker-Coleman Papers
Eleanor S. Brockenbrough Library, Museum of the Confederacy, Richmond, Va.
    Samuel Bassett French Letterbooks
    Battle Abbey Files
    Bazaar Records
    Clipping File
    Confederate Memorial Literary Society Records
    Lizzie Cary Daniel Papers
    Hollywood Memorial Association Collection
    Hospital Papers
    Ladies' Defense and Aid Association Papers
    Ladies' Ridge Benevolent Society Record Book
    Isabel Maury Papers
    Minutes of the Virginia Division, UDC
    Oakwood Memorial Association Minutes
    Pamphlet Collection
    Kate Mason Rowland Papers

Mildred Rutherford Scrapbooks

Southern Women's Collection

Fredericksburg and Spotsylvania National Military Park

Maj. Robert T. Harper Statement

Handley Regional Library, Winchester, Va.

Kate Sperry Diary

Stonewall Cemetery Records

Turner Ashby Camp Sons of Confederate Veterans Records

. United Daughters of the Confederacy Collection

Williams Family Papers

Jones Memorial Library, Lynchburg, Va.

Ladies' Memorial Association Collection

Library of Congress, Washington, D.C.

Jubal A. Early Papers

Library of Virginia, Richmond

Adeline Egerton Papers

Fredericksburg Ladies' Memorial Association Minutes

Kate Kern Letters

Lee Monument Association Records

Petersburg Ladies' Memorial Association Minutes

Perkins Library, Special Collections Library, Duke University, Durham, N.C.

Harriette Branham Diary

Lucy Muse Walton Fletcher Diary

Greenville Ladies' Association Minutes

Lucas-Ashley Papers

Munford-Ellis Family Papers

Daniel Ruggles Collection

John Rutherfoord Papers

Petersburg National Battlefield

Bessie Callender Papers

Southern Historical Collection, University of North Carolina Library, Chapel Hill

William N. Pendleton Papers

Tucker Family Papers

Virginia Historical Society, Richmond

Ashby Family Papers

Aylett Family Papers

Bagby Family Papers

Confederate Memorial Association Papers

Early Family Papers

James Henry Gardner Papers

R. E. Lee Camp, Sons of Confederate Veterans Collection

Robert E. Lee Letterbook

Marrow Family Papers

Minutes of the Annual Conventions of the United Daughters of the Confederacy, 1895–1919

Mary E. Rambant Morrison Memoir

Randolph Family Papers
Saunders Family Papers
Wynne Family Papers

Printed Sources

Averitt, Rev. James B. *The Memoirs of General Turner Ashby and His Compeers*. Baltimore,
Md.: Selby & Dulany, 1867.

Confederated Southern Memorial Association, *History of the Confederate Memorial
Associations of the South*. New Orleans: Graham Press, 1904.

Cooke, John Esten. *Stonewall Jackson: A Military Biography*. New York: D. Appleton &
Company, 1876.

Davidson, Nora Fontaine Maury. *Cullings from the Confederacy: A Collection of Southern
Poems, Original and Others, Popular during the War between the States, and Incidents and
Facts Worth Recalling*. Washington, D.C.: Rufus H. Darby Printing Co., 1903.

Elliot, Sam Davis, ed. *Doctor Quintard, Chaplain, C.S.A. and Second Bishop of Tennessee: The
Memoir and Civil War Diary of Charles Todd Quintard*. Baton Rouge: Louisiana State
University Press, 2003.

Hollywood Memorial Association. *Our Confederate Dead*. Richmond, Va.: Hollywood
Memorial Association, 1896.

Kernodle, Louise Nurney. *Guide Book of the City of Richmond*. Richmond, Va.: Central
Publishing Company, 1925.

McDonald, Cornelia Peake. *A Woman's Civil War: A Diary with Reminiscences of the War
from March 1862*. 1935; reprint with introduction by Minrose Gwin, Madison, Wis.:
University of Wisconsin Press, 1992.

McGuire, Judith White Brockenbrough. *Diary of a Southern Refugee, during the War*. 1867;
reprint, Salem, N.H.: Ayer, 1986.

Munford, Col. George Wythe. "The Jewel's of Virginia: A Lecture Delivered by Invitation of
the Hollywood Memorial Association, in Richmond, January 18, 1867." Richmond, Va.:
Gary & Clemmitt, Printers, 1867.

Parmelee, Alice Maury, ed. *The Confederate Diary of Betty Herndon Maury, 1861–1863*.
Washington, D.C.: Privately printed, 1938.

Pember, Phoebe Yates. *A Southern Woman's Story*, with introduction by George C. Rable.
1879; reprint, Columbia: University of South Carolina Press, 2002.

Pickett, LaSalle Corbell. *Pickett and His Men*. 1899; reprint, Atlanta, Ga.: Foote & Davies
Company, 1900.

Poppenheim, Mary, et al. *The History of the United Daughters of the Confederacy*. 1938;
reprint, Raleigh, N.C.: Edwards & Broughton, 1955.

Pryor, Sara Rice. *Reminiscences of Peace and War*. 1908; reprint, Freeport, N.Y.: Books for
Library Press, 1970.

Putnam, Sallie Brock. *Richmond during the War: Four Years of Personal Observation*. 1867;
reprint with introduction by Virginia Scharff, Lincoln: University of Nebraska Press,
1996.

Quinn, Silvanus Jackson. *The History of the City of Fredericksburg*. Richmond, Va.:
Hermitage Press, 1908.

Reed, James C. "'On My Way Rejoicing,' Memoir of James C. Reed." *Civil War Times*, August 2000, 56.

U.S. Bureau of the Census. *Tenth Census of the United States*, 1880.

U.S. War Department. *The War of the Rebellion: A Compilation of the Official Records of the Union and Confederate Armies*. 127 vols. Index and atlas. Washington, D.C.: GPO, 1880–1901.

Wallace, A. A. *Two Chapters of a Life: America by Comparison and Other Addresses*. Richmond, Va.: Everett Waddey, 1913.

Welton, J. Michael, ed. *"My Heart Is So Rebellious": The Caldwell Letters, 1861–1865*. Warrenton, Va.: Fauquier National Bank, n.d.

Year Book, 1926, of the Confederate Memorial Literary Society. Richmond, Va.: Whittet & Shepperson, 1926.

Periodicals

Advocate of Peace

Charleston Mercury

Confederate Veteran

Daily Progress (Charlottesville, Va.)

Fredericksburg Ledger

Fredericksburg News

Fredericksburg Star

Independent

Lynchburg Daily Virginian

Lynchburg News

Lynchburg Virginian

Montgomery Mail

New York Daily News

New York Observer and Chronicle

New York Times

Petersburg Daily Express

Petersburg Daily Index

Petersburg Daily Index-Appeal

Petersburg Index

Petersburg Index-Appeal

Republican Vindicator

Richmond Daily Dispatch

Richmond Daily Examiner

Richmond Dispatch

Richmond Enquirer

Richmond News Leader

Richmond State

Richmond Times

Richmond Times-Dispatch

Richmond Whig

Shepherdstown Register
Southern Historical Society Papers
Southern Literary Messenger
Southern Opinion (Richmond, Va.)
Staunton Spectator
Valley Virginian {Staunton, Va.)
Weekly Chronicle (Charlottesville, Va.)
Winchester Journal
Winchester News
Winchester Times

SECONDARY SOURCES

Books

Allgor, Catherine. *Parlor Politics: In Which the Ladies of Washington Help Build a City and a Government*. Charlottesville: University Press of Virginia, 2000.

Ash, Steven V. *When the Yankees Came: Conflict and Chaos in the Occupied South, 1861–1865*. Chapel Hill: University of North Carolina Press, 1995.

———. *A Year in the South: 1865, the Story of Four Ordinary People Who Lived through the Most Tumultuous Twelve Months in American History*. New York: Palgrave Macmillan, 2002.

Ayers, Edward L. *The Promise of the New South: Life after Reconstruction*. New York: Oxford University Press, 1992.

Ayers, Edward, and John C. Willis, eds. *The Edge of the South: Life in Nineteenth-Century Virginia*. Charlottesville: University of Virginia Press, 1991.

Bardaglio, Peter W. *Reconstructing the Household: Families, Sex, and the Law in the Nineteenth-Century South*. Chapel Hill: University of North Carolina Press, 1995.

Bederman, Gail. *Manliness and Civilization: A Cultural History of Gender and Race in the United States, 1880–1917*. Chicago: University of Chicago Press, 1995.

Beringer, Richard E., Herman Hattaway, Archer Jones, and William N. Still Jr. *Why the South Lost the Civil War*. Athens: University of Georgia Press, 1986.

Berry, Stephen W. II. *All That Makes a Man: Love and Ambition in the Civil War South*. New York: Oxford University Press, 2003.

Blair, William A. *Cities of the Dead: Contesting the Memory of the Civil War in the South, 1865–1914*. Chapel Hill: University of North Carolina Press, 2004.

———. *Virginia's Private War: Feeding Body and Soul in the Confederacy, 1861–1865*. New York: Oxford University Press, 1998.

Blair, William A., and William Pencak, eds. *Making and Remaking Pennsylvania's Civil War*. University Park: Pennsylvania State University Press, 2001.

Blight, David W. *Race and Reunion: The Civil War in American History*. Cambridge, Mass.: Harvard University Press, 2001.

Bonner, Robert E. *Colors and Blood: Flag Passions of the Confederate South*. Princeton, N.J.: Princeton University Press, 2002.

Breen, T. H. *The Marketplace of Revolution: How Consumer Politics Shaped American Independence*. New York: Oxford University Press, 2004.

Briggs, Martha Wren. *The Compass Windows of Old Blandford Church: A Tribute to Tiffany Glass*. Sedley, Va.: Dory Press, 1992.

Brundage, W. Fitzhugh. *The Southern Past: A Clash of Race and Memory*. Cambridge, Mass.: Harvard University Press, 2005.

————. ed. *Where These Memories Grow: History, Memory, and Southern Identity*. Chapel Hill: University of North Carolina Press, 2000.

Buck, Paul. *The Road to Reunion*. Boston: Little, Brown, 1937.

Bynum, Victoria E. *Unruly Women: The Politics of Social and Sexual Control in the Old South*. Chapel Hill: University of North Carolina Press, 1992.

Campbell, Edward D., and Kym S. Rice, eds. *A Woman's War: Southern Women, Civil War, and the Confederate Legacy*. Charlottesville: University Press of Virginia and Museum of the Confederacy, 1996.

Campbell, Jacqueline Glass. *When Sherman Marched North from the Sea: Resistance on the Confederate Home Front*. Chapel Hill: University of North Carolina Press, 2003.

Cannon, Deveraux D., Jr., *The Flags of the Confederacy: An Illustrated History*. Memphis, Tenn.: St. Lukes Press and Broadfoot, 1988.

Censer, Jane Turner. *The Reconstruction of White Southern Womanhood, 1865–1900*. Baton Rouge: Louisiana State University Press, 2003.

Chesson, Michael. *Richmond after the War, 1865–1890*. Richmond: Virginia State Library, 1981.

Christian, W. Asbury. *Lynchburg and Its People*. Lynchburg, Va.: J. P. Bell, 1900.

Clark, Kathleen. *Defining Moments: African American Commemoration and Political Culture in the South, 1863–1913*. Chapel Hill: University of North Carolina Press, 2005.

Clinton, Catherine. *The Plantation Mistress: Woman's World in the Old South*. New York: Pantheon, 1982.

Clinton, Catherine, and Nina Silber, eds. *Divided Houses: Gender and the Civil War*. New York: Oxford University Press, 1992.

Collier, Malinda W. *White House of the Confederacy: An Illustrated History*. Richmond, Va.: Cadmus Marketing, 1993.

Connelly, Thomas L. *The Marble Man: Robert E. Lee and His Image in American Society*. Baton Rouge: Louisiana State University Press, 1977.

Coryell, Janet L., Thomas H. Appleton, Anastatia Sims, Sandra Gioia Treadway, eds. *Negotiating Boundaries of Southern Womanhood: Dealing with Powers That Be*. Columbia: University of Missouri Press, 2000.

Coski, John M. *Capital Navy: The Men, Ships, and Operation of the James River Squadron*. Campbell, Calif.: Savas, 1996.

————. *The Confederate Battle Flag: America's Most Embattled Emblem*. Cambridge, Mass.: Harvard University Press, 2005.

Cox, Karen L. *Dixie's Daughters: The United Daughters of the Confederacy and the Preservation of Confederate Culture*. Gainesville: University Press of Florida, 2003.

Daniel, Pete. *Lost Revolutions: The South in the 1950s*. Chapel Hill: University of North Carolina Press, 2000.

Delauter, Roger U. *Winchester in the Civil War*. 2nd ed. Lynchburg, Va.: H. E. Howard, 1992.

Douglas, Ann. *The Feminization of American Culture*. London: Papermac, 1996.

Dubois, Ellen Carol. *Feminism and Suffrage: The Emergence of an Independent Women's Movement in America, 1848–1869*. Ithaca, N.Y.: Cornell University Press, 1978.

Edwards, Laura. *Gendered Strife and Confusion: The Political Culture of Reconstruction*. Urbana: University of Illinois Press, 1997.

———. *Scarlett Doesn't Live Here Anymore*. Urbana: University of Illinois Press, 2000.

Edwards, Rebecca. *Angels in the Machinery: Gender in American Party Politics from the Civil War to the Progressive Era*. New York: Oxford University Press, 1997.

Fahs, Alice, and Joan Waugh, eds. *The Memory of the Civil War in American Culture*. Chapel Hill: University of North Carolina Press, 2004.

Farnham, Christie Anne, ed. *Women of the American South: A Multicultural Reader*. New York: New York University Press, 1997.

Faust, Drew Gilpin. *The Creation of Confederate Nationalism: Ideology and Identity in the Civil War South*. Baton Rouge: Louisiana State University Press, 1988.

———. *Mothers of Invention: Women of the Slaveholding South in the American Civil War*. New York: Vintage Books, 1996.

Fleet, Betsy, ed. *Green Mount after the War: The Correspondence of Maria Louisa Wacker Fleet and Her Family, 1865–1900*. Charlottesville: University Press of Virginia, 1978.

Foner, Eric. *Reconstruction: America's Unfinished Revolution*. New York: Harper and Row, 1988.

Foster, Gaines M. *Ghosts of the Confederacy: Defeat, the Lost Cause, and the Emergence of the New South*. New York: Oxford University Press, 1987.

Fox-Genovese, Elizabeth. *Within the Plantation Household: Black and White Women of the Old South*. Chapel Hill: University of North Carolina Press, 1988.

Friedman, Jean. *The Enclosed Garden: Women and Community in the Evangelical South, 1830–1900*. Chapel Hill: University of North Carolina Press, 1985.

Gallagher, Gary W. *The Confederate War: How Popular Will, Nationalism, and Military Strategy Could Not Stave Off Defeat*. Cambridge, Mass.: Harvard University Press, 1997.

———. *Lee and His Generals in War and Memory*. Baton Rouge: Louisiana State University Press, 1998.

———, ed. *The Fredericksburg Campaign: Decision on the Rappahannock*. Chapel Hill: University of North Carolina Press, 1995.

Gallagher, Gary W., and Alan T. Nolan, eds. *The Myth of the Lost Cause and Civil War History*. Bloomington: Indiana University Press, 2000.

Gallman, J. Matthew. *America's Joan of Arc: The Life of Anna Elizabeth Dickinson*. New York: Oxford University Press, 2006.

Garraty, John A., and Mark C. Carnes, general ed. *American National Biography*. 24 vols. New York: Oxford University Press, 1999.

Giesberg, Judith Ann. *Civil War Sisterhood: The U.S. Sanitary Commission and Women's Politics in Transition*. Boston: Northeastern University Press, 2000.

Gilmore, Glenda Elizabeth. *Gender and Jim Crow: Women and the Politics of White Supremacy in North Carolina, 1896–1920*. Chapel Hill: University of North Carolina Press, 1996.

Gilmore, Glenda, Bryant Simon, and Jane Daily, eds. *Jumpin' Jim Crow: Southern Politics from Civil War to Civil Rights*. Princeton, N.J.: Princeton University Press, 2000.

Ginzberg, Lori D. *Women and the Work of Benevolence: Morality, Politics, and Class in the Nineteenth-Century United States*. New Haven, Conn.: Yale University Press, 1990.

Goldfield, David. *Still Fighting the Civil War: The American South and Southern History*. Baton Rouge: Louisiana State University Press, 2002.

Goolrick, John T. *Historic Fredericksburg: The Story of an Old Town*. Richmond, Va.: Whittet & Shepperson, 1922.

Greene, A. Wilson. *J. Horace Lacy: The Most Dangerous Rebel in the County*. Richmond, Va.: Ownes Publishing Company, 1988.

Green, Carol C. *Chimborazo: The Confederacy's Largest Hospital*. Knoxville: University of Tennessee Press, 2004.

Hale, Grace Elizabeth. *Making Whiteness: The Culture of Segregation in the South, 1890–1940*. New York: Pantheon, 1998.

Halsey, Don P. *Historic and Heroic Lynchburg*. Lynchburg, Va.: J. P. Bell Company, 1935.

Henderson, William D. *Gilded Age City: Politics, Life, and Labor in Petersburg, Virginia, 1874–1889*. Washington, D.C.: University Press of America, 1980.

———. *Petersburg in the Civil War: War at the Door*. Lynchburg, Va.: H. E. Howard, 1988.

Hesseltine, William B. *Confederate Leaders in the New South*. Baton Rouge: Louisiana State University Press, 1950.

Jones, Katherine M. *Ladies of Richmond, Confederate Capital*. Indianapolis: Bobbs-Merrill, 1962.

Kammen, Michael. *Mystic Chords of Memory: The Transformation of Tradition in American Culture*. New York: Vintage Books, 1993.

Kantrowitz, Stephen. *Ben Tillman and the Reconstruction of White Supremacy*. Chapel Hill: University of North Carolina Press, 2000.

Kerber, Linda K. *No Constitutional Right to Be Ladies: Women and the Obligation of Citizenship*. New York: Hill and Wang, 1998.

Kierner, Cynthia A. *Beyond the Household: Women's Place in the Early South, 1700–1835*. Ithaca, N.Y.: Cornell University Press, 1998.

Kneebone, John T., J. Jefferson Looney, Brent Tarter, and Sandra Gioia Treadway, eds. *Dictionary of Virginia Biography*, 3 vols. to date. Richmond: Library of Virginia, 1998–.

Krick, Robert K. *The Fredericksburg Artillery*. Lynchburg, Va.: H. E. Howard, 1986.

———. *The Smoothbore Volley That Doomed the Confederacy: The Death of Stonewall Jackson and Other Chapters on the Army of Northern Virginia*. Baton Rouge: Louisiana State University Press, 2002.

Laderman, Gary. *The Sacred Remains: American Attitudes toward Death, 1799–1883*. New Haven, Conn.: Yale University Press, 1996.

Lawson, Melinda. *Patriot Fires: Forging a New American Nationalism in the Civil War North*. Lawrence: University Press of Kansas, 2002.

Lebsock, Suzanne. *The Free Women of Petersburg: Status and Culture in a Southern Town, 1784–1860*. New York: W. W. Norton, 1984.

———. *A Murder in Virginia: Southern Justice on Trial*. New York: W. W. Norton, 2003.

———. *Share of Honour: Virginia Women, 1600–1945*. Richmond: Virginia Women's Cultural History Project, 1984.

Leonard, Elizabeth D. *All the Daring of a Soldier: Women of the Civil War Armies*. New York: W. W. Norton, 1999.

Loughridge, Patricia R., and Edward D. C. Campbell Jr. *Women in Mourning*. Richmond, Va.: Museum of the Confederacy, 1985.

Mahon, Michael G., ed. *Winchester Divided: The Civil War Diaries of Julia Chase and Laura Lee*. Mechanicsburg, Pa.: Stackpole Books, 2002.

McConnell, Stuart. *Glorious Contentment: The Grand Army of the Republic, 1865–1900*. Chapel Hill: University of North Carolina Press, 1992.

McDonough, James L. *Schofield: Union General in the Civil War and Reconstruction*. Tallahassee: Florida State University Press, 1972.

McPherson, James M. *For Cause and Comrades: Why Men Fought in the Civil War*. New York: Oxford University Press, 1997.

———. *What They Fought For, 1861–1865*. 1994; reprint, New York: Doubleday, 1995.

Mills, Cynthia, and Pamela H. Simpson, eds. *Monuments to the Lost Cause: Women, Art, and the Landscapes of Southern Memory*. Knoxville: University of Tennessee Press, 2003.

Mitchell, Mary H. *Hollywood Cemetery: The History of a Southern Shrine*. Richmond: Virginia State Library, 1985.

Mitchell, Reid. *Civil War Soldiers*. 1988; reprint, New York: Penguin Books, 1997.

Moore, Evelyn Lee, and Lucy Harrison Miller Baber. *Behind the Old Brick Wall: A Cemetery Story*. Lynchburg, Va.: Lynchburg Committee of the Colonial Dames, 1968.

Morris, George G., and Susan L. Foutz. *Lynchburg in the Civil War: The City, the People, and the Battle*. Lynchburg, Va.: H. E. Howard, 1984.

Morton, Frederic. *The Story of Winchester in Virginia: The Oldest Town in the Shenandoah Valley*. Strasburg, Va.: Shenandoah Publishing House, 1925.

Neff, John R. *Honoring the Civil War Dead: Commemoration and the Problem of Reconciliation*. Lawrence: University Press of Kansas, 2005.

Nichols, Janet Bernard. *Sketch of Old Blandford Church: Built in 1735, Created a Shrine 1901*. 1957; reprint, Petersburg, Va.: Ladies Memorial Association, 1990.

Oates, Stephen B. *A Woman of Valor: Clara Barton and the Civil War*. New York: Free Press, 1994.

Odem, Mary E., *Delinquent Daughters: Protecting and Policing Adolescent Female Sexuality in the United States, 1885–1920*. Chapel Hill: University of North Carolina Press, 1995.

O'Leary, Cecilia Elizabeth. *To Die For: The Paradox of American Patriotism*. Princeton, N.J.: Princeton University Press, 1999.

Osborne, Charles C. *Jubal: The Life and Times of General Jubal A. Early, CSA, Defender of the Lost Cause*. Chapel Hill, N.C.: Algonquin Books, 1992.

Osterweis, Rollin G. *The Myth of the Lost Cause, 1865–1900*. Hamden, Conn.: Archon Books, 1973.

Owen, Richard, and James Owen. *Generals at Rest: The Grave Sites of the 425 Official Confederate Generals*. Shippensburg, Penn.: White Man Publishing, 1997.

Piehler, G. Kurt. *Remembering War the American Way, 1783–1993*. Washington, D.C.: Smithsonian Institution Press, 1996.

Pryor, Elizabeth Brown. *Clara Barton: Professional Angel*. Philadelphia: University of Pennsylvania Press, 1987.

Quarles, Garland R. *Occupied Winchester, 1861–1865: Prepared for Farmers & Merchants National Bank, Winchester, Virginia*. Winchester, Va.: n.p., 1976.

———. *Some Worthy Lives: Mini Biographies, Winchester and Frederick County*. Winchester, Va.: Winchester--Frederick County Historical Society, 1988.

Quinn, S. J. *The History of the City of Fredericksburg, Virginia*. Richmond, Va.: Hermitage Press, 1908.

Rable, George C. *Civil Wars: Women and the Crisis of Southern Nationalism*. Urbana: University of Illinois Press, 1989.

———. *Fredericksburg! Fredericksburg!* Chapel Hill: University of North Carolina Press, 2002.

Reardon, Carol. *Pickett's Charge in History and Memory*. Chapel Hill: University of North Carolina Press, 1997.

Rubin, Anne Sarah. *A Shattered Nation: The Rise and Fall of the Confederacy, 1861–1868*. Chapel Hill: University of North Carolina Press, 2005.

Ryan, Mary P. *Women in Public: Between Banners and Ballots, 1825–1880*. Baltimore: Johns Hopkins University Press, 1990.

Savage, Kirk. *Standing Soldiers, Kneeling Slaves: Race, War, and Monument in Nineteenth-Century America*. Princeton, N.J.: Princeton University Press, 1997.

Schultz, Jane E. *Women at the Front: Hospital Workers in Civil War America*. Chapel Hill: University of North Carolina Press, 2004.

Scott, Anne Firor. *Natural Allies: Women's Associations in American History*. Urbana: University of Illinois Press, 1991.

———. *The Southern Lady: From Pedestal to Politics, 1830–1930*. Charlottesville: University Press of Virginia, 1970.

Silber, Nina. *Daughters of the Union: Northern Women Fight the Civil War*. Cambridge, Mass.: Harvard University Press, 2005.

———. *Romance of Reunion: Northerners and the South, 1865–1900*. Chapel Hill: University of North Carolina Press, 1993.

Skocpol, Theda. *Protecting Soldiers and Mothers: The Political Origins of Social Policy in the United States*. Cambridge, Mass.: Harvard University Press, 1992.

Swint, Henry L. *Dear Ones at Home: Letters from Contraband Camps*. Nashville, Tenn.: Vanderbilt University Press, 1966.

Thomas, Emory M. *The Confederacy as a Revolutionary Experience*. 1971; reprint, Columbia: University of South Carolina Press, 1991.

———. *Robert E. Lee: A Biography*. New York: W. W. Norton, 1995.

Treadway, Sandra Gioia. *Women of the Mark: A History of the Woman's Club Movement of Richmond, Virginia, 1894–1994*. Richmond: Library of Virginia, 1995.

Tripp, Steven Elliot. *Yankee Town, Southern City: Race and Class Relations in Civil War Lynchburg*. New York: New York University Press, 1997.

Trudeau, Noah Andre. *The Siege of Petersburg*. National Park Service Civil War Series. Harpers Ferry, W.V.: Eastern National, 1995.

Varon, Elizabeth R. *Southern Lady, Yankee Spy: The True Story of Elizabeth Van Lew, A Union Agent in the Heart of the Confederacy*. New York: Oxford University Press, 2003.

———. *We Mean to Be Counted: White Women and Politics in Antebellum Virginia*. Chapel Hill: University of North Carolina Press, 1998.

Wheeler, Marjorie Spruill. *New Women of the New South: The Leaders of the Woman Suffrage Movement in the Southern States*. New York: Oxford University Press, 1993.

Whites, LeeAnn. *The Civil War as a Crisis in Gender: Augusta, Georgia, 1860–1890*. Athens: University of Georgia Press, 1995.

Wilson, Charles Reagan. *Baptized in Blood: The Religion of the Lost Cause*. Athens: University of Georgia Press, 1980.

Woodward, C. Vann. *Origins of the New South, 1877–1913*. Baton Rouge: Louisiana State University Press, 1951.

————. *The Strange Career of Jim Crow*. New York: Oxford University Press, 1974.

————, ed. *Mary Chesnut's Civil War*. New Haven, Conn.: Yale University Press, 1981.

Woodward, C. Vann, and Elisabeth Muhlenfeld, eds. *The Private Mary Chesnut: The Unpublished Civil War Diaries*. New York: Oxford University Press, 1984.

Wyatt-Brown, Bertram. *Honor and Violence in the Old South*. New York: Oxford University Press, 1986.

Wyatt-Brown, Bertram, and Peter Wallenstein, eds. *Virginia's Civil War*. Charlottesville: University Press of Virginia, 2005.

Younger, Edward, ed. *The Governors of Virginia, 1860–1978*. Charlottesville: University Press of Virginia, 1982.

Articles

Attie, Jeanie. "Warwork and the Crisis of Domesticity in the North." In *Divided Houses: Gender and the Civil War*, edited by Catherine Clinton and Nina Silber, 247–59. New York: Oxford University Press, 1992.

Baker, Paula. "The Domestication of Politics: Women and the American Political Society, 1780–1920." *American Historical Review* 89 (June 1984): 620–47.

Barber, E. Susan. "Anxious Care and Constant Struggle: The Female Humane Association and Richmond's White Civil War Orphans." In *Before the New Deal: Social Welfare in the South, 1830–1930*, edited by Elna C. Green, 120–37. Athens: University of Georgia Press, 1999.

Bishir, Catherine W. "'A Strong Force of Ladies': Women, Politics, and Confederate Memorial Associations in Nineteenth-Century Raleigh." In *Monuments to the Lost Cause: Women, Art, and the Landscapes of Southern Memory*, edited by Cynthia Mills and Pamela H. Simpson, 3–26. Knoxville: University of Tennessee Press, 2003.

Blair, William A. "Barbarians at Fredericksburg's Gate: The Impact of the Union Army on Civilians." In *The Fredericksburg Campaign: Decision on the Rappahannock*, edited by Gary W. Gallagher, 142–70. Chapel Hill: University of North Carolina Press, 1995.

Brundage, W. Fitzhugh. "White Women and the Politics of Historical Memory in the New South." In *Jumpin' Jim Crow: Southern Politics from Civil War to Civil Rights*, edited by Glenda Gilmore, Bryant Simon, and Jane Daily, 115–39. Princeton, N.J.: Princeton University Press, 2000.

————. "'Woman's Hand and Heart and Deathless Love': White Women and the Commemorative Impulse in the New South." In *Monuments to the Lost Cause: Women, Art, and the Landscapes of Southern Memory*, edited by Cynthia Mills and Pamela H. Simpson, 64–82. Knoxville: University of Tennessee Press, 2003.

Calkins, Chris. "History of Poplar Grove National Cemetery." In *The Siege of Petersburg*, edited by Noah Andre Trudeau. Harpers Ferry, W.V.: Eastern National, 1995.

Clark, Kathleen. "Celebrating Freedom: Emancipation Day Celebrations and African American Memory in the Early Reconstruction South." In *Where These Memories Grow: History, Memory, and Southern Identity*, edited by W. Fitzhugh Brundage, 107–32. Chapel Hill: University of North Carolina Press, 2000.

Coski, John M. "A Century of Collecting: The History of the Museum of the Confederacy." *Museum of the Confederacy Journal* 74 (1996): 2–24.

Coski, John M., and Amy R. Feely. "A Monument to Southern Womanhood: The Founding Generation of the Confederate Museum." In *A Woman's War: Southern Women, Civil War, and the Confederate Legacy*, edited by Edward D. Campbell and Kym S. Rice, 130–63. Charlottesville: University Press of Virginia and Museum of the Confederacy, 1996.

Currey, David. "The Virtuous Soldier: Constructing a Useable Past in Franklin, Tennessee." In *Monuments to the Lost Cause: Women, Art, and the Landscapes of Southern Memory*, edited by Cynthia Mills and Pamela H. Simpson, 133–46. Knoxville: University of Tennessee Press, 2003.

Dailey, Jane. "The Limits of Liberalism in the New South: The Politics of Race, Sex, and Patronage in Virginia, 1879–1883." In *Jumpin' Jim Crow: Southern Politics from Civil War to Civil Rights*, edited by Glenda Gilmore, Bryant Simon, and Jane Daily, 88–114. Princeton, N.J.: Princeton University Press, 2000.

Fariello, M. Anna. "Personalizing the Political: The Davis Family Circle in Richmond's Hollywood Cemetery." In *Monuments to the Lost Cause: Women, Art, and the Landscapes of Southern Memory*, edited by Cynthia Mills and Pamela H. Simpson, 116–32. Knoxville: University of Tennessee Press, 2003.

Faust, Drew Gilpin. "The Civil War Soldier and the Art of Dying." *Journal of Southern History* 67 (February 2001): 3–38.

———. "'The Dread Void of Uncertainty': Naming the Dead in the American Civil War." *Southern Cultures* (Summer 2005): 7–32.

———. *"A Riddle of Death": Mortality and Meaning in the American Civil War*. 34th Annual Robert Fortenbaugh Memorial Lecture. Gettysburg, Penn.: Gettysburg College, 1995.

Faust, Drew Gilpin, Thavolia Glymph, and George C. Rable. "A Woman's War: Southern Women in the Civil War." In *A Woman's War: Southern Women, Civil War, and the Confederate Legacy*, edited by Edward D. Campbell and Kym S. Rice. Charlottesville: University Press of Virginia and Museum of the Confederacy, 1996.

Gay, Thomas E., Jr. "James Hoge Tyler: Rebellious Regular." In *The Governors of Virginia, 1860–1978*, edited by Edward Younger. Charlottesville: University Press of Virginia, 1982.

Hall, Virginius Cornick, Jr. "The Virginia Historical Society: An Anniversary Narrative of Its First Century and a Half." *Virginia Magazine of History and Biography* 90 (January 1982): 100–105.

Hartzell, Lawrence L. "The Exploration of Freedom in Black Petersburg, Virginia, 1865–1902." In *The Edge of the South: Life in Nineteenth-Century Virginia*, edited by Edward L. Ayers and John C. Willis, 134–56. Charlottesville: University of Virginia Press, 1991.

Janney, Caroline E. "To Honor Her Noble Sons: The Ladies' Memorial Association of Petersburg, Virginia." In *Virginia's Civil War*, edited by Bertram Wyatt-Brown and Peter Wallenstein, 256–69. Charlottesville: University of Virginia Press, December 2004.

————. "Written in Stone: Gender, Race, and the Heyward Shepherd Memorial." *Civil War History* 52, no. 2 (June 2006): 117–41.

Johnson, Joan Marie. "The Colors of Social Welfare in the New South: Black and White Clubwomen in South Carolina, 1900–1930." In *Before the New Deal: Social Welfare in the South, 1830–1930*, edited by Elna C. Green, 160–80. Athens: University of Georgia Press, 1999.

Lebsock, Suzanne. "Foreword." In *A Woman's War: Southern Women, Civil War, and the Confederate Legacy*, edited by Edward D. Campbell and Kym S. Rice. Charlottesville: University Press of Virginia and Museum of the Confederacy, 1996.

McPherson, James M. "The Long-Legged Yankee Lies: The Southern Textbook Crusade." In *The Memory of the Civil War in American Culture*, edited by Alice Fahs and Joan Waugh, 64–93. Chapel Hill: University of North Carolina Press, 2004.

Mills, Cynthia. "Gratitude and Gender Wars: Monuments to Women of the Sixties." In *Monuments to the Lost Cause: Women, Art, and the Landscapes of Southern Memory*, edited by Cynthia Mills and Pamela H. Simpson, 183–200. Knoxville: University of Tennessee Press, 2003.

Parrott, Angie. "'Love Makes Memory Eternal': The United Daughters of the Confederacy in Richmond, Virginia, 1897–1920." In *The Edge of the South: Life in Nineteenth-Century Virginia*, edited by Edward Ayers and John C. Willis, 219–38. Charlottesville: University Press of Virginia, 1991.

Rasmussen, William M. S. "Planning a Temple to the Lost Cause: The Confederate 'Battle Abbey.'" In *Monuments to the Lost Cause: Women, Art, and the Landscapes of Southern Memory*, edited by Cynthia Mills and Pamela H. Simpson, 163–82. Knoxville: University of Tennessee Press, 2003.

Ribblet, David L. "From Mount Vernon to Charlotte County: The Evolution of Historic Preservation in Virginia." *Southsider: Local History and Genealogy of Southside Virginia* 11 (1992): 3–14.

Seidman, Rachel Filene. "'We Were Enlisted for the War': Ladies' Aid Societies and the Politics of Women's Work during the Civil War." In *Making and Remaking Pennsylvania's Civil War*, edited by William A. Blair and William Pencak, 59–80. University Park: Pennsylvania State University Press, 2001.

Sklar, Kathryn Kish. "Florence Kelly and Women's Activism in the Progressive Era." In *Women's America: Refocusing the Past*, edited by Linda K. Kerber and Jane Sherron De Hart, 327–39. New York: Oxford University Press, 2004.

Van Zelm, Antoinette G. "Virginia Women as Public Citizens: Emancipation Day Celebrations and Lost Cause Commemorations, 1863–1890." In *Negotiating Boundaries of Southern Womanhood: Dealing with Powers That Be*, edited by Janet L. Coryell, Thomas H. Appleton, Anastatia Sims, and Sandra Gioia Treadway. Columbia: University of Missouri Press, 2000.

Whites, LeeAnn. "'Stand by Your Man': The Ladies Memorial Association and the Reconstruction of Southern White Manhood." In *Women of the American South: A Multicultural Reader*, edited by Christie Anne Farnham, 133–49. New York: New York University Press, 1997.

Theses and Dissertations

Ballou, Charles F., III. "Hospital Medicine in Richmond, Virginia during the Civil War: A Case Study of Hospital No. 21, Howard's Grove, and Winder Hospitals." M.A. Thesis, Virginia Polytechnic Institute and State University, May 1992.

Barber, Edna Susan. "'Sisters of the Capital': White Women in Richmond, Virginia, 1860–1880." Ph.D. diss., University of Maryland, 1997.

Bell, Diana. "Female Benevolence and the Paradox of Southern Nationalism." Honor's Thesis, Davidson College, April 2003.

Harcourt, Edward John. "The Civil War and Social Change: White Women in Fredericksburg, Virginia." M.A. Thesis, University of Richmond, 1997.

Morsman, Amy Feely. "The Big House after Slavery: Virginia's Plantation Elite and Their Postbellum Domestic Experiment." Ph.D. diss., University of Virginia, 2004.

Murrell, Amy. "Two Armies: Women's Activism in Civil War Richmond." Honor's Thesis, Duke University, Spring 1993.

Smith, James Douglas. "Virginia during Reconstruction, 1865–1870: A Political, Economic, and Social Study." Ph.D. diss., University of Virginia, 1960.

Websites

"Call for the First Anniversary of the American Equal Rights Association," Library of Congress, <http://rs6.loc.gov/learn/features/timeline/civilwar/freedmen/mott.html>. May 24, 2007.

The Camp Jackson Incident, <http://www.nps.gov/jeff/historyculture/upload/camp-jackson.pdf>. May 24, 2007.

Civil War Hospitals in Lynchburg, <http://www.gravegarden.org/hospitals.htm>. May 24, 2007.

Documenting the American South, University of North Carolina, Chapel Hill, <http://docsouth.unc.edu>. May 24, 2007.

Museum of the Confederacy, <http://www.moc.org>, March 10, 2005. May 24, 2007.

The Political Graveyard, <http://politicalgraveyard.com>. May 24, 2007.

"Pyramids in Fredericksburg," Off the Beaten Path, Vol. 3, <http://www.simplyfredericksburg.com/offpath/pyramid.shtm>. May 24, 2007.

Ruffin and Meade Family Papers, SHC, University of North Carolina at Chapel Hill, <http://www.lib.unc.edu/mss/inv/r/Ruffin_and_Meade_Family.html>. May 24, 2007.

"We Say No to the Proposed Lincoln Statue in Richmond," <http://www.petitiononline.com/noabe/petition.html>. May 24, 2007.

Women's Relief Corps Michigan, <http://www.mifamilyhistory.org/civilwar/wrc/default.asp>. May 24, 2007.

Index

Button, Charles, 57
Button, Mary, 57

Cabell, Mary, 37–38, 42
Caldwell, Susan, 31
Callender, Bessie Meade, 17–18, 30, 38, 52–53, 169
Callender, David, 52
Campbell, Jacqueline Glass, 28, 212 (n. 49)
Canby, E. R. S., 102
Carrington, Maria Louisa, 71–72
Carrington, William C., 125–26, 238 (n. 59)
Carter, Edwin, 226 (n. 36)
Carter, Martha, 211 (n. 39)
Cemeteries. *See* Confederate cemeteries; National cemeteries; *and specific cemeteries*
Censer, Jane Turner, 87, 204 (n. 3), 226 (n. 36), 228 (n. 57), 241 (n. 14), 248 (n. 1)
Chancellorsville, battle of, 9, 57
Charlottesville, Va., 50
Chesnut, Mary Boykin, 18, 23, 211 (n. 39)
Chesson, Michael B., 214 (n. 2), 219 (n. 41), 224 (n. 6)
Chew, Ellen P., 57
Chew, Robert S., 57
Chieves, Mrs. Shelton, 180, 183
Children. *See* Schools and schoolchildren
Christian, Cornelia, 54
Christian, Emma, 148
Christian, George L., 131, 186
Christian, Julia Jackson, 186
Christian, William H., 218 (n. 30)
Church associations, 129
Civil War: Confederate women's role during, 5–6, 15–38; casualties in, 9, 11, 32; Confederate women's resistance to Union army during, 15, 27–29, 36, 212 (n. 52), 215 (n. 6); knowledge of, by southern women, 16; sewing and aid societies during, 16–21, 29, 207–8 (n. 8); uniforms and supplies for Confederate soldiers during, 17, 29–30; patriotism of women during, 20–24, 29–30, 213

(n. 53); and flag of Confederacy, 21, 24, 208 (n. 21); gunboat societies during, 21–23, 26, 49, 53, 208–9 (n. 22); communication among women during, 23–24; newspapers during, 23–24; Confederate women's relationship to state during, 24–27; and Lee's surrender, 30, 37–38, 39, 40, 42, 116; mourning rituals and funerals during, 31–37; burial of soldiers during, 32–37; destruction from, in Virginia, 37, 40, 41, 54, 215 (n. 12); prisoners of war during, 44, 57, 182, 217 (n. 26), 229 (n. 61); Lee as national institution of Confederacy during, 90–91; women's petitions during, 98; and manhood of southern men, 115–16; causes of, 159, 198; in textbooks, 172–73; statistics on Virginians in, 206 (n. 18); northern women's role during, 207 (nn. 1, 5), 209 (n. 31). *See also* Hospitals; Nursing during Civil War; *and specific battles and generals*
Claiborne, John Herbert and Sarah, 137
Clark, Julia, 36
Clark, Kathleen, 12, 79
Class: and LMAs, 55, 135, 150; and ladies' auxiliaries of veterans' groups, 150; and UDC, 169, 173–74, 249 (n. 9); and Daughters of the American Revolution, 174, 249 (n. 9); and burial in Richmond cemeteries, 219 (n. 41)
Clay, Henry, monument, 94–95, 230–31 (n. 78)
Cleburne, Patrick, 125
Clopton, Adelaide, 16
Clopton, Maria, 22, 26, 210 (n. 38), 211 (nn. 40–41)
CMA. *See* Confederate Memorial Association
CMLS. *See* Confederate Memorial Literary Society
Coffin, Charles, 179–80
Coleman, Cynthia B. T., 22, 208–9 (n. 22)
Collier, C. F., 245 (n. 53)
Colston, Raleigh E., 62, 63
Colston, Mrs. Raleigh, 1

Confederacy. *See* Civil War; Lost Cause; Nationalism, Confederate; *and specific leaders, generals, and battles*

Confederate cemeteries: and LMAs, 2, 9, 13, 58, 68, 88–93, 99, 100, 131, 140, 193, 199; statistics on burials in, 9, 44, 58, 92, 201; fund-raising for, 43–44, 56, 91–92, 220 (n. 54), 230 (n. 69); collection of remains of dead and reinterment in, 44, 58, 82–83; and reburial activities of LMAs, 65–68, 82–83, 88–92, 101, 140, 199, 223 (nn. 80, 82), 229 (nn. 60, 63); reburial of Turner Ashby and other Confederate officers, 65–68, 223 (nn. 80, 82); men's work in reburial of Confederate dead, 82–83, 88, 121–26, 130, 132; and Register of Confederate Dead, 89, 97; monuments in, 90, 95, 108–10, 140, 141–42; and Confederate nationalism, 90–91; in late nineteenth century, 140; upkeep of, 140; state funds for, 176, 189–90, 253–54 (n. 64); reburial of A. S. Johnston, 224 (n. 2); Virginia legislature on, 230 (n. 70). *See also* Gettysburg reinterment project; *and specific cemeteries and cities*

Confederated Southern Memorial Association (CSMA), 178–83, 185, 194, 206 (n. 17), 251 (n. 39), 252 (nn. 44–47, 49)

Confederate Memorial Association (CMA), 191–93, 254 (nn. 66, 71)

Confederate Memorial Literary Society (CMLS): creation and charter of, 160, 247 (n. 74); relationship between HMA and, 160–61, 247 (n. 75); and Confederate Museum, 160–65, 177–78, 183, 188–93, 196–97, 199, 247 (n. 74), 255 (n. 73); officers of, 161; and preservation of Confederate legacy for future generations, 161–62, 189–90; and relics for Confederate Museum, 162–63; and fund-raising for Confederate Museum, 164–65; and Battle Abbey, 167, 190–93; and UDC, 177–78; and opening and dedication of Confederate Museum, 188–89, 190; and building markers associated with

Civil War, 189; and railroads' battlefield markers, 189, 253 (n. 62); and state funds for Confederate cemeteries, 189–90; current projects of, 196; men and African Americans on board of, 196; and name changes for Confederate Museum, 196, 197

Confederate Museum (Richmond): and male-female cooperation, 160, 164–65; and CMLS, 160–65, 177–78, 183, 188–93, 196–97, 199, 247 (n. 74), 255 (n. 73); relics for, 162–63; as monument to southern womanhood, 175; fund-raising for, 164–65; and Lost Cause, 175, 188, 190, 194, 255 (n. 73); and UDC, 176, 177–78; opening and dedication of, 188–89, 190; and Battle Abbey, 190–93; name changes for, 196, 197; current problems of, 196–97; visitor statistics for, 255 (n. 3)

Confederate museums, 163, 168, 190. *See also* Confederate Museum

Confederate nationalism. *See* Nationalism, Confederate

Confederate Relief and Historical Association of Memphis, 232–33 (n. 97)

Confederate Survivors' Association of South Carolina, 232–33 (n. 97)

Congressional Reconstruction. *See* Reconstruction

Conrad, Holmes, 227 (n. 45)

Coski, John M., 151, 163, 204 (n. 3), 250 (n. 26), 251 (n. 29)

Courtney, Mrs. Alfred, 245 (n. 49)

Cox, Karen L., 137, 159, 169, 173–74, 205 (n. 6), 233 (n. 9), 248 (n. 4), 249 (n. 9), 250 (n. 25)

Crenshaw, Lewis, 247 (n. 72)

Crenshaw, Mrs. Lewis, 54

Cunningham, Ann Pamela, 218 (n. 37)

Cutshaw, Wilfred Emory, 141

Dabney, Robert L., 218 (n. 36)

Daniels, Lizzie Cary, 178, 191

Daughters of the American Revolution, 4, 137, 170, 172, 174, 249 (n. 9)

American freedom celebrations, 78–79; men's involvement in fund-raising for LMAs, 82, 114–15; men's work in reburial of Confederate dead, 82–83, 88, 121–26, 130, 132; in Progressive Era, 92, 130; and monument building, 94–98, 107–18, 127, 134, 236 (n. 38); LMAs' role in public sphere, 99–100; male-female conflict over leadership of Lost Cause, 105–32; male-female conflict over Lee monument, 107–18, 134; Early on women's role, 114; Civil War and manhood, 115–16; Early on manhood, 115–16; male-female conflict over Gettysburg reinterment project, 125–27, 131–32, 134, 241 (n. 1); men's involvement in Memorial Days, 133–34; New South women, 137–38, 159; male-female cooperation for Gettysburg reinterment project, 142–46; cooperation between veterans' associations and LMAs, 147–49; division of responsibilities between men and women on Lost Cause, 148, 158; and ladies' auxiliaries of veterans' associations, 149–52; resistance to joint Memorial Days by women, 153–56; men's perception of women as apolitical, 155–56; and LMA junior associations, 158, 246 (n. 69); male-female cooperation for Confederate Museum, 160, 164–65; male-female cooperation for Blandford Church, 183–84; and Battle Abbey, 191–93; history and public culture as women's sphere, 236 (n. 38); southern white women and men's honor, 239 (n. 71). *See also* Ladies' Memorial Associations; Women; Women's rights and woman suffrage

General Federation of Women's Clubs, 154, 170, 249 (n. 12)

Georgia: LMAs in, 8, 62, 221 (n. 57), 226 (n. 36); national cemetery in, 44; Andersonville prison in, 44, 229 (n. 61); and funds for Virginia LMAs, 92, 97, 112; and Lee's death, 106; and Lee monu-

ment, 112; Confederate battle flag debate in, 198; during Civil War, 206 (n. 18)

Gettysburg National Cemetery, 44, 90

Gettysburg reinterment project: need for, 119–21; and *Southern Opinion*, 121, 237 (n. 45); financing of, 121–22, 124–27, 130, 132, 143–46, 243 (nn. 35–36); Rufus Weaver's work on and payment for, 121–26, 130, 132, 143–46, 177, 237 (n. 47), 243 (n. 35); and HMA, 121–27, 130, 132, 134, 142–46, 177, 232 (n. 93), 237 (n. 45); and ceremony for burial of remains in Hollywood Cemetery, 123–24; lack of funds for, 124, 126–27, 130, 143–44; conflicts with veterans' groups over, 125–27, 132, 134, 241 (n. 1); male-female cooperation on, during late nineteenth century, 142–46; and UDC, 177

Gibson, Rev. Churchill, 32

Giesberg, Judith Ann, 205 (n. 12), 227 (n. 46), 238 (n. 66)

Gilmore, Glenda, 255 (n. 6)

Ginzberg, Lori D., 5, 98, 129, 239 (n. 67)

Glasgow, Ellen, 241 (n. 14)

Goolrick, Charles Tackett, 57, 81, 226 (n. 36)

Goolrick, Virginia, 57

Gordon, Elizabeth, 19

Gordon, John Brown, 116, 147

Grammer, John, 184

Grand Army of the Republic (GAR): and Memorial Days, 76–78, 226 (n. 28); mission of, 127; decline of, 130–31, 240 (n. 73); and reconciliation activities, 147, 154; and WRC, 150–51; and textbooks on Civil War, 172; revival of, in late nineteenth century, 240 (n. 73); and pensions for Union veterans, 244 (n. 40)

Grant, Anne, 54

Grant, Harriet Chesnut, 23

Grant, Ulysses S., 30

Grant Monument, 254 (n. 66)

Groveton Confederate Cemetery, 1–2

Gunboat societies, 21–23, 26, 49, 53, 208–9 (n. 22)

Gwathmey, Abby, 19

Gwathmey, Mrs. George, 53, 128

Hale, Grace Elizabeth, 139, 174, 243 (n. 26)

Hampton, Wade, 163, 232 (n. 97)

Hanna, J. Marshall, 228 (n. 52)

Hardee, William J., 51

Harper, Robert T., 229 (n. 60)

Harrison, Constance Cary, 32

Hart, Mrs. William T., 21

Hattaway, Herman, 213 (n. 53)

Haxall, Alice Brown, 54

Hebrew Memorial Association: founding and objectives of, 48, 220 (n. 53); and Memorial Days, 74, 101, 178; and Confederate Museum, 160, 164, 247 (n. 82); membership of, 201; dates of, as unknown, 255 (n. 2)

Herndon, Ellen Mercer, 21

Hill, A. P., 101, 232 (n. 96)

Hill, D. H., 232 (n. 97)

Hill, Mrs. D. H., 252 (n. 44)

HMA. *See* Hollywood Memorial Association

Hoge, Rev. Dr. Moses, 124, 142

Holliday, F. W. M., 227 (n. 45), 233 (n. 6)

Hollywood Cemetery: Confederate soldiers buried in, 32, 33, 101, 201, 217 (n. 29), 238 (n. 54); Union soldiers buried in, 44; tending of, 48; and Memorial Days, 63–64, 67–68; pyramid monument in, 95–97, 189, 193; Confederate generals buried in, 101, 232 (n. 96); Lee monument in, 108–10; Gettysburg dead in, 121–27, 241 (n. 1); Jefferson Davis buried in, 140, 242 (n. 21); monument of Philadelphia chapter of UDC in, 177; state funds for, 189, 253 (n. 64); establishment of, 217 (n. 29); social class of residents buried in, 219 (n. 41); Soldiers' Monument in, 241 (n. 2)

Hollywood Memorial Association (Richmond; HMA): leaders of, 24, 26, 51, 53, 57, 128, 136, 219 (n. 42); beginnings of, 48, 62, 217–18 (n. 30); constitution of, 49; unification attempt between OMA and, 49, 81; and Confederate nationalism, 51; membership of, 51, 53, 54, 57, 128, 135–38, 148, 150, 169, 175, 201, 216 (n. 26), 218 (n. 30), 240 (n. 72), 245 (n. 49); funds for and fund-raising by, 56, 82, 93–94, 101, 111–13, 121–22, 124, 141, 144–45; and Memorial Days and other memorial celebrations, 58, 63–64, 68, 73, 74, 95, 101, 133–34, 223 (n. 83); men's involvement in, 80, 81, 82, 109, 141, 142–46, 234 (n. 10), 243 (n. 30); and Register of Confederate Dead, 89, 97; and monument building, 93–97, 101, 134, 141, 231 (nn. 80–81, 83); and reburial activities, 101, 121–27; and Lee monument, 108–18, 127, 131, 134, 140–41, 148, 165, 193, 232 (n. 93); and Gettysburg reinterment project, 119–27, 131–32, 134, 142–46, 177, 232 (n. 93), 243 (nn. 35–36); decline of, 128; in late nineteenth century, 134, 135, 142–46, 156–65, 241 (n. 4); and Confederate Museum, 134, 150, 160–65, 167, 183, 188–89; and junior associations, 134, 156–59; and Soldiers' and Sailors' Monument, 141, 142, 144, 148, 194; cooperation between veterans and, 148; and White House of the Confederacy project, 156, 159–65, 194, 243 (n. 30), 247 (n. 82); and state funds for Confederate cemeteries, 176, 189–90; and UDC, 177; and CSMA, 178; and Arlington National Cemetery, 182; end of, 196, 255 (n. 2); and cemetery for Confederate dead, 217 (n. 29), 241 (n. 2); reorganization of, in late nineteenth century, 241 (n. 4). *See also* Confederate Memorial Literary Society; Ladies' Lee Monument Committee

Hood, John Bell, 224 (n. 2)

Hospitals, 11, 24–26, 30, 34, 53, 54, 136, 210–11 (nn. 37–42). *See also* Nursing during Civil War

Hotchkiss, Jedediah, 82

Huck, Lewis N., 227 (n. 45)

Hunter, David, 206 (n. 24)

127, 131, 140–41, 147, 148, 165, 193, 199;
and UDC, 127, 168, 177; Soldiers' and
Sailors' Monument, 141, 142, 144, 148,
165, 194, 199; by veterans' groups, 141–42;
and Lost Cause, 142; purposes of, 142,
161–62, 242–43 (n. 26); Jefferson Davis
monument, 154, 177, 181, 246 (n. 60), 252
(n. 47); and Daughters of the American
Revolution, 172; of women, 175, 244–45
(n. 43); Pollard on, 228 (n. 54); and
southern white women generally, 236
(n. 38); of Confederate soldiers in late
nineteenth century, 242–43 (nn. 25–26);
Grant Monument, 254 (n. 66)
Moore, B. Frank, 112–13, 235 (n. 22)
Moore, James, 44
Moore, Lewis T., 35
Moore, Patrick T., 124
Morris, Robert G., 93
Morrison, Mary Rambant, 32, 37
Morson, James M., 246 (n. 72)
Mosby, John S., 233 (n. 6)
Mosby, Sally, 19–20
Mott, Lucretia, 61, 227 (n. 46)
Mount Vernon, 218 (n. 37), 231 (n. 78)
Mourning rituals: in antebellum period,
30; in Victorian period, 30–31; funerals
during Civil War, 31–32, 34; during Civil
War, 31–37; for Stonewall Jackson, 35–36,
48; and Confederate motherhood, 50;
and Lee's death, 105–6, 109, 233 (n. 1);
and authority of women and ministers,
213 (n. 54). See also Burial of Confed-
erate soldiers; Burial of Union soldiers;
Ladies' Memorial Associations; Memo-
rial Days, Confederate; Memorial Days,
National; and specific cemeteries
Munford, Charles, 19
Munford, George Wythe, 82, 131
Munford, Sallie, 19, 31
Munford, Thomas T., 40–41, 102, 139–40
Murray, John B., 225 (n. 21)
Museum of the Confederacy. See Confeder-
ate Museum
Myers, Catherine, 24

Myers, E. D., 189
Myers, Mrs. F. S., 247 (n. 82)

National Association for the Advancement
of Colored People, 198
National Association of Colored Women,
249–50 (n. 20)
National cemeteries: in Georgia, 44; in
Virginia, 44–46, 77, 153, 217 (n. 26);
statistics on, 45; southern reactions to,
45–46; exclusion of Confederates from,
45–46, 216 (n. 18); and Union Memorial
Days, 77; Point Lookout National Cemetery, 198; newspaper coverage of, 215–16
(n. 14); federal legislation on, 216 (n. 16);
and CSMA, 252 (n. 49). See also Burial
of Union soldiers
Nationalism, Confederate: and Memorial
Days, 13, 60–68, 80; and women generally, 30, 85–87, 155, 156, 213 (n. 53), 223
(n. 85); and LMAs, 50, 51, 54–58, 60–68,
99, 134, 137, 140, 156, 198–99, 220 (n. 51);
scholars on, 55, 213 (n. 53); and Confederate cemeteries, 90–91; and monument
building, 94–98. See also Lost Cause
National Park Service, 1, 198
Neff, John, 4, 90, 204 (n. 3), 216 (n. 18), 225
(n. 12)
Nelson, Mrs. F., 53
Newspapers. See New York newspapers;
Richmond: newspapers in; Southern
Opinion
New York newspapers, 60, 77, 78, 79, 106,
215 (n. 12), 215–16 (n. 14), 223 (n. 80)
Nicholas, Elizabeth (Lizzie) Byrd, 108, 128,
131, 233 (n. 8)
Nicholas, Wilson Cary, 108
Norfolk, Va., 75, 216 (n. 23)
North Carolina: LMAs in, 8, 62, 72, 87, 100,
226 (n. 36); prohibition of Memorial
Days in, 72; Reconstruction in, 72; and
funds for Virginia LMAs, 92; during
Civil War, 206 (n. 18), 212 (n. 52)
Notman, John, 217 (n. 29)
Nulton, Joseph A., 152

Nursing during Civil War, 25–27, 53, 209 (n. 33), 210–11 (nn. 37–42). *See also* Hospitals

Oakwood Cemetery: Confederate soldiers buried in, 33, 36, 201, 217 (n. 26); mourning rituals in, 36; Union soldiers buried in, 44, 217 (n. 26); and Memorial Days, 62–63; monuments in, 90, 95; fund-raising for, 92; establishment of, 216 (n. 26); African Americans buried in, 217 (n. 26); social class of residents buried in, 219 (n. 41); beautification of, 242 (n. 21)

Oakwood Memorial Association (Richmond; OMA): beginnings of, 48; membership of, 48, 53, 80, 100, 101, 201, 216 (n. 26), 219 (n. 41); relationships between other LMAs and, 49; constitution of, 49, 57; unification attempt between HMA and, 49, 81; dues for, 52, 80; leaders of, 53; and Confederate nationalism, 55–56; goals of, 56, 90; and cemetery for Confederate soldiers, 56, 92, 242 (n. 21); and Memorial Days and other memorial celebrations, 58, 62–63, 73, 101, 178, 246 (n. 59), 255 (n. 2); men's involvement in, 80, 81, 82; fund-raising by, 82, 92; and monuments, 97–98, 154; decline of, 100, 101; and assistance for Confederate widows, 151, 245 (n. 53); and joint Memorial Days, 152, 153; and junior associations, 157; and White House of the Confederacy project, 160; and Confederate Museum fund-raising, 164; and Hebrew Memorial Association, 178; and CSMA, 178, 179; frequency of meetings of, 232 (n. 93); reorganization of, in late nineteenth century, 241 (n. 4)

Oaths of loyalty, 27–28, 62, 212 (n. 45)

O'Ferrall, Charles, 162, 188, 190

O'Leary, Cecilia, 151, 158, 174, 226 (n. 28), 245 (nn. 50–51), 250 (n. 24)

Olmsted, Frederick Law, 209 (n. 31)

OMA. *See* Oakwood Memorial Association

Orphan asylums, 83, 129, 210 (n. 36)

Otey, Lucy Mina, 25–26, 29, 36–37, 38, 54, 210 (nn. 36, 38–39)

Overland campaign (1864), 11

Owen, William Otway, 210 (n. 38)

Palmer, Benjamin Morgan, 102

Park, Emily Hendree, 176

Parsley, Eliza Nutt, 168

Patriotism: of southern white women during Civil War, 20–24, 29–30, 213 (n. 53); and LMAs, 39–40, 87; of southern white women immediately after Civil War, 42–43. *See also* Ladies' Memorial Associations; Lost Cause

Peeks, Maria, 29

Pegram, Helen, 57

Pegram, John, 101

Pegram, Mrs. R. G., 129

Pegram, Richard, 57

Pember, Phoebe Yates, 28, 210 (n. 38)

Pendleton, William N., 106, 108–10, 233 (n. 6), 240 (n. 73)

Peninsula campaign (1862), 11, 16

Pensions for veterans, 244 (n. 40)

Petersburg: population and economy of, 10; during Civil War, 10, 17, 30, 32; sewing societies in, 17, 207–8 (n. 8); funeral in, 32; shallow graves of soldiers near, 40; food and aid to returning soldiers in, 43; desecration by Union burial crews in, 46; Blandford Cemetery in, 46, 81, 83, 88, 90–92, 140, 184, 220 (n. 54), 253 (n. 64); Gentlemen's Memorial Society in, 84–85, 228 (n. 55); benevolent associations in antebellum period in, 85; UDC in, 168, 183, 185, 248 (n. 6); upper class in, 219 (n. 41). *See also* Petersburg LMA

Petersburg LMA: conflicts between male leaders and, 7; beginnings of, 46, 48, 53; and Confederate cemetery, 46, 81, 83, 88, 90–92, 140, 184, 220 (n. 54); and Confederate motherhood, 50; Lee as honorary member of, 51; dues for, 52; membership of, 52–53, 57, 100, 134–35, 137, 148, 169,

on, 116; and Lynchburg LMA, 128, 131, 233 (n. 8)

Randolph, Thomas and Jane, 108

Randolph, Wythe, 18

Rasmussen, William M. S., 254 (n. 66)

Rawls, Waite, 197

Readjuster Movement, 239 (n. 70)

Reburial activities. *See* Confederate cemeteries; Gettysburg reinterment project

Reconciliation between North and South: and white supremacy, 139, 242 (n. 18); and veterans' associations, 146–47, 155, 159, 244 (n. 41), 246 (n. 57); and joint Memorial Days, 152–56; women's resistance to, 153–56

Reconstruction: and treason charges, 6–7, 40, 48, 65, 80, 107, 198–99, 221 (n. 66); Johnson's policies on, 47, 69–71, 224 (n. 2); LMAs during Radical Reconstruction (1867–70), 69–103; Federal troops in Virginia during, 70, 73–74; Confederate Memorial Days and other memorial celebrations during, 72–76, 79–80; Union Memorial Days during, 76–78; men's involvement in LMAs during, 80–88; and Confederate cemeteries, 83, 88–93; monument building during, 93–98, 218 (n. 36); end of, 102, 107, 139; Ku Klux Klan during, 171, 173

Reconstruction Acts (1867), 69–72, 102

Reed, James C., 33

Richardson, Mrs. D. C., 179

Richardson, Ned, 74–75

Richmond: location of, 11; population and economy of, 11; during Civil War, 11, 17–26, 28–30, 35, 37, 40, 212 (n. 52); as state and Confederate capital, 11, 23; sewing and aid societies in, 17–20, 23, 24–25, 29–30, 209–10 (n. 34), 218 (n. 30); newspapers in, 19–20, 30, 46, 61, 72, 77, 94, 97, 124, 136, 153, 160, 246 (n. 59); Gunboat Association in, 21–22, 26, 49, 53; Soldiers' Aid Society of Virginia in, 24–25, 53, 210 (n. 34); hospitals in, 25, 26, 53, 210 (n. 38); Confederate cemeteries in, 32,

33, 36, 44; mourning rituals in, 32, 35, 36; burial of soldiers in, 32–33; destruction of, 37, 40, 215 (n. 12); women's resistance to Union occupation in, 42; care of soldiers in, following Civil War, 43; national cemetery in, 44, 46, 77, 217 (n. 26); Evacuation Day and African Americans in, 46–47, 63; Reconstruction in, 70, 72, 214 (n. 2); 1867 violence in, 71, 75; Union Memorial Days in, 77; monuments in, 93–97, 101, 107–18, 127, 131, 140–42, 144, 147, 148, 165, 193–94, 199, 230–31 (n. 78); and Lee's death, 105, 106; organizations and clubs in, 136, 138, 249 (n. 13); and UDC, 168, 177, 248 (n. 6); Woman's Club of, 170, 249 (nn. 12–13); Tredegar Ironworks in, 198; women's refusal to aid Confederacy in, 212 (n. 52); Light Infantry's demonstration in, 222 (n. 70); desegregation of public transportation in, 224 (n. 6), 230 (n. 75). *See also* Battle Abbey; Confederate Museum; Hollywood Memorial Association; Oakwood Memorial Association

Robinson, Virginia, 193, 249 (n. 12)

Rouss, Charles Broadway, 190–91, 254 (n. 66)

Rowland, Kate Mason, 29, 34, 169

Roy, T. B., 51

Rubin, Anne Sarah, 41–42, 65, 220 (n. 51), 222 (n. 76), 224 (n. 2), 228 (n. 54)

Ruffin, Mrs. Frank G., 24–25

Ruggles, Daniel, 24

Rutherford, Jane, 249 (n. 12)

Rutherford, Mildred, 168, 170, 171–72, 177

Sanitary Commission, U.S., 24, 36, 205 (n. 12), 209 (n. 31), 227 (n. 46), 238 (n. 66)

Savage, Kirk, 142, 236 (n. 37), 242–43 (n. 26)

SCB. *See* Southern Cross Brotherhood

Schofield, John M., 70–74, 94, 224 (n. 6), 230 (n. 75)

Schools and schoolchildren, 172–73, 182–83, 189, 196, 249–50 (n. 20)

Schultz, Jane E., 210 (n. 35)

Scott, Anne Firor, 5, 6, 87, 228 (n. 57)

Seddon, James, 246 (n. 72)

Segregation, 139, 156, 157–58, 159, 171, 173

Seidman, Rachel Filene, 209 (n. 31)

Sewing and aid societies, 16–21, 29, 207–8 (n. 8)

Shadow governments, 88, 224 (n. 3)

Shepherd, T. B., 89

Sheridan, Philip Henry, 28, 69, 73, 153

Sherrard, Joseph Holmes, 65, 223 (n. 78), 227 (n. 45)

SHS. *See* Southern Historical Society

Silber, Nina, 150, 215 (n. 6), 245 (n. 51)

Simmons, Mrs. William A., 37

Simpson, Jane, 17

Skocpol, Theda, 88, 230 (n. 71)

Slaughter, Sallie Braxton, 19, 21

Slavery: Richmond slave population, 11; abolition of, 41; as marker of elite status, 55; stereotypes of happy and loyal slaves, 139, 172–73, 249 (n. 18); UDC on, 172–73; as cause of Civil War, 198; hiring out slaves on New Year's Day, 215 (n. 7); and women as slaveholders, 215 (n. 8)

Smith, Mrs. B., 53

Smith, Ella, 154

Smith, James Douglas, 230 (n. 70)

Smith, James P., 192

Social class. *See* Class

Soldiers' aid societies. *See* Sewing and aid societies

Soldiers' and Sailors' Monument (Richmond), 141, 142, 144, 148, 164, 165, 194, 199

Sons and Daughters of the Confederacy, 198

Sons of Confederate Veterans, 158, 175, 195, 198, 199

Sons of the American Revolution, 250 (n. 24)

South Carolina: LMAs in, 8, 226 (n. 36); during Civil War, 23, 25; Greenville Ladies' Association, 25, 210 (n. 34), 212 (n. 52); and funds for Virginia LMAs, 92; disenfranchisement of African Ameri-

cans in, 171; Confederate battle flag debate in, 198; and *Lady Davis* (ship), 209 (n. 25); Decoration Day in, 214 (n. 1)

Southern Cross Brotherhood (SCB), 124, 125, 130, 132, 133, 238 (n. 57)

Southern Historical Society (SHS): and Lost Cause, 8, 115, 233 (n. 97); and Early, 102, 115, 131, 240 (n. 74); and women's contributions to Lost Cause, 115; decline of, 130–31, 146, 240 (nn. 73, 75); and preservation of White House of the Confederacy, 160; and Lee, 232 (n. 97); funds for, 240 (n. 73)

Southern Opinion, 2, 72, 77, 85–87, 119–21, 228 (nn. 52–54), 237 (n. 45)

Speed, Susan, 25–26, 38, 54

Sperry, Kate, 32, 34, 36

Spotsylvania, battle of, 9, 44, 50

Spotsylvania LMA, 49–50, 81

Stanton, Elizabeth Cady, 7, 61, 62, 70, 99, 231 (n. 89)

States' rights, 159, 172, 173

Stewart, John and Mary Amanda, 135–36

Stiles, Robert, 126, 143, 233 (n. 6)

Still, William N., Jr., 213 (n. 53)

Stone, Lucy, 7, 232 (n. 89)

Stonewall Cemetery (Winchester), 43–44, 66–67, 83–84, 90, 91, 140, 201, 227 (n. 45)

Stonewall Memorial Association, 169. *See also* Winchester LMA

Stuart, J. E. B. "Jeb," 34, 95, 101, 231 (n. 80), 232 (n. 96)

Sublett, Emmie, 42

Suffrage. *See* Women's rights and woman suffrage

Taylor, Nannie, 21

Taylor, Richard, 102

Temperance movement, 4, 129, 138, 154, 170, 239 (n. 69)

Tennessee: reentry of, into Union, 70, 71; Reconstruction in, 72–73; race riot in Memphis, 75; and Lee's death, 106; memorial chapel in, 183; soldiers from, in Civil War, 206 (n. 18)

Texas, 112–13

Textbooks, 172–73, 249–50 (n. 20). *See also* Schools and schoolchildren

Thompson, John R., 34

Tiffany, Louis Comfort, 184, 185–87

Tompkins, Ellen, 211 (n. 39)

Tompkins, Sally Louisa, 26, 38, 53, 211 (n. 39)

Treason charges, 6–7, 40, 48, 65, 80, 107, 198–99, 221 (n. 66)

Tripp, Steven, 71

UCV. *See* United Confederate Veterans

UDC. *See* United Daughters of the Confederacy

Unionists, 9, 69–71, 78, 79

Union Memorial Days. *See* Memorial Days, National

United Confederate Veterans (UCV): scholarship on, 3; and women's auxiliaries, 151; and Blue-Gray reunions, 154; and monument to women, 175; annual meetings of, 178, 179; and CSMA, 178, 179–80; founding of, 244 (n. 38); and Jefferson Davis monument, 246 (n. 60)

United Daughters of the Confederacy (UDC): and Groveton Confederate Cemetery, 1–2; LMAs predating, 1–2, 3, 4, 168, 170, 194, 199, 205 (n. 6), 248 (n. 4); founding of, 4, 127, 167, 168; and white supremacy, 13, 171–73; and monument building, 127, 168; membership of, 137, 168–71, 173–76, 194, 249 (nn. 9–10), 250 (nn. 23, 25), 251 (n. 34); goals and objectives of, 157, 168, 170, 205 (n. 6); success of, 167; relationship between LMAs and, 167–68, 169, 170, 176–78, 249 (nn. 8, 14); and Confederate museums, 168, 176, 177–78; and Memorial Days, 168, 177; chapters of, 168–69, 171, 248 (n. 6), 249 (n. 14); motivations of members of, 169, 173; and class status, 169, 173–74, 249 (n. 9); and flag display and pledge, 172; and Lost Cause, 172–73; on slavery, 172–73, 249 (n. 18); eligibility requirements for, 174, 250 (n. 25); and

state funds for Confederate cemeteries, 176, 189; and Gettysburg reinterment project, 177; Richmond as site for national convention of, 177; and Jefferson Davis monument, 177, 181, 246 (n. 60); and CSMA, 179–81; and Arlington National Cemetery, 182, 252 (n. 49); and Blandford Church, 185; and essay contest on Confederate topics, 189

University of Virginia, 175

Valentine, Edward, 118

Vandervoort, Paul, 150

Van Zelm, Antoinette, 12

Varon, Elizabeth, 6, 207 (n. 3), 208 (n. 19), 214 (n. 4)

Venable, Charles, 131, 233 (n. 6)

Veterans' associations: monument building by, 141–42, 175, 244–45 (n. 43); goals of, 146; and reconciliation between Union and Confederate veterans, 146–47, 155, 159, 244 (n. 41), 246 (n. 57); cooperation between LMAs and, 147–49; ladies' auxiliaries of, 149–52; and White House of the Confederacy, 160; and Confederate Museum fund-raising, 164. *See also specific associations*

Victorian period: mourning rituals in, 30–31; women's role in, 64–65

Violence. *See* Lynching; Race riots

Virginia. *See* Civil War; Ladies' Memorial Associations; Reconstruction; *and specific cities and LMAs*

Virginia Federation of Women's Clubs, 249 (n. 13)

Wade, Frances Kirby-Smith, 252 (n. 44)

Walker, Evelyn, 17

Walker, John Stewart, 210 (n. 36)

Walker, Lucy Otey, 210 (n. 36)

Walker, Sue H., 181

Walker, Thomas L., 210 (n. 38)

Wallace, John H., 18, 53, 219 (n. 42)

Wallace, Mary Gordon, 18, 20–21, 38, 53, 88, 219 (n. 42)

Women: and Lost Cause generally, 2–4, 16, 40, 68, 85–87, 114–15, 137, 140, 155, 156, 158–59, 188, 190, 199; organizations for, in postwar period, 4, 51–52, 128–30, 138, 154, 157, 170–71, 197–98, 249 (n. 13); northern women's involvement in politics, 7, 61; resistance of, to Union army, 15, 27–29, 36, 212 (n. 52), 215 (n. 6); in antebellum period, 16, 23, 30, 55, 88, 208 (n. 19), 239 (n. 67); patriotism of southern women during Civil War, 20–24, 29–30, 213 (n. 53); petitioning government by, 21, 25–26, 98, 138, 160, 172, 184; and hospitals and nursing during Civil War, 25–27, 53, 209 (n. 33), 210–11 (nn. 37–42); and Confederate nationalism, 30, 50, 51, 54–58, 60–68, 85–87, 99, 134, 137, 140, 213 (n. 53), 220 (n. 51), 223 (n. 85); and mourning rituals, 30–37, 50, 82–83, 84, 213 (n. 54); and Confederate motherhood, 50, 159; southern "lady"/southern belle during antebellum period, 55, 137, 138, 139; and abolitionism, 61, 98, 227 (n. 46); in Victorian period, 64–65; African American women and freedom celebrations, 78–79; employment laws for protection of, 98, 230 (n. 71); Early's attitudes about, 114–19; and generations of LMA members, 135–38; of New South, 137–38, 159; resistance of, to joint Memorial Days, 153–56; higher education of, 175; monuments in honor of, 175, 244–45 (n. 43); northern women during Civil War, 207 (nn. 1, 5), 209 (n. 31); as slaveholders, 215 (n. 8); use of husbands' names for married women, 228 (n. 51); and public speaking, 228 (n. 51). *See also* Gender; Ladies' Memorial Associations; Women's rights and woman suffrage

Women's Association for the Liquidation of the Virginia State Debt, 129–30, 239–40 (n. 72)

Women's auxiliaries of veterans' associations, 149–52

Women's Christian Temperance Union, 4, 129, 138, 154, 170, 239 (n. 69)

Women's club movement, 154, 170, 171, 197, 249 (n. 13)

Women's organizations, 4, 51–52, 128–30, 154, 157, 170–71, 197, 249 (n. 13). *See also specific organizations*

Women's Relief Corps (WRC): as auxiliary of GAR, 78, 127, 150–51, 245 (n. 51); founding of, 150; goals of, 150, 154–55; LMAs' lack of relationship with, 154–55; segregation of, 157–58; membership of, 157–58, 174; in South, 157–58, 245 (n. 51); and display and pledge in schools, 172; organizational structure of, 248 (n. 2)

Women's rights and woman suffrage, 7, 61, 62, 70, 99, 138, 139, 155, 190, 198, 231–32 (n. 89)

Woodward, Miss M. E., 18

WRC. *See* Women's Relief Corps

Wright, Uriel, 64–65, 222 (n. 74)

Wyatt, Henry Lawson, 32

Wyatt-Brown, Bertram, 239 (n. 71)

Wynne, Henry, 128

Young Women's Christian Association, 138, 154, 175

Youth organizations. *See* Junior associations of LMAs